THE RIVER WAR

Copyright © BiblioBazaar, LLC

BiblioBazaar Reproduction Series: Our goal at BiblioBazaar is to help readers, educators and researchers by bringing back in print hard-to-find original publications at a reasonable price and, at the same time, preserve the legacy of literary history. The following book represents an authentic reproduction of the text as printed by the original publisher and may contain prior copyright references. While we have attempted to accurately maintain the integrity of the original work(s), from time to time there are problems with the original book scan that may result in minor errors in the reproduction, including imperfections such as missing and blurred pages, poor pictures, markings and other reproduction issues beyond our control. Because this work is culturally important, we have made it available as a part of our commitment to protecting, preserving and promoting the world's literature.

All of our books are in the "public domain" and many are derived from Open Source projects dedicated to digitizing historic literature. We believe that when we undertake the difficult task of re-creating them as attractive, readable and affordable books, we further the mutual goal of sharing these works with a larger audience. A portion of Bibliobazaar profits go back to Open Source projects in the form of a donation to the groups that do this important work around the world. If you would like to make a donation to these worthy Open Source projects, or would just like to get more information about these important initiatives, please visit www.bibliobazaar.com/opensource.

WINSTON S. CHURCHILL

THE RIVER WAR

AN ACCOUNT OF THE RECONQUEST OF THE SUDAN

THE RIVER WAR

CONTENTS

CHAPTER
- I. THE REBELLION OF THE MAHDI 11
- II. THE FATE OF THE ENVOY 40
- III. THE DERVISH EMPIRE 68
- IV. THE YEARS OF PREPARATION 84
- V. THE BEGINNING OF THE WAR 99
- VI. FIRKET 115
- VII. THE RECOVERY OF THE DONGOLA PROVINCE 123
- VIII. THE DESERT RAILWAY 142
- IX. ABU HAMED 159
- X. BERBER 174
- XI. RECONNAISSANCE 187
- XII. THE BATTLE OF THE ATBARA 199
- XIII. THE GRAND ADVANCE 210
- XIV. THE OPERATIONS OF THE FIRST OF SEPTEMBER 221
- XV. THE BATTLE OF OMDURMAN 231
- XVI. THE FALL OF THE CITY 258
- XVII. 'THE FASHODA INCIDENT' 266
- XVIII. ON THE BLUE NILE 278
- XIX. THE END OF THE KHALIFA 294

APPENDIX 309

# THE SOUDAN
>>> to illustrate the military operations <<<
1896-1898

CHAPTER I:

THE REBELLION OF THE MAHDI

The north-eastern quarter of the continent of Africa is drained and watered by the Nile. Among and about the headstreams and tributaries of this mighty river lie the wide and fertile provinces of the Egyptian Soudan. Situated in the very centre of the land, these remote regions are on every side divided from the seas by five hundred miles of mountain, swamp, or desert. The great river is their only means of growth, their only channel of progress. It is by the Nile alone that their commerce can reach the outer markets, or European civilisation can penetrate the inner darkness. The Soudan is joined to Egypt by the Nile, as a diver is connected with the surface by his air-pipe. Without it there is only suffocation. Aut Nilus, aut nihil!

The town of Khartoum, at the confluence of the Blue and White Niles, is the point on which the trade of the south must inevitably converge. It is the great spout through which the merchandise collected from a wide area streams northwards to the Mediterranean shore. It marks the extreme northern limit of the fertile Soudan. Between Khartoum and Assuan the river flows for twelve hundred miles through deserts of surpassing desolation. At last the wilderness recedes and the living world broadens out again into Egypt and the Delta. It is with events that have occurred in the intervening waste that these pages are concerned.

The real Soudan, known to the statesman and the explorer, lies far to the south—moist, undulating, and exuberant. But there is another Soudan, which some mistake for the true, whose solitudes oppress the Nile from the Egyptian frontier to Omdurman. This is the Soudan of the soldier. Destitute of wealth or future, it is rich in history. The names of its squalid villages are familiar to distant and enlightened peoples. The barrenness of its scenery has been drawn by skilful pen and pencil. Its ample deserts have tasted the blood of brave men.

Its hot, black rocks have witnessed famous tragedies. It is the scene of the war.

This great tract, which may conveniently be called 'The Military Soudan,' stretches with apparent indefiniteness over the face of the continent. Level plains of smooth sand—a little rosier than buff, a little paler than salmon—are interrupted only by occasional peaks of rock—black, stark, and shapeless. Rainless storms dance tirelessly over the hot, crisp surface of the ground. The fine sand, driven by the wind, gathers into deep drifts, and silts among the dark rocks of the hills, exactly as snow hangs about an Alpine summit; only it is a fiery snow, such as might fall in hell. The earth burns with the quenchless thirst of ages, and in the steel-blue sky scarcely a cloud obstructs the unrelenting triumph of the sun.

Through the desert flows the river—a thread of blue silk drawn across an enormous brown drugget; and even this thread is brown for half the year. Where the water laps the sand and soaks into the banks there grows an avenue of vegetation which seems very beautiful and luxuriant by contrast with what lies beyond. The Nile, through all the three thousand miles of its course vital to everything that lives beside it, is never so precious as here. The traveller clings to the strong river as to an old friend, staunch in the hour of need. All the world blazes, but here is shade. The deserts are hot, but the Nile is cool. The land is parched, but here is abundant water. The picture painted in burnt sienna is relieved by a grateful flash of green.

Yet he who had not seen the desert or felt the sun heavily on his shoulders would hardly admire the fertility of the riparian scrub. Unnourishing reeds and grasses grow rank and coarse from the water's edge. The dark, rotten soil between the tussocks is cracked and granulated by the drying up of the annual flood. The character of the vegetation is inhospitable. Thorn-bushes, bristling like hedgehogs and thriving arrogantly, everywhere predominate and with their prickly tangles obstruct or forbid the path. Only the palms by the brink are kindly, and men journeying along the Nile must look often towards their bushy tops, where among the spreading foliage the red and yellow glint of date clusters proclaims the ripening of a generous crop, and protests that Nature is not always mischievous and cruel.

The banks of the Nile, except by contrast with the desert, display an abundance of barrenness. Their characteristic is monotony. Their attraction is their sadness. Yet there is one hour when all is changed. Just before the sun sets towards the western cliffs a delicious flush brightens and enlivens the landscape. It is as though some Titanic artist in an hour of inspiration were retouching the picture, painting in dark purple shadows among the rocks, strengthening the lights on the sands, gilding and beautifying everything, and making the whole scene live. The river, whose windings make it look like a lake, turns from muddy brown to silver-grey. The sky from a dull blue deepens into violet in the west. Everything under that magic touch becomes vivid and alive. And then the sun sinks altogether behind the rocks, the colors fade out of the sky, the flush off the sands, and gradually everything darkens and grows grey—like a man's cheek when he is bleeding to death. We are left sad and sorrowful in the dark, until the stars light up and remind us that there is always something beyond.

In a land whose beauty is the beauty of a moment, whose face is desolate, and whose character is strangely stern, the curse of war was hardly needed to produce a melancholy effect. Why should there be caustic plants where everything is hot and burning? In deserts where thirst is enthroned, and where the rocks and sand appeal to a pitiless sky for moisture, it was a savage trick to add the mockery of mirage.

The area multiplies the desolation. There is life only by the Nile. If a man were to leave the river, he might journey westward and find no human habitation, nor the smoke of a cooking fire, except the lonely tent of a Kabbabish Arab or the encampment of a trader's caravan, till he reached the coast-line of America. Or he might go east and find nothing but sand and sea and sun until Bombay rose above the horizon. The thread of fresh water is itself solitary in regions where all living things lack company.

In the account of the River War the Nile is naturally supreme. It is the great melody that recurs throughout the whole opera. The general purposing military operations, the statesman who would decide upon grave policies, and the reader desirous of studying the course and results of either, must think of the Nile. It is the life of the lands through which it flows. It is the cause of the war: the means by which we fight; the end at which we aim. Imagination should paint the river through every page in the story. It glitters between the palm-trees during the actions. It is the explanation of nearly every military movement. By its banks the armies camp at night. Backed or flanked on its unfordable stream they offer or accept battle by day. To its brink, morning and evening, long lines of camels, horses, mules, and slaughter cattle hurry eagerly. Emir and Dervish, officer and soldier, friend and foe, kneel alike to this god of ancient Egypt and draw each day their daily water in goatskin or canteen. Without the river none would have started. Without it none might have continued. Without it none could ever have returned.

All who journey on the Nile, whether in commerce or war, will pay their tribute of respect and gratitude; for the great river has befriended all races and every age. Through all the centuries it has performed the annual miracle of its flood. Every year when the rains fall and the mountain snows of Central Africa begin to melt, the head-streams become torrents and the great lakes are filled to the brim. A vast expanse of low, swampy lands, crossed by secondary channels and flooded for many miles, regulates the flow, and by a sponge-like action prevents the excess of one year from causing the deficiency of the next. Far away in Egypt, prince, priest, and peasant look southwards with anxious attention for the fluctuating yet certain rise. Gradually the flood begins. The Bahr-el-Ghazal from a channel of stagnant pools and marshes becomes a broad and navigable stream. The Sobat and the Atbara from dry watercourses with occasional pools, in which the fish and crocodiles are crowded, turn to rushing rivers. But all this is remote from Egypt. After its confluence with the Atbara no drop of water reaches the Nile, and it flows for seven hundred miles through the sands or rushes in cataracts among the rocks of the Nubian desert. Nevertheless, in spite of the tremendous diminution in volume caused by the dryness of the earth and air and the heat of the sun—all of which drink greedily—the river below Assuan is sufficiently great to supply nine millions of people with as much water as their utmost science and energies can draw, and yet to pour into the Mediterranean a low-water surplus current of 61,500 cubic feet per second. Nor is its water its only gift. As the Nile rises its complexion is changed. The clear blue river becomes thick and red, laden with the magic mud that can raise cities from the desert sand and make the wilderness a garden. The geographer may still in the arrogance of science describe the Nile as 'a great, steady-flowing river, fed by the rains of the tropics, controlled by the existence of a vast head reservoir and several areas of repose, and annually flooded by the accession of a great body of water with which its eastern tributaries are flushed' [ENCYCLOPAEDIA BRITANNICA]; but all who have drunk deeply of its soft yet fateful waters—fateful, since they give both life and death—will understand why the old Egyptians worshipped the river, nor will they even in modern days easily dissociate from their minds a feeling of mystic reverence.

South of Khartoum and of 'The Military Soudan' the land becomes more fruitful. The tributaries of the Nile multiply the areas of riparian fertility. A considerable rainfall, increasing as the Equator is approached, enables the intervening spaces to support vegetation and consequently human life. The greater part of the country is feverish and unhealthy, nor can Europeans long sustain the attacks of its climate. Nevertheless it is by no means valueless. On the east the province of Sennar used to produce abundant grain, and might easily produce no less abundant cotton. Westward the vast territories of Kordofan and Darfur afford grazing-grounds to a multitude of cattle, and give means of livelihood to great numbers of Baggara or cow-herd Arabs, who may also pursue with activity and stratagem the fleet giraffe and the still fleeter ostrich. To the south-east lies Bahr-el-Ghazal, a great tract of country occupied by dense woods and plentifully watered. Further south and nearer the Equator the forests and marshes become exuberant with tropical growths, and the whole face of the land is moist and green. Amid groves of gigantic trees and through plains of high waving grass the stately elephant roams in herds which occasionally number four hundred, hardly ever disturbed by a well-armed hunter. The ivory of their tusks constitutes the wealth of the Equatorial Province. So greatly they abound that Emin Pasha is provoked to complain of a pest of these valuable pachyderms [LIFE OF EMIN PASHA, vol.i chapter ix.]: and although they are only assailed by the natives with spear and gun, no less than twelve thousand hundredweight of ivory has been exported in a single year [Ibid.] All other kinds of large beasts known to man inhabit these obscure retreats. The fierce rhinoceros crashes through the undergrowth. Among the reeds of melancholy swamps huge hippopotami, crocodiles, and buffaloes prosper and increase. Antelope of every known and many unclassified species; serpents of peculiar venom; countless millions of birds, butterflies, and beetles are among the offspring of prolific Nature. And the daring sportsman who should survive his expedition would not fail to add to the achievements of science and the extent of natural history as well as to his own reputation.

The human inhabitants of the Soudan would not, but for their vices and misfortunes, be disproportioned in numbers to the fauna or less happy. War, slavery, and oppression have, however, afflicted them until the total population of the whole country does not exceed at the most liberal estimate three million souls. The huge area contains many differences of climate and conditions, and these have produced peculiar and diverse breeds of men. The Soudanese are of many tribes, but two main races can be clearly distinguished: the aboriginal natives, and the Arab settlers. The indigenous inhabitants of the country were negroes as black as coal. Strong, virile, and simple-minded savages, they lived as we may imagine prehistoric men—hunting, fighting, marrying, and dying, with no ideas beyond the gratification of their physical desires, and no fears save those engendered by ghosts, witchcraft, the worship of ancestors, and other forms of superstition common among peoples of low development. They displayed the virtues of barbarism. They were brave and honest. The smallness of their intelligence excused the degradation of their habits. Their ignorance secured their innocence. Yet their eulogy must be short, for though their customs, language, and appearance vary with the districts they inhabit and the subdivisions to which they belong, the history of all is a confused legend of strife and misery, their natures are uniformly cruel and thriftless, and their condition is one of equal squalor and want.

Although the negroes are the more numerous, the Arabs exceed in power. The bravery of the aboriginals is outweighed by the intelligence of the invaders and their superior force of character. During the second century of the Mohammedan era, when the inhabitants of Arabia went forth to conquer the world, one adventurous army struck south. The first pioneers were followed at intervals by continual immigrations of Arabs not only from Arabia but also across the deserts from Egypt and Marocco. The element thus introduced has spread and is spreading throughout the Soudan, as water soaks into a dry sponge. The aboriginals absorbed the invaders they could not repel. The stronger race imposed its customs and language on the negroes. The vigour of their blood sensibly altered the facial appearance of the Soudanese. For more than a thousand years the influence of Mohammedanism, which appears to possess a strange fascination for negroid races, has been permeating the Soudan, and, although ignorance and natural obstacles impede the progress of new ideas, the whole of the black race is gradually adopting the new religion and developing Arab characteristics. In the districts of the north, where the original invaders settled, the evolution is complete, and the Arabs of the Soudan are a race formed by the interbreeding of negro and Arab, and yet distinct from both. In the more remote and inaccessible regions which lie to the south and west the negro race remains as yet unchanged by the Arab influence. And between these extremes every degree of mixture is to be found. In some tribes pure Arabic is spoken, and prior to the rise of the Mahdi the orthodox Moslem faith was practised. In others Arabic has merely modified the ancient dialects, and the Mohammedan religion has been adapted to the older superstitions; but although the gap between the Arab-negro and the negro-pure is thus filled by every intermediate blend, the two races were at an early date quite distinct.

The qualities of mongrels are rarely admirable, and the mixture of the Arab and negro types has produced a debased and cruel breed, more shocking because they are more intelligent than the primitive savages. The stronger race soon began to prey upon the simple aboriginals; some of the Arab tribes were camel-breeders; some were goat-herds; some were Baggaras or cow-herds. But all, without exception, were hunters of men. To the great slave-market at Jedda a continual stream of negro captives has flowed for hundreds of years. The invention of gunpowder and the adoption by the Arabs of firearms facilitated the traffic by placing the ignorant negroes at a further disadvantage. Thus the situation in the Soudan for several centuries may be summed up as follows: The dominant race of Arab invaders was unceasingly spreading its blood, religion, customs, and language among the black aboriginal population, and at the same time it harried and enslaved them.

The state of society that arose out of this may be easily imagined. The warlike Arab tribes fought and brawled among themselves in ceaseless feud and strife. The negroes trembled in apprehension of capture, or rose locally against their oppressors. Occasionally an important Sheikh would effect the combination of many tribes, and a kingdom came into existence—a community consisting of a military class armed with guns and of multitudes of slaves, at once their servants and their merchandise, and sometimes trained as soldiers. The dominion might prosper viciously till it was overthrown by some more powerful league.

All this was unheeded by the outer world, from which the Soudan is separated by the deserts, and it seemed that the slow, painful course of development would be unaided and uninterrupted. But at last the populations of Europe changed. Another civilisation reared itself above the ruins of Roman triumph and Mohammedan aspiration—a civilisation more powerful, more glorious, but no less aggressive. The impulse of conquest which hurried the French and

English to Canada and the Indies, which sent the Dutch to the Cape and the Spaniards to Peru, spread to Africa and led the Egyptians to the Soudan. In the year 1819 Mohammed Ali, availing himself of the disorders alike as an excuse and an opportunity, sent his son Ismail up the Nile with a great army. The Arab tribes, torn by dissension, exhausted by thirty years of general war, and no longer inspired by their neglected religion, offered a weak resistance. Their slaves, having known the worst of life, were apathetic. The black aboriginals were silent and afraid. The whole vast territory was conquered with very little fighting, and the victorious army, leaving garrisons, returned in triumph to the Delta.

What enterprise that an enlightened community may attempt is more noble and more profitable than the reclamation from barbarism of fertile regions and large populations? To give peace to warring tribes, to administer justice where all was violence, to strike the chains off the slave, to draw the richness from the soil, to plant the earliest seeds of commerce and learning, to increase in whole peoples their capacities for pleasure and diminish their chances of pain—what more beautiful ideal or more valuable reward can inspire human effort? The act is virtuous, the exercise invigorating, and the result often extremely profitable. Yet as the mind turns from the wonderful cloudland of aspiration to the ugly scaffolding of attempt and achievement, a succession of opposite ideas arises. Industrious races are displayed stinted and starved for the sake of an expensive Imperialism which they can only enjoy if they are well fed. Wild peoples, ignorant of their barbarism, callous of suffering, careless of life but tenacious of liberty, are seen to resist with fury the philanthropic invaders, and to perish in thousands before they are convinced of their mistake. The inevitable gap between conquest and dominion becomes filled with the figures of the greedy trader, the inopportune missionary, the ambitious soldier, and the lying speculator, who disquiet the minds of the conquered and excite the sordid appetites of the conquerors. And as the eye of thought rests on these sinister features, it hardly seems possible for us to believe that any fair prospect is approached by so foul a path.

From 1819 to 1883 Egypt ruled the Soudan. Her rule was not kindly, wise, or profitable. Its aim was to exploit, not to improve the local population. The miseries of the people were aggravated rather than lessened: but they were concealed. For the rough injustice of the sword there were substituted the intricacies of corruption and bribery. Violence and plunder were more hideous, since they were cloaked with legality and armed with authority. The land was undeveloped and poor. It barely sustained its inhabitants. The additional burden of a considerable foreign garrison and a crowd of rapacious officials increased the severity of the economic conditions. Scarcity was frequent. Famines were periodical. Corrupt and incapable Governors-General succeeded each other at Khartoum with bewildering rapidity. The constant changes, while they prevented the continuity of any wise policy, did not interrupt the misrule. With hardly any exceptions, the Pashas were consistent in oppression. The success of their administration was measured by the Ministries in Egypt by the amount of money they could extort from the natives; among the officials in the Soudan, by the number of useless offices they could create. There were a few bright examples of honest men, but these, by providing a contrast, only increased the discontents.

The rule of Egypt was iniquitous: yet it preserved the magnificent appearance of Imperial dominion. The Egyptian Pro-consul lived in state at the confluence of the Niles. The representatives of foreign Powers established themselves in the city. The trade of the south converged upon Khartoum. Thither the subordinate governors, Beys and Mudirs, repaired at intervals to report the state of their provinces and to receive instructions. Thither were sent the ivory of Equatoria, the ostrich feathers of Kordofan, gum from Darfur, grain from Sennar, and taxes collected from all the regions. Strange beasts, entrapped in the swamps and forests, passed through the capital on their journey to Cairo and Europe. Complex and imposing reports of revenue and expenditure were annually compiled. An elaborate and dignified correspondence was maintained between Egypt and its great dependency. The casual observer, astonished at the unusual capacity for government displayed by an Oriental people, was tempted to accept the famous assertion which Nubar Pasha put into the mouth of the Khedive Ismail: 'We are no longer in Africa, but in Europe.' Yet all was a hateful sham ['The government of the Egyptians in these far-off countries is nothing else but one of brigandage of the very worst description.'—COLONEL GORDON IN CENTRAL AFRICA, April 11, 1879.] The arbitrary and excessive taxes were collected only at the point of the bayonet. If a petty chief fell into arrears, his neighbours were raised against him. If an Arab tribe were recalcitrant, a military expedition was despatched. Moreover, the ability of the

Arabs to pay depended on their success as slave-hunters. When there had been a good catch, the revenue profited. The Egyptian Government had joined the International League against the slave trade. They combined, however, indirectly but deliberately, to make money out of it. [EGYPT, No.11, 1883.]

In the miserable, harassing warfare that accompanied the collection of taxes the Viceregal commanders gained more from fraud than force. No subterfuge, no treachery, was too mean for them to adopt: no oath or treaty was too sacred for them to break. Their methods were cruel, and if honour did not impede the achievement, mercy did not restrict the effects of their inglorious successes; and the effete administrators delighted to order their timid soldiery to carry out the most savage executions. The political methods and social style of the Governors-General were imitated more or less exactly by the subordinate officials according to their degree in the provinces. Since they were completely hidden from the eye of civilisation, they enjoyed a greater licence in their administration. As their education was inferior, so their habits became more gross. Meanwhile the volcano on which they disported themselves was ominously silent. The Arab tribes obeyed, and the black population cowered.

The authority of a tyrannical Government was supported by the presence of a worthless army. Nearly forty thousand men were distributed among eight main and numerous minor garrisons. Isolated in a roadless country by enormous distances and natural obstacles, and living in the midst of large savage populations of fanatical character and warlike habits, whose exasperation was yearly growing with their miseries, the Viceregal forces might depend for their safety only on the skill of their officers, the excellence of their discipline, and the superiority of their weapons. But the Egyptian officers were at that time distinguished for nothing but their public incapacity and private misbehaviour. The evil reputation of the Soudan and its climate deterred the more educated or more wealthy from serving in such distant regions, and none went south who could avoid it. The army which the Khedives maintained in the Delta was, judged by European standards, only a rabble. It was badly trained, rarely paid, and very cowardly; and the scum of the army of the Delta was the cream of the army of the Soudan. The officers remained for long periods, many all their lives, in the obscurity of the remote provinces. Some had been sent there in disgrace, others in disfavour. Some had been forced to serve out of Egypt by extreme poverty, others were drawn to the Soudan by the hopes of gratifying peculiar tastes. The majority had harems of the women of the country, which were limited only by the amount of money they could lay their hands on by any method. Many were hopeless and habitual drunkards. Nearly all were dishonest. All were indolent and incapable.

Under such leadership the finest soldiery would have soon degenerated. The Egyptians in the Soudan were not fine soldiers. Like their officers, they were the worst part of the Khedivial army. Like them, they had been driven to the south. Like them, they were slothful and effete. Their training was imperfect; their discipline was lax; their courage was low. Nor was even this all the weakness and peril of their position; for while the regular troops were thus demoralised, there existed a powerful local irregular force of Bazingers (Soudanese riflemen), as well armed as the soldiers, more numerous, more courageous, and who regarded the alien garrisons with fear that continually diminished and hate that continually grew. And behind regulars and irregulars alike the wild Arab tribes of the desert and the hardy blacks of the forests, goaded by suffering and injustice, thought the foreigners the cause of all their woes, and were delayed only by their inability to combine from sweeping them off the face of the earth. Never was there such a house of cards as the Egyptian dominion in the Soudan. The marvel is that it stood so long, not that it fell so soon.

The names of two men of character and fame are forever connected with the actual outburst. One was an English general, the other an Arab priest; yet, in spite of the great gulf and vivid contrast between their conditions, they resembled each other in many respects. Both were earnest and enthusiastic men of keen sympathies and passionate emotions. Both were powerfully swayed by religious fervour. Both exerted great personal influence on all who came in contact with them. Both were reformers. The Arab was an African reproduction of the Englishman; the Englishman a superior and civilised development of the Arab. In the end they fought to the death, but for an important part of their lives their influence on the fortunes of the Soudan was exerted in the same direction. Mohammed Ahmed, 'The Mahdi,' will be discussed in his own place. Charles Gordon needs little introduction. Long before this tale begins his reputation was European, and the fame of the 'Ever-victorious Army' had spread far beyond the Great Wall of China.

The misgovernment of the Egyptians and the misery of the Soudanese reached their greatest extreme in the seventh decade of the present century.

From such a situation there seemed to be no issue other than by force of arms. The Arab tribes lacked no provocation. Yet they were destitute of two moral forces essential to all rebellions. The first was the knowledge that better things existed. The second was a spirit of combination. General Gordon showed them the first. The Mahdi provided the second.

It is impossible to study any part of Charles Gordon's career without being drawn to all the rest. As his wild and varied fortunes lead him from Sebastopol to Pekin, from Gravesend to South Africa, from Mauritius to the Soudan, the reader follows fascinated. Every scene is strange, terrible, or dramatic. Yet, remarkable as are the scenes, the actor is the more extraordinary; a type without comparison in modern times and with few likenesses in history. Rare and precious is the truly disinterested man. Potentates of many lands and different degree—the Emperor of China, the King of the Belgians, the Premier of Cape Colony, the Khedive of Egypt—competed to secure his services. The importance of his offices varied no less than their nature. One day he was a subaltern of sappers; on another he commanded the Chinese army; the next he directed an orphanage; or was Governor-General of the Soudan, with supreme powers of life and death and peace and war; or served as private secretary to Lord Ripon. But in whatever capacity he laboured he was true to his reputation. Whether he is portrayed bitterly criticising to Graham the tactics of the assault on the Redan; or pulling the head of Lar Wang from under his bedstead and waving it in paroxysms of indignation before the astonished eyes of Sir Halliday Macartney; or riding alone into the camp of the rebel Suliman and receiving the respectful salutes of those who had meant to kill him; or telling the Khedive Ismail that he 'must have the whole Soudan to govern'; or reducing his salary to half the regulation amount because 'he thought it was too much'; or ruling a country as large as Europe; or collecting facts for Lord Ripon's rhetorical efforts—we perceive a man careless alike of the frowns of men or the smiles of women, of life or comfort, wealth or fame.

It was a pity that one, thus gloriously free from the ordinary restraining influences of human society, should have found in his own character so little mental ballast. His moods were capricious and uncertain, his passions violent, his impulses sudden and inconsistent. The mortal enemy of the morning had become a trusted ally before the night. The friend he loved to-day he loathed to-morrow. Scheme after scheme formed in his fertile brain, and jostled confusingly together. All in succession were pressed with enthusiasm. All at times were rejected with disdain. A temperament naturally neurotic had been aggravated by an acquired habit of smoking; and the General carried this to so great an extreme that he was rarely seen without a cigarette. His virtues are famous among men; his daring and resource might turn the tide or war; his energy would have animated a whole people; his achievements are upon record; but it must also be set down that few more uncertain and impracticable forces than Gordon have ever been introduced into administration and diplomacy.

Although the Egyptian Government might loudly proclaim their detestation of slavery, their behaviour in the Soudan was viewed with suspicion by the European Powers, and particularly by Great Britain. To vindicate his sincerity the Khedive Ismail in 1874 appointed Gordon to be Governor of the Equatorial Province in succession to Sir Samuel Baker. The name of the General was a sufficient guarantee that the slave trade was being earnestly attacked. The Khedive would gladly have stopped at the guarantee, and satisfied the world without disturbing 'vested interests.' But the mission, which may have been originally instituted as a pretence, soon became in Gordon's energetic hands very real. Circumstances, moreover, soon enlisted the sympathies of the Egyptian Government on the side of their zealous agent. The slave dealers had committed every variety of atrocity for which the most odious traffic in the world afforded occasion; but when, under the leadership of Zubehr Rahamna, they refused to pay their annual tribute, it was felt in Cairo that their crimes had cried aloud for chastisement.

Zubehr is sufficiently described when it has been said that he was the most notorious slave dealer Africa has ever produced. His infamy had spread beyond the limits of the continent which was the scene of his exploits to the distant nations of the north and west. In reality, his rule was a distinct advance on the anarchy which had preceded it, and certainly he was no worse than others of his vile trade. His scale of business was, however, more extended. What William Whiteley was in respect of goods and chattels, that was Zubehr in respect of slaves—a universal provider. Magnitude lends a certain grandeur to crime; and Zubehr in the height of his power, at the head of the slave merchants' confederacy, might boast the retinue of a king and exercise authority over wide regions and a powerful army.

As early as 1869 he was practically the independent ruler of the Bahr-el-Ghazal. The Khedive resolved to assert his rights. A small Egyptian force was sent to subdue the rebel slaver who not only disgraced humanity but refused to pay tribute. Like most of the Khedivial expeditions the troops under Bellal Bey met with ill-fortune. They came, they saw, they ran away. Some, less speedy than the rest, fell on the field of dishonour. The rebellion was open. Nevertheless it was the Khedive who sought peace. Zubehr apologised for defeating the Viceregal soldiers and remained supreme in the Bahr-el-Ghazal. Thence he planned the conquest of Darfur, at that time an independent kingdom. The Egyptian Government were glad to join with him in the enterprise. The man they had been unable to conquer, they found it expedient to assist. The operations were successful. The King of Darfur, who was distinguished no less for his valour than for his folly, was killed. The whole country was subdued. The whole population available after the battles became slaves. Zubehr thus wielded a formidable power. The Khedivial Government, thinking to ensure his loyalty, created him a Pasha—a rank which he could scarcely disgrace; and the authority of the rebel was thus unwillingly recognised by the ruler. Such was the situation when Gordon first came to the Soudan.

It was beyond the power of the new Governor of the Equatorial Province at once to destroy the slave-hunting confederacy. Yet he struck heavy blows at the slave trade, and when in 1877, after a short visit to England, he returned to the Soudan as Governor-General and with absolute power, he assailed it with redoubled energy. Fortune assisted his efforts, for the able Zubehr was enticed to Cairo, and, once there, the Government refused to allow their faithful ally and distinguished guest to go back to his happy-hunting grounds. Although the slave dealers were thus robbed of their great leader, they were still strong, and Zubehr's son, the brave Suliman, found a considerable following. Furious at his father's captivity, and alarmed lest his own should follow, he meditated revolt. But the Governor-General, mounted on a swift camel and attired in full uniform, rode alone into the rebel camp and compelled the submission of its chiefs before they could recover from their amazement. The confederacy was severely shaken, and when, in the following year, Suliman again revolted, the Egyptian troops under Gessi Pasha were able to disperse his forces and induce him to surrender on terms. The terms were broken, and Suliman and ten of his companions suffered death by shooting [von Slatin, Baron Rudolf Karl. FIRE

AND SWORD IN THE SOUDAN, p.28.] The league of the slave dealers was thus destroyed.

Towards the end of 1879 Gordon left the Soudan. With short intervals he had spent five busy years in its provinces. His energy had stirred the country. He had struck at the root of the slave trade, he had attacked the system of slavery, and, as slavery was the greatest institution in the land, he had undermined the whole social system. Indignation had stimulated his activity to an extraordinary degree. In a climate usually fatal to Europeans he discharged the work of five officers. Careless of his methods, he bought slaves himself, drilled them, and with the soldiers thus formed pounced on the caravans of the hunters. Traversing the country on a fleet dromedary—on which in a single year he is said to have covered 3,840 miles—he scattered justice and freedom among the astonished natives. He fed the infirm, protected the weak, executed the wicked. To some he gave actual help, to many freedom, to all new hopes and aspirations. Nor were the tribes ungrateful. The fiercest savages and cannibals respected the life of the strange white man. The women blessed him. He could ride unarmed and alone where a brigade of soldiers dared not venture. But he was, as he knew himself, the herald of the storm. Oppressed yet ferocious races had learned that they had rights; the misery of the Soudanese was lessened, but their knowledge had increased. The whole population was unsettled, and the wheels of change began slowly to revolve; nor did they stop until they had accomplished an enormous revolution.

The part played by the second force is more obscure. Few facts are so encouraging to the student of human development as the desire, which most men and all communities manifest at all times, to associate with their actions at least the appearance of moral right. However distorted may be their conceptions of virtue, however feeble their efforts to attain even to their own ideals, it is a pleasing feature and a hopeful augury that they should wish to be justified. No community embarks on a great enterprise without fortifying itself with the belief that from some points of view its motives are lofty and disinterested. It is an involuntary tribute, the humble tribute of imperfect beings, to the eternal temples of Truth and Beauty. The sufferings of a people or a class may be intolerable, but before they will take up arms and risk their lives some unselfish and impersonal spirit must animate them. In countries where there is education and mental activity or refinement, this high motive is found in the pride of glorious traditions or in a keen sympathy with surrounding misery. Ignorance deprives savage nations of such incentives. Yet in the marvellous economy of nature this very ignorance is a source of greater strength. It affords them the mighty stimulus of fanaticism. The French Communists might plead that they upheld the rights of man. The desert tribes proclaimed that they fought for the glory of God. But although the force of fanatical passion is far greater than that exerted by any philosophical belief, its sanction is just the same. It gives men something which they think is sublime to fight for, and this serves them as an excuse for wars which it is desirable to begin for totally different reasons. Fanaticism is not a cause of war. It is the means which helps savage peoples to fight. It is the spirit which enables them to combine—the great common object before which all personal or tribal disputes become insignificant. What the horn is to the rhinoceros, what the sting is to the wasp, the Mohammedan faith was to the Arabs of the Soudan—a faculty of offence or defence.

It was all this and no more. It was not the reason of the revolt. It strengthened, it characterised, but it did not cause. ['I do not believe that fanaticism exists as it used to do in the world, judging from what I have seen in this so-called fanatic land. It is far more a question of property, and is more like Communism under the flag of religion.'—GENERAL GORDON'S JOURNALS AT KHARTOUM, bk.i. p.13.] Those whose practice it is to regard their own nation as possessing a monopoly of virtue and common-sense, are wont to ascribe every military enterprise of savage peoples to fanaticism. They calmly ignore obvious and legitimate motives. The most rational conduct is considered mad. It has therefore been freely stated, and is to some extent believed, that the revolt in the Soudan was entirely religious. If the worst untruths are those that have some appearance of veracity, this impression must be very false indeed. It is, perhaps, an historical fact that the revolt of a large population has never been caused solely or even mainly by religious enthusiasm.

The reasons which forced the peoples of the Soudan to revolt were as strong as the defence which their oppressors could offer was feeble. Looking at the question from a purely political standpoint, we may say that upon the whole there exists no record of a better case for rebellion than presented itself to the Soudanese. Their country was being ruined; their property was plundered; their women were ravished; their liberties were curtailed; even their lives were threatened. Aliens ruled the inhabitants; the few oppressed the many; brave men were harried by cowards; the weak compelled the strong. Here were sufficient reasons. Since any armed movement against an established Government can be justified only by success, strength is an important revolutionary virtue. It was a virtue that the Arabs might boast. They were indeed far stronger than they, their persecutors, or the outside world had yet learned. All were soon to be enlightened.

The storm gathered and the waters rose. Three great waves impelled the living tide against the tottering house founded on the desert sand. The Arab suffered acutely from poverty, misgovernment, and oppression. Infuriated, he looked up and perceived that the cause of all his miseries was a weak and cowardly foreigner, a despicable 'Turk.' The antagonism of races increased the hatred sprung from social evils. The moment was at hand. Then, and not till then, the third wave came—the wave of fanaticism, which, catching up and surmounting the other waves, covered all the flood with its white foam, and, bearing on with the momentum of the waters, beat in thunder against the weak house so that it fell; and great was the fall thereof.

Down to the year 1881 there was no fanatical movement in the Soudan. In their utter misery the hopeless inhabitants had neglected even the practices of religion. They were nevertheless prepared for any enterprise, however desperate, which might free them from the Egyptian yoke. All that delayed them was the want of some leader who could combine the tribes and restore their broken spirits, and in the summer of 1881 the leader appeared. His subsequent career is within the limits of this account, and since his life throws a strong light on the thoughts and habits of the Arabs of the Soudan it may be worth while to trace it from the beginning.

The man who was the proximate cause of the River War was born by the banks of the Nile, not very far from Dongola. His family were poor and of no account in the province. But as the Prophet had claimed a royal descent, and as a Sacred Example was sprung from David's line, Mohammed Ahmed asserted that he was of the 'Ashraf,'(descendants of the Prophet) and the assertion, since it cannot be disproved, may be accepted. His father was a humble priest; yet he contrived to give his son some education in the practices of religion, the principles of the Koran, and the art of writing. Then he died at Kerreri while on a journey to Khartoum, and left the future Mahdi, still a child, to the mercies of the world. Solitary trees, if they grow at all, grow strong; and a boy deprived of a father's care often develops, if he escape the perils of youth, an independence and vigour of thought which may restore in after life the heavy loss of early days. It was so with Mohammed Ahmed. He looked around for an occupation and subsistence. A large proportion of the population of religious countries pass their lives at leisure, supported by the patient labour of the devout. The young man determined to follow the profession for which he felt his talents suited, and which would afford him the widest scope. He became a priest. Many of the religious teachers of heathen and other countries are devoid of enthusiasm and turn their attention to the next world because doing so affords them an easy living in this. Happily this is not true of all. It was not true of Mohammed. Even at an early age he manifested a zeal for God's service, and displayed a peculiar aptitude for learning the tenets and dogmas of the Mohammedan belief. So promising a pupil did not long lack a master in a country where intelligence and enthusiasm were scarce. His aspirations growing with his years and knowledge, he journeyed to Khartoum as soon as his religious education was completed, and became a disciple of the renowned and holy Sheikh, Mohammed Sherif.

His devotion to his superior, to his studies and to the practice of austerities, and a strange personal influence he was already beginning to show, won him by degrees a few disciples of his own: and with them he retired to the island of Abba. Here by the waters of the White Nile Mohammed Ahmed lived for several years. His two brothers, who were boat-builders in the neighbourhood, supported him by their industry. But it must have been an easy burden, for we read that he 'hollowed out for himself a cave in the mud bank, and lived in almost entire seclusion, fasting often for days, and occasionally paying a visit to the head of the order to assure him of his devotion and obedience.' [I take this passage from FIRE AND SWORD IN THE SOUDAN, by Slatin. His account is the most graphic and trustworthy of all known records of the Mahdi. He had terrible opportunities of collecting information. I have followed his version (chapter iv.) very closely on this subject.] Meanwhile his sanctity increased, and the labour and charity of the brothers were assisted by the alms of godly travellers on the river.

This virtuous and frugal existence was disturbed and terminated by an untoward event. The renowned and holy Sheikh made a feast to celebrate the circumcision of his sons. That the merriment of the auspicious occasion and the entertainment of the guests might be increased, Sherif, according to the lax practice of the time, granted a dispensation from any sins committed during the festivities, and proclaimed in God's name the suspension of the rules against singing and dancing by which the religious orders were bound. The ascetic of Abba island did not join in these seemingly innocent dissipations. With the recklessness of the reformer he protested against the demoralisation of the age, and loudly affirmed the doctrine that God alone could forgive sins. These things were speedily brought to the ears of the renowned Sheikh, and in all the righteous indignation that accompanies detected wrong-doing, he summoned Mohammed Ahmed before him. The latter obeyed. He respected his superior. He was under obligations to him. His ire had disappeared as soon as it had been expressed. He submissively entreated forgiveness; but in vain. Sherif felt that some sort of discipline must be maintained among his flock. He had connived at disobedience to the divine law. All the more must he uphold his own authority. Rising in anger, he drove the presumptuous disciple from his presence with bitter words, and expunged his name from the order of the elect.

Mohammed went home. He was greatly distressed. Yet his fortunes were not ruined. His sanctity was still a valuable and, unless he chose otherwise, an inalienable asset. The renowned Sheikh had a rival—nearly as holy and more enterprising than himself. From him the young priest might expect a warm welcome. Nevertheless he did not yet abandon his former superior. Placing a heavy wooden collar on his neck, clad in sackcloth and sprinkled with ashes, he again returned to his spiritual leader, and in this penitential guise implored pardon. He was ignominiously ejected. Nor did he venture to revisit the unforgiving Sheikh. But it happened that in a few weeks Sherif had occasion to journey to the island of Abba. His former disciple appeared suddenly before him, still clad in sackcloth and defiled by ashes. Careless of his plain misery, and unmoved by his loyalty, which was the more remarkable since it was disinterested, the implacable Sheikh poured forth a stream of invective. Among many insults, one went home: 'Be off, you wretched Dongolawi.'

Although the natives of the Dongola province were despised and disliked in the Southern Soudan, it is not at first apparent why Mohammed should have resented so bitterly the allusion to his birthplace. But abuse by class is a dangerous though effective practice. A man will perhaps tolerate an offensive word applied to himself, but will be infuriated if his nation, his rank, or his profession is insulted.

Mohammed Ahmed rose. All that man could do to make amends he had done. Now he had been publicly called 'a wretched Dongolawi.' Henceforth he would afflict Sherif with his repentance no longer. Reaching his house, he informed his disciples—for they had not abandoned him in all his trouble—that the Sheikh had finally cast him off, and that he would now take his discarded allegiance elsewhere. The rival, the Sheikh el Koreishi, lived near Mesalamia. He was jealous of Sherif and envied him his sanctimonious disciples. He was therefore delighted to receive a letter from Mohammed Ahmed announcing his breach with his former superior and offering his most devoted services. He returned a cordial invitation, and the priest of Abba island made all preparation for the journey.

This new development seems to have startled the unforgiving Sherif. It was no part of his policy to alienate his followers, still less to add to those of his rival. After all, the quality of mercy was high and noble. He would at last graciously forgive the impulsive but repentant disciple. He wrote him a letter to this effect. But it was now too late. Mohammed replied with grave dignity that he had committed no crime, that he sought no forgiveness, and that 'a wretched Dongolawi' would not offend by his presence the renowned Sheikh el Sherif. After this indulgence he departed to Mesalamia.

But the fame of his doings spread far and wide throughout the land. 'Even in distant Darfur it was the principal topic of conversation' [Slatin, FIRE AND SWORD]. Rarely had a Fiki been known to offend his superior; never to refuse his forgiveness. Mohammed did not hesitate to declare that he had done what he had done as a protest against the decay of religious fervour and the torpor of the times. Since his conduct had actually caused his dismissal, it appears that he was quite justified in making a virtue of necessity. At any rate he was believed, and the people groaning under oppression looked from all the regions to the figure that began to grow on the political horizon. His fame grew. Rumour, loud-tongued, carried it about the land that a great Reformer was come to purify the faith and break the stony apathy which paralysed the hearts of Islam. Whisperings added that a man was found who should break from off the necks of the tribes the hateful yoke of Egypt. Mohammed now deliberately entered upon the path of ambition.

Throughout Nubia the Shukri belief prevails: some day, in a time of shame and trouble, a second great Prophet will arise—a Mahdi who shall lead the faithful nearer God and sustain the religion. The people of the Soudan always look inquiringly to any ascetic who rises to fame, and the question is often repeated, 'Art thou he that should come, or do we look for another?' Of this powerful element of disturbance Mohammed Ahmed resolved to avail himself. He requested and obtained the permission of the Sheikh Koreishi to return to Abba, where he was well known, and with which island village his name was connected, and so came back in triumph to the scene of his disgrace. Thither many pilgrims began to resort. He received valuable presents, which he distributed to the poor, who acclaimed him as 'Zahed'—a renouncer of earthly pleasures. He journeyed preaching through Kordofan, and received the respect of the priesthood and the homage of the people. And while he spoke of the purification of the religion, they thought that the burning words might be applied to the freedom of the soil. He supported his sermons by writings, which were widely read. When a few months later the Sheikh Koreishi died, the priest of Abba proceeded forthwith to erect a tomb to his memory, directing and controlling the voluntary labours of the reverent Arabs who carried the stones.

While Mohammed was thus occupied he received the support of a man, less virtuous than but nearly as famous as himself. Abdullah was one of four brothers, the sons of an obscure priest; but he inherited no great love of religion or devotion to its observances. He was a man of determination and capacity. He set before himself two distinct ambitions, both of which he accomplished: to free the Soudan of foreigners, and to rule it himself. He seems to have had a queer presentiment of his career. This much he knew: there would be a great religious leader, and he would be his lieutenant and his successor. When Zubehr conquered Darfur, Abdullah presented himself before him and hailed him as 'the expected Mahdi.' Zubehr, however, protested with superfluous energy that he was no saint, and the impulsive patriot was compelled to accept his assurances. So soon as he saw Mohammed Ahmed rising to fame and displaying qualities of courage and energy, he hastened to throw himself at his feet and assure him of his devotion.

No part of Slatin Pasha's fascinating account of his perils and sufferings is so entertaining as that in which Abdullah, then become Khalifa of the whole Soudan, describes his early struggles and adversity:

'Indeed it was a very troublesome journey. At that time my entire property consisted of one donkey, and he had a gall on his back, so that I could not ride him. But I made him carry my water-skin and bag of corn, over which I spread my rough cotton garment, and drove him along in front of me. At that time I wore the white cotton shirt, like the rest of my tribe. My clothes and my dialect at once marked me out as a stranger wherever I went; and when I crossed the Nile I was frequently greeted with "What do you want? Go back to your own country. There is nothing to steal here."'

What a life of ups and downs! It was a long stride from the ownership of one saddle-galled donkey to the undisputed rule of an empire. The weary wayfarer may have dreamed of this, for ambition stirs imagination nearly as much as imagination excites ambition. But further he could not expect or wish to see. Nor could he anticipate as, in the complacency of a man who had done with evil days, he told the story of his rise to the submissive Slatin, that the day would come when he would lead an army of more than fifty thousand men to destruction, and that the night would follow when, almost alone, his empire shrunk again to the saddle-galled donkey, he would seek his home in distant Kordofan, while this same Slatin who knelt so humbly before him would lay the fierce pursuing squadrons on the trail.

Mohammed Ahmed received his new adherent kindly, but without enthusiasm. For some months Abdullah carried stones to build the tomb of the Sheikh el Koreishi. Gradually they got to know each other. 'But long before he entrusted me with his secret,' said Abdullah to Slatin, 'I knew that he was "the expected Guide."' [Slatin, FIRE AND SWORD, p.131.] And though the world might think that the 'Messenger of God' was sent to lead men to happiness in heaven, Abdullah attached to the phrase a significance of his own, and knew that he should lead him to power on earth. The two formed a strong combination. The Mahdi—for such Mohammed Ahmed had already in secret announced himself—brought the wild enthusiasm of religion, the glamour of a stainless life, and the influence of superstition into the movement. But if he were the soul of the plot, Abdullah was the brain. He was the man of the world, the practical politician, the general.

There now commenced a great conspiracy against the Egyptian Government. It was fostered by the discontents and justified by the miseries of the people of the Soudan. The Mahdi began to collect adherents and to extend his influence in all parts of the country. He made a second journey through Kordofan, and received everywhere promises of support from all classes. The most distant tribes sent assurances of devotion and reverence, and, what was of more importance, of armed assistance. The secret could not be long confined to those who welcomed the movement. As the ramifications of the plot spread they were perceived by the renowned Sheikh Sherif, who still nursed his chagrin and thirsted for revenge. He warned the Egyptian Government. They, knowing his envy and hatred of his former disciple, discounted his evidence and for some time paid no attention to the gathering of the storm. But presently more trustworthy witnesses confirmed his statements, and Raouf Pasha, then Governor-General, finding himself confronted with a growing agitation, determined to act. He accordingly sent a messenger to the island of Abba, to summon Mohammed Ahmed to Khartoum to justify his behaviour and explain his intentions. The news of the despatch of the messenger was swiftly carried to the Mahdi! He consulted with his trusty lieutenant. They decided to risk everything, and without further delay to defy the Government. When it is remembered how easily an organised army, even though it be in a bad condition, can stamp out the beginnings of revolt among a population, the courage of their resolve must be admired.

The messenger arrived. He was received with courtesy by Abdullah, and forthwith conducted before the Mahdi. He delivered his message, and urged Mohammed Ahmed to comply with the orders of the Governor-General. The Mahdi listened for some time in silence, but with increasing emotion; and when the messenger advised him, as he valued his own safety, to journey to Khartoum, if only to justify himself, his passion overcame him. 'What!' he shouted, rising suddenly and striking his breast with his hand. 'By the grace of God and his Prophet I am master of this country, and never shall I go to Khartoum to justify myself.' [Slatin, FIRE AND SWORD, p.135.] The terrified messenger withdrew. The rebellion of the Mahdi had begun.

Both the priest and the Governor-General prepared for military enterprise. The Mahdi proclaimed a holy war against the foreigners, alike the enemies of God and the scourge of men. He collected his followers. He roused the local tribes. He wrote letters to all parts of the Soudan, calling upon the people to fight for a purified religion, the freedom of the soil, and God's holy prophet 'the expected Mahdi.' He promised the honour of men to those who lived, the favour of God to those who fell, and lastly that the land should be cleared of the miserable 'Turk.' 'Better,' he said, and it became the watchword of the revolt, 'thousands of graves than a dollar tax.' [Ohrwalder, TEN YEARS' CAPTIVITY IN THE MAHDI'S CAMP.]

Nor was Raouf Pasha idle. He sent two companies of infantry with one gun by steamer to Abba to arrest the fanatic who disturbed the public peace. What followed is characteristically Egyptian. Each company was commanded by a captain. To encourage their efforts, whichever officer captured the Mahdi was promised promotion. At sunset on an August evening in 1881 the steamer arrived at Abba. The promise of the Governor-General had provoked the strife, not the emulation of the officers. Both landed with their companies and proceeded by different routes under the cover of darkness to the village where the Mahdi dwelt. Arriving simultaneously from opposite directions, they fired into each other, and, in the midst of this mistaken combat, the Mahdi rushed upon them with his scanty following and destroyed them impartially. A few soldiers succeeded in reaching the bank of the river. But the captain of the steamer would run no risks, and those who could not swim out to the vessel were left to their fate. With such tidings the expedition returned to Khartoum.

Mohammed Ahmed had been himself wounded in the attack, but the faithful Abdullah bound up the injury, so that none might know that God's Prophet had been pierced by carnal weapons. The effect of the success was electrical. The news spread throughout the Soudan. Men with sticks had slain men with rifles. A priest had destroyed the soldiers of the Government. Surely this was the Expected One. The Mahdi, however, profited by his victory only to accomplish a retreat without loss of prestige. Abdullah had no illusions. More troops would be sent. They were too near to Khartoum. Prudence counselled flight to regions more remote. But before this new Hegira the Mahdi appointed his four Khalifas, in accordance with prophecy and precedent. The first was Abdullah. Of the others it is only necessary at this moment to notice Ali-Wad-Helu, the chief of one of the local tribes, and among the first to rally to the standard of revolt.

Then the retreat began; but it was more like a triumphal progress. Attended by a considerable following, and preceded by tales of the most wonderful miracles and prodigies, the Mahdi retired to a mountain in Kordofan to which he gave the name of Jebel Masa, that being the mountain whence 'the expected Guide' is declared in the Koran sooner or later to appear. He was now out of reach of Khartoum, but within reach of Fashoda. The Egyptian Governor of that town, Rashid Bey, a man of more enterprise and even less military knowledge than is usual in his race, determined to make all attempt to seize the rebel and disperse his following. Taking no precautions, he fell on the 9th of December into an ambush, was attacked unprepared, and was himself, with fourteen hundred men, slaughtered by the ill-armed but valiant Arabs.

The whole country stirred. The Government, thoroughly alarmed by the serious aspect the revolt had assumed, organised a great expedition. Four thousand troops under Yusef, a Pasha of distinguished reputation, were sent against the rebels. Meanwhile the Mahdi and his followers suffered the extremes of want. Their cause was as yet too perilous for the rich to join. Only the poor flocked to the holy standard. All that Mohammed possessed he gave away, keeping nothing for himself, excepting only a horse to lead his followers in battle. Abdullah walked. Nevertheless the rebels were half-famished, and armed with scarcely any more deadly weapons than sticks and stones. The army of the Government approached slowly. Their leaders anticipated an easy victory. Their contempt for the enemy was supreme. They did not even trouble themselves to post sentries by night, but slept calmly inside a slender thorn fence, unwatched save by their tireless foes. And so it came to pass that in the half-light of the early morning of the 7th of June the Mahdi, his ragged Khalifas, and his almost naked army rushed upon them, and slew them to a man.

The victory was decisive. Southern Kordofan was at the feet of the priest of Abba. Stores of arms and ammunition had fallen into his hands. Thousands of every class hastened to join his standard. No one doubted that he was the divine messenger sent to free them from their oppressors. The whole of the Arab tribes all over the Soudan rose at once. The revolt broke out simultaneously in Sennar and Darfur, and spread to provinces still more remote. The smaller Egyptian posts, the tax-gatherers and local administrators, were massacred in every district. Only the larger garrisons maintained themselves in the principal towns. They were at once blockaded. All communications were interrupted. All legal authority was defied. Only the Mahdi was obeyed.

It is now necessary to look for a moment to Egypt. The misgovernment which in the Soudan had caused the rebellion of the Mahdi, in Egypt produced the revolt of Arabi Pasha. As the people of the Soudan longed to be rid of the foreign oppressors—the so-called 'Turks'—so those of the Delta were eager to free themselves from the foreign regulators and the real Turkish influence. While men who lived by the sources of the Nile asserted that tribes did not exist for officials to harry, others who dwelt at its mouth protested that nations were not made to be exploited by creditors or aliens. The ignorant south found their leader in a priest: the more educated north looked to a soldier. Mohammed Ahmed broke the Egyptian yoke; Arabi gave expression to the hatred of the Egyptians for the Turks. But although the hardy Arabs might scatter the effete Egyptians, the effete Egyptians were not likely to disturb the solid battalions of Europe. After much hesitation and many attempts at compromise, the Liberal Administration of Mr. Gladstone sent a fleet which reduced the forts of Alexandria to silence and the city to anarchy. The bombardment of the fleet was followed by the invasion of a powerful army. Twenty-five thousand men were landed in Egypt. The campaign was conducted with celerity and skill. The Egyptian armies were slaughtered or captured. Their patriotic but commonplace leader was sentenced to death and condemned to exile, and Great Britain assumed the direction of Egyptian affairs.

The British soon restored law and order in Egypt, and the question of the revolt in the Soudan came before the English advisers of the Khedive. Notwithstanding the poverty and military misfortunes which depressed the people of the Delta, the desire to hold their southern provinces was evident. The British Government, which at that time was determined to pursue a policy of non-interference in the Soudan, gave a tacit consent, and another great expedition was prepared to suppress the False Prophet, as the English and Egyptians deemed him—'the expected Mahdi,' as the people of the Soudan believed.

A retired officer of the Indian Staff Corps and a few European officers of various nationalities were sent to Khartoum to organise the new field force. Meanwhile the Mahdi, having failed to take by storm, laid siege to El Obeid, the chief town of Kordofan. During the summer of 1883 the Egyptian troops gradually concentrated at Khartoum until a considerable army was formed. It was perhaps the worst army that has ever marched to war. One extract from General Hicks's letters will suffice. Writing on the 8th of June, 1883, to Sir E. Wood, he says incidentally: 'Fifty-one men of the Krupp battery deserted on the way here, although in chains.' The officers and men who had been defeated fighting for their own liberties at Tel-el-Kebir were sent to be destroyed, fighting to take away the liberties of others in the Soudan. They had no spirit, no discipline, hardly any training, and in a force of over eight thousand men there were scarcely a dozen capable officers. The two who were the most notable of these few—General Hicks, who commanded, and Colonel Farquhar, the Chief of the Staff—must be remarked.

El Obeid had fallen before the ill-fated expedition left Khartoum; but the fact that Slatin Bey, an Austrian officer in the Egyptian service, was still maintaining himself in Darfur provided it with an object. On the 9th of September Hicks and his army (the actual strength of which was 7,000 infantry, 400 mounted Bashi Bazuks, 500 cavalry, 100 Circassians, 10 mounted guns, 4 Krupps, and 6 Nordenfeldt machine guns) left Omdurman and marched to Duem. Although the actual command of the expedition was vested in the English officer, Ala-ed-Din Pasha, the Governor-General who had succeeded Raouf Pasha, exercised an uncertain authority. Differences of opinion were frequent, though all the officers were agreed in taking the darkest views of their chances. The miserable host toiled slowly onward towards its destruction, marching in a south-westerly direction through Shat and Rahad. Here the condition of the force was so obviously demoralised that a German servant (Gustav Klootz, the servant of Baron Seckendorf) actually deserted to the Mahdi's camp. He was paraded in triumph as an English officer.

On the approach of the Government troops the Mahdi had marched out of El Obeid and established himself in the open country, where he made his followers live under military conditions and continually practised them in warlike evolutions. More than forty thousand men collected round his standard, and the Arabs were now armed with several thousand rifles and a few cannon, as well as a great number of swords and spears. To these proportions had the little band of followers who fought at Abba grown! The disparity of the forces was apparent before the battle. The Mahdi thereupon wrote to Hicks, calling on him to surrender and offering terms. His proposals were treated with disdain, although the probable result of an engagement was clear.

Until the expedition reached Rahad only a few cavalry patrols had watched its slow advance. But on the 1st of November the Mahdi left El Obeid and marched with his whole power to meet his adversary. The collision took place on the 3rd of November. All through that day the Egyptians struggled slowly forward, in great want of water, losing continually from the fire of the Soudanese riflemen, and leaving several guns behind them. On the next morning they were confronted by the main body of the Arab army, and their attempts to advance further were defeated with heavy loss. The force began to break up. Yet another day was consumed before it was completely destroyed. Scarcely five hundred Egyptians escaped death; hardly as many of the Arabs fell. The European officers perished fighting to the end; and the general met his fate sword in hand, at the head of the last formed body of his troops, his personal valour and physical strength exciting the admiration even of the fearless enemy, so that in chivalrous respect they buried his body with barbaric honours. Mohammed Ahmed celebrated his victory with a salute of one hundred guns; and well he might, for the Soudan was now his, and his boast that, by God's grace and the favour of the Prophet, he was the master of all the land had been made good by force of arms.

No further attempt was made to subdue the country. The people of the Soudan had won their freedom by their valour and by the skill and courage of their saintly leader. It only remained to evacuate the towns and withdraw the garrisons safely. But what looked like the winding-up of one story was really the beginning of another, much longer, just as bloody, commencing in shame and disaster, but ending in triumph and, let us hope, in peace.

I desire for a moment to take a more general view of the Mahdi's movement than the narrative has allowed. The original causes were social and racial. But, great as was the misery of the people, their spirit was low, and they would not have taken up arms merely on material grounds. Then came the Mahdi. He gave the tribes the enthusiasm they lacked. The war broke out. It is customary to lay to the charge of Mohammed Ahmed all the blood that was spilled. To my mind it seems that he may divide the responsibility with the unjust rulers who oppressed the land, with the incapable commanders who muddled away the lives of their men, with the vacillating Ministers who aggravated the misfortunes. But, whatever is set to the Mahdi's account, it should not be forgotten that he put life and soul into the hearts of his countrymen, and freed his native land of foreigners. The poor miserable natives, eating only a handful of grain, toiling half-naked and without hope, found a new, if terrible magnificence added to life. Within their humble breasts the spirit of the Mahdi roused the fires of patriotism and religion. Life became filled with thrilling, exhilarating terrors. They existed in a new and wonderful world of imagination. While they lived there were great things to be done; and when they died, whether it were slaying the Egyptians or charging the British squares, a Paradise which they could understand awaited them. There are many Christians who reverence the faith of Islam and yet regard the Mahdi merely as a commonplace religious impostor whom force of circumstances elevated to notoriety. In a certain sense, this may be true. But I know not how a genuine may be distinguished from a spurious Prophet, except by the measure of his success. The triumphs of the Mahdi were in his lifetime far greater than those of the founder of the Mohammedan faith; and the chief difference between orthodox Mohammedanism and Mahdism was that the original impulse was opposed only by decaying systems of government and society and the recent movement came in contact with civilisation and the machinery of science. Recognising this, I do not share the popular opinion, and I believe that if in future years prosperity should come to the peoples of the Upper Nile, and learning and happiness follow in its train, then the first Arab historian who shall investigate the early annals of that new nation will not forget, foremost among the heroes of his race, to write the name of Mohammed Ahmed.

CHAPTER II:

THE FATE OF THE ENVOY

All great movements, every vigorous impulse that a community may feel, become perverted and distorted as time passes, and the atmosphere of the earth seems fatal to the noble aspirations of its peoples. A wide humanitarian sympathy in a nation easily degenerates into hysteria. A military spirit tends towards brutality. Liberty leads to licence, restraint to tyranny. The pride of race is distended to blustering arrogance. The fear of God produces bigotry and superstition. There appears no exception to the mournful rule, and the best efforts of men, however glorious their early results, have dismal endings, like plants which shoot and bud and put forth beautiful flowers, and then grow rank and coarse and are withered by the winter. It is only when we reflect that the decay gives birth to fresh life, and that new enthusiasms spring up to take the places of those that die, as the acorn is nourished by the dead leaves of the oak, the hope strengthens that the rise and fall of men and their movements are only the changing foliage of the ever-growing tree of life, while underneath a greater evolution goes on continually.

The movement which Mohammed Ahmed created did not escape the common fate of human enterprise; nor was it long before the warm generous blood of a patriotic and religious revolt congealed into the dark clot of a military empire. With the expulsion or destruction of the foreign officials, soldiers, and traders, the racial element began to subside. The reason for its existence was removed. With the increasing disorders the social agitation dwindled; for communism pre-supposes wealth, and the wealth of the Soudan was greatly diminished. There remained only the fanatical fury which the belief in the divine mission of the Mahdi had excited; and as the necessity for a leader passed away, the belief in his sanctity grew weaker. But meanwhile a new force was making itself felt on the character of the revolt. The triumph no less than the plunder which had rewarded the Mahdi's victories had called into existence a military spirit distinct from the warlike passions of the tribesmen—the spirit of the professional soldier.

The siege of Khartoum was carried on while this new influence was taking the place of the original forces of revolt. There was a period when a neutral point was obtained and the Mahdist power languished. But the invasion of the Eastern Soudan by the British troops in the spring and the necessary advance of the relieving columns in the winter of 1884 revived the patriotic element. The tribes who had made a great effort to free themselves from foreign domination saw in the operations of Sir Gerald Graham and Lord Wolseley an attempt to bring them again under the yoke. The impulse which was given to the Mahdi's cause was sufficient to raise a fierce opposition to the invading forces. The delay in the despatch of the relief expedition had sealed the fate of Khartoum, and the fall of the town established the supremacy of the military spirit on which the Dervish Empire was afterwards founded.

All the warlike operations of Mohammedan peoples are characterised by fanaticism, but with this general reservation it may be said—that the Arabs who destroyed Yusef, who assaulted El Obeid, who annihilated Hicks fought in the glory of religious zeal; that the Arabs who opposed Graham, Earle, and Stewart fought in defence of the soil; and that the Arabs who were conquered by Kitchener fought in the pride of an army. Fanatics charged at Shekan; patriots at Abu Klea; warriors at Omdurman.

In order to describe conveniently the changing character of the revolt, I have anticipated the story and must revert to a period when the social and racial influences were already weakening and the military spirit was not yet grown strong. If the defeat of Yusef Pasha decided the whole people of the Soudan to rise in arms and strike for their liberties, the defeat of Hicks satisfied the British Government that those liberties were won. The powerful influence of the desire to rule prompted the Khedive's Ministers to make still further efforts to preserve their country's possessions. Had Egypt been left to herself, other desperate efforts would have been made. But the British Government had finally abandoned the policy of non-interference with Egyptian action in the Soudan. They 'advised' its abandonment. The protests of Sherif Pasha provoked Lord Granville to explain the meaning of the word 'advice.' The Khedive bowed to superior authority. The Minister resigned. The policy of evacuation was firmly adopted. 'Let us,' said the Ministers, 'collect the garrisons and come away.' It was simple to decide on the course to be pursued, but almost impossible to follow it. Several of the Egyptian garrisons, as in Darfur and El Obeid, had already fallen. The others were either besieged, like Sennar, Tokar, and Sinkat, or cut off from the north, as in the case of the Equatorial Province, by the area of rebellion. The capital of the Soudan was, however, as yet unmolested; and as its Egyptian population exceeded the aggregate of the provincial towns, the first task of the Egyptian Government was obvious.

Mr. Gladstone's Administration had repressed the revolt of Arabi Pasha. Through their policy the British were in armed occupation of Egypt. British officers were reorganising the army. A British official supervised the finances. A British plenipotentiary 'advised' the re-established Tewfik. A British fleet lay attentive before the ruins of Alexandria, and it was evident that Great Britain could annex the country in name as well as in fact. But Imperialism was not the object of the Radical Cabinet. Their aim was philanthropic and disinterested. As they were now determined that the Egyptians should evacuate the Soudan, so they had always been resolved that the British should evacuate Egypt.

Throughout this chapter it will be seen that the desire to get out of the country at once is the keynote of the British policy. Every act, whether of war or administration, is intended to be final. Every despatch is directed to breaking the connection between the two countries and winding up the severed strings. But responsibilities which had been lightly assumed clung like the shirt of Nessus. The ordinary practice of civilised nations demanded that some attempt should be made to justify interference by reorganisation. The British Government watched therefore with anxious solicitude the efforts of Egypt to evacuate the Soudan and bring the garrisons safely home. They utterly declined to assist with military force, but they were generous with their advice. Everybody at that time distrusted the capacities of the Egyptians, and it was thought the evacuation might be accomplished if it were entrusted to stronger and more honest men than were bred by the banks of the Nile. The Ministers looked about them, wondering how they could assist the Egyptian Government without risk or expense to themselves, and in an evil hour for their fame and fortunes someone whispered the word 'Gordon.' Forthwith they proceeded to telegraph to Cairo: 'Would General Charles Gordon be of any use to you or to the Egyptian Government; and, if so, in what capacity'? The Egyptian

Government replied through Sir Evelyn Baring that as the movement in the Soudan was partly religious they were 'very much averse' from the appointment of a Christian in high command. The eyes of all those who possessed local knowledge were turned to a different person. There was one man who might stem the tide of Mahdism, who might perhaps restore the falling dominion of Egypt, who might at least save the garrisons of the Soudan. In their necessity and distress the Khedivial advisers and the British plenipotentiary looked as a desperate remedy to the man whose liberty they had curtailed, whose property they had confiscated, and whose son they had executed—Zubehr Pasha.

This was the agent for whom the Government of Egypt hankered. The idea was supported by all who were acquainted with the local conditions. A week after Sir Evelyn Baring had declined General Gordon's services he wrote: 'Whatever may be Zubehr's faults, he is said to be a man of great energy and resolution. The Egyptian Government considers that his services may be very useful . . . Baker Pasha is anxious to avail himself of Zubehr Pasha's services.'[Sir Evelyn Baring, letter of December 9, 1883.] It is certain that had the Egyptian Government been a free agent, Zubehr would have been sent to the Soudan as its Sultan, and assisted by arms, money, and perhaps by men, to make head against the Mahdi. It is probable that at this particular period the Mahdi would have collapsed before a man whose fame was nearly equal to, and whose resources would have been much greater than, his own. But the British Ministry would countenance no dealings with such a man. They scouted the idea of Zubehr, and by so doing increased their obligation to suggest an alternative. Zubehr being rejected, Gordon remained. It is scarcely possible to conceive a greater contrast than that which these two men presented. It was a leap from the Equator to the North Pole.

When difficulties and dangers perplex all minds, it has often happened in history that many men by different lines of thought arrive at the same conclusion. No complete record has yet been published of the telegrams which passed between the Government and their agent at this juncture. The Blue-books preserve a disingenuous discretion. But it is known that from the very first Sir Evelyn Baring was bitterly opposed to General Gordon's appointment. No personal friendship existed between them, and the Administrator dreaded the return to the feverish complications of Egyptian politics of the man who had always been identified with unrest, improvisation, and disturbance. The pressure was, however, too strong for him to withstand. Nubar Pasha, the Foreign Office, the British public, everyone clamoured for the appointment. Had Baring refused to give way, it is probable that he would have been overruled. At length he yielded, and, as soon as his consent had been obtained, the government turned with delight to Gordon. On the 17th of January Lord Wolseley requested him to come to England. On the 18th he met the Cabinet. That same night he started on the long journey from which he was never to return.

Gordon embarked on his mission in high spirits, sustained by that belief in personality which too often misleads great men and beautiful women. It was, he said, the greatest honour ever conferred upon him. Everything smiled. The nation was delighted. The Ministers were intensely relieved. The most unbounded confidence was reposed in the envoy. His interview with the Khedive was 'very satisfactory.' His complete authority was proclaimed to all the notables and natives of the Soudan [Proclamation of the Khedive, January 26, 1884.] He was assured of the support of the Egyptian Government [Sir E. Baring to Major-General Gordon, January 25, 1884.] The London Foreign Office, having with becoming modesty admitted that they had not 'sufficient local knowledge,' [Earl Granville to Sir E. Baring, January 22, 1884.] accorded him 'widest discretionary power.' [Sir E. Baring to Earl Granville, February 1, 1884.] One hundred thousand pounds was placed to his credit, and he was informed that further sums would be supplied when this was exhausted. He was assured that no effort would be wanting on the part of the Cairene authorities, whether English or Egyptian, to afford him all the support and co-operation in their power [Sir E. Baring to Major-General Gordon, January 25, 1884.] 'There is no sort of difference,' wrote Sir Evelyn Baring, 'between General Gordon's views and those entertained by Nubar Pasha and myself.' [Sir E. Baring to Earl Granville, February 1,1884.] Under these propitious auguries the dismal and disastrous enterprise began.

His task, though difficult and, as it ultimately proved, impossible, was clearly defined. 'You will bear in mind,' wrote Sir Evelyn Baring, 'that the main end to be pursued is the evacuation of the Soudan.' 'The object . . . of your mission to the Soudan,' declared the Khedive, 'is to carry into execution the evacuation of those territories and to withdraw our troops, civil officials, and such of the inhabitants . . . as may wish to leave for Egypt . . . and after the evacuation to take the necessary steps for establishing an organised Government in the different provinces.' Nor was he himself under any misconception. He drew up a memorandum when on board the Tanjore in which he fully acquiesced in the evacuation of the Soudan. In a sentence which breathes the same spirit as Mr. Gladstone's famous expression, 'a people rightly struggling to be free,' he wrote: 'I must say that it would be an iniquity to conquer these peoples and then hand them back to the Egyptians without guarantees of future good government.' Finally, he unhesitatingly asserted: 'No one who has ever lived in the Soudan can escape the reflection "What a useless possession is this land!"' And Colonel Stewart, who accompanied him and endorsed the memorandum, added: 'And what a huge encumbrance to Egypt!' Thus far there was complete agreement between the British envoy and the Liberal Cabinet.

It is beyond the scope of these pages to describe his long ride across the desert from Korosko to Abu Hamed, his interview with the notables at Berber, or his proclamation of the abandonment of the Soudan, which some affirm to have been an important cause of his ruin. On the 22nd of February he arrived at Khartoum. He was received with rejoicing by the whole population. They recognised again their just Governor-General and their present deliverer. Those who had been about to fly for the north took fresh heart. They believed that behind the figure of the envoy stood the resources of an Empire. The Mahdi and the gathering Dervishes were perplexed and alarmed. Confusion and hesitancy disturbed their councils and delayed their movements. Gordon had come. The armies would follow. Both friends and foes were deceived. The great man was at Khartoum, but there he would remain—alone.

Whatever confidence the General had felt in the power of his personal influence had been dispelled on the journey to Khartoum. He had no more illusions. His experienced eye reviewed the whole situation. He saw himself confronted with a tremendous racial movement. The people of the Soudan had risen against foreigners. His only troops were Soudanese. He was himself a foreigner. Foremost among the leaders of the revolt were the Arab slave dealers, furious at the attempted suppression of their trade. No one, not even Sir Samuel Baker, had tried harder to suppress it than Gordon. Lastly, the whole movement had assumed a fanatical character. Islam marched against the infidel. Gordon was a Christian. His own soldiers were under the spell they were to try to destroy. To them their commander was accursed. Every influence was hostile, and in particular hostile to his person. The combined forces of race, class, and religion were against him. He bowed before their irresistible strength. On the very day of his arrival at Khartoum, while the townsfolk were cheering his name in the streets and the batteries were firing joyful salutes, while the people of England thought his mission already accomplished and the Government congratulated themselves on the wisdom of their action, General Gordon sat himself down and telegraphed a formal request to Cairo for Zubehr Pasha.

The whole story of his relations with Zubehr is extremely characteristic. Zubehr's son, Suliman, had been executed, if not by Gordon's orders, at least during his administration of the Soudan and with his complete approval. 'Thus,' he had said, 'does God make gaps in the ranks of His enemies.' He had hardly started from London on his new mission, when he telegraphed to Sir Evelyn Baring, telling him that Zubehr was a most dangerous man and requesting that he might be at once deported to Cyprus. This was, of course, quite beyond the powers or intention of the British Agent. The General arrived in Cairo like a whirlwind close behind his telegram, and was very angry to hear that Zubehr was still in Egypt. Before starting up the river he went to see Sherif Pasha. In the ex-Minister's ante-room he met the very man he had determined to avoid—Zubehr. He greeted him with effusion. They had a long talk about the Soudan, after which Gordon hurried to the Agency and informed Sir Evelyn Baring that Zubehr must accompany him to Khartoum at once. Baring was amazed. He did not himself disapprove of the plan. He had, in fact, already recommended it. But he thought the change in Gordon's attitude too sudden to be relied on. To-morrow he might change again. He begged the General to think more seriously of the matter. Gordon with his usual frankness admitted that his change of mind had been very sudden. He had been conscious, he said, of a 'mystic feeling' that Zubehr was necessary to save the situation in the Soudan.

Gordon left Cairo still considering the matter. So soon as he made his formal demand from Khartoum for the assistance of Zubehr it was evident that his belief in the old slave dealer's usefulness was a sound conviction and not a mere passing caprice. Besides, he had now become 'the man on the spot,' and as such his words carried double force. Sir Evelyn Baring determined to support the recommendation with his whole influence. Never was so good a case made out for the appointment of so bad a man. The Envoy Extraordinary asked for him; Colonel Stewart, his colleague, concurred; the British Agent strongly urged the request; the Egyptian Government were unanimous; and behind all these were ranged every single person who had the slightest acquaintance with the Soudan. nothing could exceed the vigour with which the demand was made. On the 1st of March General Gordon telegraphed: 'I tell you plainly, it is impossible to get Cairo employees out of Khartoum unless the Government helps in the way I told you. They refuse Zubehr . . . but it was the only chance.' And again on the 8th: 'If you do not send Zubehr, you have no chance of getting the garrisons away.' 'I believe,' said Sir Evelyn Baring in support of these telegrams, 'that General Gordon is quite right when he says that Zubehr Pasha is the only possible man. Nubar is strongly in favour of him. Dr. Bohndorf, the African traveller, fully confirms what General Gordon says of the influence of Zubehr.' The Pasha was vile, but indispensable.

Her Majesty's Government refused absolutely to have anything to do with Zubehr. They declined to allow the Egyptian Government to employ him. They would not entertain the proposal, and scarcely consented to discuss it. The historians of the future may occupy their leisure and exercise their wits in deciding whether the Ministers and the people were right or wrong; whether they had a right to indulge their sensitiveness at so terrible a cost; whether they were not more nice than wise; whether their dignity was more offended by what was incurred or by what was avoided.

General Gordon has explained his views very clearly and concisely: 'Had Zubehr Pasha been sent up when I asked for him, Berber would in all probability never have fallen, and one might have made a Soudan Government in opposition to the Mahdi. We choose to refuse his coming up because of his antecedents in re slave trade; granted that we had reason, yet, as we take no precautions as to the future of these lands with respect to the slave trade, the above opposition seems absurd. I will not send up 'A' because he will do this, but I will leave the country to 'B', who will do exactly the same [Major-General Gordon, JOURNALS AT KHARTOUM.]

But if the justice of the decision is doubtful, its consequences were obvious. Either the British Government were concerned with the Soudan, or they were not. If they were not, then they had no reason or right to prohibit the appointment of Zubehr. If they were, they were bound to see that the garrisons were rescued. It was an open question whether Great Britain was originally responsible for the safety of the garrisons. General Gordon contended that we were bound to save them at all costs, and he backed his belief with his life. Others may hold that Governments have no right to lay, or at any rate must be very judicious in the laying of burdens on the backs of their own countrymen in order that they may indulge a refined sense of chivalry towards foreigners. England had not misgoverned the Soudan, had not raised the revolt or planted the garrisons. All that Egypt had a right to expect was commiseration. But the moment Zubehr was prohibited the situation was changed. The refusal to permit his employment was tantamount to an admission that affairs in the Soudan involved the honour of England as well as the honour of Egypt. When the British people—for this was not merely the act of the Government—adopted a high moral attitude with regard to Zubehr, they bound themselves to rescue the garrisons, peaceably if possible, forcibly if necessary.

With their refusal to allow Zubehr to go to the Soudan began the long and miserable disagreement between the Government and their envoy. Puzzled and disturbed at the reception accorded to his first request, Gordon cast about for other expedients. He had already stated that Zubehr was 'the only chance.' But it is the duty of subordinates to suggest other courses when those they recommend are rejected; and with a whole-hearted enthusiasm and unreserved loyalty the General threw himself into the affair and proposed plan after plan with apparent hope.

Gordon considered that he was personally pledged to effect the evacuation of Khartoum by the garrison and civil servants. He had appointed some of the inhabitants to positions of trust, thus compromising them with the Mahdi. Others had undoubtedly been encouraged to delay their departure by his arrival. He therefore considered that his honour was involved in their safety. Henceforward he was inflexible. Neither rewards nor threats could move him. Nothing that men could offer would induce him to leave Khartoum till its inhabitants were rescued. The Government on their side were equally stubborn. Nothing, however sacred, should induce them to send troops to Khartoum, or in any way involve themselves in the middle of Africa. The town might fall; the garrison might be slaughtered; their envoy—But what possibilities they were prepared to face as regards him will not be known until all of this and the next generation are buried and forgotten.

The deadlock was complete. To some men the Foreign Office might have suggested lines of retreat, covered by the highest official praise, and leading to preferment and reward. Others would have welcomed an order to leave so perilous a post. But the man they had sent was the one man of all others who was beyond their control, who cared nothing for what they could give or take away. So events dragged on their wretched course. Gordon's proposals became more and more impracticable as the best courses he could devise were successively vetoed by the Government, and as his irritation and disappointment increased. The editor of his Journals has enumerated them with indignant care. He had asked for Zubehr. Zubehr was refused. He had requested Turkish troops. Turkish troops were refused. He had asked for Mohammedan regiments from India. The Government regretted their inability to comply. He asked for a Firman from the Sultan to strengthen his position. It was 'peremptorily refused.' He proposed to go south in his steamers to Equatoria. The Government forbade him to proceed beyond Khartoum. He asked that 200 British troops might be sent to Berber. They were refused. He begged that a few might be sent to Assuan. None were sent. He proposed to visit the Mahdi himself and try to arrange matters with him personally. Perhaps he recognised a kindred spirit. The Government in this case very naturally forbade him.

At last the quarrel is open. He makes no effort to conceal his disgust. 'I leave you,' he says, the 'indelible disgrace of abandoning the garrisons.' [Major-General Gordon to Sir E. Baring (telegraphic), received at Cairo April 16.] Such abandonment is, he declares, 'the climax of meanness.' [Ibid, despatched April 8.] He reiterates his determination to abide with the garrison of Khartoum. 'I will not leave these people after all they have gone through.' [Major-General Gordon to Sir E. Baring, Khartoum, July 30; received at Cairo October 15.] He tosses his commission contemptuously from him: 'I would also ask her Majesty's Government to accept the resignation of my commission.' [Major-General Gordon to Sir E. Baring (telegraphic), Khartoum, March 9.] The Government 'trust that he will not resign,' [Earl Granville to Sir E. Baring, Foreign Office, March 13.] and his offer remains in abeyance. Finally, in bitterness and vexation, thinking himself abandoned and disavowed, he appeals to Sir Evelyn Baring personally: 'I feel sure, whatever you may feel diplomatically, I have your support—and that of every man professing himself a gentleman—in private'; [Major-General Gordon to Sir E. Baring (telegraphic), received at Cairo April 16.] and as a last hope he begs Sir Samuel Baker to appeal to 'British and American millionaires' to subscribe two hundred thousand pounds to enable him to carry out the evacuation without, and even in spite of, the Governments of Cairo and London; and Sir Samuel Baker writes a long letter to the Times in passionate protest and entreaty.

Such are the chief features in the wretched business. Even the Blue-books in their dry recital arouse in the reader painful and indignant emotions. But meanwhile other and still more stirring events were passing outside the world of paper and ink.

The arrival of Gordon at Khartoum had seriously perplexed and alarmed Mohammed Ahmed and his Khalifas. Their following was discouraged, and they themselves feared lest the General should be the herald of armies. His Berber proclamation reassured them, and as the weeks passed without reinforcements arriving, the Mahdi and Abdullah, with that courage which in several great emergencies drew them to the boldest courses, determined to put a brave face on the matter and blockade Khartoum itself. They were assisted in this enterprise by a revival of the patriotic impulse throughout the country and a consequent stimulus to the revolt. To discover the cause it is necessary to look to the Eastern Soudan, where the next tragedy, after the defeat of Hicks, is laid.

The Hadendoa tribe, infuriated by oppression and misgovernment, had joined the rebellion under the leadership of the celebrated, and perhaps immortal, Osman Digna. The Egyptian garrisons of Tokar and Sinkat were beleaguered and hard pressed. Her Majesty's Government disclaimed all responsibility. Yet, since these towns were not far from the coast, they did not prohibit an attempt on the part of the Egyptian Government to rescue the besieged soldiers. Accordingly an Egyptian force 3,500 strong marched from Suakin in February 1884 to relieve Tokar, under the command of General Baker, once the gallant colonel of the 10th Hussars. Hard by the wells of Teb they were, on the 5th of February, attacked by about a thousand Arabs.

'On the square being only threatened by a small force of the enemy . . . the Egyptian troops threw down their arms and ran, carrying away the black troops with them, and allowing themselves to be killed without the slightest resistance.' [General Baker to Sir E. Baring, February 6 (official despatch), telegraphic.] The British and European officers in vain endeavoured to rally them. The single Soudanese battalion fired impartially on friend and foe. The general, with that unshaken courage and high military skill which had already on the Danube gained him a continental reputation, collected some fifteen hundred men, mostly unarmed, and so returned to Suakin. Ninety-six officers and 2,250 men were killed. Krupp guns, machine guns, rifles, and a large supply of ammunition fell to the victorious Arabs. Success inflamed their ardour to the point of madness. The attack of the towns was pressed with redoubled vigour. The garrison of Sinkat, 800 strong, sallied out and attempted to fight their way to Suakin. The garrison of Tokar surrendered. Both were destroyed.

The evil was done. The slaughter was complete. Yet the British Government resolved to add to it. The garrisons they had refused to rescue they now determined to avenge. In spite of their philanthropic professions, and in spite of the advice of General Gordon, who felt that his position at Khartoum would be still further compromised by operations on his only line of retreat [Sir E. Baring to Earl Granville, Cairo, February 23.], a considerable military expedition consisting of one cavalry and two infantry brigades, was sent to Suakin. The command was entrusted to General Graham. Troops were hurriedly concentrated. The 10th Hussars, returning from India, were stopped and mounted on the horses of the gendarmerie. With admirable celerity the force took the field. Within a month of the defeat at Teb they engaged the enemy almost on the very scene of the disaster. On the 4th of March they slew 3,000 Hadendoa and drove the rest in disorder from the ground. Four weeks later a second action was fought at Tamai. Again the success of the British troops was complete; again the slaughter of the Arabs was enormous. But neither victory was bloodless. El Teb cost 24 officers and 168 men; Tamai, 13 officers and 208 men. The effect of these operations was the dispersal of Osman Digna's gathering. That astute man, not for the first or last time, made a good retreat.

Ten thousand men had thus been killed in the space of three months in the Eastern Soudan. By the discipline of their armies the Government were triumphant. The tribes of the Red Sea shore cowered before them. But as they fought without reason, so they conquered without profit.

As soon as Gordon had been finally refused the assistance of Zubehr Pasha, it was evident that the rescue of the garrisons was impossible. The General had been sent as the last hope. Rightly or wrongly, his recommendations were ignored. His mission was an admitted failure. After that the only question was how to bring him away as quickly as possible. It was certain that he would not come willingly. Force was necessary. Yet it was difficult to know how to apply it. After the victories in the Eastern Soudan the opportunity presented itself. The road was open. The local tribes were crushed. Berber had not then fallen. The

Mahdi was himself still on the road from El Obeid to Khartoum. Sir Evelyn Baring saw the chance. He did not then occupy the formidable and imposing position in Egyptian politics that he has since attained. But with all his influence he urged the despatch of a small flying column to Khartoum. His idea was simple. One thousand or twelve hundred men were to mount on camels and ride thither via Berber. Those who fell ill or whose camels broke down would have to take their chance by the roadside. The plan, however, broke down in the military detail. Only one honourable course remained—a regular expedition. This the British Agent at once began to urge. This the Government obstinately refused to admit; and meanwhile time was passing.

The situation at Khartoum became grave even before the breach between General Gordon and Mr. Gladstone's Cabinet was complete. While the British Government was indulging in vengeful operations in the Eastern Soudan, the Mahdi advanced slowly but steadily upon the town with a following variously estimated at from fifteen to twenty thousand men. On the 7th of March Colonel Stewart telegraphed from Khartoum: 'The Mahdi has attempted to raise the people of Shendi by an emissary . . . We may be cut off;' [Lieut.-Colonel Stewart to Sir E. Baring, March 7, 1884.] and on the 11th Gordon himself reported: 'The rebels are four hours distant on the Blue Nile.' [Major-General Gordon to Sir E. Baring, March 11, 1884.] Thereafter no more telegrams came, for on the 15th the wire was cut between Shendi and Berber, and the blockade had commenced.

The long and glorious defence of the town of Khartoum will always fascinate attention. That one man, a European among Africans, a Christian among Mohammedans, should by his genius have inspired the efforts of 7,000 soldiers of inferior race, and by his courage have sustained the hearts of 30,000 inhabitants of notorious timidity, and with such materials and encumbrances have offered a vigorous resistance to the increasing attacks of an enemy who, though cruel, would yet accept surrender, during a period of 317 days, is an event perhaps without parallel in history. But it may safely be predicted that no one will ever write an account which will compare in interest or in detail with that set forth by the man himself in the famous. 'Journals at Khartoum.'

The brief account has delighted thousands of readers in Europe and America. Perhaps it is because he is careless of the sympathy of men that Charles Gordon so readily wins it. Before the first of the six parts into which the Journals were divided is finished, the reader has been won. Henceforth he sees the world through Gordon's eyes. With him he scoffs at the diplomatists; despises the Government; becomes impatient—unreasonably, perhaps—with a certain Major Kitchener in the Intelligence Branch, whose information miscarried or was not despatched; is wearied by the impracticable Shaiggia Irregulars; takes interest in the turkey-cock and his harem of four wives; laughs at the 'black sluts' seeing their faces for the first time in the mirror. With him he trembles for the fate of the 'poor little beast,' the Husseinyeh, when she drifts stern foremost on the shoal, 'a penny steamer under cannon fire'; day after day he gazes through the General's powerful telescope from the palace roof down the long brown reaches of the river towards the rocks of the Shabluka Gorge, and longs for some sign of the relieving steamers; and when the end of the account is reached, no man of British birth can read the last words, 'Now mark this, if the Expeditionary Force—and I ask for no more than two hundred men—does not come within ten days, the town may fall; and I have done my best for the honour of our country. Good-bye,' without being thrilled with vain regrets and futile resolutions. And then the account stops short. Nor will the silence ever be broken. The sixth instalment of the Journals was despatched on the 14th of December; and when it is finished the reader, separated suddenly from the pleasant companionship, experiences a feeling of loss and annoyance. Imagination, long supported, is brushed aside by stern reality. Henceforward Gordon's perils were unrecorded.

I would select one episode only from the Journals as an example of the peculiarity and the sternness of Charles Gordon's character—his behaviour towards Slatin. This Austrian officer had been Governor of Darfur with the rank in the Egyptian service of Bey. For four years he had struggled vainly against the rebellion. He had fought numerous engagements with varied success. He had been several times wounded. Throughout his province and even beyond its limits he bore the reputation of a brave and capable soldier. The story of his life of suffering and adventure, written by himself, is widely known, and he is thought by those who have read it to be a man of feeling and of honour. By those who enjoy his personal acquaintance this belief is unhesitatingly confirmed. He had, however, committed an act which deprived him of Gordon's sympathy and respect. During the fighting in Darfur, after several defeats, his Mohammedan soldiers were discouraged and attributed their evil fortune to the fact that their commander was an infidel under the curse of the Almighty. Slatin therefore proclaimed himself a follower of the Prophet, and outwardly at least adopted the faith of Islam. The troops, delighted at his conversion and cheered by the hope of success, renewed their efforts, and the resistance of the Governor of Darfur was prolonged. The end, however, was deferred, not averted. After the destruction of General Hicks's army Slatin was compelled to surrender to the Dervishes. The religion he had assumed to secure victory he observed to escape death. The Arab leaders, who admired his courage, treated him at first with respect and kindness, and he was conducted to the Mahdi in his encampment before Khartoum. There during the siege he remained, closely watched but not imprisoned. Thence he wrote letters to Gordon explaining his surrender, excusing his apostasy, and begging that he might be allowed—not even assisted—to escape to Khartoum. The letters are extant, and scarcely anyone who reads them, reflecting on the twelve years of danger and degradation that lay before this man, will refuse their compassion.

Gordon was inflexible. Before the arrival of the letters his allusions to Slatin are contemptuous: 'One cannot help being amused at the Mahdi carrying all the Europeans about with him—nuns, priests, Greeks, Austrian officers—what a medley, a regular Etat-Major!' [JOURNALS AT KHARTOUM.] He is suspicious of the circumstances of his surrender. 'The Greek . . . says Slatin had 4,000 ardebs of dura, 1,500 cows, and plenty of ammunition: he has been given eight horses by the Mahdi.' He will not vouch for such a man; but he adds, with characteristic justice, 'all this information must be taken with reserve.'

At length the letters came. At the peril of his life, when ordered to write and demand the surrender of the town, Slatin substituted an appeal to Gordon to countenance his escape. This is the uncompromising minute in the Journals: 'Oct. 16. The letters of Slatin have arrived. I have no remarks to make on them, and cannot make out why he wrote them.' In the afternoon, indeed, he betrays some pity; but it is the pity of a man for a mouse. 'He is evidently not a Spartan . . . he will want some quarantine . . . one feels sorry for him.' The next day he is again inexorable, and gives his reasons clearly. 'I shall have nothing to do with Slatin's coming here to stay, unless he has the Mahdi's positive leave, which he is not likely to get; his doing so would be the breaking of his parole which should be as sacred when given to the Mahdi as to any other power, and it would jeopardise the safety of all these Europeans, prisoners with Mahdi.'

Slatin's position, it should be observed, was not that of an officer released on parole, but of a prisoner of war in durance in the enemy's camp. In such circumstances he was clearly entitled to escape at his own proper risk. If his captors gave him the chance, they had only themselves to blame. His position was not dissimilar from that of the black soldiers who had been captured by the Dervishes and were now made to serve against the Government. These deserted to Khartoum daily, and the General fully acquiesced in their doing so. As to Slatin's escape affecting the treatment of the other European prisoners, it must be observed that when at various times escapes were effected from Omdurman, and ultimately when Slatin himself escaped, no ill-treatment was inflicted on the rest of the prisoners; and even had such ill-treatment been the certain consequence of an escape, that need not have debarred a man, according to the customs of war, from attempting to regain his liberty. Nothing but his free and formal promise, obtained in return for favours received, can alienate that right. If the Mahdi chose to slaughter the remaining prisoners, the responsibility rested with the Mahdi.

Slatin was, however, in no position to argue his case. His correspondence with Gordon was discovered. For some days his life hung on a thread. For several months he was heavily chained and fed on a daily handful of uncooked doura, such as is given to horses and mules. Tidings of these things were carried to Gordon. 'Slatin,' he observes icily, 'is still in chains.' He never doubted the righteousness of the course he had adopted, never for an instant. But few will deny that there were strong arguments on both sides. Many will assert that they were nicely balanced. Gordon must have weighed them carefully. He never wavered. Yet he needed Slatin. He was alone. He had no one in whose military capacity he could put the slightest confidence. Again and again in the Journals he expresses his want of trustworthy subordinates. He could not be everywhere, he said. 'Nearly every order has to be repeated two or three times. I am weary of my life.' 'What one has felt so much here is the want of men like Gessi, or Messadaglia, or Slatin, but I have no one to whom I could entrust expeditions . . . .'

This was the man who would have employed Zubehr and bowed to expediency. But Zubehr had never 'denied his Lord.'

The actual defence of Khartoum is within the province of the Journals, nor shall I attempt a chronological account. After the 10th of September, when General Gordon sent Colonel Stewart and Messrs. Power and Herbin down the river in the ill-fated Abbas steamer, he was altogether alone. Many men have bowed to the weight of responsibility. Gordon's responsibility was undivided. There was no one to whom he could talk as an equal. There was no one to whom he could—as to a trusty subordinate—reveal his doubts. To some minds the exercise of power is pleasant, but few sensations are more painful than responsibility without control. The General could not supervise the defence. The officers robbed the soldiers of their rations. The sentries slumbered at their posts. The townspeople bewailed their misfortunes, and all ranks and classes intrigued with the enemy in the hope of securing safety when the town should fall. Frequent efforts were made to stir up the inhabitants or sap their confidence. Spies of all kinds pervaded the town. The Egyptian Pashas, despairing, meditated treason. Once an attempt was made to fire the magazine. Once no less than eighty thousand ardebs of grain was stolen from the arsenal. From time to time the restless and ceaseless activity of the commander might discover some plot and arrest the conspirators; or, checking some account, might detect some robbery; but he was fully aware that what he found out was scarcely a tithe of what he could not hope to know. The Egyptian officers were untrustworthy. Yet he had to trust them. The inhabitants were thoroughly broken by war, and many were disloyal. He had to feed and inspirit them. The town itself was scarcely defensible. It must be defended to the end. From the flat roof of his palace his telescope commanded a view of the forts and lines. Here he would spend the greater part of each day, scrutinising the defences and the surrounding country with his powerful glass. When he observed that the sentries on the forts had left their posts, he would send over to have them flogged and their superiors punished. When his 'penny steamers' engaged the Dervish batteries he would watch, 'on tenter-hooks,' a combat which might be fatal to the defence, but which, since he could not direct it, must be left to officers by turns timid and reckless: and in the dark hours of the night he could not even watch. The Journals, the only receptacle of his confidences, display the bitterness of his sufferings no less than the greatness of his character. 'There is no contagion,' he writes, 'equal to that of fear. I have been rendered furious when from anxiety I could not eat, I would find those at the same table were in like manner affected.'

To the military anxieties was added every kind of worry which may weary a man's soul. The women clamoured for bread. The townsfolk heaped reproaches upon him. The quarrel with the British Government had cut him very deeply. The belief that he was abandoned and discredited, that history would make light of his efforts, would perhaps never know of them, filled his mind with a sense of wrong and injustice which preyed upon his spirits. The miseries of the townsfolk wrung his noble, generous heart. The utter loneliness depressed him. And over all lay the shadow of uncertainty. To the very end the possibility that 'all might be well' mocked him with false hopes. The first light of any morning might reveal the longed-for steamers of relief and the uniforms of British soldiers. He was denied even the numbing anaesthetic of despair.

Yet he was sustained by two great moral and mental stimulants: his honour as a man, his faith as a Christian. The first had put all courses which he did not think right once and for all out of the question, and so allayed many doubts and prevented many vain regrets. But the second was the real source of his strength. He was sure that beyond this hazardous existence, with all its wrongs and inequalities, another life awaited him—a life which, if he had been faithful and true here upon earth, would afford him greater faculties for good and wider opportunities for their use. 'Look at me now,' he once said to a fellow-traveller, 'with small armies to command and no cities to govern. I hope that death will set me free from pain, and that great armies will be given me, and that I shall have vast cities under my command.' [Lieut.-Colonel N. Newham Davis, 'Some Gordon Reminiscences,' published in THE MAN OF THE WORLD newspaper, December 14, 1898.] Such was his bright hope of immortality.

As the severity of military operations increases, so also must the sternness of discipline. The zeal of the soldiers, their warlike instincts, and the interests and excitements of war may ensure obedience of orders and the cheerful endurance of perils and hardships during a short and prosperous campaign. But when fortune is dubious or adverse; when retreats as well as advances are necessary; when supplies fail, arrangements miscarry, and disasters impend, and when the struggle is protracted, men can only be persuaded to accept evil things by the lively realisation of the fact that greater terrors await their refusal. The ugly truth is revealed that fear is the foundation of obedience. It is certain that the influence of General Gordon upon the garrison and townspeople of Khartoum owed its greatest strength to that sinister element. 'It is quite painful,' he writes in his Journals in September, 'to see men tremble so, when they come and see me, that they cannot hold the match to their cigarette.' Yet he employed all other methods of inspiring their efforts. As the winter drew on, the sufferings of the besieged increased and their faith in their commander and his promises of relief diminished. To preserve their hopes—and, by their hopes, their courage and loyalty—was beyond the power of man. But what a great man in the utmost exercise of his faculties and authority might do, Gordon did.

His extraordinary spirit never burned more brightly than in these last, gloomy days. The money to pay the troops was exhausted. He issued notes, signing them with his own name. The citizens groaned under the triple scourge of scarcity, disease, and war. He ordered the bands to play merrily and discharged rockets. It was said that they were abandoned, that help would never come, that the expedition was a myth—the lie of a General who was disavowed by his Government. Forthwith he placarded the walls with the news of victories and of the advance of a triumphant British army; or hired all the best houses by the river's bank for the accommodation of the officers of the relieving force. A Dervish shell crashed through his palace. He ordered the date of its arrival to be inscribed above the hole. For those who served him faithfully he struck medals and presented them with pomp and circumstance. Others less laudable he shot. And by all these means and expedients the defence of the city was prolonged through the summer, autumn, and winter of 1884 and on into the year 1885.

All this time the public anxiety in England had been steadily growing. If Gordon was abandoned, he was by no means forgotten. As his mission had been followed with intense interest throughout the whole country, so its failure had caused general despondency. Disappointment soon gave place to alarm. The subject of the personal safety of the distinguished envoy was first raised in the House of Commons on the 16th of March by Lord Randolph Churchill. Availing himself of the opportunities provided by Supply, he criticised the vacillating policy of the Government, their purposeless slaughter in the Eastern Soudan, and their failure to establish the Suakin-Berber route. He proceeded to draw attention to the perilous position of General Gordon at Khartoum.

'Colonel Coetlogon has stated that Khartoum may be easily captured; we know that General Gordon is surrounded by hostile tribes and cut off from communications with Cairo and London; and under these circumstances the House has a right to ask her Majesty's Government whether they are going to do anything to relieve him. Are they going to remain indifferent to the fate of the one man on whom they have counted to extricate them from their dilemmas, to leave him to shift for himself, and not make a single effort on his behalf?' [HANSARD'S PARLIAMENTARY DEBATES, March 16, 1884.]

The Government remained impassive. Lord E. Fitzmaurice made some sort of reply, and there were Ministerial cheers. But the subject, Once raised, was not allowed to drop. Inspired and animated by the earnest energy of a young man, the Opposition were continually growing stronger. The conduct of Egyptian affairs afforded ample opportunity for criticism and attack. All through the summer months and almost every night Ministers were invited to declare whether they would rescue their envoy or leave him to his fate. Mr. Gladstone returned evasive answers. The Conservative Press took the cue. The agitation became intense. Even among the supporters of the Government there was dissatisfaction. But the Prime Minister was obdurate and unflinching. At length, at the end of the Session, the whole matter was brought forward in the gravest and most formal way by the moving of a vote of censure. The debate that followed Sir Michael Hicks Beach's motion was long and acrimonious. Mr. Gladstone's speech only increased the disquietude of his followers and the fury of the Opposition. Mr. Forster openly declared his disagreement with his leader; and although Lord Hartington in winding up the debate threw out some hopes of an expedition in the autumn, the Government majority fell on the division to twenty-eight. And after the prorogation the controversy was carried on with undiminished vigour outside the walls of Parliament, and the clamour in the country grew louder and louder.

It is usual to look upon Mr. Gladstone's conduct in the matter of the relief of Gordon as dictated by benevolent weakness. History may take another view. Strong and stubborn as was the character of the General, that of the Minister was its equal. If Gordon was the better man, Gladstone was incomparably the greater. It was easy for the First Minister of the Crown to despatch an expedition against savages. He was accustomed to the exercise of power. Compared with the resources of the Empire, the enterprise was insignificant. Few men have feared responsibility less than Gladstone. On the other hand, the expressed desire of the nation was a force to which he had always bowed—to which, indeed, he owed his political existence. Yet, in spite of the growing agitation throughout the land, he remained stern and silent. Most men do what is right, or what they persuade themselves is right; nor is it difficult to believe that Mr. Gladstone did not feel justified in involving the nation in operations in the heart of the Soudan for the purpose, not of saving the life of the envoy—for Gordon had but to embark on his steamers and come home—but simply in order to vindicate the personal honour of a man. And it is possible that a feeling of resentment against the officer whose intractable nature was bringing such odium upon the Government may have coloured his resolution with a darker tinge.

But for all his power and influence he was forced to give way. The Government which had long ignored the call of honour abroad, was driven to the Soudan by the cries of shame at home. Lord Hartington, at that time Secretary of State for War, must be dissociated from the general censure which his principal colleagues have incurred. He was the first to recognise the obligation which lay upon the Cabinet, and through the Cabinet upon the nation, and it was to his influence that the despatch of the relieving expedition was mainly due. The Commander-in-Chief and the Adjutant-General, who were fully alive to the critical position at Khartoum, added their recommendations. But even at the last moment Mr. Gladstone was induced to sanction the advance only by the belief that the scale of the operations would be small, and that only a single brigade would be necessary. The decision was taken forthwith by the Ministry and announced to the nation. The Adjutant-General, however, asked for a very different force from what the Government had anticipated, and the single brigade was expanded into an expedition of ten thousand men, selected from the whole army.

To reverse the decision was now, however, impossible, and the 'Gordon Relief Expedition' began. The commander to whom the conduct of the operations had been entrusted reviewed the situation. He saw himself confronted with a task which was easy and safe if it were undertaken at leisure, and which was doubtful and perilous if begun in haste. All the fruits of a long and successful career were staked on the result, and it is scarcely wonderful that he declined to be swift and reckless. Shrewdly estimating the military difficulties, he made his plans for a methodical and deliberate advance which would leave nothing to luck, and which resembles in character that afterwards carried out by Sir H. Kitchener. He excluded the idea of a wild glorious rush which might result in astonishing success or terrible disaster.

Troops and stores were steadily collected at Wady Halfa and along the Nile. The new Camel Corps, consisting of four regiments, practised their drills and evolutions. To pilot the boats up the Cataracts voyageurs were brought from Canada. At length, when all preparations were complete, the expedition started. The plan was simple. A strong column of infantry in boats was to work up the river. In case that should not arrive in time, the Camel Corps was to strike across the Bayuda Desert from Korti to Metemma. Having arrived there, a small detachment was to be thrown into Khartoum by Gordon's steamers to sustain the defence until the arrival of the main body in March or even April of 1885, when the town could be regularly relieved.

The dramatic character of the enterprise and its picturesque and original features fascinated the nation, and the advance was watched with breathless interest. The fortunes of the River Column have been graphically described by one who played no small part in their attempt. 'The Campaign of the Cataracts' [By Sir William Butler] is a record of hard and unceasing toil. Day after day the long lines of soldiers hauled on the tow-ropes or pulled at the oars of the broad-bottomed boats. Night after night they camped on the banks amid the grim desolation of the Monassir Desert. Yet their monotonous labours were encouraged by the knowledge that as soon as the bend of the river at Abu Hamed was reached the strong north wind would carry them swiftly to Khartoum. And it seemed a strange and bitter irony that the order to turn back and the news that all had been in vain was announced to the troops on the very day when they had cleared the cataracts and were moving forward at five times their former speed.

The Desert Column started from Korti on the 30th of December. Their strength did not exceed 1,100 officers and men, but they were the flower of the army. Dropping their communications, they set forth along the caravan route towards Metemma. The knowledge which we have since gained of the resources of the Mahdists enables the peril of their desperate venture to be fully appreciated. Although the Dervishes were neither so well armed nor trained as at a later date, they were nearly as numerous and equally devoid of fear. Their tactics were more in accordance with modern conditions: their fanaticism was at its height. The British force, on the other hand, was equipped with weapons scarcely comparable with those employed in the concluding campaigns. Instead of the powerful Lee-Metford rifle, with its smokeless powder, its magazine action, and its absence of recoil, they were armed with the Martini-Henry, which possessed none of these advantages. In place of the deadly Maxim there was the Gardner gun—the very gun that jammed at Tamai, and that jammed again at Abu Klea. The artillery was also in every respect inferior to that now in general use. Besides all this, the principles of fire-discipline and of scientific musketry were new, little understood, and hardly admitted. Nevertheless, the Camel Corps went boldly forward, and engaged an enemy whose destruction ultimately required the strength of a better-armed and better-instructed army twelve times as strong.

On the 3rd of January they reached Gakdul Wells. A hundred miles of their march was accomplished. But they were now delayed by the necessity of escorting a second column of supplies to Gakdul, and after that until the arrival of reinforcements which raised their strength to 1,800 of all ranks. The interval was employed in building two small forts and establishing an advanced depot; nor was it until the 13th that the march was resumed. The number of camels was not sufficient for the necessities of the transport. The food of the camels was too poor for the work they had to perform. By the 16th, however, they had made fifty miles, and approached the wells of Abu Klea. Here their further advance was disputed by the enemy.

The news of the advance of the Desert Column had been duly reported to the Mahdi and his Arab generals. A small party of English, it was said, with camels and some cavalry, were coming swiftly to the rescue of the accursed city. Their numbers were few, scarce 2,000 men. How should they hope to prevail against 'the expected Mahdi' and the conquering Ansar who had destroyed Hicks? They were mad; yet they should die; not one should escape. The delay in the advance offered ample opportunity. A great force of Arabs was concentrated. Slatin relates how several thousand men under important Emirs were detached from the army before Khartoum and marched northward eager for the slaughter of 'the enemies of God.' At Metemma the main strength of the Jaalin tribe was collected. With the reinforcements from Omdurman the total force of the Arabs actually at hand was not less than 10,000, and behind were many thousands more. They permitted the little column to advance until their retreat, if defeated, was impossible, and then, confident of victory, offered battle near the wells of Abu Klea.

The Camel Corps remained halted during the morning of the 16th, and built a small fort, in which they placed their reserve of stores, and made some arrangement for the reception of wounded. At one o'clock they moved leisurely forward, passed through the rocky defile which led into the valley of Abu Klea and bivouacked. Early the next morning the force moved out in square formation and advanced upon the enemy. The most savage and bloody action ever fought in the Soudan by British troops followed. Notwithstanding the numbers and the valour of the Arabs, that they penetrated the square, and that they inflicted on the troops a loss of nine officers and sixty-five men killed and nine officers and eighty-five men wounded—10 percent of the entire force—they were driven from the field with great slaughter, and the Desert Column camped at the wells.

On the morning of the 18th they rested, placed their wounded in the small fort they had built, and buried their dead. In the afternoon they continued their advance, marched all through the night, and, having covered twenty-three miles, halted exhausted, almost within sight of the river, at daylight on the 19th. Meanwhile the enemy had again collected in great strength, and an effective rifle fire was opened on the column. Sir Herbert Stewart received the wound of which a few weeks later he died. The command devolved upon Sir Charles Wilson. The position was desperate. Water was running short. The Nile was only four miles away; but the column were impeded by their wounded and stores, and between the river and the thirsty men lay the Dervish army, infuriated by their losses and fully aware of the sore straits to which their astonishing enemy was now reduced.

It now became necessary to divide the small force. Some must remain to guard the baggage and the wounded; the others must fight their way to the water. At three o'clock in the afternoon of the 19th, 900 men left the hastily made zeriba and marched towards the river. Without their camels or those of the transport they appeared insignificant, a mere speck on the broad plain of Metemma. The Dervishes hastened to clinch the matter.

The square advances slowly and painfully over the stony ground, with frequent jerky halts to preserve order and to pick up the wounded. Little puffs of white smoke dot the distant sandhills. Here and there a gaudy flag waves defiantly. In front the green tops of the palm-trees by the Nile tantalise but stimulate the soldiers. On the left the great mud labyrinth of Metemma stretches indefinitely.

Suddenly the firing stops. The low scrub in front is alive with the swarming figures of the enemy. All the flags dance forward together. Ragged white figures spring up in hundreds. Emirs on horses appear as if by magic. Everywhere are men running swiftly forward, waving their spears and calling upon the Prophet of God to speed their enterprise. The square halts. The weary men begin to fire with thoughtful care, The Dervishes drop thickly. On then, children of the desert! you are so many, they are so few. They are worn with fatigue and their throats are parched. You have drunk deeply of the Nile. One rush will trample the accursed under the feet of the faithful. The charge continues. A bugle sounds in the waiting square. The firing stops. What is this? They lose heart. Their ammunition is exhausted. On, then, and make an end. Again the smoke ripples along the line of bayonets and fire is re-opened, this time at closer range and with far greater effect. The stubborn grandeur of the British soldier is displayed by desperate circumstances. The men shoot to hit. The attack crumples. The Emirs—horse and man—collapse. The others turn and walk—for they will not run—sullenly back towards the town. The square starts forward. The road to the river is open. With dusk the water is reached, and never have victors gained a more longed-for prize. The Nile is won. Gordon remains.

Sir Charles Wilson, having collected his force, remained three days by the bank of the Nile before attempting any further advance on Khartoum. He has explained why this delay was necessary, to the satisfaction of most military critics. Nor is it easy to believe that men who had made such splendid efforts would have willingly lost a single moment. On the fourth day he embarked on two of Gordon's steamers, which awaited the relieving column, and taking with him twenty British soldiers and a few blue-jackets set forth towards the Shabluka Gorge and the town that lay beyond. On the 27th of January the rescuers came in sight of Khartoum and under the fire of the enemy. Many of their perilous adventures seem to belong to romance rather than to reality: the tiny gimcrack boats struggling with the strong stream of the cataract, running the gauntlet of the Arab guns, dropping disconsolately down the river with their terrible news, or wrecked and stranded on the sandbank; Stuart-Wortley rowing to the camp before Metemma for help; Beresford starting in the remaining steamer; the bursting of the boiler by a Dervish shell; Benbow mending it in a single day; Wilson's rescue and the return to the entrenchment at Gubat. But the scene that appeals to the imagination above all the others is that where with both banks ablaze with musketry and artillery, the black smoke pouring through the shotholes in the funnels, the water rising in spurts from the bullets, the men who had come so far and braved so much stared at the palace roof and, seeing no flag flying, knew that all was over and that they had come too late.

The news of the Dervish defeats at Abu Klea and Abu Kru impelled the Mahdi to a desperate venture. The English were but 120 miles away. They were few, but victorious. It was difficult to say what force could stop such men. In spite of the wrath of the true God and the valour of Islam they might prevail. The Mahdi depended on success for existence. The tremendous forces of fanaticism are exerted only in a forward direction. Retreat meant ruin. All must be staked on an immediate assault. And, besides, the moment was ripe. Thus the Arab chiefs reasoned, and wisely resolved to be reckless. Thus the night of the 25th of January arrived.

The band played as usual in the evening. Gradually the shadows fell and it became dark. The hungry inhabitants betook themselves to bed. The anxious but indomitable commander knew that the crisis impended, and knew also that he was powerless to avert it. Perhaps he slept, satisfied that he had done his duty; and in the silence of the night the savage enemy crawled stealthily towards the town. The weary and disheartened sentinels, weakened by famine and tired of war, maintained a doubtful vigilance along the ramparts. The subsiding waters of the river had left a bare gap between the White Nile and the wall. Perhaps there was treachery besides. On a sudden the loud explosion of musketry broke the stillness of the night and the slumbers of the people; and with a continual shouting thousands of Dervishes swarmed through the unprotected space and entered Khartoum.

One mob of assailants made their way to the palace. Gordon came out to meet them. The whole courtyard was filled with wild, harlequin figures and sharp, glittering blades. He attempted a parley. 'Where is your master, the Mahdi?' He knew his influence over native races. Perhaps he hoped to save the lives of some of the inhabitants. Perhaps in that supreme moment imagination flashed another picture before his eyes; and he saw himself confronted with the false prophet of a false religion, confronted with the European prisoners who had 'denied their Lord,' offered the choice of death or the Koran; saw himself facing that savage circle with a fanaticism equal to, and a courage greater than, their own; marching in all the pride of faith 'and with retorted scorn' to a martyr's death.

It was not to be. Mad with the joy of victory and religious frenzy, they rushed upon him and, while he disdained even to fire his revolver, stabbed him in many places. The body fell down the steps and lay—a twisted heap—at the foot. There it was decapitated. The head was carried to the Mahdi. The trunk was stabbed again and again by the infuriated creatures, till nothing but a shapeless bundle of torn flesh and bloody rags remained of what had been a great and famous man and the envoy of her Britannic Majesty. The blood soaked into the ground, and left a dark stain which was not immediately effaced. Slatin mentions that the Arabs used often to visit the place. Ohrwalder went himself, and more than six weeks after the capture of the town, saw 'black spots' upon the steps. But they have all since been obliterated.

Such, briefly, is the story of the fall of Khartoum and of the death of Gordon. The fact that the two steamers arrived only two days after the capture of the town has given colour to the belief that, but for the three days' delay at Metemma, the catastrophe might have been averted. This view appears incorrect. The Arabs had long held Khartoum at their mercy. They hoped, indeed, to compel its surrender by famine and to avoid an assault, which after their experience at El Obeid they knew must cost them dear. Gordon has stated in his Journals that the town became defenceless by the middle of December. The arrival of twenty British soldiers and a few officers could not have materially affected the situation—could only, in fact, have increased the loss. Yet nearly everyone who reads the tale will wish—in spite of reason—that some help, however little, had reached the lonely man; that before the darkness fell he had grasped an English hand, and learned that his countrymen had not abandoned him, had not forgotten—would never forget.

It may not be possible as yet to fix the exact place which Charles Gordon will occupy in English history. It is certainly a high one. Whether he will rank as a commander with Peterborough, Wolfe, and Clive, those who come after us must decide. We may, however, assert that he was a man of stainless honour and enduring courage, who in varied capacities displayed a fertile and abundant genius. He was careless alike of the honours and comforts of the world, and looked forward with firm faith to the rewards of a future state. The severity of his religion did not impair the amiability of his character. The uncertainty of his moods may have frequently affected the soundness of his opinions, but not often the justice of his actions. Gordon's statue, set up in the indignant grief of the nation in the space which is appropriated to the monuments of Great Captains by sea and land, claims the attention of the passer-by, not only because it is comparatively new. The figure, its pose, and its story are familiar even to the poorest citizens of London and to people from all parts of the United Kingdom. Serene amid the noise of the traffic, as formerly in that of the battle, the famous General seems still, with bowed head and thoughtful countenance, to revolve the problems of the dark Soudan and, inattentive to the clamour of men, inquires what is acceptable to God.

With the capture of the city and the death of the envoy the reason for the expedition disappeared. It remained only to withdraw the troops. The stores which had been brought across the desert at a terrible cost were thrown hastily into the Nile. The battered steamers which had waited so long at Metemma were hurriedly dismantled. The Camel Corps, their extraordinary efforts futile and their camels killed, marched back on foot to Korti. Their retreat was pressed by the exultant enemy. The River Column, whose boats after months of labour had just cleared the Cataracts, and who had gained a success at Kirbekan, were carried back swiftly by the strong current against which they had hopefully struggled. The whole Expeditionary Force—Guards, Highlanders, sailors, Hussars, Indian soldiers, Canadian voyageurs, mules, camels, and artillery—trooped back forlornly over the desert sands, and behind them the rising tide of barbarism followed swiftly, until the whole vast region was submerged. For several months the garrison of Kassala under a gallant Egyptian maintained a desperate resistance, but at last famine forced them to surrender, and they shared the fate of the garrisons of El Obeid, Darfur, Sobat, Tokar, Sinkat, Sennar, and Khartoum. The evacuation of the Soudan was thus completed.

CHAPTER III:

THE DERVISH EMPIRE

It might seem at first a great advantage that the peoples of the Soudan, instead of being a multitude of wild, discordant tribes, should unite of their own accord into one strong community, actuated by a common spirit, living under fixed laws, and ruled by a single sovereign. But there is one form of centralised government which is almost entirely unprogressive and beyond all other forms costly and tyrannical—the rule of an army. Such a combination depends, not on the good faith and good will of its constituents, but on their discipline and almost mechanical obedience. Mutual fear, not mutual trust, promotes the co-operation of its individual members. History records many such dominations, ancient and modern, civilised or barbaric; and though education and culture may modify, they cannot change their predominant characteristics—a continual subordination of justice to expediency, an indifference to suffering, a disdain of ethical principles, a laxity of morals, and a complete ignorance of economics. The evil qualities of military hierarchies are always the same. The results of their rule are universally unfortunate. The degree may vary with time and place, but the political supremacy of an army always leads to the formation of a great centralised capital, to the consequent impoverishment of the provinces, to the degradation of the peaceful inhabitants through oppression and want, to the ruin of commerce, the decay of learning, and the ultimate demoralisation even of the military order through overbearing pride and sensual indulgence.

Of the military dominations which history records, the Dervish Empire was probably the worst. All others have displayed compensating virtues. A high sense of personal honour has counterbalanced a low standard of public justice. An ennobling patriotism may partly repair economic follies. The miseries of the people are often concealed by the magnificence of the army. The laxity of morals is in some degree excused by the elegance of manners. But the Dervish Empire developed no virtue except courage, a quality more admirable than rare. The poverty of the land prevented magnificence. The ignorance of its inhabitants excluded refinement. The Dervish dominion was born of war, existed by war, and fell by war. It began on the night of the sack of Khartoum. It ended abruptly thirteen years later in the battle of Omdurman. Like a subsidiary volcano, it was flung up by one convulsion, blazed during the period of disturbance, and was destroyed by the still more violent shock that ended the eruption.

After the fall of Khartoum and the retreat of the British armies the Mahdi became the absolute master of the Soudan. Whatever pleasures he desired he could command, and, following the example of the founder of the Mohammedan faith, he indulged in what would seem to Western minds gross excesses. He established an extensive harem for his own peculiar use, and immured therein the fairest captives of the war. The conduct of the ruler was imitated by his subjects. The presence of women increased the vanity of the warriors: and it was not very long before the patched smock which had vaunted the holy poverty of the rebels developed into the gaudy jibba of the conquerors. Since the unhealthy situation of Khartoum amid swamps and marshes did not commend itself to the now luxurious Arabs, the Mahdi began to build on the western bank of the White Nile a new capital, which, from the detached fort which had stood there in Egyptian days, was called Omdurman. Among the first buildings which he set his subjects to construct were a mosque for the services of religion, an arsenal for the storage of military material, and a house for himself. But while he was thus entering at once upon the enjoyments of supreme power and unbridled lust, the God whom he had served, not unfaithfully, and who had given him whatever he had asked, required of Mohammed Ahmed his soul; and so all that he had won by his brains and bravery became of no more account to him.

In the middle of the month of June, scarcely five months after the completion of his victorious campaigns, the Mahdi fell sick. For a few days he did not appear at the mosque. The people were filled with alarm. They were reassured by remembering the prophecy that their liberator should not perish till he had conquered the earth. Mohammed, however, grew worse. Presently those who attended him could doubt no longer that he was attacked by typhus fever. The Khalifa Abdullah watched by his couch continually. On the sixth day the inhabitants and the soldiers were informed of the serious nature of their ruler's illness, and public prayers were offered by all classes for his recovery. On the seventh day it was evident that he was dying. All those who had shared his fortunes—the Khalifas he had appointed, the chief priests of the religion he had reformed, the leaders of the armies who had followed him to victory, and his own family whom he had hallowed—crowded the small room. For some hours he lay unconscious or in delirium, but as the end approached he rallied a little, and, collecting his faculties by a great effort, declared his faithful follower and friend the Khalifa Abdullah his successor, and adjured the rest to show him honour. 'He is of me, and I am of him; as you have obeyed me, so you should deal with him. May God have mercy upon me!' [Slatin, FIRE AND SWORD.] Then he immediately expired.

Grief and dismay filled the city. In spite of the emphatic prohibition by law of all loud lamentations, the sound of 'weeping and wailing arose from almost every house.' The whole people, deprived at once of their acknowledged sovereign and spiritual guide, were shocked and affrighted. Only the Mahdi's wives, if we may credit Slatin, 'rejoiced secretly in their hearts at the death of their husband and master,' and, since they were henceforth to be doomed to an enforced and inviolable chastity, the cause of their satisfaction is as obscure as its manifestation was unnatural. The body of the Mahdi, wrapped in linen, was reverently interred in a deep grave dug in the floor of the room in which he had died, nor was it disturbed until after the capture of Omdurman by the British forces in 1898, when by the orders of Sir H. Kitchener the sepulchre was opened and the corpse exhumed.

The Khalifa Abdullah had been declared by the Mahdi's latest breath his successor. He determined to have the choice ratified once for all by the popular vote. Hurrying to the pulpit in the courtyard of the mosque, he addressed the assembled multitude in a voice which trembled with intense excitement and emotion. His oratory, his reputation as a warrior, and the Mahdi's expressed desire aroused the enthusiasm of his hearers, and the oath of allegiance was at once sworn by thousands. The ceremony continued long after it was dark. With an amazing endurance he harangued till past midnight, and when the exhausted Slatin, who hard attended him throughout the crisis, lay down upon the ground to sleep, he knew that his master's succession was assured; for, says he, 'I heard the passers-by loud in their praises of the late Mahdi, and assuring each other of their firm resolve to support his successor.'

The sovereignty that Abdullah had obtained must be held, as it had been won, by the sword. The passionate agitation which the Mahdi had excited survived him. The whole of the Soudan was in a ferment. The success which had crowned rebellion encouraged rebels. All the turbulent and fanatical elements were aroused. As the various provinces had been cleared of the Egyptians, the new Executive had appointed military governors by whom the country was ruled and taxed, subject to the pleasure of Mohammed Ahmed. His death was the signal for a long series of revolts of all kinds—military, political, and religious. Garrisons mutinied; Emirs plotted; prophets preached. Nor was the land torn only by internal struggles. Its frontiers were threatened. On the east the tremendous power of Abyssinia loomed terrible and menacing. There was war in the north with Egypt and around Suakin with England. The Italians must be confronted from the direction of Massowa. Far to the south Emin Pasha still maintained a troublesome resistance. Yet the Khalifa triumphed over nearly all his enemies; and the greatest spectacle which the Soudan presented from 1885 to 1898 was of this strong, capable ruler bearing up against all reverses, meeting each danger, overcoming each difficulty, and offering a firm front to every foe.

It is unlikely that any complete history of these events will ever be written in a form and style which will interest a later generation. The complications of extraordinary names and the imperfection of the records might alone deter the chronicler. The universal squalor of the scenes and the ignorance of the actors add discouragements. Nor, upon the other hand, are there great incentives. The tale is one of war of the cruellest, bloodiest, and most confused type. One savage army slaughters another. One fierce general cuts his rival's throat. The same features are repeated with wearying monotony. When one battle is understood, all may be imagined. Above the tumult the figure of the Khalifa rises stern and solitary, the only object which may attract the interest of a happier world. Yet even the Khalifa's methods were oppressively monotonous. For although the nature or courage of the revolts might differ with the occasion, the results were invariable; and the heads of all his chief enemies, of many of his generals, of most of his councillors, met in the capacious pit which yawned in Omdurman.

During the thirteen years of his reign Abdullah tried nearly every device by which Oriental rulers have sought to fortify their perilous sovereignty. He shrank from nothing. Self-preservation was the guiding principle of his policy, his first object and his only excuse. Among many wicked and ingenious expedients three main methods are remarkable. First, he removed or rendered innocuous all real or potential rivals. Secondly, he pursued what Sir Alfred Milner has called 'a well-considered policy of military concentration.' Thirdly, he maintained among the desert and riverain people a balance of power on the side of his own tribe. All these three methods merit some attention or illustration.

The general massacre of all possible claimants usually follows the accession of a usurper to an Oriental throne. The Khalifa was able to avoid this extreme measure. Nevertheless he took precautions. Availing himself of the grief and terror that had followed Mohammed Ahmed's death, he had extorted the oath of allegiance from the two other Khalifas and from the 'Ashraf' or relations of the Prophet. [The Madhi had superseded the original Mohammed as 'the Prophet.' His relations consequently became 'Ashraf.'] But these complaisant men soon repented of their submission. Each Khalifa boasted his independence. Each marched attended by a numerous retinue. Each asserted his right to beat his own great copper drum. Both the unsuccessful Khalifas combined against Abdullah. But while they had been busy with the beating of war-drums and the preparation of pageants, that sagacious ruler had secured the loyalty of the Baggara tribe, to a section of which he belonged, and of a considerable force of black riflemen. At length matters reached climax. Both parties prepared for war. Abdullah drew up his array without the city, and challenged his rivals to the utmost proof. The combined forces of the ousted Khalifas were the more numerous. But the fierce Baggara waved their swords, and the Soudanese riflemen were famous for their valour. For some hours a bloody struggle appeared imminent. Then the confederacy broke up. The Khalifa Ali-Wad-Helu, a prudent man, talked of compromise and amity. The Khalif Sherif, thus seriously weakened, hastened to make peace while time remained. Eventually both bowed to the superior force of the ruler and the superior courage of his followers. Once they had submitted, their power was gone. Abdullah reduced their forces to a personal escort of fifty men each, deprived them of their flags and their war-drums—the emblems of royalty—and they became for the future the useful supporters of a Government they were unable to subvert.

To other less powerful and more stubborn enemies he showed a greater severity. The Mahdi's two uncles, named respectively Abdel Kerim and Abdel Kader, were thrown chained into prison, their houses were destroyed, and their wives and other property confiscated. The numerous persons who claimed to be of the 'Ashraf' found the saintly honour a burden upon earth; for, in order to keep them out of mischief, the Khalifa enjoined them to attend five times every day at the prayers in the mosque. Eighteen months of these devotions, declares the Christian chronicler, were considered 'the highest punishment.' [Ohrwalder, TEN YEARS' CAPTIVITY.] Still more barbarous was the treatment meted out to the unfortunate Emir who had charge of the Treasury. Ahmed Wad Suliman had been accustomed under the Mahdi's mild rule to keep no public accounts, and consequently he had amassed a large fortune. He was actively hostile to Abdullah, and proclaimed his sympathy with the Ashraf. Whereupon the Khalifa invited him to give an account of his stewardship. This he was, of course, unable to do. He was then dismissed from his appointment. His private property was taken to fill the deficiencies of the State, and the brutal population of Omdurman applauded his punishment as 'an act of justice.' [Slatin, FIRE AND SWORD.]

Although the Khalifa might establish his authority by such atrocities, its maintenance depended on the military policy which he consistently pursued. The terrible power of a standing army may usually be exerted by whoever can control its leaders, as a mighty engine is set in motion by the turning of a handle. Yet to turn the handle some muscular force is necessary. Abdullah knew that to rule the Soudan he must have a great army. To make the great army obedient he must have another separate force; for the influences which keep European armies in subjection were not present among the Dervishes. For some years, indeed, he was compelled to leave much to chance or the loyalty of his officers. But latterly, when he had perfected his organisation, he became quite independent and had no need to trust anyone. By degrees and with astonishing ability he carried out his schemes.

He invited his own tribe, the Taaisha section of the Baggara Arabs, to come and live in Omdurman. 'Come,' he wrote in numerous letters to them, 'and take possession of the lands which the Lord your God has given you.' Allured by the hopes of wealth and wives and the promise of power, the savage herdsmen came to the number of 7,000 warriors. Their path was made smooth and easy. Granaries were erected along the route. Steamers and sailing-vessels waited on the Nile. Arrived at the capital, all were newly clothed at the expense of the State. An entire district of the city was forcibly cleared of its inhabitants for the accommodation of the strangers. What the generosity of the Khalifa forgot or refused, the predatory habits of his clansmen procured; and they robbed, plundered, and swindled with all the arrogance and impunity of royal favourites. The populace of the city returned a bitter hatred for these injuries; and the Khalifa's object was attained. He had created a class in Omdurman who were indissolubly attached to him. Like him, they were detested by the local tribes. Like him, they were foreigners in the land. But, like him, they were fierce and brave and strong. His dangers, his enemies, his interests were their own. Their lives depended on their loyalty.

Here was the motor muscle which animated the rest. The Taaisha Baggara controlled the black Jehadia, once the irregular troops of the Egyptians, now become the regulars of the Khalifa. The black Jehadia overawed the Arab army in the capital. The army in the capital dominated the forces in the provinces. The forces in the provinces subdued the inhabitants. The centralisation of power was assured by the concentration of military material. Cannon, rifles, stores of ammunition, all the necessities of war were accumulated in the arsenal. Only the armies on the frontiers, the Taaisha tribe, and the khalifa's personal bodyguard habitually carried firearms and cartridges. The enormous population of Omdurman was forced to be content with spears and swords. Rifles were issued to the Soudanese whenever safe and necessary; cartridges only when they were about to be used. Thus several millions of warlike and savage people, owning scarcely any law but that of might, and scattered about a vast roadless territory, were brought into the firm grip of a single man.

The third principle of government which the Khalifa was compelled, or inclined, to adopt was to keep the relative power of the various tribes and classes conveniently proportioned. If an Emir rose to great influence and wealth, he became a possible rival, and suffered forthwith death, imprisonment, or spoliation. If a tribe threatened the supremacy of the Taaisha it was struck down while its menace was yet a menace. The regulation of classes and tribes was a far more complicated affair than the adjustment of individuals. Yet for thirteen years the Khalifa held the balance, and held it exact until the very end. Such was the statecraft of a savage from Kordofan.

His greatest triumph was the Abyssinian war. It is not likely that two great barbaric kingdoms living side by side, but differing in race and religion, will long continue at peace; nor was it difficult to discover a cause of the quarrel between the Dervishes and the Abyssinians. For some time a harassing and desultory warfare disturbed the border. At length in 1885 a Dervish—half-trader, half brigand—sacked an Abyssinian church. Bas Adal, the Governor of the Amhara province, demanded that this sacrilegious robber should be surrendered to justice. The Arabs haughtily refused. The response was swift. Collecting an army which may have amounted to 30,000 men, the Abyssinians invaded the district of Gallabat and marched on the town. Against this host the Emir Wad Arbab could muster no more than 6,000 soldiers. But, encouraged by the victories of the previous four years, the Dervishes accepted battle, in spite of the disparity of numbers. Neither valour nor discipline could withstand such odds. The Moslems, broken by the fierce onset and surrounded by the overwhelming numbers of their enemies, were destroyed, together with their intrepid leader. Scarcely any escaped. The Abyssinians indulged in all the triumphs of savagery. The wounded were massacred: the slain were mutilated: the town of Gallabat was sacked and burnt. The Women were carried into captivity. All these tidings came to Omdurman. Under this heavy and unexpected blow the Khalifa acted with prudence. He opened negotiations with King John of Abyssinia, for the ransom of the captured wives and children, and at the same time he sent the Emir Yunes with a large force to Gallabat. The immediate necessities having thus been dealt with, Abdullah prepared for revenge.

Of all the Arab leaders which fifteen years of continual war and tumult throughout the Soudan produced, none displayed higher ability, none obtained greater successes, and none were more honourable, though several were more famous, than the man whom the Khalifa selected to avenge the destruction of the Gallabat army. Abu Anga had been a slave in Abdullah's family long before the Mahdi had preached at Abba island and while Egypt yet oppressed the country. After the revolt had broken out, his adventurous master summoned him from the distant Kordofan home to attend him in the war, and Abu Anga came with that ready obedience and strange devotion for which he was always distinguished. Nominally as a slave, really as a comrade, he fought by Abdullah's side in all the earlier battles of the rebellion. Nor was it until after the capture of El Obeid that he rose suddenly to power and place. The Khalifa was a judge of men. He saw very clearly that the black Soudanese troops, who had surrendered and were surrendering as town after town was taken, might be welded into a powerful weapon. And in Abu Anga he knew a man who could not only fashion the blade, but would hold it ever loyally at his master's disposal. The former slave threw himself into the duties of his command with extraordinary energy. His humble origin pleased the hardy blacks, who recognised in their leader their equal in birth, their superior in prowess. More than any other Emir, Abu Anga contributed to the destruction of Hicks's army. The Jehadia, as his soldiers were called—because they had joined in the Jehad, or Holy War—were armed with Remington rifles, and their harassing fire inflicted heavy losses on the struggling column until it was finally brought to a standstill, and the moment for the spearmen to charge arrived. Henceforward the troops of Abu Anga became famous throughout the land for their weapons, their courage, and their cruelty. Their numbers at first did not exceed 5,000; but as more towns were taken and more slaves were turned into soldiers they increased, until at one time they reached the formidable total of 15,000 men. During the siege of Khartoum the black riflemen distinguished themselves by the capture of Omdurman fort, but their violent natures and predatory instincts made them an undesirable garrison even for the Dervish capital, and they were despatched under their general to Kordofan, where they increased their reputation by a series of bloody fights with the Nubas, an aboriginal mountain people who cared for nothing but their independence.

At the end of June Abu Anga reached Omdurman with an army variously estimated at from 22,000 to 31,000 men, of whom at least 10,000 were armed with Remington rifles. The Khalifa received him with the utmost honour. After a private interview, which lasted for several hours, a formal entry into the town was arranged. At daybreak on the following morning the whole force marched into the city and camped along the northern suburbs, applauded and welcomed alike by the population and their ruler. A few days after this a great review was held under the Kerreri hills, on the very ground where the Dervish Empire was doomed to be shattered. But the fateful place oppressed the Khalifa with no forebodings. He exulted in his power: and well he might, for after the cannon had thundered indefinite salutes, no fewer than 100,000 armed men defiled to the music of the war-drums and the ombyas before the famous Black Flag. The spectacle of the enormous numbers provoked their enthusiasm. The triumphant Khalifa was cheered by his mighty host, who pressed upon him in their exuberant loyalty until he was almost crushed. It was indeed a stirring scene. The whole plain was filled with the throng. Banners of every hue and shape waved gaily in the breeze, and the sunlight glinted from innumerable spear-points. The swarming Dervishes displayed their bright parti-coloured jibbas. The wild Baggara cavalry circled on the flanks of the array. The brown dome of the Mahdi's tomb, rising above the city, seemed to assure the warriors of supernatural aid. Abdullah was at the summit of his power. The movement initiated by the priest of Abba island had attained its climax. Behind, in the plain, the frowning rocks of Surgham Hill rose ragged and gloomy, as if their silence guarded the secrets of the future.

After the feast of Bairam had been celebrated on a gigantic scale, Abu Anga was despatched to Gallabat with his army and considerable reinforcements from the troops in Omdurman, and it became evident that war with Abyssinia was imminent. The great leader relieved the Emir Yunes, much to the latter's disgust, of the chief command, and, since the strong Gallabat garrison was added to his own force, Abu Anga was able to take the field at the head of 15,000 riflemen and 45,000 spearmen. The Khalifa had embarked on a great venture in planning the invasion of Abyssinia. The vast strength of the Negus was known to the Dervishes, and has since been proved to the world. The Mahdi had forbidden such a war. An ill-omened prophecy further declared that the King of Abyssinia would tether his horse to a solitary tree by Khartoum, while his cavalry should ride through the city fetlock deep in blood. But Abdullah feared neither God nor man. He reviewed the political situation, and determined at all risks to maintain his frontiers inviolate. His Emir Wad Arbab had been killed. Blood must settle the matter.

The Abyssinians had not watched the extensive hostile preparations apathetically. Ras Adal had collected an army which in numbers actually exceeded that of the Dervishes. But the latter were far superior in rifles, and the black infantry were of invincible valour. Nevertheless, confident in his strength and relying on his powerful cavalry, the Abyssinian general allowed the Arabs to toil through all the mountainous country, to traverse the Mintik Pass, and to debouch unmolested on to the plain of Debra Sin. Abu Anga neglected no precaution. He knew that since he must fight in the heart of Abyssinia, with the mountains behind him, a defeat would involve annihilation. He drew up his army swiftly and with skill. Then the Abyssinians attacked. The rifle fire of the Soudanese repulsed them. The onset was renewed with desperate gallantry. It was resisted with equal valour and superior weapons. After frightful losses the

Abyssinians wavered, and the wise Arab seized the moment for a counterstroke. In spite of the devotion of his cavalry Ras Adal was driven from the field. Great numbers of his army were drowned in the river in front of which he had recklessly elected to fight. His camp was captured, and a valuable spoil rewarded the victors, who also gratified their passions with a wholesale slaughter of the wounded—a practice commonly followed by savages. The effect of the victory was great. The whole of the Amhara province submitted to the invaders, and in the spring of 1887 Abu Anga was able to advance without further fighting to the capture and sack of Gondar, the ancient capital of Abyssinia.

Meanwhile the Khalifa had been anxiously expecting tidings of his army. The long silence of thirty days which followed their plunge into the mountains filled him with fear, and Ohrwalder relates that he 'aged visibly' during that period. But his judgment was proved by the event, and the arrival of a selected assortment of heads turned doubt to triumph. The Dervishes did not long remain in Abyssinia, as they suffered from the climate. In December the army returned to Gallabat, which they commenced to fortify, and their victorious general followed his grisly but convincing despatch to Omdurman, where he received the usual welcome accorded by warlike peoples to military heroes. But the famous and faithful slave may have been more gratified by the tears of joy which his master and sovereign shed on beholding him again safe and successful.

The greater struggle was still to come. The whole of Abyssinia was convulsed with fury, and King John in person prepared to take the field and settle the quarrel for ever. He assembled a mighty host, which is said to have amounted to 130,000 foot and 20,000 horsemen. The rumours of this formidable concentration reached Gallabat and Omdurman, and in spite of the recent victory caused deep alarm. The Khalifa saw his frontiers—even his existence—menaced, for King John had declared that he would sweep the Dervishes from off the face of the earth: and in the hour of need the general on whom so much depended died of some poisonous medicine with which he had endeavoured to cure himself of indigestion. Abu Anga was buried in his red-brick house at Gallabat amid the lamentations of his brave black soldiers, and gloom pervaded the whole army. But, since the enemy were approaching, the danger had to be faced. The Khalifa appointed Zeki Tummal, one of Anga's lieutenants, to the command of the forces at Gallabat, which by strenuous exertions he brought up to a total of 85,000 men. King John sent word that he was coming, lest any should say that he had come secretly as a thief. The Dervishes resolved to remain on the defensive, and, fortifying themselves in an enormous zeriba around the town, awaited the onslaught.

At dawn on the 9th of March, 1889, the Abyssinians came within sight of their enemies, and early the next morning the battle began. Great clouds of dust obscured the scene, and all intelligible sounds were lost in the appalling din. The Abyssinians, undaunted by the rifle fire of the Soudanese, succeeded in setting the zeriba alight. Then, concentrating all their force on one part of the defence, they burst into the enclosure and town. The division of Wad Ali, a fourth part of the entire Dervish army, which bore the brunt of this attack, was almost completely destroyed. The interior of the zeriba was crowded with women and children, who were ruthlessly butchered by the exultant Abyssinians. The assailants scattered in all directions in search of plunder, and they even had time to begin to disinter the body of Abu Anga, which they were eager to insult in revenge for Gondar. The Dervishes already wavered; their ammunition began to fail, when suddenly a rumour spread about among the Abyssinians that the King was killed. Seizing what booty they could snatch, the victorious army began a general retreat, and the zeriba was soon cleared. The Arabs were too exhausted to pursue, but when on the following day the attack was not renewed they learned, to their surprise, that they were the victors and that their enemy was falling back towards the Atbara river. Zeki Tummal resolved to pursue, and his army were further incited to the chase by the fact that the Abyssinians had carried off with them a large number of Dervish women, including the harem of the late beloved Abu Anga. Two days after the battle the Dervishes overtook the enemy's rearguard and, surprising their camp, inflicted severe loss and captured much booty. The temporary Negus who had been appointed to fill the vacancy caused by the death of King John was among the killed. The body of that courageous monarch fell into the hands of the Dervishes, who struck off the head and sent it—a tangible proof of victory—to Omdurman. The Abyssinians, still formidable, made good their retreat; nor did Zeki Tummal venture to follow into the mountains. Internal difficulties within his dominions prevented the new Negus from resuming the offensive, and thus the Dervish-Abyssinian war dwindled down to, as it had arisen out of, frontier raids.

The arrival in Omdurman of King John's head intoxicated the Khalifa with joy. Abyssinia was regarded throughout the Soudan as a far greater power than

Egypt, and here was its mighty ruler slain and decapitated. But the victory had been dearly purchased. The two great battles had been fought with indescribable ferocity by both sides, and the slaughter was appalling. No reliable statistics are avaliable, but it may be reasonably asserted that neither side sustained a loss in killed during the war of fewer than 15,000 fighting men. The flower of the Dervish army, the heroic blacks of Abu Anga, were almost destroyed. The Khalifa had won a Pyrrhic triumph. Never again was he able to put so great a force in the field, and, although the army which was shattered at Omdurman was better armed and better drilled, it was less formidable than that which broke the might of Abyssinia.

During the progress of the struggle with Abyssinia the war against Egypt languished. The Mahdi, counting upon the support of the population, had always declared that he would free the Delta from 'the Turks,' and was already planning its invasion when he and his schemes were interrupted by death. His successor inherited all the quarrel, but not all the power. Much of Mohammed Ahmed's influence died with him. Alive, he might conquer the Moslem world; dead, he was only a saint. All fanatical feeling in Egypt soon subsided. Nevertheless the Khalifa persisted in the enterprise. The success of the Abyssinian war encouraged and enabled him to resume the offensive on his northern frontier, and he immediately ordered Wad-el-Nejumi, who commanded in Dongola, to march with his scanty force to the invasion of Egypt. The mad enterprise ended, as might have been foreseen, in the destruction of both Emir and army at Toski. The Khalifa received the news with apparent grief, but it is difficult to avoid suspecting him of dark schemes. He was far too clever to believe that Egypt could be conquered by five thousand men. He knew that besides the Egyptians there was a strange white tribe of men, the same that had so nearly saved Khartoum. 'But for the English,' he exclaimed on several occasions, 'I would have conquered Egypt.' Yet, knowing of the British occupation, he deliberately sent an army to its inevitable ruin. It is difficult to reconcile such conduct with the character for sagacity and intelligence which Abdullah has deserved. There is no doubt that he wanted to conquer Egypt. Possibly by some extraordinary chance Wad-el-Nejumi might succeed, even with his small force. If so, then the glory of God and the power of the Khalifa would advance together. If not—and herein lies the true reason for the venture—the riverain tribes would have received a crippling blow.

The terrible slaughter of the Abyssinian war had fallen mainly on the Jehadia and the eastern Arabs. The jealous tribes in the north had not suffered. The balance of power was in need of re-adjustment. The Jaalin and Barabra were fast becoming dangerous. Nejumi's army was recruited almost entirely from these sources. The reinforcements sent from Omdurman consisted of men selected from the flag of the Khalifa Sherif, who was growing too powerful, and of the Batahin tribe, who had shown a mutinous spirit [Ohrwalder, TEN YEARS' CAPTIVITY.] The success of such an army in Egypt would be glorious. Its destruction anywhere would be convenient. Whatever Abdullah's motives may have been, his advantage was certain. But the life of the empire thus compelled to prey upon itself must necessarily be short.

Other forces were soon added to the work of exhaustion. The year following the end of the Abyssinian war was marked by a fearful famine. Slatin and Ohrwalder vie with each other in relating its horrors—men eating the raw entrails of donkeys; mothers devouring their babies; scores dying in the streets, all the more ghastly in the bright sunlight; hundreds of corpses floating down the Nile—these are among the hideous features. The depopulation caused by the scarcity was even greater than that produced by the fighting. The famine area extended over the whole Soudan and ran along the banks of the river as far as Lower Egypt. The effects of the famine were everywhere appalling. Entire districts between Omdurman and Berber became wholly depopulated. In the salt regions near Shendi almost all the inhabitants died of hunger. The camel-breeding tribes ate their she-camels. The riverain peoples devoured their seed-corn. The population of Gallabat, Gedaref, and Kassala was reduced by nine-tenths, and these once considerable towns shrank to the size of hamlets. Everywhere the deserted mud houses crumbled back into the plain. The frightful mortality, general throughout the whole country, may be gauged by the fact that Zeki Tummal's army, which before the famine numbered not fewer than 87,000, could scarcely muster 10,000 men in the spring of 1890.

The new harvest came only in time to save the inhabitants of the Soudan from becoming extinct. The remnant were preserved for further misfortunes. War, scarcity, and oppression there had always been. But strange and mysterious troubles began to afflict the tortured tribes. The face of heaven was pitiless or averted. In 1890 innumerable swarms of locusts descended on the impoverished soil. The multitude of their red or yellow bodies veiled the sun and darkened the air, and although their flesh, tasting when roasted like fried shrimps, might afford a delicate meal to the natives, they took so heavy a toll of the crops that the famine was prolonged and scarcity became constant. Since their first appearance the locusts are said to have returned annually [Ohrwalder, TEN YEARS' CAPTIVITY.] Their destructive efforts were aided by millions of little red mice, who destroyed the seeds before they could grow. So vast and immeasurable was the number of these tiny pests that after a heavy rain the whole country was strewn with, and almost tinted by, the squirrel-coloured corpses of the drowned.

Yet, in spite of all the strokes of fate, the Khalifa maintained his authority unshaken. The centralisation which always occurs in military States was accelerated by the famine. The provincial towns dwindled; thousands and tens of thousands perished; but Omdurman continually grew, and its ruler still directed the energies of a powerful army. Thus for the present we might leave the Dervish Empire. Yet the gloomy city of blood, mud, and filth that arose by the confluence of the Niles deserves a final glance while still in the pride of independent barbarism.

It is early morning, and the sun, lifting above the horizon, throws the shadows of the Khartoum ruins on the brimful waters of the Nile. The old capital is solitary and deserted. No sound of man breaks the silence of its streets. Only memory broods in the garden where the Pashas used to walk, and the courtyard where the Imperial envoy fell. Across the river miles of mud houses, lining the banks as far as Khor Shambat, and stretching back into the desert and towards the dark hills, display the extent of the Arab metropolis. As the sun rises, the city begins to live. Along the road from Kerreri a score of camels pad to market with village produce. The north wind is driving a dozen sailing-boats, laden to the water's edge with merchandise, to the wharves. One of Gordon's old steamers lies moored by the bank. Another, worked by the crew that manned it in Egyptian days, is threshing up the Blue Nile, sent by the Khalifa to Sennar on some errand of State. Far away to the southward the dust of a Darfur caravan breaks the clear-cut skyline with a misty blur.

The prolonged beating of war-drums and loud booming notes of horns chase away the silence of the night. It is Friday, and after the hour of prayer all grown men must attend the review on the plain without the city. Already the streets are crowded with devout and obedient warriors. soon the great square of the mosque—for no roof could shelter so many thousand worshippers—is filled with armed men, kneeling in humble supplication to the stern God of Islam and his most holy Mahdi. It is finished. They rise and hurry to the parade. The Emirs plant their flags, and all form in the ranks. Woe to the laggard; and let the speedy see that he wear his newest jibba, and carry a sharp sword and at least three spears. Presently the array is complete.

A salute of seven guns is fired. Mounted on a fine camel, which is led by a gigantic Nubian, and attended by perhaps two hundred horsemen in chain armour, the Khalifa rides on to the ground and along the ranks. It is a good muster. Few have dared absent themselves. Yet his brow is clouded. What has happened? Is there another revolt in the west? Do the Abyssinians threaten Gallabat? Have the black troops mutinied; or is it only some harem quarrel?

The parade is over. The troops march back to the arsenal. The rifles are collected, and the warriors disperse to their homes. Many hurry to the marketplace to make purchases, to hear the latest rumour, or to watch the executions—for there are usually executions. Others stroll to the Suk-er-Rekik and criticise the points of the slave girls as the dealers offer them for sale. But the Khalifa has returned to his house, and his council have been summoned. The room is small, and the ruler sits cross-legged upon his couch. Before him squat the Emirs and Kadis. Yakub is there, with Ali-Wad-Helu and the Khalifa Sherif. Only the Sheikh-ed-Din is absent, for he is a dissolute youth and much given to drinking.

Abdullah is grave and anxious. A messenger has come from the north. The Turks are on the move. Advancing beyond their frontier, they have established themselves at Akasha. Wad Bishara fears lest they may attack the faithful who hold Firket. In itself this is but a small matter, for all these years there has been frontier fighting. But what follows is full of menacing significance. The 'enemies of God' have begun to repair the railway—have repaired it, so that the train already runs beyond Sarras. Even now they push their iron road out into the desert towards their position at Akasha and to the south. What is the object of their toil? Are they coming again? Will they bring those terrible white soldiers who broke the hearts of the Hadendoa and almost destroyed the Degheim and Kenana? What should draw them up the Nile? Is it for plunder, or in sheer love of war; or is it a blood feud that brings them? True, they are now far off. Perchance they will return, as they returned before. Yet the iron road is not built in a day, nor for a day, and of a surety there are war-clouds in the north.

CHAPTER IV:

THE YEARS OF PREPARATION

In the summer of 1886, when all the troops had retreated to Wady Halfa and all the Soudan garrisons had been massacred, the British people averted their eyes in shame and vexation from the valley of the Nile. A long succession of disasters had reached their disgraceful culmination. The dramatic features added much to the bitterness and nothing to the grandeur of the tragedy. The cost was heavy. Besides the pain produced by the death of General Gordon, the heavy losses in officers and men, and the serious expenditure of public money, the nation smarted under failure and disappointment, and were, moreover, deeply sensible that they had been humiliated before the whole world. The situation in Egypt was scarcely more pleasing. The reforms initiated by the British Administrators had as yet only caused unpopularity. Baring's interference galled the Khedive and his Ministers. Vincent's parsimony excited contempt. Moncrieff's energy had convulsed the Irrigation Department. Wood's army was the laughing-stock of Europe. Among and beneath the rotten weeds and garbage of old systems and abuses the new seed was being sown. But England saw no signs of the crop; saw only the stubborn husbandmen begrimed with the dust and dirt, and herself hopelessly involved in the Egyptian muddle: and so in utter weariness and disgust, stopping her ears to the gibes and cat-calls of the Powers, she turned towards other lands and other matters.

When the attention of the nation was again directed to Egypt the scene was transformed. It was as though at the touch of an angel the dark morasses of the Slough of Despond had been changed to the breezy slopes of the Delectable Mountains. The Khedive and his Ministers lay quiet and docile in the firm grasp of the Consul-General. The bankrupt State was spending surpluses upon internal improvement. The disturbed Irrigation Department was vivifying the land. The derided army held the frontier against all comers.

Astonishment gave place to satisfaction, and satisfaction grew into delight. The haunting nightmare of Egyptian politics ended. Another dream began—a bright if vague vision of Imperial power, of trans-continental railways, of African Viceroys, of conquest and commerce. The interest of the British people in the work of regeneration grew continually. Each new reform was hailed with applause. Each annual Budget was scrutinised with pride. England exulted in the triumph of failure turned into success. There was a general wish to know more about Egypt and the men who had done these great things. In 1893 this desire was satisfied, and yet stimulated by the publication of Sir Alfred Milner's 'England in Egypt.' His skilful pen displayed what had been overcome, no less than what was accomplished. By explaining the difficulties he enhanced the achievement. He showed how, while Great Britain was occupied elsewhere, her brilliant, persevering sons had repeated on a lesser scale in Egypt the marvellous evolution which is working out in India. Smaller systems circulate more rapidly. The administrators were guided by experience. The movement had been far swifter, and the results were more surprising. Such was the wonderful story, and it was told in a happy moment. The audience were eager and sympathetic. The subject was enthralling. The story-teller had a wit and a style that might have brightened the dullest theme. In these propitious circumstances the book was more than a book. The words rang like the trumpet-call which rallies the soldiers after the parapets are stormed, and summons them to complete the victory.

The regeneration of Egypt is not a theme which would fall within the limits of this account, even if it had not been fully dealt with by Sir Alfred Milner. But the reorganisation of the Egyptian army, the forging of the weapon of reconquest, is an essential feature. On the 20th of December, 1882, the old Egyptian army—or, rather, such parts as had escaped destruction—was disbanded by a single sentence of a British decree, and it was evident that some military body must replace that which had been swept away. All sorts of schemes for the employment of foreign legions or Turkish janissaries were devised. But Lord Dufferin adhered firmly to the principle of entrusting the defence of a country to its inhabitants, and it was determined to form a new Egyptian army. The poverty of the government, no less than the apparent folly of the experiment, demanded that the new army should be small. The force was intended only for the preservation of internal order and the defence of the southern and western frontiers of Egypt against the Bedouin Arabs. The Soudan still slumbered out its long nightmare. Six thousand men was the number originally drawn by conscription—for there are no volunteers in Egypt—from a population of more than 6,000,000. Twenty-six British officers—either poor men attracted by the high rates of pay, or ambitious allured by the increased authority—and a score of excellent drill-sergeants undertook the duty of teaching the recruits to fight. Sir Evelyn Wood directed the enterprise, and became the first British Sirdar of the Egyptian army. The work began and immediately prospered. Within three months of its formation the army had its first review. The whole 6,000 paraded in their battalions and marched past the Khedive and their country's flag. Their bearing and their drill extorted the half-contemptuous praise of the indifferent spectators. Experienced soldiers noticed other points. Indeed, the new army differed greatly from the old. In the first place, it was paid. The recruits were treated with justice. Their rations were not stolen by the officers. The men were given leave to go to their villages from time to time. When they fell sick, they were sent to hospital instead of being flogged. In short, the European system was substituted for the Oriental.

It was hardly possible that the fertile soil and enervating climate of the Delta would have evolved a warrior race. Ages of oppression and poverty rarely produce proud and warlike spirits. Patriotism does not grow under the 'Kourbash.' The fellah soldier lacks the desire to kill. Even the Mohammedan religion has failed to excite his ferocity. He may be cruel. He is never fierce. Yet he is not without courage—a courage which bears pain and hardship in patience, which confronts ill-fortune with indifference, and which looks on death with apathetic composure. It is the courage of down-trodden peoples, and one which stronger breeds may often envy, though they can scarcely be expected to admire. He has other military virtues. He is obedient, honest, sober, well-behaved, quick to learn, and, above all, physically strong. Generations of toiling ancestors, though they could not brace his nerves, have braced his muscles. Under the pressure of local circumstances there has been developed a creature who can work with little food, with little incentive, very hard for long hours under a merciless sun. Throughout the river campaigns, if the intellect of the army, if the spirit of the troops, have come from without, Egypt herself has provided the sinews of war.

Such was the material out of which the British officers have formed the new Egyptian army. At first, indeed, their task was embittered by the ridicule of their comrades in the British and Indian Services; but as the drill and bearing of the force improved, the thoughtless scorn would have been diverted from the Englishmen to fall only upon the Egyptian soldiers. But this was not allowed. The British officers identified themselves with their men. Those who abused the fellah soldier were reminded that they insulted English gentlemen. Thus a strange bond of union was established between the officers and soldiers of the Egyptian Service; and although material forces may have accomplished much, without this moral factor the extraordinary results would never have been achieved.

It was not long before the new military organisation was exposed to the stern test of war. The army that was raised to preserve internal order was soon called upon to guard the frontier. The revolt in the Soudan, which in its earlier stages seemed the least of the Egyptian difficulties, speedily dwarfed all the rest. The value of the new force was soon recognised. In June 1883 we find General Hicks, then preparing for his fatal march, writing to Sir Evelyn Wood: 'Send me four battalions of your new army, and I shall be content.' But fortune protected the infant organisation from such a disastrous beginning. The 'new army' remained for a space in Cairo; and although during the Nile expedition of 1884-85 the Egyptians were employed guarding the lines of communication, it was not until the British troops had been withdrawn from Dongola that they received at Ginniss their baptism of fire. Henceforth their place was on the frontier, and from 1886 onward the Egyptian troops proved equal to the task of resisting the northward pressure of the Dervishes.

The numbers of the army grew with its responsibilities. Up to the end of 1883 the infantry still consisted of eight fellahin battalions. In 1884 the first Soudanese battalion was raised. The black soldier was of a very different type from the fellahin. The Egyptian was strong, patient, healthy, and docile. The negro was in all these respects his inferior. His delicate lungs, slim legs, and loosely knit figure contrasted unfavourably with the massive frame and iron constitution of the peasant of the Delta. Always excitable and often insubordinate, he required the strictest discipline. At once slovenly and uxorious, he detested his drills and loved his wives with equal earnestness; and altogether 'Sambo'—for such is the Soudanese equivalent of 'Tommy'—was a lazy, fierce, disreputable child. But he possessed two tremendous military virtues. To the faithful loyalty of a dog he added the heart of a lion. He loved his officer, and feared nothing in the world.

With the introduction of this element the Egyptian army became a formidable military machine. Chance or design has placed the blacks ever in the forefront of the battle, and in Lord Kitchener's campaigns on the Nile the losses in the six Soudanese battalions have exceeded the aggregate of the whole of the rest of the army.

It was well that the Egyptian troops were strengthened by these valiant auxiliaries, for years of weary war lay before them. Sir Reginald Wingate, in his exhaustive account of the struggle of Egypt with the Mahdist power, [MAHDISM AND THE EGYPTIAN SOUDAN, Sir Reginald Wingate] has described the successive actions which accompanied the defence of the Wady Halfa frontier and of Suakin.

The ten years that elapsed between Ginniss and the first movements of the expedition of re-conquest were the dreary years of the Egyptian army. The service was hard and continual. Though the operations were petty, an untiring vigilance was imperative. The public eye was averted. A pitiless economy was everywhere enforced. The British officer was deprived of his leave and the Egyptian private of his rations, that a few pounds might be saved to the Egyptian Treasury. The clothing of the battalions wore thin and threadbare, and sometimes their boots were so bad that the soldiers' feet bled from the cutting edges of the rocks, and the convoy escorts left their trails behind them. But preparation was ever going forward. The army improved in efficiency, and the constant warfare began to produce, even among the fellahin infantry, experienced soldiers. The officers, sweltering at weary Wady Halfa and Suakin, looked at the gathering resources of Egypt and out into the deserts of the declining Dervish Empire and knew that some day their turn would come. The sword of re-conquest which Evelyn Wood had forged, and Grenfell had tested, was gradually sharpened; and when the process was almost complete, the man who was to wield it presented himself.

Horatio Herbert Kitchener, the eldest son of a lieutenant-colonel, was born in 1850, and, after being privately educated, entered in 1869 the Royal Military Academy at Woolwich as a cadet of the Royal Engineers. In the spring of 1871 he obtained his commission, and for the first ten years of his military service remained an obscure officer, performing his duties with regularity, but giving no promise of the talents and character which he was afterwards to display. One powerful weapon, however, he acquired in this time of waiting. In 1874 accident or instinct led him to seek employment in the surveys that were being made of Cyprus and Palestine, and in the latter country he learned Arabic. For six years the advantage of knowing a language with which few British officers were familiar brought him no profit. For procuring military preferment Arabic was in 1874 as valueless as Patagonian. All this was swiftly changed by the unexpected course of events. The year 1882 brought the British fleet to Alexandria, and the connection between England and Egypt began to be apparent. Kitchener did not neglect his opportunity. Securing leave of absence, he hurried to the scene of crisis. Alexandria was bombarded. Detachments from the fleet were landed to restore order. The British Government decided to send an army to Egypt. British officers and soldiers were badly wanted at the seat of war; an officer who could speak Arabic was indispensable.

Thus Kitchener came to Egypt and set his feet firmly on the high road to fortune. He came to Egypt when she was plunged in misery and shame, when hopeless ruin seemed already the only outcome of the public disasters, and when even greater misfortunes impended. He remained to see her prosperous and powerful; to restore empire to her people, peace to her empire, honour to her army; and among those clear-minded men of action by whom the marvellous work of regeneration has been accomplished, Herbert Kitchener will certainly occupy the second place. Lord Wolseley on his arrival soon found employment for the active officer who could speak Arabic. He served through the campaign of 1882 as a major. He joined the new army which was formed at the conclusion of the war, as one of the original twenty-six officers. In the Nile expedition of 1885 Arabic again led him to the front, and in the service of the Intelligence Department he found ample opportunity for his daring and energy. His efforts to communicate with Gordon in Khartoum did not, however, meet with much success, and the Journals bristle with so many sarcastic comments that their editor has been at pains to explain in his preface that there was really no cause for complaint. Major Kitchener, however, gave satisfaction to his superiors in Cairo, if not to the exacting General at Khartoum, and in 1886 he was appointed Governor of Suakin. This post, always one of responsibility and danger, did not satisfy Kitchener, whose ambition was now taking definite form. Eager for more responsibility and more danger, he harried and raided the surrounding tribes; he restricted and almost destroyed the slender trade which was again springing up, and in consequence of his measures the neighbourhood of Suakin was soon in even greater ferment than usual. This culminated at the end of 1887 in the re-appearance and advance of Osman Digna. The movements of the Dervishes were, however, uncertain. The defences of the town had been greatly strengthened and improved by the skill and activity of its new Governor. [See dispatch from Major-General Dormer to War Office, Cairo, April 22, 1888: 'With regard to the military works and defenses of the town, I was much struck with the great improvement that has been effected by Colonel Kitchener since my last visit to Suakin in the autumn of 1884.] Osman Digna retreated. The 'friendlies' were incited to follow, and Kitchener, although he had been instructed not to employ British officers or Egyptian regulars in offensive operations, went out in support. At Handub on the morning of the 17th of January, 1888, the friendlies attacked the camp of Osman Digna. They were at first successful; but while they dispersed to plunder the enemy rallied and, returning, drove them back with loss. Kitchener arrived on the field with the support, to find a defeat instead of a victory awaiting him. He bravely endeavoured to cover the retreat of the friendlies, and in so doing was severely—as it first seemed dangerously—wounded in the jaw. The loss among the friendlies and the support amounted to twenty men killed and two British officers and twenty-eight men wounded. The Governor returned in great pain and some discomfiture to Suakin. In spite of his wound and his reverse he was impatient to renew the conflict, but this was definitely forbidden by the British Government. Colonel Kitchener's military conduct was praised, but his policy was prevented. 'The policy which it is desirable to follow . . . in the Eastern Soudan,' wrote Sir Evelyn Baring on the 17th of March, in measured rebuke, 'should consist in standing purely on the defensive against any hostile movement or combination of the Arab tribes, in avoiding any course of action which might involve the ultimate necessity of offensive action, and in encouraging legitimate trade by every means in our power.' [Sir E. Baring to Consul Cameron, March 14, 1888.]

The Governor could scarcely be expected to carry out a policy so much at variance with his views and inclinations, and in the summer of 1888 he was transferred to a purely military appointment and became Adjutant-General of the Egyptian army. For the next four years he worked busily in the War Office at Cairo, effecting many useful reforms and hard economies, and revealing powers of organisation which, although not yet appreciated by his comrades in the Egyptian service, were noticed by one vigilant eye. In 1892 Sir F. Grenfell resigned the post of Sirdar, and the chief command of the Egyptian army was vacant. Two men stood out prominently as candidates—Colonel Wodehouse, who held the command of the Halfa Field Force, and the Adjutant-General. Colonel Wodehouse had undoubtedly the greater claims. He had been for several years in command of a large force in continual contact with the enemy. He had won the action of Argin, and was known throughout the Soudan as 'the conqueror of Wad-el-Nejumi.' He had conducted the civil administration of the frontier province with conspicuous success, and he was popular with all ranks of the Egyptian army. Kitchener had little to set against this. He had shown himself a brave and active soldier. He was known to be a good official. But he had not been in accord with the Government in his civil administration, and was, moreover, little known to his brother officers. Sir Evelyn Baring's influence, however, turned the scale. Somewhat, therefore, to the astonishment of the Egyptian army, Kitchener was promoted Sirdar. Lord Cromer had found the military officer whom he considered capable of re-conquering the Soudan when the opportunity should come.

The years of preparation, wasted by no one in Egypt, were employed by no department better than by the Intelligence Branch. The greatest disadvantage from which Lord Wolseley had suffered was the general ignorance of the Soudan and its peoples. The British soldiers had had to learn the details of Dervish fighting by bitter experience. But the experience, once gained, was carefully preserved. The Intelligence Branch of the Egyptian army rose under the direction of Colonel (now Sir Reginald) Wingate to an extraordinary efficiency. For ten years the history, climate, geography, and inhabitants of the Soudan were the objects of a ceaseless scrutiny. The sharp line between civilisation and savagery was drawn at Wady Halfa; but beyond that line, up the great river, within the great wall of Omdurman, into the arsenal, into the treasury, into the mosque, into the Khalifa's house itself, the spies and secret agents of the Government—disguised as traders, as warriors, or as women—worked their stealthy way. Sometimes the road by the Nile was blocked, and the messengers must toil across the deserts to Darfur, and so by a tremendous journey creep into Omdurman. At others a trader might work his way from Suakin or from the Italian settlements. But by whatever route it came, information—whispered at Halfa, catalogued at Cairo—steadily accumulated, and the diaries of the Intelligence Department grew in weight and number, until at last every important

Emir was watched and located, every garrison estimated, and even the endless intrigues and brawls in Omdurman were carefully recorded.

The reports of the spies were at length confirmed and amplified by two most important witnesses. At the end of 1891 Father Ohrwalder made his escape from Omdurman and reached the Egyptian territory. Besides giving the Intelligence Department much valuable information, he published a thrilling account of his captivity [TEN YEARS' CAPTIVITY, Father Ohrwalder], which created a wide and profound impression in England. In 1895 a still more welcome fugitive reached Assuan. Early on the 16th of March a weary, travel-stained Arab, in a tattered jibba and mounted on a lame and emaciated camel, presented himself to the Commandant. He was received with delighted wonder, and forthwith conducted to the best bath-room available. Two hours later a little Austrian gentleman stepped forth, and the telegraph hastened to tell the news that Slatin, sometime Governor of Darfur, had escaped from the Khalifa's clutches. Here at last was a man who knew everything that concerned the Dervish Empire— Slatin, the Khalifa's trusted and confidential servant, almost his friend, who had lived with him, who was even permitted to dine with him alone, who had heard all his counsels, who knew all his Emirs, and moreover Slatin, the soldier and administrator, who could appreciate all he had learned, was added with the rank of Pasha to the Staff of the Intelligence Department. While his accurate knowledge confirmed the belief of the Egyptian authorities that the Dervish power was declining, his tale of 'Fire and Sword in the Soudan' increased the horror and anger of thoughtful people in England at the cruelties of the Khalifa. Public opinion began to veer towards the policy of re-conquest.

The year 1895 brought in a Conservative and Unionist Administration. A Government came into office supported by a majority which was so strong that there seemed little reason to expect a transference of power for five or six years. Ministers were likely to be able to carry to a definite conclusion any projects they might devise. They belonged chiefly to that party in the State which had consistently assailed Mr. Gladstone's Egyptian policy. Here was an opportunity of repairing the damage done by their opponents. The comparisons that would follow such an accomplishment were self-evident and agreeable even to anticipate. The idea of re-conquering the Soudan presented itself indefinitely, but not unpleasingly, alike to the Government and the people of Great Britain. The unforeseen course of events crystallised the idea into a policy.

On the 1st of March, 1896, the battle of Adowa was fought, and Italy at the hands of Abyssinia sustained a crushing defeat. Two results followed which affected other nations. First, a great blow had been struck at European prestige in North Africa. It seemed probable that the Abyssinian success would encourage the Dervishes to attack the Italians at Kassala. It was possible that they might also attack the Egyptians at Suakin or on the Wady Halfa frontier. Secondly, the value of Italy as a factor in European politics was depreciated. The fact that her defeat had been assisted by the arms and munitions of war which had been supplied to the Abyssinians from French and Russian sources complicated the situation. The Triple Alliance was concerned. The third partner had been weakened. The balance might be restored if Great Britain would make some open sign of sympathy.

Moreover, the expectations of the Egyptian military authorities were soon fulfilled. The Dervishes threatened Kassala as soon as the news of Adowa reached them, and indeed there were signs of increased activity in Omdurman itself. In these circumstances the British Government determined to assist Italy by making a demonstration on the Wady Halfa frontier. They turned to Egypt. It had always been recognised that the recovery of the lost provinces was a natural and legitimate aspiration. 'The doubtful point was to decide the time when the military and financial resources of the country were sufficiently developed to justify an assumption of the offensive.' [LORD CROMER'S REPORTS: EGYPT, No. 2, 1896.] From a purely Egyptian point of view the best possible moment had not yet arrived. A few more years of recuperation were needed. The country would fight the Soudan campaigns more easily if first refreshed by the great reservoirs which were projected. For more than two years both projects had been pressed upon the Government of his Highness the Khedive—or, to write definitely, upon Lord Cromer. At regular intervals Sir Herbert Kitchener and Sir William Garstin would successively visit the British Agency (it would be treason to call it 'Government House')—the one to urge the case for a war, the other to plead for a reservoir. The reservoir had won. Only a few weeks before the advance to Dongola was ordered Garstin met Kitchener returning from the Agency. The engineer inquired the result of the General's interview. 'I'm beaten,' said Kitchener abruptly; 'you've got your dam'—and Garstin went on his way rejoicing.

The decision of the British Government came therefore as a complete surprise to the Cairene authorities. The season of the year was unfavourable to military operations. The hot weather was at hand. The Nile was low. Lord Cromer's report, which had been published in the early days of March, had in no way foreshadowed the event. The frontier was tranquil. With the exception of a small raid on a village in the Wady Halfa district and an insignificant incursion into the Tokar Delta the Dervish forces had during the year maintained 'a strictly defensive attitude.' [EGYPT, No. 1, 1896.] Lord Cromer, however, realised that while the case for the reservoirs would always claim attention, the re-conquest of the Soudan might not receive the support of a Liberal Government. The increasing possibility of French intrigues upon the Upper Nile had also to be considered. All politics are series of compromises and bargains, and while the historian may easily mark what would have been the best possible moment for any great undertaking, a good moment must content the administrator. Those who guarded the interests of Egypt could hardly consent to an empty demonstration on the Wady Halfa frontier at her expense, and the original intention of the British Government was at once extended to the re-conquest of the Dongola province—a definite and justifiable enterprise which must in any case be the first step towards the recovery of the Soudan.

* * * * *

It will be convenient, before embarking upon the actual chronicle of the military operations, to explain how the money was obtained to pay for the war. I desire to avoid the intricate though fascinating tangles of Egyptian finance. Yet even when the subject is treated in the most general way the difficulties which harass and impede the British administrators and insult the sovereign power of Egypt—the mischievous interference of a vindictive nation, the galling and almost intolerable financial fetters in which a prosperous country is bound—may arouse in the sympathetic reader a flush of annoyance, or at any rate a smile of pitying wonder.

About half the revenue of Egypt is devoted to the development and government of the country, and the other half to the payment of the interest on the debt and other external charges; and, with a view to preventing in the future the extravagance of the past, the London Convention in 1885 prescribed that the annual expenditure of Egypt shall not exceed a certain sum. When the expenditure exceeds this amount, for every pound that is spent on the government or development of Egypt another pound must be paid to the Commissioners of the Debt; so that, after the limit is reached, for every pound that is required to promote Egyptian interests two pounds must be raised by taxation from an already heavily taxed community. But the working of this law was found to be so severe that, like all laws which exceed the human conception of justice, it has been somewhat modified. By an arrangement which was effected in 1888, the Caisse de la Dette are empowered, instead of devoting their surplus pound to the sinking fund, to pay it into a general reserve fund, from which the Commissioners may make grants to meet 'extraordinary expenses'; those expenses, that is to say, which may be considered 'once for all'(capital) expenditure and not ordinary annual charges.

The Dongola expedition was begun, as has been said, without reference to the immediate internal condition of Egypt. The moment was a good one, but not the best. It was obviously impossible for Egypt to provide for the extraordinary expenses of the military operations out of revenue. The Ministry of Finance therefore appealed to the Caisse de la Dette for a grant from the general reserve fund. Here was an obvious case of 'extraordinary expenses.' The Egyptian Government asked for 500,000 Egyptian pounds (EP500,000).

The Caisse met in council. Six Commissioners—representing England, France, Russia, Germany, Austria, and Italy—duly discussed the application. Four Commissioners considered that the grant should be made. Two Commissioners, those representing France and Russia, voted against it. The majority decided. The grant was made. The money was handed to the Egyptian Government and devoted to the prosecution of the war.

Egypt as a sovereign power had already humbly begged to be allowed to devote part of the surplus of her own revenues to her own objects. A greater humiliation remained. The Commissioners of France and Russia, who had been out-voted, brought an action against their colleagues on the grounds that the grant was ultra vires; and against the Egyptian Government for the return of the money thus wrongly obtained. Other actions were brought at French instigation by various people purporting to represent the bondholders, who declared that their interests were threatened. The case was tried before the Mixed

Tribunals, an institution which exists in Egypt superior to and independent of the sovereign rights of that country.

On the part of the Egyptian Government and the four Commissioners it was contended that the Mixed Tribunals had no competency to try the case; that the attacking parties had no right of action; that the Egyptian Government had, in applying, done all that the law of liquidation required; and that the act of sovereignty was complete as soon as the Caisse, which was the legal representative of the bondholding interest, had pronounced its decision.

The argument was a strong one; but had it been ten times as strong, the result would have been the same. The Mixed Tribunals, an international institution, delivered its judgment on strictly political grounds, the judges taking their orders from the different countries they represented. It was solemnly pronounced that war expenses were not 'extraordinary expenses.' The proximate destruction of the Khalifa's power was treated quite as a matter of everyday occurrence. A state of war was apparently regarded as usual in Egypt. On this wise and sensible ground the Egyptian Government were condemned to pay back EP500,000, together with interest and costs. After a momentary hesitation as to whether the hour had not come to join issue on the whole subject of the financial restrictions of Egypt, it was decided to bow to this iniquitous decision. The money had now to be refunded. It had already been spent. More than that, other sums were needed for the carrying on of the war. The army was by then occupying Dongola, and was in actual expectation of a Dervish counter-attack, and it was evident that the military operations could not be suspended or arrested. It was impossible to stop; yet without money it seemed impossible to go on; and, besides, it appeared that Egypt would be unable to repay the EP500,000 which she had been granted, and of which she was now deprived.

Such was the painful and difficult situation which a friendly nation, in the utmost exercise of her wit and the extreme compass of her legal rights, had succeeded in producing in a country for whose welfare she had always professed an exaggerated regard. Such was the effect of French diplomacy. But there is a Nemesis that waits on international malpractices, however cunning. Now, as before and since, the very astuteness of the French Ministers and agents was to strike a terrible blow at French interests and French influence in Egypt. At this period France still exercised a considerable force on Egyptian politics. One Egyptian party, the weaker, but still by no means insignificant, looked towards her for support. The news of the French success cheered their hearts and raised their spirits. Orientals appreciate results. The result was a distinct reverse to the British. The conclusion to the native mind was obvious. Great Britain had been weighed in the European balances and found wanting. In all Eastern countries a large proportion of the population fluctuates uncertainly, eager only to be on the winning side. All this volume of agitation and opinion began to glide and flow towards the stronger Power, and when the Egyptian Government found their appeal from the decision of the Court of First Instance of the Mixed Tribunals to the International Court of Appeal at Alexandria quashed, and the original decision confirmed, the defeat of the British was no less complete than the triumph of the French.

But meanwhile the Consul-General acted. On the 2nd of December he telegraphed to Lord Salisbury, reporting the judgment of the Court of Appeal and asking that he might be 'authorised to state directly that her Majesty's Government will be prepared to advance the money on conditions to be hereafter arranged.' The reply was prompt, though guarded. 'You are authorised,' said Lord Salisbury, 'by the Chancellor of the Exchequer to state that though of course the primary liability for the payment of the EP500,000 rests with the Egyptian Government, her Majesty's Government will hold themselves prepared to advance, on conditions to be decided hereafter, such a sum as they feel satisfied that the Egyptian Treasury is powerless to provide.' [The original EP500,000 was afterwards increased to EP800,000; which sum was paid by the British Exchequer to the Egyptian Government, at first as a loan, and later as a gift.] This obvious development does not seem to have been foreseen by the French diplomatists, and when, on the 3rd of December, it was rumoured in Cairo that Great Britain was prepared to pay the money, a great feeling of astonishment and of uncertainty was created. But the chances of the French interference proving effective still seemed good. It was believed that the English Government would not be in a position to make an advance to the Egyptian Government until funds had been voted by Parliament for the purpose. It was also thought that Egypt would be utterly unable to find the money immediately. In the meantime the position was humiliating. France conceived herself mistress of the situation. A complete disillusionment, however, awaited the French Government. The taxes in Egypt, as in other countries, are not collected evenly over the whole year. During some months there is a large cash balance in the Exchequer. In others the money drains in slowly. It happened at this period of the year, after the cotton crop had been gathered, that a considerable balance had accumulated in the Treasury, and on the guarantee of the English Government being received, to the effect that they would ultimately assist Egypt with regard to the expenses of the expedition, Lord Cromer determined to repay the money at once.

The event was foreshadowed. On the 5th of December the Egyptian Council of Ministers, presided over by the Khedive in person, decided on their own initiative to despatch an official letter expressing in warm terms their gratitude for the financial help offered them by her Majesty's Government. 'I am desired,' said Boutros Pasha, 'to beg your lordship to be good enough to convey to his lordship the Marquess of Salisbury the expression of the lively gratitude of the Khedive and the Egyptian Government for the great kindness which her Majesty's Government has shown to them on this occasion.' [EGYPT, No. 1, 1897.]

On the 6th of December EP500,000, together with EP15,600 interest and costs, in gold, was conveyed in boxes in a cart from the Egyptian Treasury to the offices of the Caisse de la Dette. The effect was tremendous. All Cairo knew of the difficulty. All Cairo witnessed the manner in which it had been overcome. The lesson was too plain to be lost on the native mind. The reverse of the French diplomacy was far greater even than its success had appeared. For many years French influence in Egypt had not received so heavy a blow; yet even in the short space of time which this story covers it was to receive a still more terrible wound.

CHAPTER V:

THE BEGINNING OF THE WAR

Shortly before midnight on the 12th of March, 1896, the Sirdar received instructions from Lord Cromer authorising an expedition into the Dongola province and directing him to occupy Akasha. The next morning the news was published in the Times, ostensibly as coming from its correspondent in Cairo: and the Egyptian Cabinet was convened to give a formal assent by voting the decree. On the 14th the reserves were called out. On the 15th the Khedive reviewed the Cairo garrison; and at the termination of the parade Sir H. Kitchener informed him that the earliest battalions would start for the front that night.

The Egyptian frontier force had always been kept in a condition of immediate readiness by the restless activity of the enemy. The beginning of the long-expected advance was hailed with delight by the British officers sweltering at Wady Halfa and Sarras. On Sunday, the 15th of March, three days after the Sirdar had received his orders, and before the first reinforcements had started from Cairo, Colonel Hunter, who commanded on the frontier, formed a small column of all arms to seize and hold Akasha. At dawn on the 18th the column started, and the actual invasion of the territory which for ten years had been abandoned to the Dervishes began. The route lay through a wild and rocky country—the debatable ground, desolated by years of war—and the troops straggled into a long procession, and had several times for more than an hour to move in single file over passes and through narrow defiles strewn with the innumerable boulders from which the 'Belly of Stones' has derived its name. The right of their line of march was protected by the Nile, and although it was occasionally necessary to leave the bank, to avoid difficult ground, the column camped each night by the river. The cavalry and the Camel Corps searched the country to the south and east; for it was expected that the Dervishes would resist the advance. Creeping along the bank, and prepared at a moment's notice to stand at bay at the water's edge, the small force proceeded on its way. Wady Atira was reached on the 18th, Tanjore on the 19th, and on the 20th the column marched into Akasha.

The huts of the mud village were crumbling back into the desert sand. The old British fort and a number of storehouses—relics of the Gordon Relief Expedition—were in ruins. The railway from Sarras had been pulled to pieces. Most of the sleepers had disappeared, but the rails lay scattered along the track. All was deserted: yet one grim object proclaimed the Dervish occupation. Beyond the old station and near the river a single rail had been fixed nearly upright in the ground. From one of the holes for the fishplate bolts there dangled a rotten cord, and on the sand beneath this improvised yet apparently effective gallows lay a human skull and bones, quite white and beautifully polished by the action of sun and wind. Half-a-dozen friendly Arabs, who had taken refuge on the island below the cataract, were the only inhabitants of the district.

The troops began to place themselves in a defensive position without delay. On the 22nd the cavalry and Camel Corps returned with the empty convoy to Sarras to escort to the front a second and larger column, under the command of Major MacDonald, and consisting of the XIth and XIIth Soudanese, one company of the 3rd Egyptians (dropped as a garrison at Ambigole Wells), and a heavy convoy of stores numbering six hundred camels. Starting from Sarras on the 24th, the column, after four days' marching, arrived without accident or attack, and MacDonald assumed command of the whole advanced force.

Akasha was now converted into a strong entrenched camp, in which an advanced base was formed. Its garrison of three battalions, a battery, and the mounted troops, drew their supplies by camel transport from Sarras. The country to the south and east was continually patrolled, to guard against a turning movement, and the communications were further strengthened by the establishment of fortified posts at Semna, Wady Atira, and Tanjore. The friendly Arab tribes—Bedouin, Kabbabish, and Foggara—ranged still more widely in the deserts and occupied the scattered wells. All this time the Dervishes watched supinely from their position at Fuket, and although they were within a single march of Akasha they remained inactive and made no attempt to disturb the operations.

Meanwhile the concentration of the Egyptian army on the frontier was proceeding. The reservists obeyed the summons to the colours of their own free will and with gratifying promptness, instead of being tardily dragged from their homes in chains as in the days of Ismail. All the battalions of the army were brought up to war strength. Two new battalions of reservists were formed, the 15th and 16th. The 15th was placed at Assuan and Korosko on the line of communications. The 16th was despatched to Suakin to release the two battalions in garrison there for service on the Nile. The 1st Battalion of the North Staffordshire Regiment was moved up the river from Cairo to take the place of the Wady Halfa garrison of six battalions, which had moved on to Sarras and Akasha. A Maxim battery of four guns was formed from the machine-gun sections of the Staffordshires and Connaught Rangers and hurried south. The 2nd, 4th, 5th, and 6th Egyptian Battalions from Cairo were passed in a continual succession along the railway and river to the front. In all this busy and complicated movement of troops the Egyptian War Office worked smoothly, and clearly showed the ability with which it was organised.

The line of communications from Cairo, the permanent base, to the advanced post at Akasha was 825 miles in length. But of this distance only the section lying south of Assuan could be considered as within the theatre of war. The ordinary broad-gauge railway ran from Cairo to Balliana, where a river base was established. From Balliana to Assuan reinforcements and supplies were forwarded by Messrs. Cook's fleet of steamers, by barges towed by small tugs, and by a number of native sailing craft. A stretch of seven miles of railway avoids the First Cataract, and joins Assuan and Shellal. Above Shellal a second flotilla of gunboats, steamers, barges, and Nile boats was collected to ply between Shellal and Halfa. The military railway ran from Halfa to Sarras. South of Sarras supplies were forwarded by camels. To meet the increased demands of transport, 4,500 camels were purchased in Egypt and forwarded in boats to Assuan, whence they marched via Korosko to the front. The British Government had authorised the construction of the military railway to Akasha, and a special railway battalion was collected at Assuan, through which place sleepers and other material at once began to pass to Sarras. The strategic railway construction will, however, form the subject of a later chapter, which I shall not anticipate.

By the 1st of April, less than three weeks from the commencement of the advance, the whole line of communications had been organised and was working efficiently, although still crowded with the concentrating troops.

As soon as the 16th Battalion of reservists arrived at Suakin, the IXth Soudanese were conveyed by transports to Kossier, and marched thence across the desert to Kena. The distance was 120 miles, and the fact that in spite of two heavy thunderstorms—rare phenomena in Egypt—it was covered in four days is a notable example of the marching powers of the black soldiers. It had been determined that the Xth Soudanese should follow at once, but circumstances occurred which detained them on the Red Sea littoral and must draw the attention of the reader thither.

The aspect and history of the town and port of Suakin might afford a useful instance to a cynical politician. Most of the houses stand on a small barren island which is connected with the mainland by a narrow causeway. At a distance the tall buildings of white coral, often five storeys high, present an imposing appearance, and the prominent chimneys of the condensing machinery—for there is scarcely any fresh water—seem to suggest manufacturing activity. But a nearer view reveals the melancholy squalor of the scene. A large part of the town is deserted. The narrow streets wind among tumbled-down and neglected houses. The quaintly carved projecting windows of the facades are boarded up. The soil exhales an odour of stagnation and decay. The atmosphere is rank with memories of waste and failure. The scenes that meet the eye intensify these impressions. The traveller who lands on Quarantine Island is first confronted with the debris of the projected Suakin-Berber Railway. Two or three locomotives that have neither felt the pressure of steam nor tasted oil for a decade lie rusting in the ruined workshops. Huge piles of railway material rot, unguarded and neglected, on the shore. Rolling stock of all kinds—carriages, trucks, vans, and ballast waggons—are strewn or heaped near the sheds. The Christian cemetery alone shows a decided progress, and the long lines of white crosses which mark the graves of British soldiers and sailors who lost their lives in action or by disease during the various campaigns, no less than the large and newly enclosed areas to meet future demands, increase the depression of the visitor. The numerous graves of Greek traders—a study of whose epitaphs may conveniently refresh a classical education—protest that the climate of the island is pestilential. The high loopholed walls declare that the desolate scrub of the mainland is inhabited only by fierce and valiant savages who love their liberty.

For eleven years all trade had been practically stopped, and the only merchants remaining were those who carried on an illicit traffic with the Arabs or, with Eastern apathy, were content to wait for better days. Being utterly unproductive, Suakin had been wisely starved by the Egyptian Government, and the gloom of the situation was matched by the poverty of its inhabitants.

The island on which the town stands is joined to the mainland by a causeway, at the further end of which is an arched gateway of curious design called 'the Gate of the Soudan.' Upon the mainland stands the crescent-shaped suburb of El Kaff. It comprises a few mean coral-built houses, a large area covered with mud huts inhabited by Arabs and fishermen, and all the barracks and military buildings. The whole is surrounded by a strong wall a mile and a half long, fifteen feet high, six feet thick, with a parapet pierced for musketry and strengthened at intervals by bastions armed with Krupp guns.

Three strong detached posts complete the defences of Suakin. Ten miles to the northward, on the scene of Sir H. Kitchener's unfortunate enterprise, is the fort of Handub. Tambuk is twenty-five miles inland and among the hills. Situate upon a high rock, and consisting only of a store, a formidable blockhouse, and a lookout tower, this place is safe from any enemy unprovided with artillery. Both Handub and Tambuk were at the outset of the campaign provisioned for four months. The third post, Tokar Fort, lies fifty miles along the coast to the south. Its function is to deprive the Arabs of a base in the fertile delta of the Tokar river. The fort is strong, defended by artillery, and requires for its garrison an entire battalion of infantry.

No description of Suakin would be complete without some allusion to the man to whom it owes its fame. Osman Digna had been for many years a most successful and enterprising Arab slave dealer. The attempted suppression of his trade by the Egyptian Government drove him naturally into opposition. He joined in the revolt of the Mahdi, and by his influence roused the whole of the Hadendoa and other powerful tribes of the Red Sea shore. The rest is upon record. Year after year, at a horrid sacrifice of men and money, the Imperial Government and the old slaver fought like wolves over the dry bone of Suakin. Baker's Teb, El Teb, Tamai, Tofrek, Hashin, Handub, Gemaiza, Afafit—such were the fights of Osman Digna, and through all he passed unscathed. Often defeated, but never crushed, the wily Arab might justly boast to have run further and fought more than any Emir in the Dervish armies.

It had scarcely seemed possible that the advance on Dongola could influence the situation around Kassala, yet the course of events encouraged the belief that the British diversion in favour of Italy had been effective; for at the end of March—as soon, that is to say, as the news of the occupation of Akasha reached him—Osman Digna separated himself from the army threatening Kassala, and marched with 300 cavalry, 70 camelry, and 2,500 foot towards his old base in the Tokar Delta. On the first rumour of his advance the orders of the Xth Soudanese to move via Kossier and Kena to the Nile were cancelled, and they remained in garrison at Tokar. At home the War Office, touched in a tender spot, quivered apprehensively, and began forthwith to make plans to strengthen the Suakin garrison with powerful forces.

The state of affairs in the Eastern Soudan has always been turbulent. The authority of the Governor of the Red Sea Littoral was not at this time respected beyond the extreme range of the guns of Suakin. The Hadendoa and other tribes who lived under the walls of the town professed loyalty to the Egyptian Government, not from any conviction that their rule was preferable to that of Osman Digna, but simply for the sake of a quiet life. As their distance from Suakin increased, the loyalty of the tribesmen became even less pronounced, and at a radius of twenty miles all the Sheikhs oscillated alternately between Osman Digna and the Egyptian Government, and tried to avoid open hostilities with either. Omar Tita, Sheikh of the district round about Erkowit, found himself situated on this fringe of intriguing neutrality. Although he was known to have dealings with Osman, it was believed that if he had the power to choose he would side with the Egyptian Government. Early in April Omar Tita reported that Osman Digna was in the neighbourhood of Erkowit with a small force, and that he, the faithful ally of the Government, had on the 3rd of the month defeated him with a loss of four camels. He also said that if the Egyptian Government would send up a force to fight Osman, he, the aforesaid ally, would keep him in play until it arrived.

After a few days of hesitation and telegraphic communication with the Sirdar, Colonel Lloyd, the Governor of Suakin, who was then in very bad health, decided that he had not enough troops to justify him in taking the risk of going up to Erkowit to fight Osman. Around Suakin, as along the Indian frontier, a battle was always procurable on the shortest notice. When a raid has taken place, the Government may choose the scale of their reprisals. If they are poor, they will arrange a counter-raid by means of 'friendlies,' and nothing more will be heard of the affair. If they are rich, they will mobilise two or three brigades, and make an expedition or fight a pitched battle, so that another glory may be added to the annals of the British army. In the present instance the Egyptian Government were poor, and as the British Government did not desire to profit by the opportunity it was determined to have only a small-scale operation. The Governor therefore arranged a plan for a demonstration at the foot of the hills near Khor Wintri by means of combined movements from Suakin and Tokar. The garrison of Suakin consisted of the 1st and half the 5th Egyptian Battalions; the 16th Egyptian reservists, who had just replaced the IXth Soudanese, and were as yet hardly formed into a military body; one squadron of cavalry, one company of Camel Corps, and some detachments of artillery. The garrison of Tokar consisted of the Xth Soudanese and a few gunners. From these troops there was organised in the second week in April, with all due ceremony, a 'Suakin Field Force.'

The plan of campaign was simple. Colonel Lloyd was to march out from Suakin and effect a junction with the 'Tokar Column' at Khor Wintri, where the Erkowit road enters the hills. It was then hoped that Osman Digna would descend and fight a battle of the required dimensions in the open; after which, if victorious, the force would return to Suakin and Tokar.

In order to make the Suakin Column as mobile as possible, the whole force was mounted on camels, of which more than 1,000 were requisitioned, as well as 60 mules and 120 donkeys. Two hundred Arabs accompanied the column to hold these beasts when necessary. Six days' forage and rations, one day's reserve of water, 200 rounds per man, and 100 shell per gun were carried. At five o'clock on the afternoon of Tuesday, the 14th of April, the troops paraded outside the walls of Suakin, and bivouacked in the open ready to march at daylight.

The next morning the column, which numbered about 1,200 men of all arms, started. After marching for four or five hours in the direction of Khor Wintri the cavalry, who covered the advance, came in contact with the Dervish scouts. The force thereupon assumed an oblong formation: the mixed Soudanese company and the two guns in front, three Egyptian companies on each flank, the Camel Corps company in the rear, and the transport in the centre. The pace was slow, and, since few of the camels had ever been saddled or ridden, progress was often interrupted by their behaviour and by the broken and difficult nature of the country. Nevertheless at about four o'clock in the afternoon, Teroi Wells, eight miles from Khor Wintri, were reached; and here, having marched nineteen miles, Colonel Lloyd determined to halt. While the infantry were making the zeriba, the cavalry were sent on under Captain Fenwick (an infantry officer employed on the Staff) to gain touch with the Tokar force, who were expected to have already reached the rendezvous. Apparently under the belief that Omar Tita and his Arabs would give timely notice of an attack, the cavalry seem to have neglected many of the usual precautions, and in consequence at about five o'clock, when approaching Khor Wintri, they found themselves suddenly confronted with a force of about 200 Dervish horsemen supported by a large body of infantry. The squadron wheeled about with promptitude, and began to retire at a trot. The Dervish horsemen immediately pursued. The result was that the Egyptians began a disorderly flight at a gallop through the thick and treacherous scrub and over broken, dangerous ground. Sixteen horses fell; their riders were instantly speared by the pursuers. Rallying thirty-eight troopers, Captain Fenwick seized a rocky hillock, and dismounting with the natural instinct of an infantry soldier, prepared to defend himself to the last. The remainder of the squadron continued their flight, and thirty-two troopers, under an Egyptian officer (whose horse is said to have bolted), arrived at the Teroi zeriba with the news that their comrades had been destroyed, or had perhaps 'returned to Suakin,' and that they themselves had been closely followed by the enemy. The news caused the gravest anxiety, which was not diminished when it was found that the bush around the zeriba was being strongly occupied by Dervish spearmen. Two mounted men, who volunteered for the perilous duty, were sent to make their way through this savage cordon, and try to find either the remainder of the cavalry or the Tokar Column. Both were hunted down and killed. The rest of the force continued in hourly expectation of an attack.

Their suspense was aggravated towards midnight, when the Dervishes began to approach the zeriba. In the darkness what was thought to be a body of horsemen was seen moving along a shallow khor opposite the right face of the defence. At the same moment a loud yell was raised by the enemy on the other side. An uncontrolled musketry fire immediately broke out. The guns fired blindly up the valley; the infantry wildly on all sides. The fusillade continued furiously for some time, and when by the efforts of the British officers the troops were restrained, it was found that the Dervishes had retired, leaving behind them a single wounded man. Occasional shots were fired from the scrub until the morning, but no fresh attack was attempted by the Dervishes.

Meanwhile Captain Fenwick maintained his solitary and perilous position on the hillock. He was soon surrounded by considerable bodies of the enemy, and as soon as it became dark he was sharply attacked. But the Dervishes fortunately possessed few rifles, and the officers and troopers, by firing steady volleys, succeeded in holding their ground and repulsing them. The sound of the guns at Teroi encouraged the Egyptians and revealed the direction of their friends. With the daylight the Dervishes, who seem throughout the affair to have been poor-spirited fellows, drew off, and the detachment, remounting, made haste to rejoin the main body.

The force, again united, pursued their way to Khor Wintri, where they found the column from Tokar already arrived. Marching early on the 15th, Major Sidney with 250 men of the Xth Soudanese, the only really trustworthy troops in the force, had reached Khor Wintri the same afternoon. He drove out the small Dervish post occupying the khor, and was about to bivouac, when he was sharply attacked by a force of Arabs said to have numbered 80 horsemen and 500 foot. The Soudanese fought with their usual courage, and the Dervishes were repulsed, leaving thirty dead upon the ground. The regulars had three men wounded.

Up to this point Colonel Lloyd's plan had been successfully carried out. The columns from Suakin and Tokar had effected a junction at Khor Wintri on the Erkowit road. It now remained to await the attack of Osman Digna, and inflict a heavy blow upon him. It was decided, however, in view of what had occurred, to omit this part of the scheme, and both forces returned together without delay to Suakin, which they reached on the 18th, having lost in the operations eighteen Egyptian soldiers killed and three wounded.

Their arrival terminated a period of anxious doubt as to their fate. The town, which had been almost entirely denuded of troops, was left in charge of Captain Ford-Hutchinson. At about two o'clock in the afternoon of the 16th a few stragglers from the Egyptian cavalry with half-a-dozen riderless horses knocked at the gates, and vague but sinister rumours spread on all sides. The belief that a disaster had overtaken the Egyptian force greatly excited the Arabs living within the walls, and it appeared that they were about to rise, plunder the town, and massacre the Christians. Her Majesty's ship Scout was, however, by good fortune in the harbour. Strong parties of bluejackets were landed to patrol the streets. The guns of the warship were laid on the Arab quarter. These measures had a tranquillising effect, and order reigned in Suakin until the return of the Field Force, when their victory was celebrated with appropriate festivities.

It was announced that as a result of the successful operations the Dervish enterprise against the Tokai Delta had collapsed, and that Osman Digna's power was for ever broken. In order, however, that no unfortunate incident should mar the triumph, the Xth Soudanese were sent back to Tokar by sea via Trinkitat, instead of marching direct and the garrison of Suakin confined themselves henceforward strictly to their defences. Osman Digna remained in the neighbourhood and raided the friendly villages. On the arrival of the Indian contingent he was supposed to be within twelve miles of the town, but thereafter he retired to Adarama on the Atbara river, where he remained during the Dongola campaign. The fact that no further offensive operations were undertaken in the Eastern Soudan prevented all fighting, for the Dervishes were, of course, unable to assail the strong permanent fortifications behind which the Egyptians took shelter. They nevertheless remained in actual possession of the surrounding country, until the whole situation was altered by the successful advance of powerful forces behind them along the Nile and by the occupation of Berber.

After the affair of Khor Wintri it was evident that it would not be possible to leave Suakin to the defence only of the 16th Battalion of reservists. On the other hand, Sir H. Kitchener required every soldier the Egyptian army could muster to carry out the operations on the Nile. It was therefore determined to send Indian troops to Suakin to garrison the town and forts, and thus release the Xth Soudanese and the Egyptian battalions for the Dongola Expedition. Accordingly early in the month of May the Indian Army authorities were ordered to prepare a brigade of all arms for service in Egypt.

The troops selected were as follow: 26th Bengal Infantry, 35th Sikhs, 1st Bombay Lancers, 5th Bombay Mountain Battery, two Maxim guns, one section Queen's Own (Madras) Sappers and Miners—in all about 4,000 men. The command was entrusted to Colonel Egerton, of the Corps of Guides.

On the 30th of May the dreary town of Suakin was enlivened by the arrival of the first detachments, and during the following week the whole force disembarked at the rotten piers and assumed the duties of the defence. It is mournful to tell how this gallant brigade, which landed so full of high hope and warlike enthusiasm, and which was certainly during the summer the most efficient force in the Soudan, was reduced in seven months to the sullen band who returned to India wasted by disease, embittered by disappointment, and inflamed by feelings of resentment and envy.

The Indian contingent landed in the full expectation of being immediately employed against the enemy. After a week, when all the stores had been landed, officers and men spent their time speculating when the order to march would come. It was true that there was no transport in Suakin, but that difficulty was easily overcome by rumours that 5,000 camels were on their way from the Somali coast to enable the force to move on Kassala or Berber. As these did not arrive, General Egerton sent in a proposed scheme to the Sirdar, in which he undertook to hold all the advanced posts up to the Kokreb range, if he were supplied with 1,000 camels for transport. A characteristic answer was returned, to the effect that it was not intended to use the Indian contingent as a mobile force. They had come as a garrison for Suakin, and a garrison for Suakin they should remain. This information was not, however, communicated to the troops, who continued to hope for orders to advance until the fall of Dongola.

The heat when the contingent arrived was not great, but as the months wore on the temperature rose steadily, until in August and September the thermometer rarely fell below 103 degrees during the night, and often rose to 115 degrees by day. Dust storms were frequent. A veritable plague of flies tormented the unhappy soldiers. The unhealthy climate, the depressing inactivity, and the scantiness of fresh meat or the use of condensed water, provoked an outbreak of scurvy. At one time nearly all the followers and 50 per cent of the troops were affected. Several large drafts were invalided to India. The symptoms were painful and disgusting—open wounds, loosening of the teeth, curious fungoid growths on the gums and legs. The cavalry horses and transport animals suffered from bursati, and even a pinprick expanded into a large open sore. It is doubtful whether the brigade could have been considered fit for active service after September. All the Europeans suffered acutely from prickly heat. Malarial fever was common. There were numerous cases of abscess on the liver. Twenty-five per cent of the British officers were invalided to England or India, and only six escaped a stay in hospital. The experiences of the battalion holding Tokar Fort were even worse than those of the troops in Suakin. At length the longed-for time of departure arrived. With feelings of relief and delight the Indian contingent shook the dust of Suakin off their feet and returned to India. It is a satisfaction to pass from the dismal narrative of events in the Eastern Soudan to the successful campaign on the Nile.

By the middle of April the concentration on the frontier was completed. The communications were cleared of their human freight, and occupied only by supplies and railway material, which continued to pour south at the utmost capacity of the transport. Eleven thousand troops had been massed at and beyond Wady Halfa. But no serious operations could take place until a strong reserve of stores had been accumulated at the front. Meanwhile the army waited, and the railway grew steadily. The battalions were distributed in three principal fortified camps—Halfa, Sarras, and Akasha—and detachments held the chain of small posts which linked them together.

Including the North Staffordshire Regiment, the garrison of Wady Halfa numbered about 3,000 men. The town and cantonment, nowhere more than 400 yards in width, straggle along the river-bank, squeezed in between the water and the desert, for nearly three miles. The houses, offices, and barracks are all built of mud, and the aspect of the place is brown and squalid. A few buildings, however, attain to the dignity of two storeys. At the northern end of the town a group of fairly well-built houses occupy the river-front, and a distant view of the clusters of palm-trees, of the white walls, and the minaret of the mosque refreshes the weary traveller from Korosko or Shellal with the hopes of civilised entertainment. The whole town is protected towards the deserts by a ditch and mud wall; and heavy Krupp field-pieces are mounted on little bastions where the ends of the rampart rest upon the river. Five small detached forts strengthen the land front, and the futility of an Arab attack at this time was evident. Halfa had now become the terminus of a railway, which was rapidly extending; and the continual arrival and despatch of tons of material, the building of sheds, workshops, and storehouses lent the African slum the bustle and activity of a civilised city.

Sarras Fort is an extensive building, perched on a crag of black rock rising on the banks of the Nile about thirty miles south of Halfa. During the long years of preparation it had been Egypt's most advanced outpost and the southern terminus of the military railway. The beginning of the expedition swelled it into an entrenched camp, holding nearly 6,000 men. From each end of the black rock on which the fort stood a strong stone wall and wire entanglement ran back to the river. The space thus enclosed was crowded with rows of tents and lines of animals and horses; and in the fort Colonel Hunter, commanding the district known as 'Sarras and the South,' had his headquarters.

From Sarras the army seemed to have chosen a double line of advance. The railway reconstruction followed the old track which had been prepared through the desert in 1885. The convoy route wound along by the river. Both were protected from attack. The 7th Egyptians guarded Railhead, while the chain of small posts secured the road by the Nile to Akasha. The advanced base grew during the months of April and May into a strong position. Only once did the Arabs venture to approach within artillery range. A small body of horse and camel men made a sort of haphazard reconnaissance, and, being seen from the outpost line, were fired on at a great distance by a field-gun. They fell back immediately, but it was believed that the range was too great for the projectile to have harmed them; and it was not until two days later that the discovery on the spot of a swollen, blistering corpse, clad in bright jibba, apprised the delighted gunners of the effect of their fire. Warned by this lucky shot the Dervishes came no more, or came unseen.

The Sirdar, accompanied by Colonel Bundle, his Chief of Staff, had left Cairo on the 22nd of March, and after a short stay at Assuan reached Wady Halfa on the 29th. Here he remained during the month of April, superintending and pressing the extension of the railroad and the accumulation of supplies. On the 1st of May he arrived at Akasha, with a squadron of cavalry, under Major Burn-Murdoch, as his escort. It happened that a convoy had come in the previous day, so that there were two extra cavalry squadrons at the advanced post. Almost at the same moment that Sir H. Kitchener entered the camp, a party of friendly Arabs came in with the news that they had been surprised some four miles to the eastward by a score of Dervish camel-men, and had only succeeded in escaping with the loss of two of their number. In the belief that the enemy in the immediate vicinity were not in force, the Sirdar ordered the three squadrons of Egyptian cavalry, supported by the XIth Soudanese, to go out and reconnoitre towards Firket and endeavour to cut off any hostile patrols that might be found.

At ten o'clock Major Burn-Murdoch started with four British officers and 240 lances. After moving for seven or eight miles among the hills which surround Akasha, the cavalry passed through a long, sandy defile, flanked on either side by rocky peaks and impracticable ravines. As the head of the column was about to debouch from this, the advanced scouts reported that there was a body of Dervishes in the open ground in front of the defile. The cavalry commander rode forward to look at them, and found himself confronted, not, as he had expected, by a score of camel-men, but by a strong force of Dervishes, numbering at least 1,500 foot and 250 horse. The cavalry, by trotting, had left the supporting infantry some distance behind them. The appearance of the enemy was threatening. The horsemen, who were drawn up scarcely 300 yards away, were already advancing to the attack, their right flank protected by a small force of camelry; and behind was the solid array of the spearmen.

Major Burn-Murdoch determined to fall back on his infantry support and escape from the bad ground. He gave the order, and the squadrons wheeled about by troops and began to retire. Forthwith the Dervish horse charged, and, galloping furiously into the defile, attacked the cavalry in rear. Both sides were crowded in the narrow space. The wildest confusion followed, and the dust raised by the horses' hoofs hung over all like a yellow London fog, amid which the bewildered combatants discharged their pistols and thrust at random. The Egyptian cavalry, thus highly tried, showed at first no disposition to turn to meet the attack. The tumult drowned all words of command. A disaster appeared imminent. But the British officers, who had naturally been at the head of the column during its advance, were now at the rear and nearest the enemy. Collecting a score of troopers, they made such resistance with their swords and revolvers that they actually held the defile and beat back the Dervish horse, who retired on their infantry, leaving a dozen dead upon the ground. Two of the Egyptian squadrons continued to retreat until clear of the defile, a distance of 700 yards; but the third and rearmost was compelled by the British officers to face about, and, galloping with this force down the ravine, Major Burn-Murdoch drove the Arabs pell-mell out of it. The other two squadrons had now returned, and the whole force dismounted, and, taking up a position among the sandhills near the mouth of the defile, opened fire with their carbines. The repulse of their cavalry seemed to have disheartened the Dervishes, for they made no attempt to attack the dismounted troopers, and contented themselves with maintaining a desultory fire, which was so ill-aimed that but little loss was caused. The heat of the weather was terrific, and both men and horses suffered acutely from thirst. The squadron which had escorted the Sirdar had performed a long march before the reconnaissance and was exhausted. The cavalry, however, held their position among the sandhills and easily defeated a feeble attempt to turn their right. At a quarter past twelve the Dervishes began to retire slowly and deliberately, and by one o'clock, when the XIth Soudanese arrived, eager and agog, the last Arab had disappeared. The force then returned to camp, bearing many spears and leading six captured horses as trophies of victory. The intensity of the heat may be gauged by the fact that one of the Soudanese soldiers—that is to say, an African negro—died of sunstroke. Such was the affair of the 1st of May, and it is pleasing to relate that in this fierce fight the loss was not severe. One British officer, Captain Fitton, was slightly wounded. One native soldier was killed; one was mortally and eight severely wounded.

During May the preparations for the advance on the Dervish position at Firket continued, and towards the end of the month it became evident that they were nearly complete. The steady accumulation of stores at Akasha had turned that post into a convenient base from which the force might operate for a month without drawing supplies of any kind from the north. The railway, which had progressed at the rate of about half a mile a day, had reached and was working to Ambigole Wells, where a four-gun fort and entrenchment had been built. The distance over which convoys must plod was reduced by half, and the business of supply was doubly accelerated. By degrees the battalions and squadrons began to move forward towards Akasha. Sarras, deprived of its short-lived glory, became again the solitary fort on a crag. Wady Halfa was also deserted, and, except for the British battalion in garrison, could scarcely boast a soldier. Both the Egyptian battalions from Suakin had arrived on the Nile. The Xth Soudanese were on their way. The country beyond Akasha had been thoroughly reconnoitred and mapped to within three miles of the Dervish position. Everything was ready.

The actual concentration may be said to have begun on the 1st of June, when the Sirdar started for the front from Halfa, whither he had returned after the cavalry skirmish. Construction work on the railway came to a full stop. The railway battalions, dropping their picks and shovels, shouldered their Remington rifles and became the garrisons of the posts on the line of communications. On the 2nd of June the correspondents were permitted to proceed to Akasha. On the 3rd the Xth Soudanese passed through Ambigole and marched south. The Horse battery from Halfa followed. The Egyptian battalions and squadrons which had been camped along the river at convenient spots from Ambigole to Akasha marched to a point opposite Okma. Between this place and the advanced post an extensive camp, stretching three miles along the Nile bank, arose with magic swiftness. On the 4th the 7th Egyptians moved from Railhead, and with these the last battalion reached the front. Nine thousand men, with ample supplies, were collected within striking distance of the enemy.

All this time the Dervishes at Firket watched in senseless apathy the deliberate, machine-like preparations for their destruction. They should have had good information, for although the Egyptian cavalry patrolled ceaselessly, and the outpost line was impassable to scouts, their spies, as camel-drivers, water-carriers, and the like, were in the camp. They may not, perhaps, have known the exact moment of the intended blow, for the utmost secrecy was observed. But though they must have realised that it was imminent, they did nothing. There was, indeed, no course open to them but retreat. Once the army was concentrated with sufficient supplies at Akasha, their position was utterly untenable. The Emir-in-Chief, Hammuda, then had scarcely 3,000 men around his flag. Their rifles and ammunition were bad; their supplies scanty. Nor could the valour of fifty-seven notable Emirs sustain the odds against them. There was still time to fall back on Kosheh, or even on Suarda—anywhere outside the sweep of their terrible enemy's sword. They would not budge. Obstinate and fatuous to the last, they dallied and paltered on the fatal ground, until sudden, blinding, inevitable catastrophe fell upon them from all sides at once, and swept them out of existence as a military force.

CHAPTER VI:

FIRKET

June 7, 1896

Since the end of 1895 the Dervish force in Firket had been under the command of the Emir Hammuda, and it was through the indolence and neglect of this dissipated Arab that the Egyptian army had been able to make good its position at Akasha without any fighting. Week after week the convoys had straggled unmolested through the difficult country between Sarras and the advanced base. No attack had been made upon the brigade at Akasha. No enterprise was directed against its communications. This fatal inactivity did not pass unnoticed by Wad Bishara, the Governor of Dongola; but although he was nominally in supreme command of all the Dervish forces in the province he had hardly any means of enforcing his authority. His rebukes and exhortations, however, gradually roused Hammuda, and during May two or three minor raids were planned and executed, and the Egyptian position at Akasha was several times reconnoitred.

Bishara remained unsatisfied, and at length, despairing of infusing energy into Hammuda, he ordered his subordinate Osman Azrak to supersede him. Osman was a Dervish of very different type. He was a fanatical and devoted believer in the Mahdi and a loyal follower of the Khalifa. For many years he had served on the northern frontier of the Dervish Empire, and his name was well known to the Egyptian Government as the contriver of the most daring and the most brutal raids. His cruelty to the wretched inhabitants of the border villages had excluded him from all hope of mercy should he ever fall into the hands of the enemy. His crafty skill, however, protected him, and among the Emirs gathered at Firket there was none whose death would have given greater satisfaction to the military authorities than the man who was now to replace Hammuda.

Whether Osman Azrak had actually assumed command on the 6th of June is uncertain. It seems more likely that Hammuda declined to admit his right, and that the matter still stood in dispute. But in any case Osman was determined to justify his appointment by his activity, and about midday he started from the camp at Firket, and, accompanied by a strong patrol of camel-men, set out to reconnoitre Akasha. Moving cautiously, he arrived unperceived within sight of the position at about three o'clock in the afternoon. The columns which were to storm Firket at dawn were then actually parading. But the clouds of dust which the high wind drove across or whirled about the camp obscured the view, and the Dervish could distinguish nothing unusual. He therefore made the customary pentagonal mark on the sand to ensure good luck, and so returned to Firket to renew his dispute with Hammuda, bearing the reassuring news that 'the Turks lay quiet.'

The force which the Sirdar had concentrated for the capture of Firket amounted to about nine thousand men, and was organised as follows:—

Commander-in-Chief: THE SIRDAR

The Infantry Division: COLONEL HUNTER Commanding

1st Brigade	2nd Brigade	3rd Brigade
Major LEWIS	MAJOR MACDONALD	MAJOR MAXWELL
3rd Egyptians	IXth Soudanese	2nd Egyptians
4th "	XIth "	7th "
Xth Soudanese	XIIth "	8th "
	XIIIth "	

Mounted Forces: MAJOR BURN-MURDOCH

| Egyptian Cavalry | . | . | . | . | 7 squadrons |
| Camel Corps | . | . | . | . | 8 companies |

Artillery

Horse Artillery	. . . .	1 battery
Field Artillery	. . . .	2 batteries
Maxim Guns	. . . . .	1 battery

Two roads led from Akasha to Firket—one by the bank of the river, the other inland and along the projected railway line. The Sirdar determined to avail himself of both. The force was therefore divided into two columns. The main column, under command of the Sirdar, was to move by the river road, and consisted of the infantry division, the Field Artillery, and the Maxim guns. The Desert Column, under command of Major Burn-Murdoch, consisted of the mounted forces, the Horse Artillery, and one battalion of infantry (the XIIth Soudanese) drawn from MacDonald's brigade and mounted upon camels: in all about two thousand men. Very precise orders were given to the smaller column, and Burn-Murdoch was instructed to occupy the hills to the south-east of the centre of Firket village by 4.30 A.M.; to dispose his force facing west, with the cavalry on the left, the Camel Corps in the centre, and the XIIth Soudanese on the right. The only point left to his discretion was the position to be occupied by the Horse battery. He was especially warned not to come under the fire of the main infantry force. As soon as the enemy should be routed, the XIIth Soudanese were to return to the Sirdar. The cavalry, camelry, and Horse Artillery were to pursue—the objective being, firstly, Koyeka, and, secondly, Suarda.

The infantry column began to march out of Akasha at 3.30 in the afternoon of the 6th, and trailed southwards along the track by the river in the following order: Lewis's brigade, with the Xth Soudanese leading; two Maxim guns and the artillery; MacDonald's brigade; Maxwell's brigade; and, lastly, the field hospitals and a half-battalion forming rearguard. The Sirdar marched behind the artillery. The rear of the long column was clear of the camp by 4.30, and about two hours later the mounted force started by the desert road. The River Column made good progress till dark, but thereafter the advance was slow and tedious. The track led through broken rocky ground, and was so narrow that it nowhere allowed a larger front to be formed than of four men abreast. In some places the sharp rocks and crumbling heaps of stone almost stopped the gun-mules altogether, while the infantry tripped and stumbled painfully. The moon had not risen, and the darkness was intense. Still the long procession of men, winding like a whiplash between the jagged hills, toiled onward through the night, with no sound except the tramping of feet and the rattle of accoutrements. At half-past ten the head of Lewis's brigade debouched into a smooth sandy plain about a mile to the north of Sarkamatto village. This was the spot—scarcely three miles from the enemy's position—where the Sirdar had decided to halt and bivouac. The bank and foreshore of the river were convenient for watering; all bottles and skins were filled, and soldiers and animals drank. A little food was eaten, and then, battalion by battalion, as the force arrived at the halting-place, they lay down to rest. The tail of Maxwell's brigade reached the bivouac about midnight, and the whole column was then concentrated.

Meanwhile the mounted force were also on their way. Like the River Column, they were disordered by the broken ground, and the XIIth Soudanese, who were unused to camel riding and mounted only on transport saddles, were soon wearied. After one o'clock many men, both in the Camel Corps and in the battalion, fell asleep on their camels, and the officers had great difficulty in keeping them awake. However, the force reached their point of concentration—about three miles to the south-east of Firket—at a quarter to three. Here the XIIth Soudanese dismounted from their camels and became again a fighting unit. Leaving the extra camels under a guard, Major Burn-Murdoch then advanced towards his appointed position on the hills overlooking Firket.

The Sirdar moved on again with the infantry at 2.30. The moon had risen over the rocks to the left of the line of march, but it was only a thin crescent and did not give much light. The very worst part of the whole track was encountered immediately the bivouac was left, and the column of nearly six thousand men had to trickle through one narrow place in single file. There were already signs of the approach of dawn; the Dervish camp was near; the Sirdar and his Staff began to look anxious. He sent many messages to the leading battalions to hurry; and the soldiers, although now very weary, ran and scrambled through the difficult passage like sheep crowding through a gate. By four o'clock the leading brigade had cleared the obstacle, and the most critical moment seemed to have passed.

Suddenly, a mile to the southward, rose the sound of the beating of drums. Everyone held his breath. The Dervishes were prepared. Perhaps they would attack the column before it could deploy. Then the sound died away, and but for the clatter of the marching columns all was again silent. It was no alarm, but only the call to the morning prayer; and the Dervishes, still ignorant that their enemies approached and that swift destruction was upon them, trooped from their huts to obey the pious summons.

The great mass of Firket mountain, still dark in the half-light, now rose up on the left of the line of march. Between it and the river stretched a narrow strip of scrub-covered ground; and here, though obstructed by the long grass, bushes, palm-trees, and holes, the leading brigade was ordered to deploy. There was, however, as yet only room for the Xth Soudanese to form line, and the 3rd and 4th Egyptians contented themselves with widening to column of companies—the 3rd in rear of the right of the Xth, the 4th in rear of the centre. The force now began to emerge from the narrow space between the hills and the river, and debouch into open country. As the space widened No. 1 field battery came into line on the left, and No. 2 On the right of the Xth Soudanese. A swell of ground hid Firket village, though it was known to be within a mile, and it was now daylight. Still there was no sign that the Dervishes were prepared. It seemed scarcely possible to believe that the advance had not yet been discovered. The silence seemed to forbode some unexpected attack. The leading brigade and guns halted for a few minutes to allow MacDonald to form his battalions from 'fours' into column of companies. Then at five o'clock the advance was resumed, and at this moment from the shoulder of Firket mountain there rang out a solitary shot. The Dervish outposts had at last learned their danger. Several other shots followed in quick succession, and were answered by a volley from the Xth, and then from far away to the southeast came the report of a field-gun. The Horse Artillery battery had come into action. The operation of the two columns was simultaneous: the surpise of the enemy was complete.

The great object was now to push on and deploy as fast as possible. The popping of musketry broke out from many points, and the repeated explosions of the Horse battery added to the eager excitement of the troops. For what is more thrilling than the sudden and swift development of an attack at dawn? The Xth Soudanese had now reached the top of the rise which had hidden Firket, and the whole scene came into view. To the right front the village of Firket stretched by the side of the river—a confusion of mud houses nearly a mile in length and perhaps 300 yards broad. On the landward side the tents and straw shelters of the Dervish force showed white and yellow. A system of mud walls and loop-holed houses strengthened the northern end of the village. Behind it as a background stood lines and clusters of palm-trees, through which the broad river and the masts of the Arab boats might be seen. In front of the troops, but a little to their left, rose a low rocky ridge surmounted with flags and defended by a stone breastwork running along its base. Across the open space between the village and the hill hundreds of Dervishes on horse and on foot were hurrying to man their defences, and others scrambled up the rocks to see for themselves the numbers of the enemy. Scores of little puffs of smoke already speckled the black rocks of the ridge and the brown houses of the village.

The attack developed very rapidly. The narrow passage between the mountain and the river poured forth its brigades and battalions, and the firing-line stretched away to the right and left with extraordinary speed. The Xth Soudanese opened fire on the village as soon as they topped the rise. The 3rd and 4th Egyptians deployed on the right and left of the leading regiment, two companies of the 4th extending down on to the foreshore below the steep river-bank. Peake's battery (No. 1) and the Maxim guns, coming into action from a spur of Firket mountain, began to fire over the heads of the advancing infantry.

The whole of Lewis's brigade now swung to the right and attacked the village; MacDonald's, coming up at the double in line of battalion columns, deployed to the left, inland, round the shoulder of the mountain, and, bearing away still more to the left, advanced swiftly upon the rocky ridge. The ground in MacDonald's front was much broken by boulders and scrub, and a deep khor delayed the advance. The enemy, though taken at obvious disadvantage, maintained an irregular fire; but the Soudanese, greatly excited, pressed on eagerly towards the breastworks. When the brigade was still 200 yards from the ridge, about fifty Dervish horsemen dashed out from among the rocks and charged the left flank. All were immediately shot down by a wild but heavy independent fire. With joyful yells the blacks broke into a run and carried the breastworks at the bayonet. The Dervishes did not await the shock. As soon as they saw their horsemen—among whom was the Emir Hammuda himself and Yusef Angar, Emir of the Jehadia—swept away, they abandoned the first ridge and fell back on another which lay behind. The Soudanese followed closely, and pursued the outnumbered enemy up one and down the other side of the rocky hills, up again and down again, continually shouldering and bringing round the left of the brigade; until at last the hills were cleared of all except the dead, and the fugitives were running towards the river-bank. Then the scattered battalions re-formed facing west, and the panting soldiers looked about them.

While MacDonald's brigade was storming the hills, Lewis's had advanced on the village and the Dervish camp. The Arabs from their loopholed houses made a stubborn resistance, and the 4th battalion by the river-bank were sharply engaged, their commanding officer, Captain Sparkes, having his horse shot in four places. Encouraged by their enormous superiority in number and weapons, the Egyptians showed considerable zeal in the attack, and their conduct on this occasion was regarded as a very happy augury for the war, of which this was the first general engagement.

As Lewis's brigade had swung to its right, and MacDonald's had borne away to the left, a wide gap had opened in the centre of the attack. This was immediately filled by Maxwell's brigade, so that the whole force was now formed in one line, which curved and wheeled continually to the right until, by the time the rocky hills had been taken, all three brigades practically faced west and were advancing together towards the Nile. The Dervishes—penned between the river and the enemy, and unable to prevent the remorseless advance, which every moment restricted them to narrower limits—now thought only of flight, and they could be seen galloping hither and thither seeking for some means of escape. The position of the Desert Column would have enabled the XIIth Soudanese, by moving down to the river, to cut off this line of retreat; but the foreshore of the river at the southern end of Firket is concealed from a landward view by the steep bank, and by this sandy path the greater number of the fugitives found safety.

The cavalry and the Camel Corps, instead of cutting at the flank, contented themselves with making a direct pursuit after the enemy had crossed their front, and in consequence several hundred Arabs made good their escape to the south. Others swam the river and fled by the west bank. The wicked Osman Azrak, his authority now no longer disputed, for his rival was a corpse, galloped from the field and reached Suarda. The rest of the Dervish force held to the houses, and variously prepared to fight to the death or surrender to their conquerors.

The three brigades now closed upon the village and, clearing it step by step, advanced to the water's edge. MacDonald's brigade did not indeed stop until they had crossed the swampy isthmus and occupied the island. The Arabs, many of whom refused quarter, resisted desperately, though without much effect, and more than eighty corpses were afterwards found in one group of buildings. By 7.20 o'clock all firing had ceased; the entire Dervish camp was in the hands of the Egyptian troops, and the engagement of Firket was over.

The Sirdar now busied himself with the pursuit, and proceeded with the mounted troops as far as Mograka, five miles south of Firket. The whole cavalry force, with the Camel Corps and Horse Artillery, pressed the retreat vigorously to Suarda. Osman Azrak, however, succeeded in transporting the women and children and some stores, with a sufficient escort, to the west bank before the arrival of the troops. On the approach of the cavalry he retired along the east bank, with a small mounted force, without fighting. The Emir in charge of the escort on the other side delayed, and was in consequence shelled at long range by the Horse battery. The local inhabitants, tired of the ceaseless war which had desolated the frontier province for so long, welcomed their new masters with an appearance of enthusiasm. The main pursuit stopped at Suarda, but a week later two squadrons and sixteen men of the Camel Corps, under Captain Mahon, were pushed out twenty miles further south, and an Arab store of grain was captured.

The Dervish loss in the action was severe. More than 800 dead were left on the field, and there were besides 500 wounded and 600 prisoners. The casualties in the Egyptian army were 1 British officer—Captain Legge—wounded, 20 native soldiers killed and 83 wounded.

Firket is officially classed as a general action: special despatches were written, and a special clasp struck. The reader will have formed his own estimate of the magnitude and severity of the fight. The whole operation was well and carefully planned, and its success in execution was complete. The long and difficult night march, the accurate arrival and combination of the two columns, the swift deployment, the enveloping movement, proved alike the discipline and training of the troops and the skill of their officers. The only point on which criticism may be made is the failure of the Desert Column to intercept the flying Dervishes. But it should be remembered they had marched far, and it was not at that time certain what the powers of the mounted troops were. The brilliant aspect of the affair caused great satisfaction in England, and the further prosecution of the campaign was looked for with increasing interest.

CHAPTER VII:

THE RECOVERY OF THE DONGOLA PROVINCE

Countless and inestimable are the chances of war. Those who read the story, and still more those who share the dangers, of a campaign feel that every incident is surrounded with a host of possibilities, any one of which, had it become real, would have changed the whole course of events. The influence of Fortune is powerfully and continually exerted. In the flickering light of conflict the outlines of solid fact throw on every side the vague shadows of possibility. We live in a world of 'ifs.' 'What happened,' is singular; 'what might have happened,' legion. But to try to gauge the influence of this uncertain force were utterly futile, and it is perhaps wise, and indisputably convenient, to assume that the favourable and adverse chances equate, and then eliminate them both from the calculation.

The 'Sirdar's luck' became almost proverbial in the Soudan. As the account progresses numerous instances will suggest themselves. It was lucky that the Dervishes did not harass the communications, or assail Akasha before it was fortified. It was lucky that they fought at Firket; that they retired from Berber; that Mahmud did not advance in January; that he advanced in March; that he did not retire before the battle of the Atbara; that the Khalifa did not hold the Shabluka; that he did not attack on the night before Omdurman, and that he did attack at dawn.

But after Firket all things were contrary. One unexpected misfortune succeeded another. Difficulties were replaced by others as soon as they had been overcome. The autumn of 1896 was marked by delay and disappointment. The state of the Nile, the storms, the floods, the cholera, and many minor obstacles, vexed but did not weary the commander. The victory at Firket was succeeded by a long pause in the operations. The army had made one spring forward; it must now gather energy for another. The preparations, however, proceeded rapidly. A strong camp was formed at Firket. MacDonald's brigade occupied

Suarda two days after the fight, and this place now became the advanced post, just as Akasha had been in the first phase of the campaign. The accumluation of stores at Firket and Suarda began forthwith. Owing to the arrangements which had been made before the engagement it was possible to collect within one week of the action two months' supplies at Suarda for the garrison of 2,000 men, and one month's at Firket for the 7,000 troops encamped there. Thereafter, however, the necessity of hurrying the railway construction and the considerable daily demands of 9,000 men only allowed this margin to be increased very gradually.

The army had now passed beyond the scope of a camel, or other pack-animal, system of supply, except for very short distances, and it was obvious that they could only advance in future along either the railway or a navigable reach of the river, and preferably along both. From the Dal Cataract near Kosheh there is a clear waterway at high Nile to Merawi. To Kosheh, therefore, the railway must be extended before active operations could recommence. A third condition had also to be observed. For the expulsion of the Dervishes from Kerma and Dongola it was desirable that a flotilla of gunboats should co-operate with the land forces. Four of these vessels—the Tamai, El Teb, the Metemma, and the Abu Klea; and three steamers—the Kaibar, Dal, and Akasha, which it was proposed to arm—had, since 1885, patrolled the river from Assuan to Wady Halfa, and assisted in protecting the frontier from Dervish raids. All seven were now collected at the foot of the Second Cataract, and awaited the rise of the river to attempt the passage. To strengthen the flotilla three new and very powerful gunboats had been ordered in England. These were to be brought in sections over the railway to a point above the Second Cataract, and be fitted together there. It was thus necessary to wait, firstly, for the railway to reach Kosheh; secondly, for the Nile to rise; thirdly, for the old gunboats to ascend the Cataract; fourthly, for the new gunboats to be launched on the clear waterway; and, fifthly, for the accumulation of supplies. With all of these matters the Sirdar now busied himself.

The reconstruction of the railway to Akasha and its extension beyond this place towards Kosheh was pressed forward. By the 26th of June Akasha was reached. Thenceforward the engineers no longer followed an existing track, but were obliged to survey, and to make the formation for themselves. Strong fatigue parties from the Egyptian and Soudanese battalions were, however, employed on the embankments, and the line grew daily longer. On the 24th of July the first train ran across the battlefield of Firket; and on the 4th of August the railway was working to Kosheh.

Kosheh is six miles south of Firket, and consists, like most places in the 'Military Soudan,' of little more than a name and a few ruined mud-huts which were once a village. On the 5th of July the whole camp was moved thither from the scene of the action. The reasons were clear and apparent. Kosheh is a point on the river above the Dal Cataract whence a clear waterway runs at high Nile to beyond Dongola. The camp at Firket had become foul and insanitary. The bodies of the dead, swelling and decaying in their shallow graves, assailed, as if in revenge, the bodies of the living. The dysentery which had broken out was probably due to the 'green' water of the Nile; for during the early period of the flood what is known as 'the false rise' washes the filth and sewage off the foreshore all along the river, and brings down the green and rotting vegetation from the spongy swamps of Equatoria. The water is then dangerous and impure. There was nothing else for the army to drink; but it was undesirable to aggravate the evil by keeping the troops in a dirty camp.

The earliest freight which the railway carried to Kosheh was the first of the new stern-wheel gunboats. Train after train arrived with its load of steel and iron, or with the cumbrous sections of the hull, and a warship in pieces—engines, armaments, fittings and stores—soon lay stacked by the side of the river. An improvised dockyard, equipped with powerful twenty-ton shears and other appliances, was established, and the work—complicated as a Chinese puzzle—of fitting and riveting together the hundreds of various parts proceeded swiftly. Gradually the strange heaps of parts began to evolve a mighty engine of war. The new gunboats were in every way remarkable. The old vessels had been 90 feet long. These were 140 feet. Their breadth was 24 feet. They steamed twelve miles an hour. They had a command of 30 feet. Their decks were all protected by steel plates, and prepared by loopholed shields for musketry. Their armament was formidable. Each carried one twelve-pounder quick-firing gun forward, two six-pounder quick-firing guns in the central battery, and four Maxim guns. Every modern improvement—such as ammunition hoists, telegraphs, search-lights, and steam-winches—was added. Yet with all this they drew only thirty-nine inches of water.

The contract specified that these vessels should be delivered at Alexandria by the 5th of September, but, by exertions, the first boat, the Zafir, reached Egypt on the 23rd of July, having been made in eight weeks, and in time to have assisted in the advance on Dongola. The vessels and machinery had been constructed and erected in the works in London; they were then marked, numbered, and taken to pieces, and after being shipped to Alexandria and transported to the front were finally put together at Kosheh. Although in a journey of 4,000 miles they were seven times transhipped, not a single important piece was lost.

The convenience of Kosheh on the clear waterway, and the dirty condition of Firket, were in themselves sufficient reasons for the change of camp; but another and graver cause lay behind. During the month of June an epidemic of cholera began to creep up the Nile from Cairo. On the 29th there were some cases at Assuan. On the 30th it reached Wady Halfa. In consequence of this the North Staffordshire Regiment marched into camp at Gemai. Their three months' occupation of the town had not improved their health or their spirits. During the sixteen-mile march along the railway track to Gemai the first fatal case occurred, and thereafter the sickness clung to the regiment until the middle of August, causing continual deaths.

The cholera spread steadily southward up the river, claiming successive victims in each camp. In the second week of July it reached the new camp at Kosheh, whence all possible precautions to exclude it had proved vain. The epidemic was at first of a virulent form. As is usual, when it had expended its destructive energy, the recoveries became more frequent. But of the first thousand cases between Assuan and Suarda nearly eight hundred proved fatal. Nor were the lives thus lost to be altogether measured by the number. [The attacks and deaths from cholera in the Dongola Expeditionary Force were as follow: British troops - 24 attacks, 19 deaths; Native troops - 406 attacks, 260 deaths; Followers - 788 attacks, 640 deaths.] To all, the time was one of trial, almost of terror. The violence of the battle may be cheaply braved, but the insidious attacks of disease appal the boldest. Death moved continually about the ranks of the army—not the death they had been trained to meet unflinchingly, the death in high enthusiasm and the pride of life, with all the world to weep or cheer; but a silent, unnoticed, almost ignominious summons, scarcely less sudden and far more painful than the bullet or the sword-cut. The Egyptians, in spite of their fatalistic creed, manifested profound depression. The English soldiers were moody and ill-tempered. Even the light-hearted Soudanese lost their spirits; their merry grins were seen no longer; their laughter and their drums were stilled. Only the British officers preserved a stony cheerfulness, and ceaselessly endeavoured by energy and example to sustain the courage of their men. Yet they suffered most of all. Their education had developed their imaginations; and imagination, elsewhere a priceless gift, is amid such circumstances a dangerous burden.

It was, indeed, a time of sore trouble. To find the servant dead in the camp kitchen; to catch a hurried glimpse of blanketed shapes hustled quickly to the desert on a stretcher; to hold the lantern over the grave into which a friend or comrade—alive and well six hours before—was hastily lowered, even though it was still night; and through it all to work incessantly at pressure in the solid, roaring heat, with a mind ever on the watch for the earliest of the fatal symptoms and a thirst that could only be quenched by drinking of the deadly and contaminated Nile: all these things combined to produce an experience which those who endured are unwilling to remember, but unlikely to forget. One by one some of the best of the field army and the communication Staff were stricken down. Gallant Fenwick, of whom they used to say that he was 'twice a V.C. without a gazette'; Polwhele, the railway subaltern, whose strange knowledge of the Egyptian soldiers had won their stranger love; Trask, an heroic doctor, indifferent alike to pestilence or bullets; Mr. Vallom, the chief superintendent of engines at Halfa; Farmer, a young officer already on his fourth campaign; Mr. Nicholson, the London engineer; long, quaint, kind-hearted 'Roddy' Owen—all filled graves in Halfa cemetery or at the foot of Firket mountain. At length the epidemic was stamped out, and by the middle of August it had practically ceased to be a serious danger. But the necessity of enforcing quarantine and other precautions had hampered movement up and down the line of communications, and so delayed the progress of the preparations for an advance.

Other unexpected hindrances arose. Sir H. Kitchener had clearly recognised that the railway, equipped as it then was, would be at the best a doubtful means for the continual supply of a large force many miles ahead of it. He therefore organised an auxiliary boat service and passed gyassas and nuggurs [native sailing craft] freely up the Second Cataract. During the summer months, in the Soudan, a strong north wind prevails, which not only drives the sailing-boats up against the stream—sometimes at the rate of twenty miles a day—but also gratefully cools the air. This year, for forty consecutive days, at the critical period of the campaign, the wind blew hot and adverse from the south. The whole auxiliary boat service was thus practically arrested. But in spite of these aggravating obstacles the preparations for the advance were forced onwards, and it soon became necessary for the gunboats and steamers to be brought on to the upper reach of the river.

The Second Cataract has a total descent of sixty feet, and is about nine miles long. For this distance the Nile flows down a rugged stairway formed by successive ledges of black granite. The flood river deeply submerges these steps, and rushes along above them with tremendous force, but with a smooth though swirling surface. As the Nile subsides, the steps begin to show, until the river tumbles violently from ledge to ledge, its whole surface for miles churned to the white foam of broken water, and thickly studded with black rocks. At the Second Cataract, moreover, the only deep channel of the Nile is choked between narrow limits, and the stream struggles furiously between stern walls of rock. These dark gorges present many perils to the navigator. The most formidable, the Bab-el-Kebir, is only thirty-five feet wide. The river here takes a plunge of ten feet in seventy yards, and drops five feet at a single bound. An extensive pool above, formed by the junction of two arms of the river, increases the volume of the water and the force of the stream, so that the 'Gate' constitutes an obstacle of difficulty and danger which might well have been considered insurmountable.

It had been expected that in the beginning of July enough water would be passing down the Second Cataract to enable the gunboats and steamers waiting below to make the passage. Everything depended upon the rise of the river, and in the perversity of circumstances the river this year rose much later and slower than usual. By the middle of August, however, the attempt appeared possible. On the 14th the first gunboat, the Metemma, approached the Cataract. The North Staffordshire Regiment from Gemai, and the 6th and 7th Egyptian Battalions from Kosheh, marched to the 'Gate' to draw the vessel bodily up in spite of the current. The best native pilots had been procured. Colonel Hunter and the naval officers under Commander Colville directed the work. The boat had been carefully prepared for the ordeal. To reduce, by raising the free-board, the risk of swamping, the bows were heightened and strengthened, and stout wooden bulwarks were built running from bow to stern. Guns and ammunition were then removed, and the vessel lightened by every possible means. A strop of wire rope was passed completely round the hull, and to this strong belt the five cables were fastened—two on each side and one at the bow. So steep was the slope of the water that it was found necessary to draw all the fires, and the steamer was thus dependent entirely upon external force. It was luckily possible to obtain a direct pull, for a crag of black rock rose above the surface of the pool opposite the 'Gate.' On this a steel block was fixed, and the hawser was led away at right angles until it reached the east bank, where a smooth stretch of sand afforded a convenient place for the hauling parties. Two thousand men were then set to pull at the cables, yet such was the extraordinary force of the current that, although the actual distance in which these great efforts were necessary was scarcely one hundred yards, the passage of each steamer occupied an hour and a half, and required the most strenuous exertions of the soldiers. No accident, however, occurred, and the six other vessels accomplished the ascent on successive days. In a week the whole flotilla steamed safely in the open water of the upper reach.

And now for a moment it seemed that the luck of the expedition had returned. The cholera was practically extinct. The new gunboat Zafir was nearly ready at Kosheh, and her imposing appearance delighted and impressed the army. On the 23rd of August all the seven steamers which had passed the Cataract arrived in a stately procession opposite the camp. Almost at the same time the wind changed to the north, and a cool and delicious breeze refreshed the weary men and bore southward to Suarda a whole fleet of sailing boats laden with supplies, which had been lying weather-bound during the previous six weeks at the head of the rapids. The preparatory orders for the advance tinkled along the telegraph. The North Staffordshire Regiment were, to the intense relief of officers and men, warned to hold themselves in readiness for an immediate move. The mounted troops had already returned to the front from the camps in which they had been distributed. At last the miserable delay was over.

From Koshch to Kerma, the first Dervish position, the distance by river is 127 miles. A study of the map shows that by land marches this can be shortened by nearly forty-one miles; thirty miles being saved by cutting across the great loop of the Nile from Kosheh to Sadin Fanti, and eleven miles by avoiding the angle from Fereig to Abu Fatmeh. From Kerma to Dongola, which latter town was the objective of the expedition, a further distance of thirty-five miles must be traversed, making a total of 120 miles by land or 161 by river. The long desert march from Kosheh to Sadin Fanti was the only natural difficulty by land. Although the river from Kosheh to Kerma is broken by continual rapids, it is, with one interval, freely navigable at half Nile. The Amara Cataract, ten miles beyond Kosheh, is easily ascended by sailing boats with a fair wind, and by steamers without assistance. From Amara to the Kaibar Cataract stretches a reach of sixty-five miles of open water. The Kaibar Cataract is, during the flood, scarcely any hindrance to navigation; but at Hannek, about thirty miles further on, the three miles of islands, rocks, rapids, and broken water which are called the Third Cataract are, except at high Nile, a formidable barrier, Once this is passed, there is open water for more than 200 miles at all seasons to Merawi. The banks of the river, except near Sadin Fanti, where the hills close in, are flat and low. The Eastern bank is lined with a fringe of palm-trees and a thin strip of cultivation, which constitutes what is called 'the fertile province of Dongola.' On the other side the desert reaches the water's edge. Along the right bank of this part of the river the army was now to move.

The first act of the advance was the occupation of Absarat, and on the 23rd of August MacDonald's brigade marched thither from Suarda, cutting across the desert to Sadin Fanti, and then following the bank of the Nile. The occupation of Absarat covered the next movement. On the 26th Lewis's brigade was ordered to march across the loop from Kosheh to Sadin Fanti, and reinforce the brigade at Absarat. The distance of thirty-seven miles was far too great to be accomplished without a system of watering-places. This the Sirdar rapidly organised. Water-depots were formed by carrying tanks and water-skins on camels to two points in the desert, and replenishing them by daily convoys. But now a heavy calamity descended on the arrangements of the General and the hopes of the troops.

During the afternoon of the 25th the wind veered suddenly to the south, and thereupon a terrific storm of sand and rain, accompanied by thunder and lightning, burst over the whole of the Nubian desert, and swept along the line of communications from Suarda to Halfa. On the next day a second deluge delayed the march of Lewis's brigade. But late on the 27th they started, with disastrous results. Before they had reached the first watering-place a third tempest, preceded by its choking sandstorm, overtook them. Nearly 300 men fell out during the early part of the night, and crawled and staggered back to

Kosheh. Before the column reached Sadin Fanti 1,700 more sank exhausted to the ground. Out of one battalion 700 strong, only sixty men marched in. Nine deaths and eighty serious cases of prostration occurred, and the movement of the brigade from Kosheh to Absarat was grimly called 'The Death March.'

The 'Death March' was the least of the misfortunes caused by the storms. The violent rains produced floods such as had not been seen in the Soudan for fifty years. The water, pouring down the broad valleys, formed furious torrents in the narrower gorges. More than twelve miles of the railway was washed away. The rails were twisted and bent; the formation entirely destroyed. The telegraph wires were broken. The work of weeks was lost in a few hours. The advance was stopped as soon as it had been begun. At the moment when every military reason demanded speed and suddenness, a hideous delay became inevitable.

In this time of crisis the success of the whole campaign hung in the balance. Sir Herbert Kitchener did not then possess that measure of the confidence and affection of his officers which his military successes have since compelled. Public opinion was still undecided on the general question of the war. The initial bad luck had frightened many. All the croakers were ready. 'A Jingo Government'—'An incapable general'—'Another disaster in the Soudan'—such were the whispers. A check would be the signal for an outcry. The accounts of 'The Death March' had not yet reached England; but the correspondents, irritated at being 'chained to headquarters,' were going to see about that. And, besides all this, there were the army to feed and the Dervishes to fight. In this serious emergency, which threatened to wreck his schemes, the Sirdar's organising talents shone more brilliantly than at any other moment in this account. Travelling swiftly to Moghrat, he possessed himself of the telephone, which luckily still worked. He knew the exact position or every soldier, coolie, camel, or donkey at his disposal. In a few hours, in spite of his crippled transport, he concentrated 5,000 men on the damaged sections of the line, and thereafter fed them until the work was finished. In seven days traffic was resumed. The advance had been delayed, but it was not prevented.

On the 5th of September the 1st (Lewis) and 2nd (MacDonald) Brigades moved to Dulgo, and at the same time the remainder of the army began to march across the loop from Kosheh by Sadin Fanti to Absarat. Every available soldier had been collected for the final operation of the campaign.

The Expeditionary Force was organised as follows:

Commander-in-Chief: The SIRDAR

The Infantry Division: COLONEL HUNTER Commanding

1st Brigade	2nd Brigade	3rd Brigade	4th Brigade
MAJOR LEWIS	MAJOR MACDONALD	MAJOR MAXWELL	AJOR DAVID
3rd Egyptians	XIth Soudanese	2nd Egyptians	1st Egyptians
4th "	XIIth "	7th "	5th "
IXth Soudanese	XIIIth "	8th "	15th "
	Xth "		

Cavalry Brigade and Mounted Forces: MAJOR BURN-MURDOCH

Cavalry	. . . . .	8 squadrons
Camel Corps	. . . .	6 companies
Horse Artillery	. . .	1 battery

Artillery: MAJOR PARSONS

Field Artillery	. . .	2 batteries
Maxims	. . . .	1 battery (British)

Divisional Troops: MAJOR CURRIE

North Staffordshire Regiment . . . . 1st Battalion

The Flotilla: COMMANDER COLVILLE

Gunboats	. .	Zafir, Tamai, Abu Klea, Metemma, El Teb
Armed Steamers	. . .	Kaibar, Dal, Akasha

Total: 15,000 men, 8 war-vessels, and 36 guns

Thus thirteen of the sixteen battalions of the Egyptian Army were employed at the front. Two others, the 6th and XIVth, were disposed along the line of communication, holding the various fortified posts. The 16th Battalion of reservists remained at Suakin. The whole native army was engaged in the war, and the preservation of domestic order in the capital and throughout the Khedive's dominions was left entirely to the police and to the British Army of Occupation. By the 9th all four brigades had reached the rendezvous at Dulgo; on the 10th the British regiment, which it was determined to send up in the steamers, was moved to Kosheh by rail from Sarras and Gemai. The Sirdar prepared to start with the flotilla on the 12th.

But a culminating disappointment remained. By tremendous exertions the Zafir had been finished in time to take part in the operations. Throughout the army it was expected that the Zafir would be the feature of the campaign. At length the work was finished, and the Zafir floated, powerful and majestic, on the waters of the Nile. On the afternoon of the 11th of September many officers and men came to witness her trial trip. The bank was lined with spectators. Colville took command. The Sirdar and his Staff embarked. Flags were hoisted and amid general cheering the moorings were cast off. But the stern paddle had hardly revolved twice when there was a loud report, like that of a heavy gun, clouds of steam rushed up from the boilers, and the engines stopped. Sir H. Kitchener and Commander Colville were on the upper deck. The latter rushed below to learn what had happened, and found that she had burst her low-pressure cylinder, a misfortune impossible to repair until a new one could be obtained from Halfa and fitted.

In spite of this, however, the advance was not delayed. On the 13th the 1st, 2nd, and 3rd Brigades occupied Kaderma. Here the flotilla overtook them, and henceforward the boats on the river kept pace with the army on the bank. Fareig was reached on the 14th, and as the numerous palms by the water afforded a pleasant shade a halt of two days was ordered. On the 16th the 4th Brigade arrived, and the concentration of the force was then complete.

After the annihilation of his strong advanced post at Firket, the Dervish Emir, Wad Bishara, concentrated his remaining forces in Dongola. Here during the summer he had awaited, and in the middle of August some small reinforcements under one Emir of low rank reached him from Omdurman. The Khalifa, indeed, promised that many more should follow, but his promises long remained unfulfilled, and the greatest strength that Bishara could muster was 900 Jehadia, 800 Baggara Arabs, 2,800 spearmen, 450 camelmen, 650 cavalry—in all 5,600 men, with six small brass cannon and one mitrailleuse gun. To augment in numbers, if not in strength, this small force of regular soldiers, he impressed a large number of the local tribesmen; but as these were, for the most part, anxious to join the Government troops at the first opportunity, their effect in the conflict was inconsiderable.

The first sign that the forces were drawing closer was the cutting of the telegraph-wire by a Dervish patrol on the 6th of September. On the 10th the Sirdar heard that Kerma was strongly held. On the 15th of September the Egyptian cavalry first established contact with the Dervish scouts, and a slight skirmish took place. On the 18th the whole force advanced to Sardek, and as Bishara still held his position at Kerma it looked as if an action was imminent. It was resolved to attack the Dervish position at Kerma at dawn. Although it seemed that only four miles separated the combatants, the night passed quietly. With the first light the army began to move, and when the sun rose the spectacle of the moving masses of men and artillery, with the gunboats on the right, was inspiring. The soldiers braced themselves for the expected action. But no sooner were the village and fort of Kerma visible than the report passed along the ranks that they were deserted. Rumour was soon merged in certainty, for on reaching Kerma it was found that the Dervishes had evacuated the place, and only the strong, well-built mud fort attested the recent presence of Bishara. Whither had he gone? The question was not left unanswered.

Half a mile to the southward, on the opposite bank of the river, among the groves of palm-trees ran a long and continuous line of shelter trenches and loopholed walls. The flanks of this new position rested on the deep morasses which extend from the river both on the north and south sides of Hafir. A small steamer, a fleet of large gyassas and other sailing vessels moored to the further shore explained what had happened. Conscious of his weakness, the prudent Emir had adroitly transported himself across the river, and had thus placed that broad flood between his troops and their destruction.

Meanwhile the three gunboats—all that now remained of the armed flotilla, for the Teb had run on a rock in the Hannek Cataract—were steaming gradually nearer the enemy, and the army swung to the right, and, forming along the river bank, became spectators of a scene of fascinating interest. At half-past six the Horse battery unlimbered at the water's edge, and began to fire obliquely up and across the river. As soon as the first few shells had reached the Arab entrenchment the whole line of shelter trenches was edged with smoke, and the Dervishes replied with a heavy rifle fire. The distance was, however, too great for their bad rifles and inferior ammunition, and their bullets, although they occasionally struck the ground on which the infantry were drawn up, did not during the day cause any loss to the watching army.

The Dervish position was about half a mile in length. As the gunboats approached the northern end they opened fire with their guns, striking the mud entrenchments at every shot, and driving clouds of dust and splinters into the air. The Maxim guns began to search the parapets, and two companies of the Staffordshire Regiment on board the unarmoured steamers Dal and Akasha fired long-range volleys. Now, as on other occasions throughout the war, the Dervishes by their military behaviour excited the admiration of their enemies. Encouraged by the arrival in the morning of a reinforcement from Omdurman of 1,000 Black Jehadia and 500 spearmen under Abdel Baki, the Dervish gunners stood to their guns and the riflemen to their trenches, and, although suffering severely, maintained a formidable fire.

The gunboats continued to advance, beating up slowly against the strong current. As they came opposite Hafir, where the channel narrows to about 600 yards, they were received by a very heavy fire from guns placed in cleverly screened batteries, and from the riflemen sheltered in deep pits by the water's edge or concealed amid the foliage of the tops of the palm-trees. These aerial skirmishers commanded the decks of the vessels, and the shields of the guns were thus rendered of little protection. All the water round the gunboats was torn into foam by the projectiles. The bullets pattered against their sides, and, except where they were protected by steel plates, penetrated. One shell struck the Abu Klea on the water-line, and entered the magazine. Luckily it did not explode, the Dervishes having forgotten to set the fuse. Three shells struck the Metemma. On board the Tamai, which was leading, Commander Colville was severely wounded in the wrist; Armourer-Sergeant Richardson was killed at his Maxim gun, and on each boat some casualties occurred. So hot was the fire that it was thought doubtful whether to proceed with the bombardment, and the Tamai swung round, and hurried down the river with the current and at full steam to report to the Sirdar. The other gunboats remained in action, and continued to shell the Dervish defences. The Tamai soon returned to the fight, and, steaming again up the river, was immediately hotly re-engaged.

The sight which the army witnessed was thrilling. Beyond the flood waters of the river, backed against a sky of staring blue and in the blazing sunlight, the whole of the enemy's position was plainly visible. The long row of shelter trenches was outlined by the white smoke of musketry and dotted with the bright-coloured flags waving defiantly in the wind and with the still brighter flashes of the guns. Behind the entrenchments and among the mud houses and enclosures strong bodies of the jibba-clad Arabs were arrayed. Still further back in the plain a large force of cavalry—conspicuous by the gleams of light reflected from their broad-bladed spears—wheeled and manoeuvred. By the Nile all the tops of the palm-trees were crowded with daring riflemen, whose positions were indicated by the smoke-puffs of their rifles, or when some tiny black figure fell, like a shot rook, to the ground. In the foreground the gunboats, panting and puffing up the river, were surrounded on all sides by spouts and spurts of water, thrown up by the shells and bullets. Again the flotilla drew near the narrow channel; again the watching army held their breath; and again they saw the leading boat, the Metemma, turn and run down stream towards safety, pursued by the wild cheers of the Arabs. It was evident that the gunboats were not strong enough to silence the Dervish fire. The want of the terrible Zafir was acutely felt.

The firing had lasted two hours and a half, and the enemy's resistance was no less vigorous than at the beginning of the action. The Sirdar now altered his plans. He saw that his flotilla could not hope to silence the Dervishes. He therefore ordered De Rougemont—who had assumed the command after Colville was wounded—to run past the entrenchments without trying to crush their fire, and steam on to Dongola. To support and cover the movement, the three batteries of artillery under Major Parsons were brought into action from the swampy island of Artagasha, which was connected at this season with the right bank by a shoal. At the same time three battalions of infantry were moved along the river until opposite the Arab position. At 9 A.M. the eighteen guns on the island opened a tremendous bombardment at 1,200 yards range on the entrenchments, and at the same time the infantry and a rocket detachment concentrated their fire on the tops of the palm-trees. The artillery now succeeded in silencing three of the five Dervish guns and in sinking the little Dervish steamer Tahra, while the infantry by a tremendous long-range fire drove the riflemen out of the palms. Profiting by this, the gunboats at ten o'clock moved up the river in line, and, disregarding the fusillade which the Arabs still stubbornly maintained, passed by the entrenchment and steamed on towards Dongola. After this the firing on both sides became intermittent, and the fight may be said to have ended.

Both forces remained during the day facing each other on opposite sides of the river, and the Dervishes, who evidently did not admit a defeat, brandished their rifles and waved their flags, and their shouts of loud defiance floated across the water to the troops. But they had suffered very heavily. Their brave and skilful leader was severely wounded by the splinters of a shell. The wicked Osman Azrak had been struck by a bullet, and more than 200 Ansar had fallen, including several Emirs. Moreover, a long train of wounded was seen to start during the afternoon for the south. It is doubtful, however, whether Bishara would have retreated, if he had not feared being cut off. He seems to have believed that the Sirdar would march along the right bank at once to Dongola, and cross there under cover of his gunboats. Like all Moslem soldiers, he was nervous about his line of retreat. Nor, considering the overwhelming force against him, can we wonder. There was, besides this strategic reason for retiring, a more concrete cause. All his supplies of grain were accumulated in the gyassas which lay moored to the west bank. These vessels were under the close and accurate fire of the artillery and Maxim guns on Artagasha island. Several times during the night the hungry Dervishes attempted to reach their store; but the moon was bright and the gunners watchful. Each time the enemy exposed themselves, a vigorous fire was opened and they were driven back. When morning dawned, it was found that Hafir was evacuated, and that the enemy had retreated on Dongola.

Wad Bishara's anxiety about his line of retreat was unnecessary, for the Sirdar could not advance on Dongola with a strong Dervish force on his line of communications: and it was not desirable to divide the army and mask Hafir with a covering force. But as soon as the Dervishes had left their entrenchments the situation was simplified. At daybreak all the Arab boats were brought over to the right bank by the villagers, who reported that Bishara and his soldiers had abandoned the defence and were retreating to Dongola. Thereupon the Sirdar, relieved of the necessity of forcing the passage, transported his army peacefully to the other bank. The operation afforded scope to his powers of organisation, and the whole force—complete with cavalry, camels, and guns—was moved across the broad, rushing river in less than thirty-six hours and without any apparent difficulty.

The casualties on the 19th were not numerous, and in a force of nearly 15,000 men they appear insignificant. Commander Colville was wounded. One British sergeant and one Egyptian officer were killed. Eleven native soldiers were wounded. The total—fourteen—amounted to less than one per thousand of the troops engaged. Nevertheless this picturesque and bloodless affair has been solemnly called the 'Battle of Hafir.' Special despatches were written for it. It is officially counted in records of service as a 'general action.' Telegrams of congratulation were received from her Majesty and the Khedive. A special clasp was struck. Of all the instances of cheaply bought glory which the military history of recent years affords, Hafir is the most remarkable.

The 20th and part of the 21st were occupied by the passage of the army across the Nile. The troops were still crossing when the gunboats returned from Dongola. The distance of this place by water from Hafir is about thirty-six miles, and the flotilla had arrived opposite the town during the afternoon of the 19th. A few shells expelled the small Dervish garrison, and a large number of sailing vessels were captured. The results of the movement of the gunboats to Dongola must, however, be looked for at Hafir. In consequence of the Sirdar's manoeuvre that place was evacuated and the unopposed passage of the river secured.

Bishara continued his retreat during the 20th, and, marching all day, reached Dongola in the evening. Wounded as he was, he re-occupied the town and began forthwith to make preparations for the defence of its considerable fortifications. The knowledge of his employment was not hidden from his enemy, and during the 21st the gunboat Abu Klea, under Lieutenant Beatty, R.N., arrived with the design of keeping him occupied. Throughout the day a desultory duel was maintained between the entrenchments and the steamer. At daylight on the 22nd, Beatty was reinforced by another gunboat, and an unceasing bombardment was made on the town and its defences.

Notwithstanding that the army did not finish crossing the river until the afternoon of the 21st, the Sirdar determined to continue his advance without delay, and the force accordingly marched twelve miles further south and camped opposite the middle of the large island of Argo. At daybreak the troops started again, and before the sun had attained its greatest power reached Zowarat. This place was scarcely six miles from Dongola, and, as it was expected that an action would be fought the next day, the rest of eighteen hours was welcomed by the weary soldiers. All day long the army remained halted by the palms of the Nile bank. Looking through their glasses up the river, the officers might watch the gunboats methodically bombarding Dongola, and the sound of the guns was clearly heard. At intervals during the day odd parties of Dervishes, both horse and foot, approached the outpost line and shots were exchanged.

All these things, together with the consciousness that the culmination of the campaign was now at hand, raised the excitement of the army to a high pitch, and everyone lay down that night warmed by keen anticipations. An atmosphere of unrest hung over the bivouac, and few slept soundly. At three o'clock the troops were aroused, and at half-past four the final advance on Dongola had begun.

It was still night. The full moon, shining with tropical brilliancy in a cloudless sky, vaguely revealed the rolling plains of sand and the huge moving mass of the army. As long as it was dark the battalions were closely formed in quarter columns. But presently the warmer, yellower light of dawn began to grow across the river and through the palms, and gradually, as the sun rose and it became daylight, the dense formation of the army was extended to an array more than two miles long. On the left, nearest the river, marched Lewis's brigade—three battalions in line and the fourth in column as a reserve. Next in order Maxwell's three battalions prolonged the line. The artillery were in the centre, supported by the North Staffordshire Regiment. The gunners of the Maxim battery had donned their tunics, so that the lines and columns of yellow and brown were relieved by a vivid flash of British red. MacDonald's brigade was on the right. David's brigade followed in rear of the centre as a reserve. The cavalry, the Camel Corps, and the Horse Artillery watched the right flank; and on the left the gunboats steamed along the river.

For two hours the army were the only living things visible on the smooth sand, but at seven o'clock a large body of Dervish horse appeared on the right flank. The further advance of half a mile discovered the Arab forces. Their numbers were less than those of the Egyptians, but their white uniforms, conspicuous on the sand, and the rows of flags of many colours lent an imposing appearance to their array. Their determined aspect, no less than the reputation of Bishara, encouraged the belief that they were about to charge.

The disparity of the forces was, however, too great; and as the Egyptian army steadily advanced, the Dervishes slowly retired. Their retreat was cleverly covered by the Baggara horse, who, by continually threatening the desert flank, delayed the progress of the troops. Bishara did not attempt to re-enter the town, on which the gunboats were now concentrating their fire, but continued to retire in excellent order towards the south and Debba.

The Egyptian infantry halted in Dongola, which when they arrived they found already in the hands of detachments from the flotilla. The red flag with the Crescent and star waved once again from the roof of the Mudiria. The garrison of 400 black Jehadia had capitulated, and were already fraternising with their Soudanese captors, whose comrades in arms they were soon to be. While the infantry occupied the town the cavalry and Camel Corps were despatched in pursuit. The Baggara horse, however, maintained a firm attitude, and attempted several charges to cover the retreat of their infantry. In one of these an actual collision occurred, and Captain Adams's squadron of Egyptian cavalry inflicted a loss of six killed on the enemy at a cost to themselves of eight men wounded. The cavalry and Camel corps had about twenty casualties in the pursuit. But although the Dervishes thus withdrew in an orderly manner from the field, the demoralising influence of retreat soon impaired their discipline and order, and many small parties, becoming detached from the main body, were captured by the pursuers. The line of retreat was strewn with weapons and other effects, and so many babies were abandoned by their parents that an artillery waggon had to be employed to collect and carry them. Wad Bishara, Osman Azrak, and the Baggara horse, however, made good their flight across the desert to Metemma, and, in spite of terrible sufferings from thirst, retained sufficient discipline to detach a force to hold Abu Klea Wells in case the retreat was followed. The Dervish infantry made their way along the river to Abu Hamed, and were much harassed by the gunboats until they reached the Fourth Cataract, when the pursuit was brought to an end.

The Egyptian losses in the capture of Dongola and in the subsequent pursuit were: British, nil. Native ranks: killed, 1; wounded, 25. Total, 26.

The occupation of Dongola terminated the campaign of 1896. About 900 prisoners, mostly the Black Jehadia, all the six brass cannon, large stores of grain, and a great quantity of flags, spears, and swords fell to the victors, and the whole of the province, said to be the most fertile in the Soudan, was restored to the Egyptian authority. The existence of a perpetual clear waterway from the head of the Third Cataract to Merawi enabled the gunboats at once to steam up the river for more than 200 miles, and in the course of the following month the greater part of the army was established in Merawi below the Fourth Cataract, at Debba, or at Korti, drawing supplies along the railway, and from Railhead by a boat service on the long reach of open water. The position of a strong force at Merawi—only 120 miles along the river bank from Abu Hamed, the northern Dervish post—was, as will be seen, convenient to the continuance of the campaign whenever the time should arrive. But a long delay in the advance was now inevitable, and nearly a year was destined to pass without any collision between the forces of the Khedive and those of the Khalifa.

The success of the operations caused great public satisfaction in England. The first step had been taken. The Soudan was re-entered. After ten years of defensive war the Dervishes had been attacked, and it was clear that when they were attacked with adequate forces they were not so very terrible after all. The croakers were silent. A general desire was manifested in the country that the operations should continue, and although the Government did not yet abandon their tentative policy, or resolve utterly to destroy the Khalifa's power, it was decided that, as the road had so far been safe and pleasant, there was at present no need to stop or turn back.

A generous gazette of honours was published. With a single exception, which it would be invidious to specify, all the officers of the Egyptian army were mentioned in despatches. Sir H. Kitchener, Colonel Hunter, and Colonel Rundle were promoted Major-Generals for distinguished service in the field; a special medal—on whose ribbon the Blue Nile is shown flowing through the yellow desert—was struck; and both the engagement at Firket and the affair at Hafir were commemorated by clasps. The casualties during the campaign, including the fighting round Suakin, were 43 killed and 139 wounded; 130 officers and men died from cholera; and there were 126 deaths from other causes. A large number of British officers were also invalided.

CHAPTER VIII:

THE DESERT RAILWAY

It often happens that in prosperous public enterprises the applause of the nation and the rewards of the sovereign are bestowed on those whose offices are splendid and whose duties have been dramatic. Others whose labours were no less difficult, responsible, and vital to success are unnoticed. If this be true of men, it is also true of things. In a tale of war the reader's mind is filled with the fighting. The battle—with its vivid scenes, its moving incidents, its plain and tremendous results—excites imagination and commands attention. The eye is fixed on the fighting brigades as they move amid the smoke; on the swarming figures of the enemy; on the General, serene and determined, mounted in the middle of his Staff. The long trailing line of communications is unnoticed. The fierce glory that plays on red, triumphant bayonets dazzles the observer; nor does he care to look behind to where, along a thousand miles of rail, road, and river, the convoys are crawling to the front in uninterrupted succession. Victory is the beautiful, bright-coloured flower. Transport is the stem without which it could never have blossomed. Yet even the military student, in his zeal to master the fascinating combinations of the actual conflict, often forgets the far more intricate complications of supply.

It cannot be denied that a battle, the climax to which all military operations tend, is an event which is not controlled by strategy or organisation. The scheme may be well planned, the troops well fed, the ammunition plentiful, and the enemy entangled, famished, or numerically inferior. The glorious uncertainties of the field can yet reverse everything. The human element—in defiance of experience and probability—may produce a wholly irrational result, and a starving, out-manoeuvred army win food, safety, and honour by their bravery. But such considerations apply with greater force to wars where both sides are equal in equipment and discipline. In savage warfare in a flat country the power of modern machinery is such that flesh and blood can scarcely prevail, and the chances of battle are reduced to a minimum. Fighting the Dervishes was primarily a matter of transport. The Khalifa was conquered on the railway.

Hitherto, as the operations have progressed, it has been convenient to speak of the railway in a general manner as having been laid or extended to various points, and merely to indicate the direction of the lines of communication. The reader is now invited to take a closer view. This chapter is concerned with boats, railways, and pack animals, but particularly with railways.

Throughout the Dongola campaign in 1896 the Nile was the main channel of communication between the Expeditionary Force and its base in Egypt. All supplies were brought to the front as far as possible by water transport. Wherever the Nile was navigable, it was used. Other means of conveyance— by railways and pack animals—though essential, were merely supplementary. Boats carry more and cost less than any other form of transport. The service is not so liable to interruption; the plant needs only simple repair; the waterway is ready-made. But the Nile is not always available. Frequent cataracts obstruct its course for many miles. Other long reaches are only navigable when the river is in flood. To join the navigable reaches, and thus preserve the continuity of the communications, a complex system of railways and caravans was necessary.

In the expedition to Dongola a line of railway was required to connect the two navigable reaches of the Nile which extend from Assuan to Wady Halfa, and from Kerma to Merawi. Before the capture of Dongola, however, this distance was shortened by the fact that the river at high Nile is navigable between the Third Cataract and Kerma. In consequence it was at first only necessary to construct the stretch of 108 miles between Wady Halfa and Kosheh. During the years when Wady Halfa was the southernmost garrison of the Egyptian forces a strong post had been maintained at Sarras. In the Nile expeditions of 1885 the railway from Halfa had been completed through Sarras and as far as Akasha, a distance of eighty-six miles. After the abandonment of the Soudan the Dervishes destroyed the line as far north as Sarras. The old embankments were still standing, but the sleepers had been burnt and the rails torn up, and in many cases bent or twisted. The position in 1896 may, in fact, be summed up as follows: The section of thirty-three miles from Wady Halfa to Sarras was immediately available and in working order. The section of fifty-three miles from Sarras to Akasha required partial reconstruction. The section of thirty-two miles from Akasha to Kosheh must, with the exception of ten miles of embankment completed in 1885, at once be newly made. And, finally, the section from Kosheh to Kerma must be completed before the Nile flood subsided.

The first duty, therefore, which the Engineer officers had to perform was the reconstruction of the line from Sarras to Akasha. No trained staff or skilled workmen were available. The lack of men with technical knowledge was doubtfully supplied by the enlistment of a 'Railway Battalion' 800 strong. These men were drawn from many tribes and classes. Their only qualification was capacity and willingness for work. They presented a motley appearance. Dervish prisoners, released but still wearing their jibbas, assisted stalwart Egyptians in unloading rails and sleepers. Dinkas, Shillooks, Jaalin, and Barabras shovelled contentedly together at the embankments. One hundred civilian Soudanese—chiefly time-expired soldiers—were also employed; and these, since they were trustworthy and took an especial pride in their work, soon learned the arts of spiking rails and sleepers, fishing rails together, and straightening. To direct and control the labours of these men of varied race and language, but of equal inexperience, some civilian foremen platelayers were obtained at high rates of pay from Lower Egypt. These, however, with very few exceptions were not satisfactory, and they were gradually replaced by intelligent men of the 'Railway Battalion,' who had learned their trade as the line progressed. The projection, direction, and execution of the whole work were entrusted to a few subalterns of Engineers, of whom the best-known was Edouard Girouard.

Work was begun south of Sarras at the latter end of March. At first the efforts of so many unskilled workmen, instructed by few experienced officers, were productive of results ridiculous rather than important. Gradually, however, the knowledge and energy of the young director and the intelligence and devotion of his still more youthful subordinates began to take effect. The pace of construction increased, and the labour was lightened by the contrivances of experience and skill.

As the line grew longer, native officers and non-commissioned officers from the active and reserve lists of the Egyptian Army were appointed station-masters. Intelligent non-commissioned officers and men were converted into shunters, guards, and pointsmen. Traffic was controlled by telephone. To work the telephone, men were discovered who could read and write—very often who could read and write only their own names, and even that with such difficulty that they usually preferred a seal. They developed into clerks by a simple process of selection. To improve their education, and to train a staff in the office work of a railway, two schools were instituted at Halfa. In these establishments, which were formed by the shade of two palm-trees, twenty pupils received the beginnings of knowledge. The simplicity of the instruction was aided by the zeal of the students, and learning grew beneath the palm-trees more quickly perhaps than in the magnificent schools of civilisation.

The rolling stock of the Halfa-Sarras line was in good order and sufficient quantity, but the eight locomotives were out of all repair, and had to be patched up again and again with painful repetition. The regularity of their break-downs prevented the regularity of the road, and the Soudan military railway gained a doubtful reputation during the Dongola expedition and in its early days. Nor were there wanting those who employed their wits in scoffing at the undertaking and in pouring thoughtless indignation on the engineers. Nevertheless the work went on continually.

The initial difficulties of the task were aggravated by an unexpected calamity. On the 26th of August the violent cyclonic rain-storm of which some account has been given in the last chapter broke over the Dongola province.

A writer on the earlier phases of the war [A. Hilliard Atteridge, TOWARDS FREEDOM.] has forcibly explained why the consequences were so serious:

'In a country where rain is an ordinary event the engineer lays his railway line, not in the bottom of a valley, but at a higher level on one slope or the other. Where he passes across branching side valleys, he takes care to leave in all his embankments large culverts to carry off flood-water. But here, in what was thought to be the rainless Soudan, the line south of Sarras followed for mile after mile the bottom of the long valley of Khor Ahrusa, and no provision had been made, or had been thought necessary, for culverts in the embankments where minor hollows were crossed. Thus, when the flood came, it was not merely that the railway was cut through here and there by the rushing deluge. It was covered deep in water, the ballast was swept away, and some of the banks so destroyed that in places rails and sleepers were left hanging in the air across a wide gap.'

Nearly fourteen miles of track were destroyed. The camp of the construction gangs was wrecked and flooded. Some of the rifles of the escort—for the conditions of war were never absent—were afterwards recovered from a depth of three feet of sand. In one place, where the embankment had partly withstood the deluge, a great lake several miles square appeared. By extraordinary exertions the damage was repaired in a week.

As soon as the line as far as Kosheh was completed, the advance towards Dongola began. After the army had been victorious at Hafir the whole province was cleared of Dervishes, and the Egyptian forces pushed on to Merawi. Here they were dependent on river transport. But the Nile was falling rapidly, and the army were soon in danger of being stranded by the interruption of river traffic between the Third Cataract and Kenna. The extension of the line from Kosheh to Kerma was therefore of vital importance. The survey was at once undertaken, and a suitable route was chosen through the newly acquired and unmapped territory. Of the ninety-five miles of extended track, fifty-six were through the desert, and the constructors here gained the experience which was afterwards of value on the great Desert Railway from Wady Halfa to the Atbara. Battalions of troops were distributed along the line and ordered to begin to make the embankments. Track-laying commenced south of Kosheh on the 9th of October, and the whole work was carried forward with feverish energy. As it progressed, and before it was completed, the reach of the river from the Third Cataract to Kenna ceased to be navigable. The army were now dependent for their existence on the partly finished railway, from the head of which supplies were conveyed by an elaborate system of camel transport. Every week the line grew, Railhead moved forward, and the strain upon the pack animals diminished. But the problem of feeding the field army without interfering with the railway construction was one of extraordinary intricacy and difficulty. The carrying capacity of the line was strictly limited. The worn-out engines frequently broke down. On many occasions only three were in working order, and the other five undergoing 'heavy repairs' which might secure them another short span of usefulness. Three times the construction had to be suspended to allow the army to be revictualled. Every difficulty was, however, overcome. By the beginning of May the line to Kenna was finished, and the whole of the Railway Battalion, its subalterns and its director, turned their attention to a greater enterprise.

In the first week in December the Sirdar returned from England with instructions or permission to continue the advance towards Khartoum, and the momentous question of the route to be followed arose. It may at first seem that the plain course was to continue to work along the Nile, connecting its navigable reaches by sections of railway. But from Merawi to Abu Hamed the river is broken by continual cataracts, and the broken ground of both banks made a railway nearly an impossibility. The movements of the French expeditions towards the Upper Nile counselled speed. The poverty of Egypt compelled economy. The Nile route, though sure, would be slow and very expensive. A short cut must be found. Three daring and ambitious schemes presented themselves: (1) the line followed by the Desert Column in 1884 from Korti to Metemma; (2) the celebrated, if not notorious, route from Suakin to Berber; (3) across the Nubian desert from Korosko or Wady Halfa to Abu Hamed.

The question involved the whole strategy of the war. No more important decision was ever taken by Sir Herbert Kitchener, whether in office or in action. The request for a British division, the attack On Mahmud's zeriba, the great left wheel towards Omdurman during that battle, the treatment of the Marchand expedition, were matters of lesser resolve than the selection of the line of advance. The known strength of the Khalifa made it evident that a powerful force would be required for the destruction of his army and the capture of his capital. The use of railway transport to some point on the Nile whence there was a clear waterway was therefore imperative. Berber and Metemma were known, and Abu Hamed was believed, to fulfil this condition. But both Berber and Metemma were important strategic points. It was improbable that the Dervishes would abandon these keys to Khartoum and the Soudan without severe resistance. It seemed likely, indeed, that the Khalifa would strongly reinforce both towns, and desperately contest their possession. The deserts between Korti and Metemma, and between Suakin and Berber, contained scattered wells, and small raiding parties might have cut the railway and perhaps have starved the army at its head. It was therefore too dangerous to project the railway towards either Berber or Metemma until they were actually in our hands. The argument is circular. The towns could not be taken without a strong force; so strong a force could not advance until the railway was made; and the railway could not be made till the towns were taken.

Both the Korti-Metemma and the Suakin-Berber routes were therefore rejected. The resolution to exclude the latter was further strengthened by the fact that the labour of building a railway over the hills behind Suakin would have been very great.

The route via Abu Hamed was selected by the exclusion of the alternatives. But it had distinct and apparent advantages. Abu Hamed was within striking distance of the army at Merawi. It was not a point essential to the Dervish defences, and not, therefore, likely to be so strongly garrisoned as Berber or Metemma. It might, therefore, be captured by a column marching along the river, and sufficiently small to be equipped with only camel transport. The deserts through which the railway to Abu Hamed would pass contain few wells, and therefore it would be difficult for small raiding parties to cut the line or attack the construction gangs; and before the line got within reach of the Dervish garrison at Abu Hamed, that garrison would be dislodged and the place seized.

The plan was perfect, and the argument in its favour conclusive. It turned, however, on one point: Was the Desert Railway a possibility? With this question the General was now confronted. He appealed to expert opinion. Eminent railway engineers in England were consulted. They replied with unanimity that, having due regard to the circumstances, and remembering the conditions of war under which the work must be executed, it was impossible to construct such a line. Distinguished soldiers were approached on the subject. They replied that the scheme was not only impossible, but absurd. Many other persons who were not consulted volunteered the opinion that the whole idea was that of a lunatic, and predicted ruin and disaster to the expedition. Having received this advice, and reflected on it duly, the Sirdar ordered the railway to be constructed without more delay.

A further question immediately arose: Should the railway to Abu Hamed start from Korosko or from Wady Halfa? There were arguments on both sides. The adoption of the Korosko line would reduce the river stage from Assuan by forty-eight hours up stream. The old caravan route, by which General Gordon had travelled to Khartoum on his last journey, had been from Korosko via Murat Wells to Abu Hamed. On the other hand, many workshops and appliances for construction were already existing at Wady Halfa. It was the northern terminus of the Dongola railway. This was an enormous advantage. Both routes were reconnoitred: that from Wady Halfa was selected. The decision having been taken, the enterprise was at once begun.

Lieutenant Girouard, to whom everything was entrusted, was told to make the necessary estimates. Sitting in his hut at Wady Halfa, he drew up a comprehensive list. Nothing was forgotten. Every want was provided for; every difficulty was foreseen; every requisite was noted. The questions to be decided were numerous and involved. How much carrying capacity was required? How much rolling stock? How many engines? What spare parts? How much oil? How many lathes? How many cutters? How many punching and shearing machines? What arrangements of signals would be necessary? How many lamps? How many points? How many trolleys? What amount of coal should be ordered? How much water would be wanted? How should it be carried? To what extent would its carriage affect the hauling power and influence all previous calculations? How much railway plant was needed? How many miles of rail? How many thousand sleepers? Where could they be procured at such short notice? How many fishplates were necessary? What tools would be required? What appliances? What machinery? How much skilled labour was wanted? How much of the class of labour available? How were the workmen to be fed and watered? How much food would they want? How many trains a day must be run to feed them and their escort? How many must be run to carry plant? How did these requirements affect the estimate for rolling stock? The answers to all these questions, and to many others with which I will not inflict the reader, were set forth by Lieutenant Girouard in a ponderous volume several inches thick; and such was the comprehensive accuracy of the estimate that the working parties were never delayed by the want even of a piece of brass wire.

In any circumstances the task would have been enormous. It was, however, complicated by five important considerations: It had to be executed with military precautions. There was apparently no water along the line. The feeding of 2,000 platelayers in a barren desert was a problem in itself. The work had to be completed before the winter. And, finally, the money voted was not to be outrun. The Sirdar attended to the last condition.

Girouard was sent to England to buy the plant and rolling stock. Fifteen new engines and two hundred trucks were ordered. The necessary new workshops were commenced at Halfa. Experienced mechanics were procured to direct them. Fifteen hundred additional men were enlisted in the Railway Battalion and trained. Then the water question was dealt with. The reconnoitring surveys had reported that though the line was certainly 'good and easy' for 110 miles— and, according to Arab accounts, for the remaining 120 miles—no drop of water was to be found, and only two likely spots for wells were noted. Camel transport was, of course, out of the question. Each engine must first of all haul enough water to carry it to Railhead and back, besides a reserve against accidents. It was evident that the quantity of water required by any locomotive would continually increase as the work progressed and the distance grew greater, until finally the material trains would have one-third of their carrying power absorbed in transporting the water for their own consumption. The amount of water necessary is largely dependent on the grades of the line. The 'flat desert' proved to be a steady slope up to a height of 1,600 feet above Halfa, and the calculations were further complicated. The difficulty had, however, to be faced, and a hundred 1,500-gallon tanks were procured. These were mounted on trucks and connected by hose; and the most striking characteristic of the trains of the Soudan military railway was the long succession of enormous boxes on wheels, on which the motive power of the engine and the lives of the passengers depended.

The first spadeful of sand of the Desert Railway was turned on the first day of 1897; but until May, when the line to Kerma was finished, no great efforts were made, and only forty miles of track had been laid. In the meanwhile the men of the new Railway Battalion were being trained; the plant was steadily accumulating; engines, rolling stock, and material of all sorts had arrived from England. From the growing workshops at Wady Halfa the continual clatter and clang of hammers and the black smoke of manufacture rose to the African sky. The malodorous incense of civilisation was offered to the startled gods of Egypt. All this was preparation; nor was it until the 8th of May that track-laying into the desert was begun in earnest. The whole of the construction gangs and railroad staff were brought from Kerma to Wady Halfa, and the daring pioneers of modern war started on their long march through the wilderness, dragging their railway behind them—safe and sure road which infantry, cavalry, guns, and gunboats might follow with speed and convenience.

It is scarcely within the power of words to describe the savage desolation of the regions into which the line and its constructors plunged. A smooth ocean of bright-coloured sand spread far and wide to distant horizons. The tropical sun beat with senseless perseverance upon the level surface until it could scarcely be touched with a naked hand, and the filmy air glittered and shimmered as over a furnace. Here and there huge masses of crumbling rock rose from the plain, like islands of cinders in a sea of fire. Alone in this vast expanse stood

Railhead—a canvas town of 2,500 inhabitants, complete with station, stores, post-office, telegraph-office, and canteen, and only connected with the living world of men and ideas by two parallel iron streaks, three feet six inches apart, growing dim and narrower in a long perspective until they were twisted and blurred by the mirage and vanished in the indefinite distance.

Every morning in the remote nothingness there appeared a black speck growing larger and clearer, until with a whistle and a welcome clatter, amid the aching silence of ages, the 'material' train arrived, carrying its own water and 2,500 yards of rails, sleepers, and accessories. At noon came another speck, developing in a similar manner into a supply train, also carrying its own water, food and water for the half-battalion of the escort and the 2,000 artificers and platelayers, and the letters, newspapers, sausages, jam, whisky, soda-water, and cigarettes which enable the Briton to conquer the world without discomfort. And presently the empty trains would depart, reversing the process of their arrival, and vanishing gradually along a line which appeared at last to turn up into the air and run at a tangent into an unreal world.

The life of the strange and lonely town was characterised by a machine-like regularity, born perhaps of the iron road from which it derived its nourishment. Daily at three o'clock in the morning the 'camp-engine' started with the 'bank parties.' With the dawn the 'material' train arrived, the platelaying gangs swarmed over it like clusters of flies, and were carried to the extreme limit of the track. Every man knew his task, and knew, too, that he would return to camp when it was finished, and not before. Forthwith they set busily to work without the necessity of an order. A hundred yards of material was unloaded. The sleepers were arranged in a long succession. The rails were spiked to every alternate sleeper, and then the great 80-ton engine moved cautiously forward along the unballasted track, like an elephant trying a doubtful bridge. The operation was repeated continually through the hours of the burning day. Behind the train there followed other gangs of platelayers, who completed the spiking and ballasting process; and when the sun sank beneath the sands of the western horizon, and the engine pushed the empty trucks and the weary men home to the Railhead camp, it came back over a finished and permanent line. There was a brief interval while the camp-fires twinkled in the waste, like the lights of a liner in mid-ocean, while the officers and men chatted over their evening meal, and then the darkness and silence of the desert was unbroken till morning brought the glare and toil of another long day.

So, week in, week out, the work went on. Every few days saw a further advance into the wilderness. The scene changed and remained unaltered—'another, yet the same.' As Wady Halfa became more remote and Abu Hamed grew near, an element of danger, the more appalling since it was peculiar, was added to the strange conditions under which the inhabitants of Railhead lived. What if the Dervishes should cut the line behind them? They had three days' reserve of water. After that, unless the obstruction were removed and traffic restored, all must wither and die in the sand, and only their bones and their cooking-pots would attest the folly of their undertaking.

By the 20th of July a hundred and thirty miles of line had been finished, and it became too dangerous to advance further until Abu Hamed had been cleared of the Dervish force. They were still a hundred miles away, but camels travel fast and far, and the resources of the enemy were uncertain. It appeared that progress would be checked, but on the 7th of August General Hunter, marching from Merawi along the river bank, attacked and took Abu Hamed—an operation which will be described hereafter. Work was at once resumed with renewed energy. The pace of construction now became remarkable. As much as 5,300 yards of track was surveyed, embanked, and laid in a single day. On the 1st of November Abu Hamed was reached, and by the banks of the Nile the men who had fought their way across the desert joined hands with those who had fought their way along the river.

The strain and hardship had not, however, been without effect on the constructors. Two of the Engineer subalterns—Polwhele and Cator—out of the eight concerned in the laying of the Dongola and the Desert railways had died. Their places were eagerly filled by others.

The completion of the line was accelerated by nearly a month through the fortunate discovery of water. At the beginning of July a well was sunk in what was thought to be a likely place at 'No. 4 Station,' seventy-seven miles from Halfa. After five weeks' work water was found in abundance at a depth of 90 feet. A steam-pump was erected, and the well yielded a continual supply. In October a second well was sunk at 'No. 6 Station,' fifty-five miles further on, whence water was obtained in still greater quantity. These discoveries modified, though they did not solve, the water question. They substantially increased the carrying capacity of the line, and reduced the danger to which the construction gangs were exposed. The sinking of the wells, an enterprise at which the friendly Arabs scoffed, was begun on the Sirdar's personal initiative; but the chronicler must impartially observe that the success was won by luck as much as by calculation, for, since the first two wells were made, eight others of greater depth have been bored and in no case has water been obtained.

As the railway had been made, the telegraph-wire had, of course, followed it. Every consignment of rails and sleepers had been accompanied by its proportion of telegraph-poles, insulators, and wire. Another subaltern of Engineers, Lieutenant Manifold, who managed this part of the military operations against the Arabs, had also laid a line from Merawi to Abu Hamed, so that immediate correspondence was effected round the entire circle of rail and river.

The labours of the Railway Battalion and its officers did not end with the completion of the line to Abu Hamed. The Desert Railway was made. It had now to be maintained, worked, and rapidly extended. The terminus at Halfa had become a busy town. A mud village was transformed into a miniature Crewe. The great workshops that had grown with the line were equipped with diverse and elaborate machines. Plant of all kinds purchased in Cairo or requisitioned from England, with odds and ends collected from Ishmail's scrap heaps, filled the depots with an extraordinary variety of stores. Foundries, lathes, dynamos, steam-hammers, hydraulic presses, cupola furnaces, screw-cutting machines, and drills had been set up and were in continual work. They needed constant attention. Every appliance for repairing each must be provided. To haul the tonnage necessary to supply the army and extend the line nearly forty engines were eventually required. Purchased at different times and from different countries, they included ten distinct patterns; each pattern needed a special reserve of spare parts. The permutations and combinations of the stores were multiplied. Some of the engines were old and already worn out. These broke down periodically. The frictional parts of all were affected by the desert sand, and needed ceaseless attention and repair. The workshops were busy night and day for seven days a week.

To the complication of machinery was added the confusion of tongues. Natives of various races were employed as operatives. Foremen had been obtained from Europe. No fewer than seven separate languages were spoken in the shops. Wady Halfa became a second Babel. Yet the undertaking prospered. The Engineer officers displayed qualities of tact and temper: their director was cool and indefatigable. Over all the Sirdar exercised a regular control. Usually ungracious, rarely impatient, never unreasonable, he moved among the workshops and about the line, satisfying himself that all was proceeding with economy and despatch. The sympathy of common labour won him the affection of the subalterns. Nowhere in the Soudan was he better known than on the railroad. Nowhere was he so ardently believed in.

It is now necessary to anticipate the course of events. As soon as the railway reached Abu Hamed, General Hunter's force, which was holding that place, dropped its slender camel communications with Merawi and drew its supplies along the new line direct from Wady Halfa. After the completion of the desert line there was still left seventeen miles of material for construction, and the railway was consequently at once extended to Dakhesh, sixteen miles south of Abu Hamed. Meanwhile Berber was seized, and military considerations compelled the concentration of a larger force to maintain that town. The four battalions which had remained at Merawi were floated down stream to Kerma, and, there entraining, were carried by Halfa and Abu Hamed to Dakhesh—a journey of 450 miles.

When the railway had been begun across the desert, it was believed that the Nile was always navigable above Abu Hamed. In former campaigns it had been reconnoitred and the waterway declared clear. But as the river fell it became evident that this was untrue. With the subsidence of the waters cataracts began to appear, and to avoid these it became necessary first of all to extend the railway to Bashtinab, later on to Abadia, and finally to the Atbara. To do this more money had to be obtained, and the usual financial difficulties presented themselves. Finally, however, the matter was settled, and the extension began at the rate of about a mile a day. The character of the country varies considerably between Abu Hamed and the Atbara River. For the first sixty miles the line ran beside the Nile, at the edge of the riparian belt. On the right was the cultivable though mostly uncultivated strip, long neglected and silted up with fine sand drifted into dunes, from which scattered, scraggy dom palms and prickly mimosa bushes grew. Between the branches of these sombre trees the river gleamed, a cool and attractive flood. On the left was the desert, here broken by frequent rocks and dry watercourses. From Bashtinab to Abadia another desert section of fifty miles was necessary to avoid some very difficult ground by the Nile bank. From Abadia to the Atbara the last stretch of the line runs across a broad alluvial expanse from whose surface plane-trees of mean appearance, but affording welcome shade, rise, watered by the autumn rains. The fact that the railway was approaching regions where rain is not an almost unknown phenomenon increased the labour of construction. To prevent the embankments from being washed away in the watercourses, ten bridges and sixty culverts had to be made; and this involved the transport over the railway of more than 1,000 tons of material in addition to the ordinary plant.

By the arrival of the reinforcements at Berber the fighting force at the front was doubled: doubled also was the business of supply. The task of providing the food of an army in a desert, a thousand miles from their base, and with no apparent means of subsistence at the end of the day's march, is less picturesque, though not less important, than the building of railways along which that nourishment is drawn to the front. Supply and transport stand or fall together; history depends on both; and in order to explain the commissariat aspect of the River War, I must again both repeat and anticipate the account. The Sirdar exercised a direct and personal supervision over the whole department of supply, but his action was restricted almost entirely to the distribution of the rations. Their accumulation and regular supply were the task of Colonel Rogers, and this officer, by three years of exact calculation and unfailing allowance for the unforeseen, has well deserved his high reputation as a feeder of armies.

The first military necessity of the war was, as has been described, to place the bulk of the Egyptian army at Akasha. In ordinary circumstances this would not have been a serious commissariat problem. The frontier reserves of food were calculated to meet such an emergency. But in 1895 the crops in Egypt had been much below the average. At the beginning of 1896 there was a great scarcity of grain. When the order for the advance was issued, the frontier grain stores were nearly exhausted. The new crops could not be garnered until the end of April. Thus while the world regarded Egypt as a vast granary, her soldiers were obliged to purchase 4,000 tons of doura and 1,000 tons of barley from India and Russia on which to begin the campaign.

The chief item of a soldier's diet in most armies is bread. In several of our wars the health, and consequently the efficiency, of the troops has been impaired by bad bread or by the too frequent substitution of hard biscuit. For more than a year the army up the river ate 20 tons of flour daily, and it is easy to imagine how bitter amid ordinary circumstances would have been the battle between the commissariat officers, whose duty it was to insist on proper quality, and the contractors—often,

I fear, meriting the epithet 'rascally'—intent only upon profit. But in the well-managed Egyptian Service no such difficulties arose. The War Department had in 1892 converted one of Ismail Pasha's gun factories near Cairo into a victualling-yard. Here were set up their own mills for grinding flour, machinery for manufacturing biscuit to the extent of 60,000 rations daily, and even for making soap. Three great advantages sprang from this wise arrangement. Firstly, the good quality of the supply was assured. Complaints about bread and biscuit were practically unknown, and the soap—since the soldier, in contrast to the mixture of rubble and grease with which the contractors had formerly furnished him, could actually wash himself and his clothes with it—was greatly prized. Secondly, all risk of contractors failing to deliver in time was avoided. Lastly, the funds resulting from the economy had been utilised to form a useful corps of 150 bakers. And thus, although the purchase of foreign grain added to the expense, the beginning of the war found the commissariat of the Egyptian Army in a thoroughly efficient state.

Vast reserves of stores were quickly accumulated at Assuan. From these not an ounce of food was issued without the Sirdar's direct sanction. At the subsidiary depot, formed at Wady Halfa, the same rule prevailed. The man who was responsible to no one took all the responsibility; and the system whereby a Chief of the Staff is subjected to the continual bombardment of heads of departments was happily avoided. Sufficient supplies having been accumulated at Akasha to allow of a forward movement, Firket was fought. After Firket the situation became difficult, and the problem of the supply officers was to keep the troops alive without delaying the progress of the railway with the carriage of their food. A small quantity of provisions was painfully dragged, with an average loss of 50 per cent from theft and water damage, up the succession of cataracts which obstruct the river-way from Halfa to Kosheh. Camel convoys from Railhead carried the rest. But until the line reached Kosheh the resources of the transport were terribly strained, and at one time it was even necessary to send the mounted troops north to avoid actual famine. The apparent inadequacy of the means to the end reached a climax when the army moved southward from Dulgo. The marches and halts to Dongola were estimated to take ten days, which was the utmost capacity of camel and steam transport, A few boat-loads of grain might be captured; a few handfuls of dates might be plucked; but scarcely any local supplies would be available. The sailing-boats, which were the only regular means of transport, were all delayed by the adverse winds.

Fortune returned at the critical moment. By good luck on the first day of the march the north wind began to blow, and twelve days' supplies, over and above those moved by camel and steamer, reached Dongola with the troops. With this reserve in hand, the occupation of the province was completed, and although the army only existed from hand to mouth until the railway reached Kerma, no further serious difficulty was experienced in supplying them.

The account of the commissariat is now complete to the end of the Dongola Expedition; but it may conveniently be carried forward with the railway construction. In the Abu Hamed phase the supplies were so regulated that a convoy travelling from Murat Wells along the caravan route arrived the day after the fight; and thereafter communications were opened with Merawi. The unexpected occupation of Berber, following Abu Hamed, created the most difficult situation of the war. Until the railway was forced on to Berber a peculiarly inconvenient line of supply had to be used; and strings of camels, scattering never less than 30 per cent of their loads, meandered through the rough and thorny country between Merawi and Abu Hamed. This line was strengthened by other convoys from Murat and the approaching Railhead, and a system of boats and camel portages filtered the supplies to their destination.

Even when the railway had reached Dakhesh the tension was only slightly relaxed. The necessity of supplying the large force at Berber, 108 miles from Railhead, still required the maintenance of a huge and complicated system of boat and camel transport. Of course, as the railway advanced, it absorbed stage after stage of river and portage, and the difficulties decreased. But the reader may gain some idea of their magnitude by following the progress of a box of biscuits from Cairo to Berber in the month of December 1897. The route was as follows: From Cairo to Nagh Hamadi (340 miles) by rail; from Nagh Hamadi to Assuan (205 miles) by boat; from Assuan to Shellal (6 miles} by rail; from Shellal to Halfa (226 miles) by boat; from Halfa to Dakhesh (Railhead)—248 miles—by military railway; from Dakhesh to Shereik (45 miles) by boat; from Shereik by camel (13 miles) round a cataract to Bashtinab; from Bashtinab by boat (25 miles) to Omsheyo; from Omsheyo round another impracticable reach (11 miles) by camel to Geneinetti, and thence (22 miles) to Berber by boat. The road taken by this box of biscuits was followed by every ton of supplies required by 10,000 men in the field. The uninterrupted working of the long and varied chain was vital to the welfare of the army and the success of the war.

It could only be maintained if every section was adequately supplied and none were either choked or starved. This problem had to be solved correctly every day by the transport officers, in spite of uncertain winds that retarded the boats, of camels that grew sick or died, and of engines that repeatedly broke down. In the face of every difficulty a regular supply was maintained. The construction of the railway was not delayed, nor the food of the troops reduced.

The line continued to grow rapidly, and as it grew the difficulties of supply decreased. The weight was shifted from the backs of the camels and the bottoms of the sailing-boats to the trucks of the iron road. The strong hands of steam were directed to the prosecution of the war, and the swiftness of the train replaced the toilsome plodding of the caravan. The advance of the Dervishes towards Berber checked the progress of the railway. Military precautions were imperative. Construction was delayed by the passage of the 1st British Brigade from Cairo to the front, and by the consequently increased volume of daily supplies. By the 10th of March, however, the line was completed to Bashtinab. On the 5th of May it had reached Abadia. On the 3rd of July the whole railway from Wady Halfa to the Atbara was finished, and the southern terminus was established in the great entrenched camp at the confluence of the rivers. The question of supply was then settled once and for all. In less than a week stores sufficient for three months were poured along the line, and the exhausting labours of the commissariat officers ended. Their relief and achievement were merged in the greater triumph of the Railway Staff. The director and his subalterns had laboured long, and their efforts were crowned with complete success. On the day that the first troop train steamed into the fortified camp at the confluence of the Nile and the Atbara rivers the doom of the Dervishes was sealed. It had now become possible with convenience and speed to send into the heart of the Soudan great armies independent of the season of the year and of the resources of the country; to supply them not only with abundant food and ammunition, but with all the varied paraphernalia of scientific war; and to support their action on land by a powerful flotilla of gunboats, which could dominate the river and command the banks, and could at any moment make their way past Khartoum even to Sennar, Fashoda, or Sobat. Though the battle was not yet fought, the victory was won. The Khalifa, his capital, and his army were now within the Sirdar's reach. It remained only to pluck the fruit in the most convenient hour, with the least trouble and at the smallest cost.

CHAPTER IX:

ABU HAMED

The last chapter carried the account of the war forward at express speed. The reader, who had already on the railway reached the Atbara encampment and was prepared for the final advance on Khartoum, must allow his mind to revert to a period when the Egyptian forces are distributed along the river in garrisons at Dongola, Debba, Korti, and Merawi; when the reorganisation of the conquered province has been begun; and when the Desert Railway is still stretching steadily forward towards Abu Hamed.

The news of the fall of Dongola created a panic in Omdurman. Great numbers of Arabs, believing that the Khalifa's power was about to collapse, fled from the city. All business was at a standstill. For several days there were no executions. Abdullah himself kept his house, and thus doubtfully concealed his vexation and alarm from his subjects. On the fifth day, however, having recovered his own confidence, he proceeded to the mosque, and after the morning prayer ascended his small wooden pulpit and addressed the assembled worshippers. After admitting the retreat of the Dervishes under Wad Bishara, he enlarged on the losses the 'Turks' had sustained and described their miserable condition. He deplored the fact that certain of the Jehadia had surrendered, and reminded his listeners with a grim satisfaction of the horrible tortures which it was the practice of the English and Egyptians to inflict upon their captives. He bewailed the lack of faith in God which had allowed even the meanest of the Ansar to abandon the Jehad against the infidel, and he condemned the lack of piety which disgraced the age. But he proclaimed his confidence in the loyalty of his subjects and his enjoyment of the favour of God and the counsels of the late Mahdi; and having by his oratory raised the fanatical multitude to a high pitch of excitement, he thus concluded his long harangue: 'It is true that our chiefs have retired from Dongola. Yet they are not defeated. Only they that disobeyed me have perished. I instructed the faithful to refrain from fighting and return to Metemma. It was by my command that they have done what they have done. For the angel of the Lord and the spirit of the Mahdi have warned me in a vision that the souls of the accursed Egyptians and of the miserable English shall leave their bodies between Dongola and Omdurman, at some spot which their bones shall whiten. Thus shall the infidels be conquered.' Then, drawing his sword, he cried with a loud voice: 'Ed din mansur! The religion is victorious! Islam shall triumph!' Whereupon the worshippers, who to the number of 20,000 filled the great quadrangle—although they could not all hear his voice—saw his sword flashing in the sunlight, and with one accord imitated him, waving their swords and spears, and raising a mighty shout of fury and defiance. When the tumult had subsided, the Khalifa announced that those who did not wish to remain faithful might go where they liked, but that he for his part would remain, knowing that God would vindicate the faith. Public confidence was thus restored.

In order that the divine favour might be assisted by human effort, Abdullah adopted every measure or precaution that energy or prudence could suggest. At first he seems to have apprehended that the Sirdar's army would advance at once upon Omdurman, following the route of the Desert Column in 1885 from Korti to Metemma. He therefore ordered Osman Azrak—in spite of his severe wound—to hold Abu Klea Wells with the survivors of his flag. Bishara, who had rallied and reorganised the remains of the Dongola army, was instructed to occupy Metemma, the headquarters of the Jaalin. Messengers were despatched to the most distant garrisons to arrange for a general concentration upon Omdurman. The Emir Ibrahim Khalil was recalled from the Ghezira, or the land between the Blue and White Niles, and with his force of about 4,000 Jehadia and Baggara soon reached the city. Another chief, Ahmed Fedil, who was actually on his way to Gedaref, was ordered to return to the capital. Thither also Osman Digna repaired from Adarama. But it appears that the Khalifa only required the advice of that wily councillor, for he did not reduce the number of Dervishes in the small forts along the line of the Atbara—Ed Darner, Adarama, Asubri, El Fasher—and after a short visit and a long consultation Osman Digna returned to his post at Adarama. Last of all, but not least in importance, Mahmud, who commanded the 'Army of the West,' was ordered to leave very reduced garrisons in Kordofan and Darfur, and march with his whole remaining force, which may have numbered 10,000 fighting men, to the Nile, and so to Omdurman. Mahmud, who was as daring and ambitious as he was conceited and incapable, received the summons with delight, and began forthwith to collect his troops.

The Khalifa saw very clearly that he could not trust the riverain tribes. The Jaalin and Barabra were discontented. He knew that they were weary of his rule and of war. In proportion as the Egyptian army advanced, so their loyalty and the taxes they paid decreased. He therefore abandoned all idea of making a stand at Berber. The Emir Yunes—who, since he had been transferred from Dongola in 1895, had ruled the district—was directed to collect all the camels, boats, grain, and other things that might assist an invading army and send them to Metemma. The duty was most thoroughly performed. The inhabitants were soon relieved of all their property and of most of their means of livelihood, and their naturally bitter resentment at this merciless treatment explains to some extent the astonishing events which followed the capture of Abu Hamed. This last place Abdullah never regarded as more than an outpost. Its garrison was not large, and although it had now become the most northerly Dervish position, only a slender reinforcement was added to the force under the command of Mohammed-ez-Zein.

The power of the gunboats and their effect in the Dongola campaign were fully appreciated by the Arabs; and the Khalifa, in the hopes of closing the Sixth Cataract, began to construct several forts at the northern end of the Shabluka gorge. The Bordein, one of Gordon's old steamers, plied busily between Omdurman and Wad Hamed, transporting guns and stores; and Ahmed Fedil was sent with a sufficient force to hold the works when they were made. But the prophecy of the Mahdi exercised a powerful effect on the Khalifa's mind, and while he neglected no detail he based his hopes on the issue of a great battle on the plains of Kerreri, when the invaders should come to the walls of the city. With this prospect continually before him he drilled and organised the increasing army at Omdurman with the utmost regularity, and every day the savage soldiery practised their evolutions upon the plain they were presently to strew with their bodies.

But after a while it became apparent that the 'Turks' were not advancing. They tarried on the lands they had won. The steamers went no further than Merawi. The iron road stopped at Kerma. Why had they not followed up their success?

Obviously because they feared the army that awaited them at Omdurman. At this the Khalifa took fresh courage, and in January 1897 he began to revolve schemes for taking the offensive and expelling the invaders from the Dongola province. The army drilled and manoeuvred continually on the plains of Kerreri; great numbers of camels were collected at Omdurman; large stores of dried kisru or 'Soudan biscuit,' the food of Dervishes on expeditions, were prepared.

The Sirdar did not remain in ignorance of these preparations. The tireless enterprise of the Intelligence Branch furnished the most complete information; and preparations were made to concentrate the troops in Dongola on any threatened point, should the enemy advance. Regular reconnaissances were made by the cavalry both into the desert towards Gakdul Wells and along the river. Towards the end of May it was reported that the Emir Yunes had crossed the Nile and was raiding the villages on the left bank below Abu Hamed. In consequence the Sirdar ordered a strong patrol under Captain Le Gallais, and consisting of three squadrons of cavalry under Captain Mahon, three companies of the Camel Corps, and 100 men of the IXth Soudanese on camels, with one Maxim gun, to reconnoitre up the Nile through the Shukuk Pass and as far as Salamat.

The outward journey was unbroken by incident; but as the patrol was returning it was attacked by an equal force of Dervishes, and a sharp little skirmish ensued in which one British officer—Captain Peyton—was severely wounded, nine Egyptian troopers were killed, and three others wounded. This proof that the Dervishes were on the move enforced the greatest vigilance in all the Dongola garrisons.

At the end of May, Mahmud with his army arrived at Omdurman. The Khalifa received him with delight, and several imposing reviews were held outside the city. Mahmud himself was eager to march against the 'Turks.' He had no experience of modern rifles, and felt confident that he could easily destroy or at least roll back the invading forces. Partly persuaded by the zeal of his lieutenant, and partly by the wavering and doubtful attitude of the Jaalin, the Khalifa determined early in June to send the Kordofan army to occupy Metemma, and thereby either to awe the tribe into loyalty, or force them to revolt while the Egyptian troops were still too distant to assist them. He summoned the chief of the Jaalin, Abdalla-Wad-Saad, to Omdurman, and informed him that the Jaalin territories were threatened by the Turks. In the goodness of his heart, therefore, and because he knew that they loved the Mahdi and practised the true religion, he was resolved to protect them from their enemies. The chief bowed his head. The Khalifa continued that the trusty Mahmud with his army would be sent for that purpose; Abdalla might show his loyalty in furnishing them with all supplies and accommodation. He intimated that the interview was over. But the Jaalin chief had the temerity to protest. He assured the Khalifa of his loyalty, and of the ability of his tribe to repel the enemy. He implored him not to impose the burden of an army upon them. He exaggerated the poverty of Metemma; he lamented the misfortunes of the times. Finally he begged forgiveness for making his protest.

The Khalifa was infuriated. Forgetting his usual self-control and the forms of public utterance, he broke out into a long and abusive harangue. He told the chief that he had long doubted his loyalty, that he despised his protestations, that he was worthy of a shameful death, that his tribe were a blot upon the face of the earth, and that he hoped Mahmud would improve their manners and those of their wives.

Abdalla-Wad-Saad crept from the presence, and returned in fury and disgust to Metemma. Having collected the head men of his tribe, he informed them of his reception and the Khalifa's intent. They did not need to be told that the quartering upon them of Mahmud's army meant the plunder of their goods, the ruin of their homes, and the rape of their women. It was resolved to revolt and join the Egyptian forces. As a result of the council the Jaalin chief wrote two letters. The first was addressed to the Sirdar, and reached General Rundle at Merawi by messenger on the 24th of June. It declared the Jaalin submission to the Government, and begged for help, if possible in men, or, failing that, in arms; but ended by saying that, help or no help, the tribe were resolved to fight the Dervishes and hold Metemma to the death. The second letter—a mad and fatal letter—carried defiance to the Khalifa.

Rundle, who was at Merawi when the Jaalin messenger found him, lost no time. A large amount of ammunition and 1,100 Remington rifles were speedily collected and hurried on camels across the desert by the Korti-Metemma route, escorted by a strong detachment of the Camel Corps. The Khalifa did not receive his letter until the 27th of June. But he acted with even greater promptitude. Part of Mahmud's army had already started for the north. Mahmud and the rest followed on the 28th. On the 30th the advanced guard arrived before Metemma.

The Jaalin prepared to resist desperately. Nearly the whole tribe had responded to the summons of their chief, and more than 2,500 men were collected behind the walls of the town. But in all this force there were only eighty serviceable rifles, and only fifteen rounds of ammunition each. Abdalla expected that the Dervishes would make their heaviest attack on the south side of Metemma, and he therefore disposed his few riflemen along that front. The defence of the rest of the town had perforce to be entrusted to the valour of the spearmen.

On the morning of the 1st of July, Mahmud, with a force variously estimated at 10,000 or 12,000 men, began his assault. The first attack fell, as the chief had anticipated, on the southern face. It was repulsed with severe loss by the Jaalin riflemen. A second attack followed immediately. The enemy had meanwhile surrounded the whole town, and just as the Jaalin ammunition was exhausted a strong force of the Dervishes penetrated the northern face of their defences, which was held only by spearmen. The whole of Mahmud's army poured in through the gap, and the garrison, after a stubborn resistance, were methodically exterminated. An inhuman butchery of the children and some of the women followed. Abdalla-Wad-Saad was among the killed.

A few of the Jaalin who had escaped from the general destruction fled towards Gakdul. Here they found the Camel Corps with their caravan of rifles and ammunition. Like another force that had advanced by this very road to carry succour to men in desperate distress, the relief had arrived too late. The remnants of the Jaalin were left in occupation of Gakdul Wells. The convoy and its escort returned to Korti.

But while the attention of the Khalifa was directed to these matters, a far more serious menace offered from another quarter. Unnoticed by the Dervishes, or, if noticed, unappreciated, the railway was stretching farther and farther into the desert. By the middle of July it had reached the 130th mile, and, as is related in the last chapter, work had to be suspended until Abu Hamed was in the hands of the Egyptian forces. The Nile was rising fast. Very soon steamers would be able to pass the Fourth Cataract. It should have been evident that the next movement in the advance of the 'Turks' impended. The Khalifa seems, indeed, to have understood that the rise of the river increased his peril, for throughout July he continued to send orders to the Emir in Berber—Yunes—that he should advance into the Monassir district, harry such villages as existed, and obstruct the frequent reconnaissances from Merawi. Yunes, however, preferred to do otherwise, and remained on the left bank opposite Berber until, at length, his master recalled him to Omdurman to explain his conduct. Meanwhile, determined with mathematical exactness by the rise of the Nile and progress of the railway, the moment of the Egyptian advance arrived.

At the end of July preparations were made, as secretly as possible, to despatch a flying column against Abu Hamed. The Dervish garrison, under Mohammed-ez-Zein, was not believed to exceed 600 men, but in order that there should be no doubt as to the result it was determined to employ a strong force.

A brigade of all arms was formed as follows:-

Commanding: MAJOR-GENERAL HUNTER

Cavalry	One troop
Artillery	No. 2 Field Battery

[This battery consisted of six Krupp guns, two Maxims, one Gardner gun, and one Nordenfeldt—an effective medley.]

Infantry	MACDONALD'S BRIGADE
	- 3rd Egyptian
	- IXth Soudanese
	- Xth "
	- XIth "

Major-General Sir Archibald Hunter, the officer to whom the operation was entrusted, was from many points of view the most imposing figure in the Egyptian army. He had served through the Nile Expedition of 1884-85, with some distinction, in the Khedive's service. Thenceforward his rise was rapid, even for an Egyptian officer, and in ten years he passed through all the grades from Captain to Major-General. His promotion was not, however, undeserved. Foremost in every action, twice wounded—once at the head of his brigade—always distinguished for valour and conduct, Hunter won the admiration of his comrades and superiors. During the River War he became, in spite of his hard severity, the darling of the Egyptian Army. All the personal popularity which great success might have brought to the Sirdar focussed itself on his daring, good-humoured subordinate, and it was to Hunter that the soldiers looked whenever there was fighting to be done. The force now placed under his command for the attack upon Abu Hamed amounted to about 3,600 men. Until that place was taken all other operations were delayed. The Sirdar awaited the issue at Merawi. The railway paused in mid-desert.

The troops composing the 'flying column' concentrated at Kassingar, a small village a few miles above Merawi, on the right (or Abu Hamed) bank of the Nile. General Hunter began his march on the 29th of July. The total distance from Kassingar to Abu Hamed is 146 miles. The greatest secrecy had been observed in the preparation of the force, but it was known that as soon as the column actually started the news would be carried to the enemy. Speed was therefore essential; for if the Dervish garrison in Abu Hamed were reinforced from Berber, the flying column might not be strong enough to take the village. On the other hand, the great heat and the certainty that the troops would have to fight an action at the end of the march imposed opposite considerations on the commander. To avoid the sun, the greater part of the distance was covered at night. Yet the advantage thus gained was to some extent neutralised by the difficulty of marching over such broken ground in the darkness.

Throughout the whole length of the course of the Nile there is no more miserable wilderness than the Monassir Desert. The stream of the river is broken and its channel obstructed by a great confusion of boulders, between and among which the water rushes in dangerous cataracts. The sandy waste approaches the very brim, and only a few palm-trees, or here and there a squalid mud hamlet, reveal the existence of life. The line of advance lay along the river; but no road relieved the labour of the march. Sometimes trailing across a broad stretch of white sand, in which the soldiers sank to their ankles, and which filled their boots with a rasping grit; sometimes winding over a pass or through a gorge of sharp-cut rocks, which, even in the moonlight, felt hot with the heat of the previous day—always in a long, jerky, and interrupted procession of men and camels, often in single file—the column toiled painfully like the serpent to whom it was said, 'On thy belly shalt thou go, and dust shalt thou eat.'

The column started at 5.30 in the evening, and by a march of sixteen and a half miles reached Mushra-el-Obiad at about midnight. Here a convenient watering-place, not commanded by the opposite bank, and the shade of eight or ten thorny bushes afforded the first suitable bivouac. At 3.30 P.M. on the 30th the march was continued eight and a half miles to a spot some little distance beyond Shebabit. The pace was slow, and the route stony and difficult. It was after dark when the halting-place was reached. Several of the men strayed from the column, wandered in the gloom, and reached the bivouac exhausted. General Hunter had proposed to push on the next day to Hosh-el-Geref, but the fatigues of his troops in the two night marches had already been severe, and as, after Abu Haraz, the track twisted away from the river so that there was no water for five miles, he resolved to halt for the day and rest. Hosh-el-Geref was therefore not reached until the 1st of August—a day later than had been expected; but the rest had proved of such benefit to the troops that the subsequent acceleration of progress fully compensated for the delay. The column moved on again at midnight and halted at daybreak at Salmi. In the small hours of the next morning the march was resumed. The road by the Nile was found too difficult for the Maxim guns, which were on wheels, and these had to make a detour of twenty-eight miles into the desert while the infantry moved ten miles along the river. In order that the Maxims should not arrive alone at Dakfilli, General Hunter had marched thither with the IXth Soudanese at 11 P.M. on the previous day. The rest of the column followed a few hours later. On the 4th, by an eighteen-mile march through deep sand, El Kab was reached. A single shot was fired from the opposite bank of the river as the cavalry patrol entered the village; and there was no longer any doubt that the Dervishes knew of the advance of the column. Both the troops and the transport were now moving admirably; nevertheless, their sufferings were severe.

The nights were consumed in movement. Without shade the soldiers could not sleep by day. All ranks wearied, and the men would frequently, during the night marches, sink down upon the ground in profound slumber, only to be sternly aroused and hurried on. But the pace of the advance continued to be swift. On the 5th, the force, by a fourteen-mile march, reached Khula. Here they were joined by Sheikh Abdel-Azim with 150 Ababda camel-men from Murat Wells. Up to this point three Egyptians had died and fifty-eight men had been left behind exhausted in depots. A double ration of meat was issued to the whole force. The column moved on during the night, and arrived at Ginnifab at 8 A.M. on the morning of the 6th. Here startling news of the enemy was received. It was known that Mohammed-ez-Zein was determined to fight, and a trustworthy report was now received that a large force was coming down from Berber to support the Abu Hamed garrison. In spite of the long marches and the fatigues of the troops, General Hunter resolved to hurry on. He had already made up the day spent at Abu Haraz. He now decided to improve on the prescribed itinerary, accelerate his own arrival and anticipate that of the Dervish reinforcements. Accordingly the troops marched all through the night of the 6-7th with only a short halt of an hour and a half, so as to attack Abu Hamed at dawn. After covering sixteen miles of bad ground, the 'flying column' reached Ginnifab, 144 miles from Kassingar and only two from the Dervish post, at 3.30 on the morning of the 7th of August. A halt of two hours was allowed for the troops to prepare themselves. Half the 3rd Egyptian Battalion remained as escort to the transport and reserve ammunition, and then the force moved off in the darkness towards the enemy's position.

The village of Abu Hamed straggles along the bank of the Nile, and consists of a central mass of mud houses, intersected by a network of winding lanes and alleys, about 500 yards long by perhaps 100 yards wide. To the north and south are detached clusters of ruined huts, and to the south there rises a large, ragged pile of rocks. The ground slopes gradually up from the river, so that at a distance of 300 yards the village is surrounded on three sides by a low plateau. Upon this plateau stand three stone watch-towers, which were erected by General Gordon. The Dervish garrison were strongly posted in shelter trenches and loop-holed houses along the eastern face of the village. The towers were held by their outposts.

Making a wide circuit to their left, and then swinging round to the right, so as to front facing the river, the brigade silently moved towards the enemy's position, and at a quarter past six occupied the plateau in a crescent-shaped formation; the XIth Soudanese on the right, opposite the north-east corner of the village; the battery, escorted by the remaining half-battalion of the 3rd Egyptians, next; then the IXth in the centre, and the Xth Soudanese on the left flank. As the troops approached the watch-towers the Dervish outposts fell back and the force continued to advance until the edge of the plateau was reached. From here the whole scene was visible.

The day was just breaking, and the mist hung low and white over the steel-grey surface of the river. The outlines of the mud houses were sharply defined on this pale background. The Dervish riflemen crouched in the shelter trench that ran round the village. Their cavalry, perhaps a hundred strong, were falling in hurriedly on the sandy ground to the south near the ragged rocks. The curve of the hills, crowned with the dark line of the troops, completed and framed the picture. Within this small amphitheatre one of the minor dramas of war was now to be enacted.

At half past six the battery came into action, and after a few shells had been fired at the loopholed houses in the left centre of the position, a general advance was ordered. In excellent order the three Soudanese battalions, with General Hunter, Lieut.-Colonel MacDonald, and the other British officers on horseback in front of their line, advanced slowly down the hill, opening a destructive fire on the entrenchment. The distance was scarcely three hundred yards; but the crescent formation of the attack made the lines of advance converge, and before half the distance was covered the Xth were compelled to halt, lest the XIth Soudanese on the right flank should fire into them. The Dervishes remained silent until the troops were within a hundred yards, when they discharged two tremendous volleys, which were chiefly effective upon the halted battalion. Major Sidney, Lieutenant Fitzclarence, and a dozen men were shot dead. More than fifty men were wounded. All the Soudanese thereupon with a loud shout rushed upon the entrenchment, stormed it, and hunted the Dervishes into the houses. In the street-fighting which followed, the numbers of the troops prevailed. The advance scarcely paused until the river bank was reached, and by 7.30 Abu Hamed was in the possession of the Egyptian forces.

The Dervish horsemen, who had remained spectators near the southern crag during the attack, fled towards Berber as soon as they saw the attack successful. Scarcely any of the infantry escaped.

In this action, besides the two British officers, Major H. M. Sidney and Lieutenant E. Fitzclarence, 21 native soldiers were killed; 61 native soldiers were wounded.

The news of the capture of Abu Hamed was carried swiftly by camel and wire to all whom it might concern. The Sirdar, anticipating the result, had already ordered the gunboats to commence the passage of the Fourth Cataract. The camp at Railhead sprang to life after an unaccustomed rest, and the line began again to grow rapidly. The Dervishes who were hurrying from Berber were only twenty miles from Abu Hamed when they met the fugitives. They immediately turned back, and retired to the foot of the Fifth Cataract, whence after a few days' halt they continued their retreat. Their proximity to the captured village shows how little time the column had to spare, and that General Hunter was wise to press his marches. The Emir who commanded at Berber heard of the loss of the outpost on the 9th. He sent the messenger on to Metemma. Mahmud replied on the 11th that he was starting at once with his whole army to reinforce Berber. Apparently, however, he did not dare to move without the Khalifa's permission; for his letters, as late as the 20th, show that he had not broken his camp, and was still asking the Emir for information as to the doings of the 'Turks.' Of a truth there was plenty to tell.

On the 4th of August the gunboats El Teb and Tamai approached the Fourth Cataract to ascend to the Abu Hamed-Berber reach of the river. Major David was in charge of the operation. Lieutenants Hood and Beatty (Royal Navy) commanded the vessels. Two hundred men of the 7th Egyptians were towed in barges to assist in hauling the steamers in the difficult places. The current was, however, too strong, and it was found necessary to leave three barges, containing 160 soldiers, at the foot of the rapids. Nevertheless, as the cataract was not considered a very formidable barrier, Major David determined to make the attempt. Early on the 5th, therefore, the Tamai tried the ascent. About 300 local Shaiggia tribesmen had been collected, and their efforts were directed—or, as the result proved, mis-directed—by those few of the Egyptian soldiers who had not been left behind. The steamer, with her engines working at full speed, succeeded in mounting half the distance. But the rush of water was then so great that her bows were swept round, and, after a narrow escape of capsizing, she was carried swiftly down the stream.

The officers thought that this failure was due to the accidental fouling of a rope at a critical moment, and to the fact that there were not enough local tribesmen pulling at the hawsers. Four hundred more Shaiggia were therefore collected from the neighbouring villages, and in the afternoon the Teb attempted the passage. Her fortunes were far worse than those of the Tamai. Owing to the lack of co-operation and discipline among the local tribesmen, their utter ignorance of what was required of them, and the want of proper supervision, the hauling power was again too weak. Again the bows of the steamer were swept round, and, as the hawsers held, a great rush of water poured over the bulwarks. In ten seconds the Teb heeled over and turned bottom upwards. The hawsers parted under this new strain, and she was swept down stream with only her keel showing. Lieutenant Beatty and most of the crew were thrown, or glad to jump, into the foaming water of the cataract, and, being carried down the river, were picked up below the rapids by the Tamai, which was luckily under steam. Their escape was extraordinary, for of the score who were flung into the water only one Egyptian was drowned. Two other men were, however, missing, and their fate seemed certain. The capsized steamer, swirled along by the current, was jammed about a mile below the cataract between two rocks, where she became a total wreck. Anxious to see if there was any chance of raising her, the officers proceeded in the Tamai to the scene. The bottom of the vessel was just visible above the surface. It was evident to all that her salvage would be a work of months. The officers were about to leave the wreck, when suddenly a knocking was heard within the hull. Tools were brought, a plate was removed, and there emerged, safe and sound from the hold in which they had been thus terribly imprisoned, the second engineer and a stoker. When the rapidity with which the steamer turned upside down, with the engines working, the fires burning, and the boilers full—the darkness, with all the floors become ceilings—the violent inrush of water—the wild career down the stream—are remembered, it will be conceded that the experience of these men was sufficiently remarkable.

Search was now made for another passage. This was found on the 6th, nearer the right bank of the river. On the 8th the Metemma arrived with 300 more men of the 7th Egyptians. Three days were spent in preparations and to allow the Nile to rise a little more. On the 13th, elaborate precautions being observed, the Metemma passed the cataract safely, and was tied up to the bank on the higher reach. The Tamai followed the next day. On the 19th and 20th the new gunboats Fateh, Naser, and Zafir, the most powerful vessels on the river, accomplished the passage. Meanwhile the Metemma and Tamai had already proceeded up stream. On the 23rd the unarmed steamer Dal made the ascent, and by the 29th the whole flotilla reached Abu Hamed safely.

After the arrival of the gunboats events began to move at the double. The sudden dart upon Abu Hamed had caused the utmost consternation among the Dervishes. Finding that Mahmud was not going to reinforce him, and fearing the treachery of the local tribes, Zeki Osman, the Emir in Berber, decided to fall back, and on the 24th he evacuated Berber and marched south. On the 27th General Hunter at Abu Hamed heard that the Dervish garrison had left the town. The next day he despatched Abdel-Azim, the chief of Irregulars, and Ahmed Bey Khalifa, his brother, with forty Ababda tribesmen, to reconnoitre. These bold fellows pushed on recklessly, and found the inhabitants everywhere terrified or acquiescent. Spreading extraordinary tales of the strength of the army who were following them, they created a panic all along the river, and, in spite of a sharp fight with a Dervish patrol, reached Berber on the 31st. As there was no armed force in the town, the enterprising allies rode into the streets and occupied the grain store—the only public building—in the name of the Government. They then sent word back to Abu Hamed of what they had done, and sat down in the town, thus audaciously captured, to await developments.

The astonishing news of the fall of Berber reached General Hunter on the 2nd of September. He immediately telegraphed to Merawi. Sir Herbert Kitchener was confronted with a momentous question: should Berber be occupied or not? It may at first seem that there could be little doubt about the matter. The objective of the expedition was Omdurman. The occupation of Berber by an Egyptian garrison would settle at once the difficulties near Suakin. The town was believed to be on the clear waterway to the Dervish capital. The moral effect of its capture upon the riverain tribes and throughout the Soudan would be enormous. Berber was, in fact, the most important strategic point on the whole line of advance. This great prize and advantage was now to be had for the asking.

The opposite considerations were, however, tremendous. Abu Hamed marked a definite stage in the advance. As long as Merawi and the other posts in Dongola were strongly held, the line from Abu Hamed to Debba was capable of easy defence. Abu Hamed could soon be made impregnable to Dervish attack. The forces in Dongola could be quickly concentrated on any threatened point. At this moment in the campaign it was possible to stop and wait with perfect safety. In the meantime the Khalifa would steadily weaken and the railway might steadily grow. When the line reached the angle of the river, it would be time to continue the systematic and cautious advance. Until then prudence and reason counselled delay. To occupy Berber was to risk much. Mahmud, with a large and victorious army, lay at Metemma. Osman Digna, with 2,000 men, held Adarama almost within striking distance. The railway still lagged in the desert. The Dongola garrisons must be weakened to provide a force for Berber. The Dervishes had the advantage of occupying the interior of the angle which the Nile forms at Abu Hamed. The troops in Berber would have to draw their supplies by a long and slender line of camel communication, winding along all the way from Merawi, and exposed, as a glance at the map will show, throughout its whole length to attack. More than all this: to advance to Berber must inevitably force the development of the whole war. The force in the town would certainly have its communications threatened, would probably have to fight for its very existence. The occupation of Berber would involve sooner or later a general action; not a fight like Firket, Hafir, or Abu Hamed, with the advantage of numbers on the side of the Egyptian troops, but an even battle. For such a struggle British troops were necessary. At this time it seemed most unlikely that they would be granted. But if Berber was occupied, the war, until the arrival of British troops, would cease to be so largely a matter of calculation, and must pass almost entirely into the sphere of chance. The whole situation was premature and unforeseen. The Sirdar had already won success. To halt was to halt in safety; to go on was to go on at hazard. Most of the officers who had served long in the Egyptian army understood the question. They waited the decision in suspense.

The Sirdar and the Consul-General unhesitatingly faced the responsibility together. On the 3rd of September General Hunter received orders to occupy Berber. He started at once with 350 men of the IXth Soudanese on board the gunboats Tamai, Zafir, Naser, and Fateh. Shortly after daybreak on the 5th the Egyptian flag was hoisted over the town. Having disembarked the infantry detachment, the flotilla steamed south to try to harass the retreating Emir. They succeeded; for on the next day they caught him, moving along the bank in considerable disorder, and, opening a heavy fire, soon drove the mixed crowd of fugitives, horse and foot, away from the river into the desert. The gunboats then returned to Berber, towing a dozen captured grain-boats. Meanwhile the Sirdar had started for the front himself. Riding swiftly with a small escort across the desert from Merawi, he crossed the Nile at the Baggara Cataract and reached Berber on the 10th of September. Having inspected the immediate arrangements for defence, he withdrew to Abu Hamed, and there busily prepared to meet the developments which he well knew might follow at once, and must follow in the course of a few months.

CHAPTER X:

BERBER

The town of Berber stands at a little distance from the Nile, on the right bank of a channel which is full only when the river is in flood. Between this occasional stream and the regular waterway there runs a long strip of rich alluvial soil, covered during the greater part of the year with the abundant crops which result from its annual submersion and the thick coating of Nile mud which it then receives. The situation of Berber is fixed by this fertile tract, and the houses stretch for more than seven miles along it and the channel by which it is caused. The town, as is usual on the Nile, is comparatively narrow, and in all its length it is only at one point broader than three-quarters of a mile. Two wide streets run longitudinally north and south from end to end, and from these many narrow twisting alleys lead to the desert or the river. The Berber of Egyptian days lies in ruins at the southern end of the main roads. The new town built by the Dervishes stands at the north. Both are foul and unhealthy; and if Old Berber is the more dilapidated, New Berber seemed to the British officers who visited it to be in a more active state of decay. The architectural style of both was similar. The houses were constructed by a simple method. A hole was dug in the ground. The excavated mud formed the walls of the building. The roof consisted of palm-leaves and thorn bushes. The hole became a convenient cesspool. Such was Berber, and this 'emporium of Soudan trade,' as it has been called by enthusiasts, contained at the time of its recapture by the Egyptian forces a miserable population of 5,000 males and 7,000 females, as destitute of property as their dwellings were of elegance.

The Egyptian garrison of Berber at first consisted only of the 350 men of the IXth Soudanese, and two companies of the Camel Corps, who arrived on the 16th of September, having marched across the desert from Merawi.

But the proximity of Osman Digna at Adarama made it necessary speedily to strengthen the force.

During the latter part of September MacDonald's brigade, with the exception of half the 3rd Egyptians, was moved south from Abu Hamed, and by the end of the month the infantry in Berber were swollen to three and a half battalions. This was further increased on the 11th of October by the arrival of the XIIIth Soudanese and the remaining half of the 3rd Egyptians, and thereafter the place was held by five battalions (3rd, IXth, Xth, XIth, XIIIth), No. 2 Field Battery, and two companies of the Camel Corps. As all the Dervishes on the right bank of the Nile had fled to the south of the Atbara, it was found possible to establish a small advanced post of Camel Corps and friendly Arabs in the village of Dakhila, at the confluence of the rivers. From this humble beginning the Atbara fort with its great entrenchment was soon to develop.

The effect of the occupation of Berber upon the tribes around Suakin was decisive, and the whole country between these towns became at once tranquil and loyal. Osman Digna's influence was destroyed. The friendly villages were no longer raided. The Governor of the town became in reality, as well as in name, the Governor of the Red Sea Littoral. The route from Suakin to Berber was opened; and a Camel Corps patrol, several small caravans of traders, and a party of war correspondents—who might boast that they were the first Europeans to make the journey for thirteen years—passed safely along it.

It is now necessary to look to the enemy. Had the Khalifa allowed the Emir Mahmud to march north immediately after the destruction of the Dervish outpost in Abu Hamed, the course of the operations would have been very different. Mahmud would certainly have defended Berber with his whole army. The advance of the Expeditionary Force must have been delayed until the Desert Railway reached the river, and probably for another year. But, as the last chapter has described, the sudden seizure of Abu Hamed, the defection of the riverain tribes, and the appearance of the gunboats above the Fourth Cataract persuaded Abdullah that the climax of the war approached, and that he was about to be attacked in his capital. He accordingly devoted himself to his preparations for defence, and forbade his lieutenant to advance north of Metemma or attempt any offensive operations. In consequence Berber fell, and its fall convinced the Khalifa that his belief was well founded. He worked with redoubled energy. An elaborate system of forts armed with artillery was constructed outside the great wall of Omdurman along the river-bank. The concentration of Arab and black soldiery from Gedaref, Kordofan, and Darfur continued. Large quantities of grain, of camels and other supplies, were requisitioned from the people of the Ghezira (the country lying between the Blue and White Niles) and stored or stabled in the city. The discontent to which this arbitrary taxation gave rise was cured by a more arbitrary remedy. As many of the doubtful and embittered tribesmen as could be caught were collected in Omdurman, where they were compelled to drill regularly, and found it prudent to protest their loyalty. The strength and tenacity of the ruler were surprisingly displayed. The Khalifa Sherif, who had been suspected of sympathising with the Jaalin, was made a prisoner at large. The direst penalties attended the appearance of sedition. A close cordon around the city, and especially towards the north, prevented much information from reaching the Egyptian troops; and though small revolts broke out in Kordofan in consequence of the withdrawal of Mahmud's army, the Dervish Empire as a whole remained submissive, and the Khalifa was able to muster all its remaining force to meet the expected onslaught of his enemies.

During the first week in October the Sirdar decided to send the gunboats—which now plied, though with some difficulty, up and down the Fifth Cataract—to reconnoitre Metemma and discover the actual strength and position of Mahmud's army. On the 14th the Zafir, Fateh, and Naser steamed south from Berber, under Commander Keppel, each carrying, besides its ordinary native crew, fifty men of the IXth Soudanese and two British sergeants of Marine Artillery. Shortly after daybreak on the 16th the flotilla approached the enemy's position. So silently had they moved that a small Dervish outpost a few miles to the north of Shendi was surprised still sleeping, and the negligent guards, aroused by a splutter of firing from the Maxim guns, awoke to find three terrible machines close upon them. The gunboats pursued their way, and, disdaining a few shots which were fired from the ruins of Shendi, arrived, at about seven o'clock, within range of Metemma. The town itself stood more than a thousand yards from the Nile, but six substantial mud forts, armed with artillery, lined and defended the riverside. Creeping leisurely forward along the east bank, remote from the Dervish works, the flotilla came into action at a range of 4,000 yards. The fire was at first concentrated on the two northern forts, and the shells, striking the mud walls in rapid succession or bursting in the interior, soon enveloped them in dust and smoke. The Dervishes immediately replied, but the inferiority of their skill and weapons was marked, and, although their projectiles reached the flotilla, very few took effect. One shell, however, crashed through the deck of the Zafir, mortally wounding a Soudanese soldier, and two struck the Fateh. After the long-range bombardment had continued for about an hour the gunboats moved forward opposite to the enemy's position, and poured a heavy and continuous fire of shrapnel and double shell into all the forts, gradually subduing their resistance. The fugitives from the batteries, and small parties of Baggara horse who galloped about on the open plain between the works and the town, afforded good targets to the Maxims, and many were licked up even at extreme ranges.

No sooner had the gunboats passed the forts than the Dervish fire ceased entirely, and it was discovered that their embrasures only commanded the northern approach. As the guns could not be pointed to the southward, the flotilla need fear nothing from any fort that had been left behind. The officers were congratulating themselves on the folly of their foes, when danger threatened from another quarter. The boats had hugged the eastern bank as closely as possible during their duel with the forts. They were scarcely a hundred yards from the shore, when suddenly a sharp fire of musketry was opened from twenty or thirty Dervish rifle-men concealed in the mimosa scrub. The bullets pattered all over the decks, but while many recorded narrow escapes no one was actually hit, and the Maxim guns, revolving quickly on their pivots, took a bloody vengeance for the surprise. The flotilla then steamed slowly past the town, and, having thoroughly reconnoitred it, turned about and ran down stream, again exchanging shells with the Dervish artillery. All firing ceased at half-past two; but six sailing-boats containing grain were captured on the return voyage, and with these the gunboats retired in triumph to a small island six miles north of Metemma, where they remained for the night.

It being now known that bombarding the Dervishes was no less enjoyable than exciting, it was determined to spend another day with them; and at four o'clock the next morning the flotilla again steamed southward, so as to be in position opposite Metemma before daylight. Fire was opened on both sides with the dawn, and it was at once evident that the Dervishes had not been idle during the night. It appeared that on the previous day Mahmud had expected a land attack from the direction of Gakdul, and had placed part of his artillery and nearly all his army in position to resist it. But as soon as he was convinced that the gunboats were unsupported he moved several of the landward guns into the river forts, and even built two new works, so that on the 17th the Dervishes brought into action eleven guns, firing from eight small round forts. The gunboats, however, contented themselves with keeping at a range at which their superior weapons enabled them to strike without being struck, and so, while inflicting heavy loss on their enemies, sustained no injury themselves. After four hours' methodical and remorseless bombardment Commander Keppel considered the reconnaissance complete, and gave the order to retire down stream. The Dervish gunners, elated in spite of their losses by the spectacle of the retreating vessels, redoubled their fire, and continued hurling shell after shell in defiance down the river until their adversaries were far beyond their range. As the gunboats floated northward their officers, looking back towards Metemma, saw an even stranger scene than the impotent but exulting forts. During the morning a few flags and figures had been distinguished moving about the low range of sandhills near the town; and as soon as the retirement of the flotilla began, the whole of the Dervish army, at least 10,000 men, both horse and foot, and formed in an array more than a mile in length, marched triumphantly into view, singing, shouting, and waving their banners amid a great cloud of dust. It was their only victory.

The loss on the gunboats was limited to the single Soudanese soldier, who died of his wounds, and a few trifling damages. The Arab slaughter is variously estimated, one account rating it at 1,000 men; but half that number would probably be no exaggeration. The gunboats fired in the two days' bombardment 650 shells and several thousand rounds of Maxim-gun ammunition. They then returned to Berber, reporting fully on the enemy's position and army.

As soon as Berber had been strongly occupied by the Egyptian troops, Osman Digna realised that his position at Adarama was not only useless but very dangerous. Mahmud had long been imperiously summoning him to join the forces at Metemma; and although he hated the Kordofan general, and resented his superior authority, the wary and cunning Osman decided that in this case it would be convenient to obey and make a virtue of necessity. Accordingly about the same time that the gunboats were making their first reconnaissance and bombardment of Metemma, he withdrew with his two thousand Hadendoa from Adarama, moved along the left bank of the Atbara until the tongue of desert between the rivers became sufficiently narrow for it to be crossed in a day, and so made his way by easy stages to Shendi.

When the Sirdar heard of the evacuation of Adarama he immediately determined to assure himself of the fact, to reconnoitre the unmapped country in that region, and to destroy any property that Osman might have left behind him. On the 23rd of October, therefore, a flying column started from Berber under the command of General Hunter, and formed as follows: XIth Soudanese (Major Jackson), two guns, one company of the Camel Corps, and Abdel-Azim and 150 irregulars. Lightly equipped, and carrying the supplies on a train of 500 camels, the small force moved rapidly along the Nile and reached the post at the confluence on the 24th, and arrived at Adarama on the 29th, after a journey of eighty-four miles. The report that Osman Digna had returned to the Nile proved to be correct. His former headquarters were deserted, and although a patrol of sixty of the Camel Corps and the Arab irregulars scouted for forty miles further up the river, not a single Dervish was to be seen. Having thus collected a great deal of negative information, and delaying only to burn Adarama to the ground, the column returned to Berber.

It was now November. The Nile was falling fast, and an impassable rapid began to appear at Um Tiur, four miles north of the confluence. The Sirdar had a few days in which to make up his mind whether he would keep his gunboats on the upper or lower reach. As in the latter case their patrolling limits would have been restricted, and they would no longer have been able to watch the army at Metemma, he determined to leave them on the enemy's side of the obstruction. This involved the formation of a depot at Dakhila ['Atbara Fort'], where simple repairs could be executed and wood and other necessities stored. To guard this little dockyard half the 3rd Egyptian battalion was moved from Berber and posted in a small entrenchment. The other half-battalion followed in a few weeks. The post at the confluence was gradually growing into the great camp of a few months later.

A regular system of gunboat patrolling was established on the upper reach, and on the 1st of November the Zafir, Naser, and Metemma, under Commander Keppel, again steamed south to reconnoitre Mahmud's position. The next day they were joined by the Fateh, and on the 3rd the three larger boats ran the gauntlet of the forts. A brisk artillery duel ensued, but the Dervish aim was, as usual, erratic, and the vessels received no injury. It was observed that the position of the Dervish force was unchanged, but that three new forts had been constructed to the south of the town. The gunboats continued on their way and proceeded as far as Wad Habeshi. The Arab cavalry kept pace with them along the bank, ready to prevent any landing. Having seen all there was to be seen, the flotilla returned and again passed the batteries at Metemma. But this time they were not unscathed, and a shell struck the Fateh, slightly wounding three men.

No other incident enlivened the monotony of November. The Khalifa continued his defensive preparations. Mahmud remained motionless at Metemma; and although he repeatedly begged to be allowed to advance against the force near Berber he was steadily refused, and had to content himself with sending raiding parties along the left bank of the Nile, and collecting large stores of grain from all the villages within his reach. Meanwhile the railway was stretching further and further to the south, and the great strain which the sudden occupation of Berber had thrown upon the transport was to some extent relieved. The tranquillity which had followed the advance to Berber was as opportune as it was unexpected. The Sirdar, delighted that no evil consequences had followed his daring move, and finding that he was neither attacked nor harassed in any way, journeyed to Kassala to arrange the details of its retrocession.

The convenient situation of Kassala—almost equally distant from Omdurman, Berber, Suakin, Massowa, and Rosaires—and the fertility of the surrounding region raise it to the dignity of the most important place in the Eastern Soudan. The soil is rich; the climate, except in the rainy season, not unhealthy. A cool night breeze relieves the heat of the day, and the presence of abundant water at the depth of a few feet below the surface supplies the deficiency of a river. In the year 1883 the population is said to have numbered more than 60,000. The Egyptians considered the town of sufficient value to require a garrison of 3,900 soldiers. A cotton mill adequately fitted with machinery and a factory chimney gave promise of the future development of manufacture. A regular revenue attested the existence of trade. But disasters fell in heavy succession on the Eastern Soudan and blighted the prosperity of its mud metropolis. In 1885, after a long siege and a stubborn resistance, Kassala was taken by the Dervishes. The garrison were massacred, enslaved, or incorporated in the Mahdi's army. The town was plundered and the trade destroyed. For nearly ten years an Arab force occupied the ruins and a camp outside them. Kassala became a frontier post of the Dervish Empire. Its population perished or fled to the Italian territory. This situation might have remained unaltered until after the battle of Omdurman if the Dervishes had been content with the possession of Kassala. But in 1893 the Emir in command of the garrison, being anxious to distinguish himself, disobeyed the Khalifa's instructions to remain on the defensive and attacked the Europeans at Agordat. The Arab force of about 8,000 men were confronted by 2,300 Italian troops, protected by strong entrenchments, under Colonel Arimondi. After a fierce but hopeless attack the Dervishes were repulsed with a loss of 3,000 men, among whom was their rash leader. The engagement was, however, as disastrous to Italy as to the Khalifa. The fatal African policy of Signor Crispi received a decided impetus, and in the next year, agreeably to their aspirations in Abyssinia, the Italians under General Baratieri advanced from Agordat and captured Kassala. The occupation was provisionally recognised by Egypt without prejudice to her sovereign rights, and 900 Italian regulars and irregulars established themselves in a well-built fort. The severe defeat at Adowa in 1896, the disgrace of Baratieri, the destruction of his army, and the fall of the Crispi Cabinet rudely dispelled the African ambitions of Italy. Kassala became an encumbrance. Nor was that all. The Dervishes, encouraged by the victory of the Abyssinians, invested the fort, and the garrison were compelled to fight hard to hold what their countrymen were anxious to abandon. In these circumstances the Italian Government offered, at a convenient opportunity, to retrocede Kassala to Egypt. The offer was accepted, and an arrangement made. The advance of the Khedivial forces into the Dongola province relieved, as has been described, the pressure of the Dervish attacks. The Arabs occupied various small posts along the Atbara and in the neighbourhood of the town, and contented themselves with raiding. The Italians remained entirely on the defensive, waiting patiently for the moment when the fort could be handed over to the Egyptian troops.

The Sirdar had no difficulty in coming to a satisfactory arrangement with General Caneva, the Italian commander. The fort was to be occupied by an Egyptian force, the stores and armament to be purchased at a valuation, and a force of Italian Arab irregulars to be transferred to the Egyptian service. Sir H. Kitchener then returned to the Nile, where the situation had suddenly become acute. During November Colonel Parsons, the 16th Egyptian Battalion, and a few native gunners marched from Suakin, and on the 20th of December arrived at Kassala. The Italian irregulars—henceforth to be known as the Arab battalion—were at once despatched to the attack of the small Dervish posts at El Fasher and Asubri, and on the next day these places were surprised and taken with scarcely any loss. The Italian officers, although a little disgusted at the turn of events, treated the Egyptian representatives with the most perfect courtesy, and the formal transference of Kassala fort was arranged to take place on Christmas Day.

An imposing ceremonial was observed, and the scene itself was strange. The fort was oblong in plan, with mud ramparts and parapets pierced for musketry. Tents and stores filled the enclosure. In the middle stood the cotton factory. Its machinery had long since been destroyed, but the substantial building formed the central keep of the fort. The tall chimney had become a convenient lookout post. The lightning-conductor acted as a flagstaff. The ruins of the old town of Kassala lay brown and confused on the plain to the southward, and behind all rose the dark rugged spurs of the Abyssinian mountains. The flags of Egypt and of Italy were hoisted. The troops of both countries, drawn up in line, exchanged military compliments. Then the Egyptian guard marched across the drawbridge into the fort and relieved the Italian soldiers. The brass band of the 16th Battalion played appropriate airs. The Italian flag was lowered, and with a salute of twenty-one guns the retrocession of Kassala was complete.

Here, then, for a year we leave Colonel Parsons and his small force to swelter in the mud fort, to carry on a partisan warfare with the Dervish raiders, to look longingly towards Gedaref, and to nurse the hope that when Omdurman has fallen their opportunity will come. The reader, like the Sirdar, must return in a hurry to the Upper Nile.

Towards the end of November the Khalifa had begun to realise that the Turks did not mean to advance any further till the next flood of the river. He perceived that the troops remained near Berber, and that the railway was only a little way south of Abu Hamed. The blow still impended, but it was delayed. As soon as he had come to this conclusion, he no longer turned a deaf ear to Mahmud's solicitations. He knew that the falling Nile would restrict the movements of the gunboats. He knew that there were only 2,000 men in Berber—a mere handful. He did not realise the tremendous power of rapid concentration which the railway had given his enemies; and he began to think of offensive operations. But Mahmud should not go alone. The whole strength of the Dervish army should be exerted to drive back the invaders. All the troops in Omdurman were ordered north. A great camp was again formed near Kerreri. Thousands of camels were collected, and once more every preparation was made for a general advance. At the beginning of December he sent his own secretary to Mahmud to explain the plan, and to assure him of early reinforcements and supplies. Lastly, Abdullah preached a new Jehad, and it is remarkable that, while all former exhortations had been directed against 'the infidel'—i.e., those who did not believe in the Mahdi—his letters and sermons on this occasion summoned the tribes to destroy not the Egyptians but the Christians. The Khalifa had no doubts as to who inspired the movement which threatened him. There were at this time scarcely 150 Europeans in the Soudan; but they had made their presence felt.

The Sirdar was returning from Kassala when the rumours of an intended Dervish advance began to grow. Every scrap of information was assiduously collected by the Intelligence Department, but it was not until the 18th of December, just as he reached Wady Halfa, that the General received apparently certain news that the Khalifa, Mahmud, all the Emirs, and the whole army were about to march north. There can be no doubt that even this tardy movement of the enemy seriously threatened the success of the operations. If the Dervishes moved swiftly, it looked as if a very critical engagement would have to be fought to avoid a damaging retreat. Sir H. Kitchener's reply to the Khalifa's open intent was to order a general concentration of the available Egyptian army towards Berber, to telegraph to Lord Cromer asking for a British brigade, and to close the Suakin-Berber route.

The gunboat depot at the confluence, with only a half-battalion escort, was now in an extremely exposed position. The gunboats could not steam north, for the cataract four miles below the confluence was already impassable. Since they must remain on the enemy's side, so must their depot; and the depot must be held by a much stronger force. Although the Sirdar felt too weak to maintain himself even on the defensive without reinforcements, he was now compelled to push still further south. On the 22nd of December Lewis's brigade of four battalions and a battery were hurried along the Nile to its junction with the Atbara, and began busily entrenching themselves in an angle formed by the rivers. The Atbara fort sprang into existence.

Meanwhile the concentration was proceeding. All the troops in Dongola, with the exception of scanty garrisons in Merawi, Korti, and Debba, were massed at

Berber. The infantry and guns, dropping down the river in boats, entrained at Kerma, were carried back to Halfa, then hustled across the invaluable Desert Railway, past Abu Hamed, and finally deposited at Railhead, which then (January 1) stood at Dakhesh. The whole journey by rail from Merawi to Dakhesh occupied four days, whereas General Hunter with his flying column had taken eight—a fact which proves that, in certain circumstances which Euclid could not have foreseen, two sides of a triangle are together shorter than the third side. The Egyptian cavalry at Merawi received their orders on the 25th of December, and the British officers hurried from their Christmas dinners to prepare for their long march across the bend of the Nile to Berber. Of the eight squadrons, three were pushed on to join Lewis's force at the position which will hereinafter be called 'the Atbara encampment,' or more familiarly 'the Atbara'; three swelled the gathering forces at Berber; and two remained for the present in the Dongola province, looking anxiously out towards Gakdul Wells and Metemma.

The War Office, who had been nervous about the situation in the Soudan since the hasty occupation of Berber, and who had a very lively recollection of the events of 1884 and 1885, lost no time in the despatch of British troops; and the speed with which a force, so suddenly called for, was concentrated shows the capacity for energy which may on occasion be developed even by our disjointed military organisation. The 1st Battalions of the Royal Warwickshire Regiment, of the Lincoln Regiment, and of the Cameron Highlanders were formed into a brigade and moved from Cairo into the Soudan. The 1st Battalion of the Seaforth Highlanders was brought from Malta to Egypt, and held in immediate readiness to reinforce the troops at the front. Other battalions were sent to take the places of those moved south, so that the Army of Occupation was not diminished.

The officer selected for the command of the British brigade was a man of high character and ability. General Gatacre had already led a brigade in the Chitral expedition, and, serving under Sir Robert Low and Sir Bindon Blood had gained so good a reputation that after the storming of the Malakand Pass and the subsequent action in the plain of Khar it was thought desirable to transpose his brigade with that of General Kinloch, and send Gatacre forward to Chitral. From the mountains of the North-West Frontier the general was ordered to Bombay, and in a stubborn struggle with the bubonic plague, which was then at its height, he turned his attention from camps of war to camps of segregation.

He left India, leaving behind him golden opinions, just before the outbreak of the great Frontier rising, and was appointed to a brigade at Aldershot. Thence we now find him hurried to the Soudan—a spare, middle-sized man, of great physical strength and energy, of marked capacity and unquestioned courage, but disturbed by a restless irritation, to which even the most inordinate activity afforded little relief, and which often left him the exhausted victim of his own vitality.

By the end of January a powerful force lay encamped along the river from Abu Hamed to the Atbara. Meanwhile the Dervishes made no forward movement. Their army was collected at Kerreri; supplies were plentiful; all preparations had been made. Yet they tarried. The burning question of the command had arisen. A dispute that was never settled ensued. When the whole army was regularly assembled, the Khalifa announced publicly that he would lead the faithful in person; but at the same time he arranged privately that many Emirs and notables should beg him not to expose his sacred person. After proper solicitation, therefore, he yielded to their appeals. Then he looked round for a subordinate. The Khalifa Ali-Wad-Helu presented himself. In the Soudan every advantage and honour accrues to the possessor of an army, and the rival chief saw a chance of regaining his lost power. This consideration was not, however, lost upon Abdullah. He accepted the offer with apparent delight, but he professed himself unable to spare any rifles for the army which Ali-Wad-Helu aspired to lead. 'Alas!' he cried, 'there are none. But that will make no difference to so famous a warrior.' Ali-Wad-Helu, however, considered that it would make a great deal of difference, and declined the command. Osman Sheikh-ed-Din offered to lead the army, if he might arm the riverain tribes and use them as auxiliaries to swell his force. This roused the disapproval of Yakub. Such a policy, he declared, was fatal. The riverain tribes were traitors—dogs—worthy only of being destroyed; and he enlarged upon the more refined methods by which his policy might be carried out. The squabble continued, until at last the Khalifa, despairing of any agreement, decided merely to reinforce Mahmud, and accordingly ordered the Emir Yunes to march to Metemma with about 5,000 men. But it was then discovered that Mahmud hated Yunes, and would have none of him. At this the Khalifa broke up his camp, and the Dervish army marched back for a second time, in vexation and disgust, to the city.

It seemed to those who were acquainted with the Dervish movements that all offensive operations on their part had been definitely abandoned. Even in the Intelligence Department it was believed that the break-up of the Kerreri camp was the end of the Khalifa's determination to move north. There would be a hot and uneventful summer, and with the flood Nile the expedition would begin its final advance. The news which was received on the 15th of February came as a great and pleasant surprise. Mahmud was crossing the Nile and proposed to advance on Berber without reinforcements of any kind. The Sirdar, highly satisfied at this astounding piece of good fortune, immediately began to mass his force nearer the confluence. On the 21st the British at Abu Dis were instructed to hold themselves in readiness. The Seaforths began their journey from Cairo, and the various battalions of the Egyptian army pressed forward towards Berber and Atbara fort. On the 25th, Mahmud being reported as having crossed to the right bank, the general concentration was ordered.

CHAPTER XI:

RECONNAISSANCE

Although the story of a campaign is made up of many details which cannot be omitted, since they are essential to the truth as well as the interest of the account, it is of paramount importance that the reader should preserve throughout a general idea. For otherwise the marches, forays, and reconnaissance will seem disconnected and purposeless affairs, and the battle simply a greater operation undertaken in the same haphazard fashion. To appreciate the tale it is less necessary to contemplate the wild scenes and stirring incidents, than thoroughly to understand the logical sequence of incidents which all tend to and ultimately culminate in a decisive trial of strength.

The hazards which were courted by the daring occupation of Berber have been discussed in the last chapter. From October to December the situation was threatening. In December it suddenly became critical. Had the Emir Mahmud advanced with the Dervishes at Metemma even as late as the middle of January, he might possibly have re-captured Berber. If the great Omdurman army had taken the field, the possibility would have become a certainty. The young Kordofan general saw his opportunity, and begged to be allowed to seize it. But it was not until the Khalifa had sent his own army back into the city that, being very badly informed of the numbers and disposition of the Egyptian force, he allowed the Metemma Dervishes to move.

Mahmud received permission to advance at the end of January. He eagerly obeyed the longed-for order. But the whole situation was now changed. The Egyptian army was concentrated; the British brigade had arrived; the railway had reached Geneinetti; the miserable hamlet of Dakhila, at the confluence, had grown from a small depot to a fort, and from a fort to an entrenched camp, against which neither Dervish science nor strength could by any possibility prevail. Perhaps Mahmud did not realise the amazing power of movement that the railway had given his foes; perhaps he still believed, with the Khalifa, that Berber was held only by 2,000 Egyptians; or else—and this is the most probable—he was reckless of danger and strong in his own conceit. At any rate, during the second week in February he began to transport himself across the Nile, with the plain design of an advance north. With all the procrastination of an Arab he crawled leisurely forward towards the confluence of the rivers. At El Aliab some idea of the strength of the Atbara entrenchment seems to have dawned upon him. He paused undecided. A council was held. Mahmud was for a continued advance and for making a direct attack on the enemy's position. Osman Digna urged a more prudent course. Many years of hard fighting against disciplined troops had taught the wily Hadendoa slaver the power of modern rifles, and much sound tactics besides. He pressed his case with jealous enthusiasm upon the commander he detested and despised. An insurmountable obstacle confronted them. Yet what could not be overcome might be avoided. The hardy Dervishes could endure privations which would destroy the soldiers of civilisation. Barren and inhospitable as was the desert, they might move round the army at the Atbara fort and so capture Berber after all. Once they were behind the Egyptians, these accursed ones were lost. The railway—that mysterious source of strength—could be cut. The host that drew its life along it must fight at a fearful disadvantage or perish miserably. Besides, he reminded Mahmud—not without reason—that they could count on help in Berber itself.

The agreement of the Emirs, called to the council, decided the Dervish leader. His confidence in himself was weakened, his hatred of Osman Digna increased. Nevertheless, following the older man's advice, he left Aliab on the 18th of March, and struck north-east into the desert towards the village and ford of Hudi on the Atbara river. Thence by a long desert march he might reach the Nile and Berber. But while his information of the Sirdar's force and movements was uncertain, the British General was better served. What Mahmud failed to derive from spies and 'friendlies,' his adversary obtained by gunboats and cavalry. As soon, therefore, as Sir H. Kitchener learned that the Dervishes had left the Nile and were making a detour around his left flank, he marched up the Atbara river to Hudi. This offered Mahmud the alternative of attacking him in a strong position or of making a still longer detour. Having determined upon caution he chose the latter, and, deflecting his march still more to the east, reached the

Atbara at Nakheila. But from this point the distance to Berber was far too great for him to cover. He could not carry enough water in his skins. The wells were few, and held against him. Further advance was impossible. So he waited and entrenched himself, sorely troubled, but uncertain what to do. Supplies were running short. His magazines at Shendi had been destroyed as soon as he had left the Nile. The Dervishes might exist, but they did not thrive, on the nuts of the dom palms. Soldiers began to desert. Osman Digna, although his advice had been followed, was at open enmity. His army dwindled.

And all this time his terrible antagonist watched him as a tiger gloats on a helpless and certain prey—silent, merciless, inexorable. Then the end came suddenly. As soon as the process of attrition was sufficiently far advanced to demoralise the Dervish host, without completely dissolving them, the Sirdar and his army moved. The victim, as if petrified, was powerless to fly. The tiger crept forward two measured strides—from Ras-el-Hudi to Abadar, from Abadar to Umdabia—crouched for a moment, and then bounded with irresistible fury upon its prey and tore it to pieces.

Such is a brief strategic account of the Atbara campaign; but the tale must be told in full.

On the 23rd of January the Khalifa, having learned of the arrival of British troops near Abu Hamed, and baffled by the disputes about the command of his army, ordered Kerreri camp to be broken up, and permitted his forces to return within the city, which he continued to fortify. A few days later he authorised Mahmud to advance against Berber. What he had not dared with 60,000 men he now attempted with 20,000. The course of action which had for three months offered a good hope of success he resolved to pursue only when it led to ruin. He forbade the advance while it was advisable. When it was already become mad and fatal he commanded it. And this was a man whose reputation for intelligence and military skill had been bloodily demonstrated!

The gunboats ceaselessly patrolled the river, and exchanged shots with the Dervish forts. Throughout January nothing of note had happened. The reports of spies showed the Khalifa to be at Kerreri or in Omdurman. Ahmed Fedil held the Shabluka Gorge, Osman Digna was at Shendi, and his presence was proved by the construction of two new forts on that side of the river. But beyond this the Dervishes had remained passive. On the 12th of February, however, it was noticed that their small outpost at Khulli had been withdrawn. This event seemed to point to a renewal of activity. It was felt that some important movement impended. But it was not until the 15th that its nature was apparent, and the gunboats were able to report definitely that Mahmud was crossing to the east bank of the Nile. The flotilla exerted itself to harass the Dervishes and impede the transportation; but although several sailing-boats and other river craft were captured, Mahmud succeeded in moving his whole army to Shendi by the 28th of February. His own headquarters were established at Hosh-ben-Naga, a little village about five miles further south. A delay of more than a fortnight followed, during which the gunboats exercised the utmost vigilance. The Suakin-Berber road was again closed for caravans, and the Sirdar himself proceeded to Berber. On the 11th of March the remnants of the Jaalin tribe, having collected at Gakdul, re-occupied the now abandoned Metemma, to find its streets and houses choked with the decaying bodies of their relations. On the 13th the Egyptian look-out station, which had been established on Shebaliya island, was attacked by the Dervishes, and in the skirmish that ensued Major Sitwell was wounded. On the same day the enemy were reported moving northwards to Aliab, and it became evident that Mahmud had begun his advance.

He started from Shendi with a force which has been estimated at 19,000 souls, but which included many women and children, and may have actually numbered 12,000 fighting men, each and all supplied with a month's rations and about ninety rounds of ammunition. The Sirdar immediately ordered the Anglo-Egyptian army, with the exception of the cavalry and Lewis's Egyptian brigade—which, with three squadrons, held the fort at the confluence—to concentrate at Kunur. Broadwood, with the remaining five squadrons, marched thither on the 16th; and the whole cavalry force, with the Camel Corps in support, on the three subsequent days reconnoitred twenty miles up the Nile and the Atbara.

Meanwhile the concentration was proceeding apace. The two Soudanese brigades, formed into a division under command of Major-General Hunter, with the artillery, reached Kunur on the night of the 15th. The British brigade—the Lincolns, the Warwicks, and the Camerons—marched thither from Dabeika. The Seaforth Highlanders, who on the 13th were still at Wady Halfa, were swiftly railed across the desert to Geneinetti. Thence the first half-battalion were brought to Kunur in steamers. The second wing—since the need was urgent and the steamers few—were jolted across the desert from Railhead on camels, an experience for which neither their training nor their clothes had prepared them. By the 16th the whole force was concentrated at Kunur, and on the following day they were reviewed by the Sirdar. The first three days at Kunur were days of eager expectation. Rumour was king. The Dervish army had crossed the Atbara at Hudi, and was within ten miles of the camp. Mahmud was already making a flank march through the desert to Berber. A battle was imminent. A collision must take place in a few hours. Officers with field-glasses scanned the sandy horizon for the first signs of the enemy. But the skyline remained unbroken, except by the wheeling dust devils, and gradually the excitement abated, and the British brigade began to regret all the useful articles they had scrupulously left behind them at Dabeika, when they marched in a hurry and the lightest possible order to Kunur.

On the 19th of March the gunboats reported that the Dervishes were leaving the Nile, and Mahmud's flanking movement became apparent. The next day the whole force at Kunur marched across the desert angle between the rivers to Hudi. The appearance of the army would have been formidable. The cavalry, the Camel Corps, and the Horse Artillery covered the front and right flank; the infantry, with the British on the right, moved in line of brigade masses; the transport followed. All was, however, shrouded in a fearful dust-storm. The distance, ten miles, was accomplished in five hours, and the army reached Hudi in time to construct a strong zeriba before the night. Here they were joined from Atbara fort by Lewis's brigade of Egyptians—with the exception of the 15th Battalion, which was left as garrison—and the troops at the Sirdar's disposal were thus raised to 14,000 men of all arms. This force was organised as follows:

Commander-in-Chief: THE SIRDAR

British Brigade: MAJOR-GENERAL GATACRE

    1st Battalion Royal Warwickshire Regiment (6 companies)
    "   "   Lincolnshire Regiment
    "   "   Seaforth Highlanders
    "   "   Cameron Highlanders

Egyptian Infantry Division: MAJOR-GENERAL HUNTER

1st Brigade	2nd Brigade	3rd Brigade
LIEUT.-COL. MAXWELL	LIEUT.-COL. MACDONALD	LIEUT.-COL. LEWIS
8th Egyptians	2nd Egyptians	3rd Egyptians
XIIth Soudanese	IXth Soudanese	4th "
XIIIth "	Xth "	7th "
XIVth "	XIth "	

Cavalry: LIEUT.-COL. BROADWOOD

>8 squadrons
>2 Maxim guns

Camel Corps: MAJOR TUDWAY

>6 companies

Artillery: LIEUT.-COL. LONG

>Detachment, No. 16 Company, E Division R.A., with 6 five-inch B.L. howitzers
>Egyptian Horse Battery (6 guns)
>Nos. 1, 2, and 3 Field Batteries Egyptian Army (18 guns)
>British Maxim Battery (4 guns)
>Rocket Detachment (2 sections)

Mahmud had early intelligence of the movement of the Anglo-Egyptian army. His original intention had been to march to Hudi. But he now learned that at Hudi he would have to fight the Sirdar's main force. Not feeling strong enough to attack them, he determined to march to Nakheila. The mobility of the Arabs was now as conspicuous as their dilatory nature had formerly been. The whole Dervish army—horse, foot, and artillery, men, women, children, and animals—actually traversed in a single day the forty miles of waterless desert which lie between Aliab and Nakheila, at which latter place they arrived on the night of the 20th. The Sirdar's next object was to keep the enemy so far up the Atbara that they could not possibly strike at Berber or Railhead. Accordingly, at dawn on the 21st, the whole force was ordered to march to Ras-el-Hudi, five miles nearer the Dervishes' supposed halting-place. The detour which the Arabs would have to make to march round the troops was nearly doubled by this movement. The utter impossibility of their flank march with a stronger enemy on the radius of the circle was now apparent.

The movement of the Anglo-Egyptian force was screened by seven squadrons of cavalry and the Horse Artillery, and Colonel Broadwood was further instructed to reconnoitre along the river and endeavour to locate the enemy. The country on either bank of the Atbara is covered with dense scrub, impassable for civilised troops. From these belts, which average a quarter of a mile in depth, the dom palms rise in great numbers. All the bush is leafy, and looks very pretty and green by contrast with the sombre vegetation of the Nile. Between the trees fly gay parrots and many other bright birds. The river itself above Ras-el-Hudi is, during March and April, only a dry bed of white sand about 400 yards broad, but dotted with deep and beautifully clear pools, in which peculiarly brilliant fish and crocodiles, deprived of their stream, are crowded together. The atmosphere is more damp than by the Nile, and produces, in the terrible heat of the summer, profuse and exhausting perspiration. The natives dislike the water of the Atbara, and declare that it does not quench the thirst like that of the great river. It has, indeed, a slightly bitter taste, which is a strong contrast with the sweet waters of the Nile. Nevertheless the British soldiers, with characteristic contrariness, declared their preference for it. Outside the bush the ground undulated gently, but the surface was either stony and uneven or else cracked and fissured by the annual overflow. Both these conditions made it hard for cavalry, and still more for artillery, to move freely; and the difficulties were complicated by frequent holes and small khors full of long grass.

Amid such scenes the squadrons moved cautiously forward. Having made the ground good for fifteen miles from Hudi, Colonel Broadwood halted his force at Abadar, an old fort, and sent one squadron under Captain Le Gallais seven miles further. At two o'clock this squadron returned, having met a few of the enemy's scouts, but no formed bodies. While the force watered by turns at the river Captain Baring's squadron was extended in a line of outposts about a mile and a quarter to the south-east. But the reconnoitring squadron had been followed homeward by several hundred Dervish horsemen. Creeping along through the dense bush by the bank and evading the vedettes, these suddenly fell on the picket line and drove in all the outposts. In this affair eight troopers were killed and seven wounded. Thirteen horses were also lost, as, having rid themselves of their riders on the broken ground, they galloped off after the Arab mares on which the Dervishes were mostly mounted.

The news of an attack on Adarama was received on this same afternoon. It appeared that the Arabs had been repulsed by the Abyssinian irregulars raised by Colonel Parsons. Glowing details were forthcoming, but I do not propose to recount the Homeric struggles of the 'friendlies.' Little in them is worthy of remembrance; much seeks oblivion.

For more than a week the Anglo-Egyptian force remained halted at Ras-el-Hudi, waiting for privation to demoralise Mahmud's army or to exasperate him into making an attack. Every morning the cavalry rode out towards the enemy's camp. All day long they skirmished with or watched the Baggara horse, and at night they returned wearily to camp. Each morning the army awoke full of the hopes of battle, waited during the long hours, and finally retired to sleep in deep disgust and profound peace. And while the army halted, the camp began to assume a more homely appearance. The zeriba grew stronger and thicker, the glacis wider, the field kitchens more elaborate, the pools of the Atbara more dirty. Over all the sun beat down in merciless persistence, till all white men quivered with weary suffering when in the open air, and even under the grass huts or improvised tents the temperature always registered 115 degrees during the hottest hours of the day. The nights were, however, cool and pleasant.

But although the main part of the force found the days long and tedious, the time which the army spent at Ras-el-Hudi was by no means uneventful. The work of the squadrons was hard, and ceased only with the night. The continual patrolling told severely on men and horses; and the fact that the Dervishes were far stronger in the mounted arm than the Sirdar's army necessitated the utmost vigilance of the cavalry commander. Employment was also found for the gunboats.

When Mahmud had left the Nile he had established a sort of depot at Shendi, in which the wives of the Emirs and the surplus stores had been deposited. This treasure house was protected only by a slender garrison of 700 riflemen and twenty-five horsemen. On ordinary military grounds, and also since the event might infuriate the Arabs, it was decided to capture this place and disperse its defenders. Accordingly, on the afternoon of the 24th the 3rd Egyptian Battalion from Lewis's brigade marched from Ras-el-Hudi to Atbara fort and relieved the 15th Egyptians then in garrison, and a small force under Commander Keppel—consisting of the 15th Egyptians under Major Hickman, two field-guns of Peake's battery, and 150 Jaalin irregulars—was embarked on, or in boats towed by, the three gunboats Zafir, Naser, and Fateh, and started the same night for Shendi.

At dawn on the 27th the flotilla appeared off Shendi. The Dervishes had been apprised of its approach and prepared to offer resistance. But the force against them was overwhelming. Under cover of the gunboats the infantry and guns were landed. The artillery then came into action, but after they had discharged two shells, the Arabs fled, firing their rifles with little effect. Shendi was occupied by the Egyptians. The pursuit was left to the Jaalin, and in it they are said to have killed 160 men—a revenge which must have been doubly sweet since it was consummated so near to the scene of the destruction of their tribe, and was also attended by scarcely any danger. Loot of all kinds fell to the victors, and the gunboats were soon laden with a miscellaneous spoil. The wives of the important Emirs made their escape to Omdurman, but upwards of 650 women and children of inferior rank were taken prisoners and transported to the Atbara, where in due course they contracted new family ties with the Soudanese soldiery and, as far as can be ascertained, lived happily ever afterwards. There were no casualties among the troops, but the Jaalin lost a few men in their pursuit. The force then returned to the Atbara.

The 3rd of April was the last day the army spent at Ras-el-Hudi. The period of waiting was over. The enemy's position had been duly reconnoitred. His strength was believed to be sufficiently impaired for a successful attack to be made. The camp at Hudi was becoming very insanitary. Moreover, the situation, satisfactory though it was, was not one which the commander could view without anxiety. All the time that the army was operating on the Atbara it drew its supplies from the fort at the confluence. Between this and the camp, convoys, protected only by a handful of Camel Corps, passed once in every four days. Only the idiotic apathy of the Dervishes allowed the communications to remain uninterrupted. Mahmud was strong in cavalry. It will be evident to anyone who looks at the map how easily a force might have moved along the left bank to attack the convoys. Such tactics would have occurred to most savage tribes. But in their last campaigns the Dervishes thought only of battles, and disregarded all smaller enterprises. Had they assailed the communications, the Sirdar might have been forced to build a chain of forts and to guard his convoys with strong infantry escorts. The fighting force would have been weakened, the troops have been wearied, and the result must have been delayed. The Dervishes had as yet attempted nothing. But there was no reason why they should not at any moment become enterprising. It was time to make an end. On the 4th of April the whole force moved to Abadar, and established themselves in a new camp five miles nearer the enemy. The tiger was tired of watching: he had taken his first stride towards his prey.

Although the information as to the enemy's strength and position was accurate and complete, the Sirdar decided to order a final reconnaissance on the 5th of April.

Starting at four o'clock Broadwood cut off the sharp angle which the Atbara forms at Umdabia, and, avoiding the thick bush, soon approached the Dervish camp. Not a sign of the enemy was seen during the march. The bush by the Atbara appeared deserted. The camp gave no sign of life; an ominous silence prevailed. The squadrons moved forward at a walk, keeping about 1,200 yards away from the enemy's zeriba and almost parallel to it. Presently, as they did so, a large force of cavalry became visible in front. It was difficult to estimate their strength, but they appeared to be superior in numbers to the reconnaissance. The Dervish horsemen continued to retire towards the south-east, always reaching round the Egyptian left flank.

And while the Egyptian force advanced, as soon as they were opposite the southern end of the zeriba, another considerable body of Dervish horse issued from the northern side and threatened the line of retreat. At the same time the camp began to swarm with men, and crowds of tiny figures were observed clambering on to the entrenchments and gun emplacements, eagerly watching the development of the fight. The cavalry had by this time approached to within 1,000 yards of the zeriba, and the Arab artillery began to fire occasional round shot and clumsily fused shells.

At nine o'clock, the enemy's position having been again sketched and the approaches reconnoitred, Colonel Broadwood ordered the retirement to begin. The Maxims and artillery were in the centre, supported by Colonel Broadwood and three squadrons. Captain Baring with three squadrons watched the left flank, now in retirement become the right. Captains Le Gallais and Persse guarded the river flank.

The cavalry retired by alternate wings in measured fashion. But the enemy pressed on impetuously, and their horsemen, soon completely enveloping the desert flank of the Egyptians, began to threaten a charge. To meet this Colonel Broadwood sent one of his squadrons from the centre to join those under Captain Baring, so that at about a quarter to ten the reconnoitring force was formed with four squadrons towards the desert, two with the guns, and two towards the river. The weakness of the river flank of the troops encouraged the Dervish horse lurking in the scrub to make a bold attempt to capture the guns. The movement was shrewd and daring, but the cavalry commander met it with admirable skill. The springing-up of dust-clouds hardly 300 yards away was his only warning. He immediately took command of the two squadrons under Persse and Le Gallais, and ordered them to 'right about wheel' and charge. Thus headed by Broadwood himself, and with their British officers several horse-lengths in front, the Egyptians broke into a gallop and encountered the Baggara line, which numbered not fewer than 400 men but was in loose order, with firmness. They struck them obliquely and perhaps a third of the way down their line, and, breaking through, routed them utterly.

While this dashing operation was carried out on the river flank the Dervish cavalry, following up the retirement, also delivered an attack towards the guns. Thereupon Captain Baring with two squadrons galloped from the desert flank across the front of the artillery, and, riding through the advancing enemy, repulsed them with loss. The charge was good and effective, but the shock and confusion broke both squadrons, and, although successful, they came through the Dervishes and back on to the river flank in some disorder. Persse and Le Gallais, who had just rallied, at once dismounted their men and opened carbine fire on the retreating Dervishes. Their action not only checked the enemy, but prevented, by getting the troopers off their horses, any chance of their being involved in the disorder of the squadrons who had just charged.

Although their horsemen were thus sharply checked, the Dervish infantry continued in spite of losses to advance rapidly, and for a few minutes a hot musketry fire was exchanged by the Arab riflemen and the two dismounted squadrons. Captain Persse was severely wounded, and several other casualties occurred. But the whole force was drawing away from the enemy, and by eleven o'clock it had passed through the gap to the north-east and had shaken off all pursuit. The casualties in the operation were fortunately small. One British officer was wounded; six Egyptian troopers were killed and ten wounded; and about thirty horses were lost or disabled.

The details of the enemy's defences were now known; his strength was estimated from trustworthy information. It was evident from the frequent desertions that his army was disheartened, and from his inactivity that he was scarcely hopeful of success. The moment for destroying him had arrived. At daybreak on the morning of the 6th the whole army broke camp at Abadar and marched to the deserted village of Umdabia, where they bivouacked close by a convenient pool of the Atbara and seven miles nearer the Dervish camp.

CHAPTER XII:

THE BATTLE OF THE ATBARA

April 8, 1898

    In the evening of Thursday, the 7th of April, the army at Umdabia paraded for the attack on Mahmud's zeriba. The camp lay in the scrub which grows by the banks of the Atbara, as by those of the Nile, and in order to profit by the open, level ground the four infantry brigades moved by parallel routes into the desert, and then formed facing south-east in column of brigade squares, the British brigade leading. The mounted forces, with four batteries of artillery, waited in camp until two o'clock the next morning, and did not break their march. The distance from the river bank to the open plain was perhaps a mile and a half, and the whole infantry force had cleared the scrub by six o'clock. The sun was setting, and the red glow, brightening the sandy hillocks, made the western horizon indefinite, so that it was hard to tell where the desert ended and the sky began. A few gazelle, intercepted on their way to the water by the unexpected movement of troops, trotted slowly away in the distance—white spots on the rosy-brown of the sand—and on the great plain 12,000 infantry, conscious of their strength and eager to encounter the enemy, were beautifully arranged in four solid masses. Then the march began. The actual distance from the camp to the Dervish position was scarcely seven miles, but the circle necessary to avoid the bushes and the gradual bends of the river added perhaps another five to the length of the road. The pace of the advance was slow, and the troops had not gone far when the sun sank and, with hardly an interval of twilight, darkness enveloped everything. In the stillness of the night the brigades moved steadily forward, and only the regular scrunching of the hard sand betrayed the advance of an overwhelming force upon their enemies.

No operation of a war is more critical than a night-march. Over and over again in every country frightful disaster has overtaken the rash or daring force that has attempted it. In the gloom the shape and aspect of the ground are altered. Places well known by daylight appear strange and unrecognisable. The smallest obstacle impedes the column, which can only crawl sluggishly forward with continual checks and halts. The effect of the gloom upon the nerves of the soldiers is not less than on the features of the country. Each man tries to walk quietly, and hence all are listening for the slightest sound. Every eye seeks to pierce the darkness. Every sense in the body is raised to a pitch of expectancy. In such hours doubts and fears come unbidden to the brain, and the marching men wonder anxiously whether all will be well with the army, and whether they themselves will survive the event. And if suddenly out of the black silence there burst the jagged glare of rifles and the crash of a volley followed by the yell of an attacking foe, the steadiest troops may be thrown into confusion, and a panic, once afoot, stops only with the destruction or dispersal of the whole force. Nevertheless, so paramount is the necessity of attacking at dawn, with all the day to finish the fight, that in spite of the recorded disasters and the known dangers, the night-march is a frequent operation.

For more than two hours the force advanced, moving across smooth swells of sand broken by rocks and with occasional small bushes. Several shallow khors traversed the road, and these rocky ditches, filled with a strange, sweet-scented grass, delayed the brigades until the pace was hardly two miles an hour. The smell of the grass was noticed by the alert senses of many, and will for ever refresh in their minds the strong impression of the night. The breeze which had sprung up at sundown gradually freshened and raised clouds of fine sand, which deepened the darkness with a whiter mist.

At nine o'clock the army halted in a previously selected space, near the deserted village of Mutrus and about two miles from the river. Nearly half the distance to Mahmud's zeriba was accomplished, and barely four miles in the direct line divided the combatants; but since it was not desirable to arrive before the dawn, the soldiers, still formed in their squares, lay down upon the ground. Meat and biscuits were served out to the men. The transport animals went by relays to the pools of the Atbara bed to drink and to replenish the tanks. All water-bottles were refilled, pickets being thrown out to cover the business. Then, after sufficient sentries had been posted, the army slept, still in array.

During the halt the moon had risen, and when at one o'clock the advance was resumed, the white beams revealed a wider prospect and, glinting on the fixed bayonets, crowned the squares with a sinister glitter. For three hours the army toiled onwards at the same slow and interrupted crawl. Strict silence was now enforced, and all smoking was forbidden. The cavalry, the Camel Corps, and the five batteries had overtaken the infantry, so that the whole attacking force was concentrated. Meanwhile the Dervishes slept.

At three o'clock the glare of fires became visible to the south, and, thus arrived before the Dervish position, the squares, with the exception of the reserve brigade, were unlocked, and the whole force, assuming formation of attack, now advanced in one long line through the scattered bush and scrub, presently to emerge upon a large plateau which overlooked Mahmud's zeriba from a distance of about 900 yards.

It was still dark, and the haze that shrouded the Dervish camp was broken only by the glare of the watch-fires. The silence was profound. It seemed impossible to believe that more than 25,000 men were ready to join battle at scarcely the distance of half a mile. Yet the advance had not been unperceived, and the Arabs knew that their terrible antagonists crouched on the ridge waiting for the morning; For a while the suspense was prolonged. At last, after what seemed to many an interminable period, the uniform blackness of the horizon was broken by the first glimmer of the dawn. Gradually the light grew stronger until, as a theatre curtain is pulled up, the darkness rolled away, the vague outlines in the haze became definite, and the whole scene was revealed.

The British and Egyptian army lay along the low ridge in the form of a great bow—the British brigade on the left, MacDonald in the centre, Maxwell curving forward on the right. The whole crest of the swell of ground was crowned with a bristle of bayonets and the tiny figures of thousands of men sitting or lying down and gazing curiously before them. Behind them, in a solid square, was the transport, guarded by Lewis's brigade. The leading squadrons of the cavalry were forming leisurely towards the left flank. The four batteries and a rocket detachment, moving between the infantry, ranged themselves on two convenient positions about a hundred yards in front of the line of battalions. All was ready. Yet everything was very quiet, and in the stillness of the dawn it almost seemed that Nature held her breath.

Half a mile away, at the foot of the ridge, a long irregular black line of thorn bushes enclosed the Dervish defences. Behind this zeriba low palisades and entrenchments bent back to the scrub by the river. Odd shapeless mounds indicated the positions of the gun-emplacements, and various casemates could be seen in the middle of the enclosure. Without, the bushes had been cleared away, and the smooth sand stretched in a gentle slope to where the army waited. Within were crowds of little straw huts and scattered bushes, growing thicker to the southward. From among this rose the palm-trees, between whose stems the dry bed of the Atbara was exposed, and a single pool of water gleamed in the early sunlight. Such was Mahmud's famous zeriba, which for more than a month had been the predominant thought in the minds of the troops. It was scarcely imposing, and at first the soldiers thought it deserted. Only a dozen stray horsemen sat silently on their horses outside the entrenchment, watching their enemies, and inside a few dirty-white figures appeared and disappeared behind the parapets. Yet, insignificant as the zeriba looked, the smoke of many fires cooking the morning meal—never to be eaten—showed that it was occupied by men; and gay banners of varied colour and device, flaunting along the entrenchments or within the enclosure, declared that some at least were prepared to die in its defence.

The hush of the hour and the suspense of the army were broken by the bang of a gun. Everyone on the ridge jumped up and looked towards the sound. A battery of Krupps a little to the right of the Cameron Highlanders had opened fire. Another gun further to the right was fired. Another shell burst over the straw huts among the palm-trees. The two Maxim-Nordenfeldt batteries had come into action. The officers looked at their watches. It was a quarter-past six. The bombardment had begun.

Explosion followed explosion in quick succession until all four batteries were busily engaged. The cannonade grew loud and continuous. The rocket detachment began to fire, and the strange projectiles hissed and screamed as they left the troughs and jerked erratically towards the zeriba. In the air above the enclosure shell after shell flashed into existence, smote the ground with its leaden shower, and dispersed—a mere film—into the haze and smoke which still hung over the Dervish encampment. At the very first shot all the dirty-white figures disappeared, bobbing down into their pits and shelters; but a few solitary horsemen remained motionless for a while in the middle of the enclosure, watching the effect of the fire, as if it had no concern with them. The British infantry stood up on tip-toe to look at the wonderful spectacle of actual war, and at first every shell was eagerly scrutinised and its probable effect discussed. But the busy gunners multiplied the projectiles until so many were alive in the air at once that all criticism was prevented. Gradually even the strange sight became monotonous. The officers shut up their glasses. The men began to sit down again. Many of them actually went to sleep. The rest were soon tired of the amazing scene, the like of which they had never looked on before, and awaited impatiently further developments and 'some new thing.'

After the bombardment had lasted about ten minutes a great cloud of dust sprang up in the zeriba, and hundreds of horsemen were seen scrambling into their saddles and galloping through a gap in the rear face out into the open sand to the right. To meet the possibility of an attempt to turn the left flank of the attack, the eight squadrons of cavalry and two Maxim guns jingled and clattered off in the direction of the danger. The dust, which the swift passage of so many horsemen raised, shut the scene from the eyes of the infantry, but continual dust-clouds above the scrub to the left and the noise of the Maxims seemed to indicate a cavalry fight. The Baggara horse, however, declined an unequal combat, and made no serious attempt to interfere with the attack. Twice they showed some sort of front, and the squadrons thought they might find opportunity to charge; but a few rounds from the Maxims effectually checked the enemy, inflicting on each occasion the loss of about twenty killed and wounded. With the exception of one squadron detached on the right, the Egyptian cavalry force, however, remained on the left flank, and shielded the operations of the assaulting infantry.

Meanwhile the bombardment—no longer watched with curiosity—continued with accuracy and precision. The batteries searched the interior of the zeriba, threshing out one section after another, and working the whole ground regularly from front to rear. The zeriba and palisades were knocked about in many places, and at a quarter to seven a cluster of straw huts caught fire and began to burn briskly. At a quarter-past seven the infantry were ordered to form in column for assault.

The plan of the attack for the army was simple. The long, deployed line were to advance steadily against the entrenchments, subduing by their continual fire that of the enemy. They were then to tear the zeriba to pieces. Covered by their musketry, the dense columns of assault which had followed the line were to enter the defences through the gaps, deploy to the right, and march through the enclosure, clearing it with the bayonet and by fire.

At twenty minutes to eight the Sirdar ordered his bugles to sound the general advance. The call was repeated by all the brigades, and the clear notes rang out above the noise of the artillery. The superior officers—with the exception of Hunter, Maxwell, and MacDonald—dismounted and placed themselves at the head of their commands. The whole mass of the infantry, numbering nearly eleven thousand men, immediately began to move forward upon the zeriba. The scene as this great force crested the ridge and advanced down the slope was magnificent and tremendous. Large solid columns of men, preceded by a long double line, with the sunlight flashing on their bayonets and displaying their ensigns, marched to the assault in regular and precise array. The pipes of the Highlanders, the bands of the Soudanese, and the drums and fifes of the English regiments added a wild and thrilling accompaniment. As soon as the advance masked the batteries, the guns were run forward with the firing line, in order effectually to support the attack. The deployed battalions opened a ceaseless and crushing fire on the entrenchment, and as the necessity of firing delayed the advance of the attacking columns, the pace did not exceed a slow march.

The Dervishes remained silent until the troops were within 300 yards. Then the smoke-puffs spurted out all along the stockades, and a sharp fusillade began, gradually and continually growing in intensity until the assaulting troops were exposed to a furious and effective fire. From 250 yards up to the position losses began to occur. The whole entrenchment was rimmed with flame and smoke, amid which the active figures of the Dervish riflemen were momentarily visible, and behind the filmy curtain solid masses of swordsmen and spearmen appeared. The fortunate interposition of a small knoll in some degree protected the advance of the Lincoln Regiment, but in both Highland battalions soldiers began to drop. The whole air was full of a strange chirping whistle. The hard pebbly sand was everywhere dashed up into dust-spurts. Numerous explosive bullets, fired by the Arabs, made queer startling reports. The roar of the rifles drowned even the noise of the artillery. All the deployed battalions began to suffer. But they and the assaulting columns, regardless of the fire, bore down on the zeriba in all the majesty of war—an avalanche of men, stern, unflinching, utterly irresistible.

Two hundred yards from the entrenchment and one hundred and fifty from the thorn bushes independent firing broke out, running along the line from end to end. Shooting continually, but without any hurry or confusion, the British and Soudanese battalions continued their slow, remorseless advance; and it was evident that, in spite of the fierce fire of the defence, which was now causing many casualties, the assault would be successful.

The loss during the passage of the zeriba and in the assault of the entrenchments was severe. Captain Findlay and Major Urquhart, of the Cameron Highlanders, were both mortally wounded in the fight at the stockades, and expired still cheering on their men. Major Napier, of the same regiment, and Captain Baillie, of the Seaforth Highlanders, received the wounds, of which they subsequently died, a few yards further on. At all points the troops broke into the enclosure. Behind the stockade there ran a treble trench. The whole interior was honeycombed with pits and holes. From these there now sprang thousands of Dervishes, desperately endeavouring to show a front to the attack. Second-Lieutenant Gore, a young officer fresh from Sandhurst, was shot dead between the thorn fence and the stockade. Other officers in the Lincoln and the Warwickshire regiments sustained severe wounds. Many soldiers were killed and wounded in the narrow space. These losses were general throughout the assaulting brigades. In the five minutes which were occupied in the passage of the obstruction about four hundred casualties occurred. The attack continued.

The British brigade had struck the extremity of the north front of the zeriba, and thus took the whole of the eastern face in enfilade, sweeping it with their terrible musketry from end to end, and strewing the ground with corpses. Although, owing to the lines of advance having converged, there was not room for more than half the force to deploy, the brigades pushed on. The conduct of the attack passed to the company commanders. All these officers kept their heads, and brought their companies up into the general line as the front gradually widened and gaps appeared. So the whole force—companies, battalions, even brigades—mixed up together and formed in one dense, ragged, but triumphant line, marched on unchecked towards the river bed, driving their enemies in hopeless confusion before them. Yet, although the Dervishes were unable to make head against the attack, they disdained to run. Many hundreds held their ground, firing their rifles valiantly till the end. Others charged with spear and sword. The greater part retired in skirmishing order, jumping over the numerous pits, walking across the open spaces, and repeatedly turning round to shoot. The XIth Soudanese encountered the most severe resistance after the defences were penetrated. As their three deployed companies pressed on through the enclosure, they were confronted by a small inner zeriba stubbornly defended by the Emir Mahmud's personal bodyguard. These poured a sudden volley into the centre company at close range, and so deadly was the effect that nearly all the company were shot, falling to the ground still in their ranks, so that a British officer passing at a little distance was provoked to inquire 'what they were doing lying down.' Notwithstanding this severe check the regiment, gallantly led by their colonel and supported by the Xth Soudanese, rushed this last defence and slew its last defenders. Mahmud was himself captured. Having duly inspected his defences and made his dispositions, he had sheltered in a specially constructed casemate. Thence he was now ignominiously dragged, and, on his being recognised, the intervention of a British officer alone saved him from the fury of the excited Soudanese.

Still the advance continued, and it seemed to those who took part in it more like a horrible nightmare than a waking reality. Captains and subalterns collected whatever men they could, heedless of corps or nationality, and strove to control and direct their fire. Jibba-clad figures sprang out of the ground, fired or charged, and were destroyed at every step. And onwards over their bodies—over pits choked with dead and dying, among heaps of mangled camels and donkeys, among decapitated or eviscerated trunks, the ghastly results of the shell fire; women and little children killed by the bombardment or praying in wild terror for mercy; blacks chained in their trenches, slaughtered in their chains—always onwards marched the conquerors, with bayonets running blood; clothes, hands, and faces all besmeared; the foul stench of a month's accumulated filth in their nostrils, and the savage whistle of random bullets in their ears.

But at about twenty minutes past eight the whole force, with the Seaforth Highlanders well forward on the left, arrived at the bank of the Atbara, having marched completely through the position, and shot or bayoneted all in their path. Hundreds of Dervishes were still visible retiring across the dry bed of the river, and making for the scrub on the opposite bank. The leading companies of the Seaforth Highlanders and Lincolns, with such odd parties of Camerons as had been carried on with the attack, opened a murderous fire on these fugitives. Since they would not run their loss was heavy, and it was a strange sight—the last vivid impression of the day—to watch them struggling through the deep sand, with the dust knocked up into clouds by the bullets which struck all round them. Very few escaped, and the bodies of the killed lay thickly dotting the river-bed with heaps of dirty-white. Then at 8.25 the 'Cease fire' sounded, and the battle of the Atbara ended.

Forthwith the battalions began to re-form, and in every company the roll was called. The losses had been severe. In the assault—a period not exceeding half an hour—eighteen British, sixteen native officers and 525 men had been killed or wounded, the greater part during the passage of the zeriba.

The actual pursuit was abortive. Colonel Lewis, with his two battalions, followed a line of advance which led south of the zeriba, and just before reaching the river bank found and fired upon a few Dervishes retreating through the scrub. All the cavalry and the Camel Corps crossed the Atbara and plunged into the bush on the further side. But so dense and tangled was the country that after three miles of peril and perplexity they abandoned he attempt, and the routed Arabs fled unmolested. The Baggara horse had ridden off during the action, headed by the prudent Osman Digna—whose position in the zeriba was conveniently suited to such a manoeuvre—and under that careful leadership suffered little loss. The rest of the army was, however, destroyed or dispersed. The fugitives fled up the Atbara river, leaving many wounded to die in the scrub, all along their line of retreat. Of the powerful force of 12,000 fighting men which Mahmud had gathered at Metemma, scarcely 4,000 reached Gedaret in safety. These survivors were added to the army of Ahmed Fedil, and thus prevented from spreading their evil tidings among the populace at Omdurman. Osman Digna, Wad Bishara, and other important Emirs whose devotion and discretion were undoubted, alone returned to the capital.

As soon as the troops were re-formed, the zeriba was evacuated and the army drew up in line along the neighbouring ridge. It was then only nine o'clock, and the air was still cool and fresh. The soldiers lit fires, made some tea, and ate their rations of biscuits and meat. Then they lay down and waited for evening. Gradually, as the hours passed, the sun became powerful. There was no shade, and only a few thin, leafless bushes rose from the sand. The hours of a day, peculiarly hot, even for the country and season, dragged wearily away. The sandy ridge beat back the rays till the air above was like the breath of a furnace and the pebbly ground burned. The water in the fantasses and bottles was hot and scarce. The pool of the Atbara was foul and tainted. In spite of the devoted efforts of the few medical officers who had been allowed to accompany the force, the wounded officers and soldiers endured the greatest miseries, and it is certain that several died of their wounds who might in happier circumstances have been saved.

Several hundred prisoners were taken. They were mostly negroes—for the Arabs refused to surrender, and fought to the last or tried to escape. The captive blacks, who fight with equal willingness on either side, were content to be enlisted in the Soudanese regiments; so that many of those who served the Khalifa on the Atbara helped to destroy him at Omdurman. The most notable prisoner was the Emir Mahmud—a tall, strong Arab, about thirty years old. Immediately after his capture he was dragged before the Sirdar. 'Why,' inquired the General, 'have you come into my country to burn and kill?' 'I have to obey my orders, and so have you,' retorted the captive sullenly, yet not without a certain dignity. To other questions he returned curt or evasive answers, and volunteered the opinion that all this slaughter would be avenged at Omdurman. He was removed in custody—a fine specimen of proud brutality, worthy perhaps of some better fate than to linger indefinitely in the gaol at Rosetta.

With the cool of the evening the army left its bed of torment on the ridge and returned to Umdabia. The homeward march was a severe trial; the troops were exhausted; the ground was broken; the guides, less careful or less fortunate than on the previous night, lost their way. The columns were encumbered with wounded, most of whom were already in a high state of fever, and whose sufferings were painful to witness. It was not until after midnight that the camp was reached. The infantry had been continuously under arms—marching, fighting, or sweltering in the sun—for thirty hours, and most of them had hardly closed their eyes for two days. Officers and soldiers—British, Soudanese, and Egyptian—struggled into their bivouacs, and fell asleep, very weary but victorious.

British and Egyptian casualties on the Atbara included 20 officers and 539 men killed or wounded. The Dervish loss was officially estimated at 40 Emirs and 3,000 dervishes killed. No statistics as to their wounded are forthcoming.

* * * * *

As the battle of the Atbara had been decisive, the whole Expeditionary Force went into summer quarters. The Egyptian army was distributed into three principal garrisons—four battalions at Atbara camp, six battalions and the cavalry at Berber, three battalions at Abadia. The artillery and transport were proportionately divided. The British brigade encamped with two battalions at Darmali and two at the village of Selim, about a mile and a half distant.

For the final phase of the campaign three new gunboats had been ordered from England. These were now sent in sections over the Desert Railway. Special arrangements were made to admit of the clumsy loads passing trains on the ordinary sidings. As usual, the contrivances of the railway subalterns were attended with success. Sir H. Kitchener himself proceeded to Abadia to accelerate by his personal activity and ingenuity the construction of the vessels on which so much depended. Here during the heat of the summer he remained, nursing his gunboats, maturing his plans, and waiting only for the rise of the river to complete the downfall of his foes.

CHAPTER XIII:

THE GRAND ADVANCE

All through the early months of the summer the preparations for the final advance were steadily proceeding. A second British brigade was ordered to the Soudan. A new battery of Howitzer artillery—the 37th—firing enormous shells charged with lyddite, was despatched from England. Two large 40-pounder guns were sent from Cairo. Another British Maxim battery of four guns was formed in Cairo from men of the Royal Irish Fusiliers. Three new screw gunboats of the largest size and most formidable pattern had been passed over the indefatigable railway in sections, and were now launched on the clear waterway south of the Atbara encampment; and last, but not least, the 21st Lancers [The author led a troop in this regiment during the final advance to Omdurman; and it is from this standpoint that the ensuing chapters are to some extent conceived] were ordered up the Nile. Events now began to move rapidly. Within three weeks of the arrival of the reinforcements the climax of the war was over; within five weeks the British troops were returning home. There was no delay at the Atbara encampment. Even before the whole of the second brigade had arrived, some of its battalions were being despatched to Wad Hamed, the new point of concentration. This place was a few miles north of Shabluka, and only fifty-eight miles from Omdurman. It was evident, therefore, that the decisive moment of the three years' war approached. The Staff, the British infantry, one squadron, the guns, and the stores were carried south in steamers and barges. The Egyptian division marched to Wad Hamed by brigades. The horses of the batteries, the transport animals of the British division (about 1,400 in number), the chargers of the officers, some cattle, and most of the war correspondents were sent along the left bank of the river escorted by two squadrons of the 21st Lancers and two Maxim guns.

All the thirteen squadrons of cavalry remained three days at Wad Hamed. After the fatigues of the march we were glad to have an opportunity of looking about, of visiting regiments known in other circumstances, and of writing a few letters. This last was the most important, for it was now known that after leaving Wad Hamed there would be no post or communication with Cairo and Europe until the action had been fought and all was over. The halt was welcome for another reason. The camp itself was well worth looking at. It lay lengthways along the river-bank, and was nearly two miles from end to end. The Nile secured it from attack towards the east. On the western and southern sides were strong lines of thorn bushes, staked down and forming a zeriba; and the north face was protected by a deep artificial watercourse which allowed the waters of the river to make a considerable inundation. From the bank of this work the whole camp could be seen. Far away to the southward the white tents of the British division; a little nearer rows and rows of grass huts and blanket shelters, the bivouacs of the Egyptian and Soudanese brigades; the Sirdar's large white tent, with the red flag of Egypt flying from a high staff, on a small eminence; and to the right the grove of palm-trees in which the officers of the Egyptian cavalry had established themselves. The whole riverside was filled by a forest of masts. Crowds of gyassas, barges, and steamers were moored closely together; and while looking at the furled sails, the tangled riggings, and the tall funnels it was easy for the spectator to imagine that this was the docks of some populous city in a well-developed and civilised land.

But the significance of the picture grew when the mind, outstripping the eye, passed beyond the long, low heights of the gorge and cataract of Shabluka and contemplated the ruins of Khartoum and the city of Omdurman. There were known to be at least 50,000 fighting men collected in their last stronghold. We might imagine the scene of excitement, rumour, and resolve in the threatened capital. The Khalifa declares that he will destroy the impudent invaders. The Mahdi has appeared to him in a dream. Countless angelic warriors will charge with those of Islam. The 'enemies of God' will perish and their bones will whiten the broad plain. Loud is the boasting, and many are the oaths which are taken, as to what treatment the infidel dogs shall have when they are come to the city walls. The streets swarm with men and resound with their voices. Everywhere is preparation and defiance. And yet over all hangs the dark shadow of fear. Nearer and nearer comes this great serpent of an army, moving so slowly and with such terrible deliberation, but always moving. A week ago it was sixty miles away, now it is but fifty. Next week only twenty miles will intervene, and then the creep of the serpent will cease, and, without argument or parley, one way or the other the end will come.

The road to the next camp was a long one; for though Royan island, opposite to which the site had been selected, was only seven miles in the direct line, it was necessary to march eight miles into the desert to avoid the Shabluka heights, and then to turn back to the Nile. The infantry were therefore provided with camel transport to carry sufficient water in small iron tanks for one night; and they were thus able to bivouac half-way, and to complete the journey on the next morning, thus making a two days' march. The mounted troops, who remained at Wad Hamed till all had gone south, were ordered to move on the 27th of August, and by a double march catch up the rest of the army.

Wad Hamed then ceased for the time being to exist except in name. All the stores and transport were moved by land or water to the south of Shabluka, and an advanced base was formed upon Royan island. Communications with the Atbara encampment and with Cairo were dropped, and the army carried with them in their boats sufficient supplies to last until after the capture of Omdurman, when the British division would be immediately sent back. It was calculated that the scope of this operation would not be greater than three weeks, and on the 27th the army were equipped with twenty-one days' supplies, of which two were carried by the troops, five by the regimental barges, and fourteen in the army transport sailing-vessels. All surplus stores were deposited at Royan island, where a field hospital was also formed.

The Expeditionary Force which was thus concentrated, equipped, and supplied for the culminating moment of the River War, was organised as follows:

Commander-in-Chief: THE SIRDAR

The British Division: MAJOR-GENERAL GATACRE Commanding

1st Brigade	2nd Brigade
BRIGADIER-GEN. WAUCHOPE	BRIGADIER-GEN. LYTTELTON
1st Btn. Royal Warwickshire Regt.	1st Btn. Grenadier Guards
" " Lincoln Regiment	" " Northumberland Fusiliers
" " Seaforth Highlanders	2nd " Lancashire Fusiliers
" " Cameron Highlanders	" " Rifle Brigade

The Egyptian Division: MAJOR-GENERAL HUNTER Commanding

1st Brigade	2nd Brigade	3rd Brigade	4th Brigade
COL. MACDONALD	COL. MAXWELL	COL. LEWIS	COL. COLLINSON
2nd Egyptians	8th Egyptians	3rd Egyptians	1st Egyptians
IXth Soudanese	XIIth Soudanese	4th "	5th (half) "
Xth "	XIIIth "	7th "	17th "
XIth "	XIVth "	15th "	18th "

Mounted Forces

21st Lancers	Camel Corps	Egyptian Cavalry
COLONEL MARTIN	MAJOR TUDWAY	COLONEL BROADWOOD
4 squadrons	8 companies	9 squadrons

Artillery: COLONEL LONG Commanding

(British)	32nd Field Battery, R.A. (with two 40-pounder guns)	8 guns
"	37th " " " (5-inch Howitzers) .	6 guns
(Egyptian)	The Horse Battery, E.A. (Krupp) . . .	6 guns
"	No. 1 Field Battery, E.A. (Maxim-Nordenfeldt)	6 guns
"	No. 2 " " "	6 guns
"	No. 3 " " "	6 guns
"	No. 4 " " "	6 guns

Machine Guns

    (British)   Detachment 16th Co. Eastern Division R.A. .   6 Maxim
      "   "   Royal Irish Fusiliers .   . 4 "
(Egyptian) 2 Maxim guns to each of the five
            Egyptian batteries   .   .   .   . 10 "

Engineers

    Detachment of Royal Engineers

The Flotilla: COMMANDER KEPPEL

1898 Class Armoured Screw Gunboats (3): the Sultan, the Melik, the Sheikh

    each carrying: 2 Nordenfeldt guns
                  1 quick-firing 12-pounder gun
                  1 Howitzer
                  4 Maxims

1896 Class Armoured Screw Gunboats (3): the Fateh, The Naser, the Zafir

    each carrying: 1 quick-firing 12-pounder gun
                  2 6-pounder guns
                  4 Maxims

Old Class Armoured Stern-wheel Gunboats (4): the Tamai, the Hafir*, the Abu Klea, the Metemma

    each carrying: 1 12-pounder gun
                  2 Maxim-Nordenfeldt guns

---

* The steamer El Teb, wrecked at the Fourth Cataract in 1897, had been refloated, and to change the luck was renamed Hafir.

Steam Transport

5 Steamers: The Dal, The Akasha, the Tahra, The Okma, the Kaibar

The total strength of the Expeditionary Force amounted to 8,200 British and 17,600 Egyptian soldiers, with 44 guns and 20 Maxims on land, with 36 guns and 24 Maxims on the river, and with 2,469 horses, 896 mules, 3,524 camels, and 229 donkeys, besides followers and private animals.

While the army were to move along the west bank of the river—the Omdurman side—a force of Arab irregulars, formed from the friendly tribes, would march along the east bank and clear it of any Dervishes. All the debris which the Egyptian advance had broken off the Dervish Empire was thus to be hurled against that falling State. Eager for plunder, anxious to be on the winning side, Sheikhs and Emirs from every tribe in the Military Soudan had hurried, with what following the years of war had left them, to Wad Hamed. On the 26th of August the force of irregulars numbered about 2,500 men, principally Jaalin survivors, but also comprising bands and individuals of Bisharin; of Hadendoa from Suakin; of Shukria, the camel-breeders; of Batahin, who had suffered a bloody diminution at the Khalifa's hands; of Shaiggia, Gordon's vexatious allies; and lastly some Gellilab Arabs under a reputed son of Zubehr Pasha. The command of the whole motley force was given to Major Stuart-Wortley, Lieutenant Wood accompanying him as Staff Officer; and the position of these officers among the cowed and untrustworthy Arabs was one of considerable peril.

While the infantry divisions were marching round the heights of Shabluka to the camp opposite Royan island, the steamers and gunboats ascended the stream and passed through the gorge, dragging up with them the whole fleet of barges and gyassas. The northern end of the narrow passage had been guarded by the five Dervish forts, which now stood deserted and dismantled. They were well built, and formed nearly a straight line—four on one bank and one on the other. Each fort had three embrasures, and might, when occupied, have been a formidable defence to the cataract.

Threshing up against the current, the gunboats and stern-wheelers one after another entered the gorge. The Nile, which below is nearly a mile across, narrows to a bare 200 yards. The pace of the stream becomes more swift. Great swirls and eddies disturb its surface. High on either side rise black, broken, and precipitous cliffs, looking like piles of gigantic stones. Through and among them the flood-river pours with a loud roaring, breaking into foam and rapids wherever the submerged rocks are near the surface. Between the barren heights and the water is a strip of green bushes and grass. The bright verdant colour seems the more brilliant by contrast with the muddy water and the sombre rocks. It is a forbidding passage. A few hundred riflemen scattered Afridiwise among the tops of the hills, a few field-guns in the mud forts by the bank, and the door would be shut.

The mounted forces marched from Wad Hamed at dawn on the 27th and, striking out into the desert, skirted the rocky hills. Besides the 21st Lancers and nine squadrons of Egyptian cavalry, the column included the Camel Corps, 800 strong, and a battery of Horse Artillery; and it was a fine sight to see all these horsemen and camel-men trotting swiftly across the sand by squadrons and companies, with a great cloud of dust rising from each and drifting away to the northward.

The zeriba of the camp at Royan had been already made and much of the ground cleared by the energy of the Soudanese division, which had been the first to arrive. An advanced depot was established at Royan island which was covered with white hospital tents, near which there was a forest of masts and sails. The barges and boats containing the stores and kits awaited the troops, and they had only to bivouac along the river-bank and shelter themselves as quickly as possible from the fierce heat of the sun. The dark hills of Shabluka, among and beneath which the camp and army nestled, lay behind us now. To the south the country appeared a level plain covered with bush and only broken by occasional peaks of rock. The eternal Nile flowed swiftly by the tents and shelters, and disappeared mysteriously in the gloom of the gorge; and on the further bank there rose a great mountain—Jebel Royan—from the top of which it was said that men might see Khartoum.

The whole army broke camp at Royan on the 28th of August at four o'clock in the afternoon, and marched to Wady el Abid six miles further south. We now moved on a broad front, which could immediately be converted into a fighting formation. This was the first time that it had been possible to see the whole force—infantry, cavalry, and guns—on the march at once. In the clear air the amazing detail of the picture was striking. There were six brigades of infantry, composed of twenty-four battalions; yet every battalion showed that it was made up of tiny figures, all perfectly defined on the plain. A Soudanese brigade had been sent on to hold the ground with pickets until the troops had constructed a zeriba. But a single Dervish horseman managed to evade these and, just as the light faded, rode up to the Warwickshire Regiment and flung his broad-bladed spear in token of defiance. So great was the astonishment which this unexpected apparition created that the bold man actually made good his escape uninjured.

On the 29th the forces remained halted opposite Um Teref, and only the Egyptian cavalry went out to reconnoitre. They searched the country for eight or nine miles, and Colonel Broadwood returned in the afternoon, having found a convenient camping-ground, but nothing else. During the day the news of two river disasters arrived—the first to ourselves, the second to our foes. On the 28th the gunboat Zafir was steaming from the Atbara to Wad Hamed, intending thereafter to ascend the Shabluka Cataract. Suddenly—overtaken now, as on the eve of the advance on Dongola, by misfortune—she sprang a leak, and, in spite of every effort to run her ashore, foundered by the head in deep water near Metemma. The officers on board—among whom was Keppel, the commander of the whole flotilla—had scarcely time to leap from the wreck, and with difficulty made their way to the shore, where they were afterwards found very cold and hungry. The Sirdar received the news at Royan. His calculations were disturbed by the loss of a powerful vessel; but he had allowed for accidents, and in consequence accepted the misfortune very phlegmatically. The days of struggling warfare were over, and the General knew that he had a safe margin of strength.

The other catastrophe afflicted the Khalifa, and its tale was brought to the advancing army by the Intelligence spies, who to the last—even when the forces were closing—tried to pass between them. Not content with building batteries along the banks, Abdullah, fearing the gunboats, had resolved to mine the river. An old officer of the old Egyptian army, long a prisoner in Omdurman, was brought from his chains and ordered to construct mines. Two iron boilers were filled with gunpowder, and it was arranged that these should be sunk in the Nile at convenient spots. Buried in the powder of each was a loaded pistol with a string attached to the trigger. On pulling the string the pistol, and consequently the mine, would be exploded. So the Khalifa argued; nor was he wrong. It was resolved to lay one mine first. On the 17th of August the Dervish steamer Ismailia moved out into the middle of the Nile, carrying one of the boilers fully charged and equipped with pistol detonator. Arrived at the selected spot, the great cylinder of powder was dropped over the side. Its efficiency as a destructive engine was immediately demonstrated, for, on the string being pulled by accident, the pistol discharged itself, the powder exploded, and the Ismailia and all on board were blown to pieces.

Undeterred by the loss of life, and encouraged by the manifest power of the contrivance, the Khalifa immediately ordered the second of the two boilers to be sunk in the stream. As the old Egyptian officer had been killed by the explosion, the Emir in charge of the arsenal was entrusted with the perilous business. He rose, however, to the occasion, and, having first taken the precaution of letting the water into the boiler so as to damp the powder, he succeeded in laying the second mine in mid-stream, to the joy and delight of Abdullah, who, not understanding that it was now useless, overwhelmed him with praise and presents.

Beguiled with such stories and diversions, the day of rest at Wady el Abid passed swiftly. Night brought beetles, bugs, and ants, and several men were stung by scorpions—a most painful though not dangerous affair. Towards morning it began to rain, and everyone was drenched and chilled when the sun rose across the river from behind a great conical hill and dispersed the clouds into wisps of creamy flame. Then we mounted and set out. This day the army moved prepared for immediate action, and all the cavalry were thrown out ten miles in front in a great screen which reached from the gunboats on the river to the Camel Corps far out in the desert.

When we had advanced a little further, there arose above the scrub the dark outlines of a rocky peak, the hill of Merreh. The whole of the 21st Lancers now concentrated, and, trotting quickly forward, occupied this position, whence a considerable tract of country was visible. We were hardly twenty-five miles from Khartoum, and of that distance at least ten miles were displayed. Yet there were no enemy. Had they all fled? Would there be no opposition? Should we find Omdurman deserted or submissive? These were questions which occurred to everyone, and many answered them affirmatively. Colonel Martin had meanwhile heliographed back to the Sirdar that all the ground was up to this point clear, and that there were no Dervishes to be seen. After some delay orders were signalled back for one squadron to remain till sunset in observation on the hill and for the rest to return to camp.

With two troops thrown out a mile in front we waited watching on the hill. Time passed slowly, for the sun was hot. Suddenly it became evident that one of the advanced troops was signalling energetically. The message was spelt out. The officer with the troop perceived Dervishes in his front. We looked through our glasses. It was true. There, on a white patch of sand among the bushes of the plain, were a lot of little brown spots, moving slowly across the front of the cavalry outposts towards an Egyptian squadron, which was watching far out to the westward. There may have been seventy horsemen altogether. We could not take our eyes off those distant specks we had travelled so far, if possible, to destroy. Presently the Dervish patrol approached our right troop, and apparently came nearer than they imagined, for the officer who commanded—Lieutenant Conolly—opened fire on them with carbines, and we saw them turn and ride back, but without hurrying.

The camp to which we returned was a very different place from the one we had left in the morning. Instead of lying along the river-bank, it was pitched in the thinner scrub. The bushes had on all sides been cut down, the ground cleared, and an immense oblong zeriba was built, around which the six brigades were drawn up, and into which cavalry, guns, and transport were closely packed.

Very early next morning the advance was continued. The army paraded by starlight, and with the first streak of the dawn the cavalry were again flung far out in advance. Secure behind the screen of horsemen and Camel Corps, the infantry advanced in regular array. Up to the 27th of August the force marched by divisions; but on and after the 30th of August the whole force commenced to march in fighting formation. The British division was on the left, the Egyptian army on the right. All the brigades marched in line, or in a slight echelon. The flank brigades kept their flank battalions in column or in fours. Other British battalions had six companies in the front line (in company column of fours) and two companies in support. The Egyptian brigades usually marched with three battalions in the front line and one in reserve, each of the three in the front line having four companies in front and two in support.

The spectacle of the moving army—the grand army of the Nile—as it advanced towards its goal was especially wonderful in the clear air of the early morning; a long row of great brown masses of infantry and artillery, with a fringe of cavalry dotting the plain for miles in front, with the Camel Corps—chocolate-coloured men on cream-coloured camels—stretching into the desert on the right, and the white gunboats stealing silently up the river on the left, scrutinising the banks with their guns; while far in rear the transport trailed away into the mirage, and far in front the field-glass disclosed the enemy's patrols. Day after day and hour after hour the advance was maintained. Arrived at the camping-ground, the zeriba had to be built; and this involved a long afternoon of fatigue. In the evening, when the dusty, tired-out squadrons returned, the troopers attended to their horses, and so went to sleep in peace. It was then that the dusty, tired-out infantry provided sentries and pickets, who in a ceaseless succession paced the zeriba and guarded its occupants.

The position of the next camp was a strong one, on a high swell of open ground which afforded a clear field of fire in every direction. Everyone that night lay down to sleep with a feeling of keen expectancy. One way or the other all doubts would be settled the next day. The cavalry would ride over the Kerreri Hills, if they were not occupied by the enemy, and right up to the walls of Omdurman. If the Dervishes had any army—if there was to be any battle—we should know within a few hours. The telegrams which were despatched that evening were the last to reach England before the event. During the night heavy rain fell, and all the country was drenched. The telegraph-wire had been laid along the ground, as there had been no time to pole it. The sand when dry is a sufficient insulator, but when wet its non-conductivity is destroyed. Hence all communications ceased, and those at home who had husbands, sons, brothers, or friends in the Expeditionary Force were left in an uncertainty as great as that in which we slept—and far more painful.

The long day had tired everyone. Indeed, the whole fortnight since the cavalry convoy had started from the Atbara had been a period of great exertion, and the Lancers, officers and men, were glad to eat a hasty meal, and forget the fatigues of the day, the hardness of the ground, and the anticipations of the morrow in deep sleep. The camp was watched by the infantry, whose labours did not end with the daylight. At two o'clock in the morning the clouds broke in rain and storm. Great blue flashes of lightning lit up the wide expanse of sleeping figures, of crowded animals, and of shelters fluttering in the wind; and from the centre of the camp it was even possible to see for an instant the continuous line of sentries who watched throughout the night with ceaseless vigilance. Nor was this all. Far away, near the Kerreri Hills, the yellow light of a burning village shot up, unquenched by the rain, and only invisible in the brightest flashes of the lightning. There was war to the southward.

CHAPTER XIV:

THE OPERATIONS OF THE FIRST OF SEPTEMBER

The British and Egyptian cavalry, supported by the Camel Corps and Horse Artillery, trotted out rapidly, and soon interposed a distance of eight miles between them and the army. As before, the 21st Lancers were on the left nearest the river, and the Khedivial squadrons curved backwards in a wide half-moon to protect the right flank. Meanwhile the gunboat flotilla was seen to be in motion. The white boats began to ascend the stream leisurely. Yet their array was significant. Hitherto they had moved at long and indefinite intervals—one following perhaps a mile, or even two miles, behind the other. Now a regular distance of about 300 yards was observed. The orders of the cavalry were to reconnoitre Omdurman; of the gunboats to bombard it.

As soon as the squadrons of the 21st Lancers had turned the shoulder of the steep Kerreri Hills, we saw in the distance a yellow-brown pointed dome rising above the blurred horizon. It was the Mahdi's Tomb, standing in the very heart of Omdurman. From the high ground the field-glass disclosed rows and rows of mud houses, making a dark patch on the brown of the plain. To the left the river, steel-grey in the morning light, forked into two channels, and on the tongue of land between them the gleam of a white building showed among the trees. Before us were the ruins of Khartoum and the confluence of the Blue and White Niles.

A black, solitary hill rose between the Kerreri position and Omdurman. A long, low ridge running from it concealed the ground beyond. For the rest there was a wide-rolling, sandy plain of great extent, surrounded on three sides by rocky hills and ridges, and patched with coarse, starveling grass or occasional bushes. By the banks of the river which framed the picture on the left stood a straggling mud village, and this, though we did not know it, was to be the field of Omdurman. It was deserted. Not a living creature could be seen. And now there were many who said once and for all that there would be no fight; for here we were arrived at the very walls of Omdurman, and never an enemy to bar our path. Then, with four squadrons looking very tiny on the broad expanse of ground, we moved steadily forward, and at the same time the Egyptian cavalry and the Camel Corps entered the plain several miles further to the west, and they too began to trot across it.

It was about three miles to the last ridge which lay between us and the city. If there was a Dervish army, if there was to be a battle, if the Khalifa would maintain his boast and accept the arbitrament of war, much must be visible from that ridge. We looked over. At first nothing was apparent except the walls and houses of Omdurman and the sandy plain sloping up from the river to distant hills. Then four miles away on our right front emerged a long black line with white spots. It was the enemy. It seemed to us, as we looked, that there might be 3,000 men behind a high dense zeriba of thorn-bushes. That, said the officers, was better than nothing. It is scarcely necessary to describe our tortuous movements towards the Dervish position. Looking at it now from one point of view, now from another, but always edging nearer, the cavalry slowly approached, and halted in the plain about three miles away—three great serpents of men— the light-coloured one, the 21st Lancers; a much longer and a blacker one, the Egyptian squadrons; a mottled one, the Camel Corps and Horse Artillery. From this distance a clearer view was possible, and we distinguished many horsemen riding about the flanks and front of the broad dark line which crowned the crest of the slope. A few of these rode carelessly towards the squadrons to look at them. They were not apparently acquainted with the long range of the Lee-Metford carbine. Several troops were dismounted, and at 800 yards fire was made on them. Two were shot and fell to the ground. Their companions, dismounting, examined them, picked up one, let the other lie, and resumed their ride, without acknowledging the bullets by even an increase of pace.

While this passed, so did the time. It was now nearly eleven o'clock. Suddenly the whole black line which seemed to be zeriba began to move. It was made of men, not bushes. Behind it other immense masses and lines of men appeared over the crest; and while we watched, amazed by the wonder of the sight, the whole face of the slope became black with swarming savages. Four miles from end to end, and, as it seemed, in five great divisions, this mighty army advanced—swiftly. The whole side of the hill seemed to move. Between the masses horsemen galloped continually; before them many patrols dotted the plain; above them waved hundreds of banners, and the sun, glinting on many thousand hostile spear-points, spread a sparkling cloud.

It is now known that the Khalifa had succeeded in concentrating at Omdurman an army of more than 60,000 men. He remembered that all the former victories over the Egyptians had been won by the Dervishes attacking. He knew that in all the recent defeats they had stood on the defensive. He therefore determined not to oppose the advance at the Shabluka or on the march thence to Omdurman. All was to be staked on the issue of a great battle on the plains of Kerreri. The Mahdi's prophecy was propitious. The strength of the Dervish army seemed overwhelming. When the 'Turks' arrived, they should be driven into the river. Accordingly the Khalifa had only watched the advance of the Expeditionary Force from Wad Hamed with a patrol of cavalry about 200 strong. On the 30th he was informed that the enemy drew near, and on the 31st he assembled his bodyguard and regular army, with the exception of the men needed for the river batteries, on the Omdurman parade ground. He harangued the leaders; and remained encamped with his troops during the night. The next day all the male population of the city were compelled to join the army in the field, and only the gunners and garrisons on the river-face remained within. In spite, however, of his utmost vigilance, nearly 6,000 men deserted during the nights of the 31st of August and the 1st of September. This and the detachments in the forts reduced the force actually engaged in the battle to 52,000 men. The host that now advanced towards the British and Egyptian cavalry was perhaps 4,000 stronger.

Their array was regular and precise, and, facing northeast, stretched for more than four miles from flank to flank. A strong detachment of the mulazemin or guard was extended in front of the centre. Ali-Wad-Helu, with his bright green flag, prolonged the line to the left; and his 5,000 warriors, chiefly of the Degheim and Kenana tribes, soon began to reach out towards the Egyptian cavalry. The centre and main force of the army was composed of the regular troops, formed in squares under Osman Sheikh-ed-Din and Osman Azrak. This great body comprised 12,000 black riflemen and about 13,000 black and Arab spearmen. In their midst rose the large, dark green flag which the Sheikh-ed-Din had adopted to annoy Ali-Wad-Helu, of whose distinctive emblem he was inordinately jealous. The Khalifa with his own bodyguard, about 2,000 strong, followed the centre.

In rear of all marched Yakub with the Black Flag and 13,000 men—nearly all swordsmen and spearmen, who with those extended in front of the army constituted the guard. The right wing was formed by the brigade of the Khalifa Sherif, consisting of 2,000 Danagla tribesmen, whose principal ensign was a broad red flag. Osman Digna, with about 1,700 Hadendoa, guarded the extreme right and the flank nearest Omdurman, and his fame needed no flag. Such was the great army which now moved swiftly towards the watching squadrons; and these, pausing on the sandy ridge, pushed out a fringe of tentative patrols, as if to assure themselves that what they saw was real.

The Egyptian cavalry had meanwhile a somewhat different view of the spectacle. Working on the right of the 21st Lancers, and keeping further from the river, the leading squadrons had reached the extreme western end of the Kerreri ridge at about seven o'clock. From here the Mahdi's Tomb was visible, and, since the rocks of Surgham did not obstruct the view from this point, the British officers, looking through their field-glasses, saw what appeared to be a long column of brown spots moving south-westwards across the wide plain which stretches away to the west of Omdurman. The telescope, an invaluable aid to reconnaissance, developed the picture. The brown objects proved to be troops of horses grazing; and beyond, to the southward, camels and white flapping tents could be distinguished. There were no signs that a retreat was in progress; but from such a distance—nearly four miles—no certain information could be obtained, and Colonel Broadwood decided to advance closer. He accordingly led his whole command south-westward towards a round-topped hill which rose about four miles from the end of the Kerreri ridge and was one of the more distant hill features bounding the plain on the western side. The Egyptian cavalry moved slowly across the desert to this new point of observation. On their way they traversed the end of the Khor Shambat, a long depression which is the natural drainage channel of the plains of Kerreri and Omdurman, and joins the Nile about four miles from the city. The heavy rain of the previous night had made the low ground swampy, and pools of water stood in the soft, wet sand. The passage, however, presented no great difficulty, and at half-past eleven the Egyptian squadrons began to climb the lower slopes of the round-topped hill. Here the whole scene burst suddenly upon them. Scarcely three miles away the Dervish army was advancing with the regularity of parade. The south wind carried the martial sound of horns and drums and—far more menacing—the deep murmur of a multitude to the astonished officers. Like the 21st Lancers—three miles away to their left, at the end of the long sandy ridge which runs westward from Surgham—the soldiers remained for a space spellbound. But all eyes were soon drawn from the thrilling spectacle of the Dervish advance by the sound of guns on the river.

At about eleven o'clock the gunboats had ascended the Nile, and now engaged the enemy's batteries on both banks. Throughout the day the loud reports of their guns could be heard, and, looking from our position on the ridge, we could see the white vessels steaming slowly forward against the current, under clouds of black smoke from their furnaces and amid other clouds of white smoke from the artillery. The forts, which mounted nearly fifty guns, replied vigorously; but the British aim was accurate and their fire crushing. The embrasures were smashed to bits and many of the Dervish guns dismounted. The rifle trenches which flanked the forts were swept by the Maxim guns. The heavier projectiles, striking the mud walls of the works and houses, dashed the red dust high into the air and scattered destruction around. Despite the tenacity and courage of the Dervish gunners, they were driven from their defences and took refuge among the streets of the city. The great wall of Omdurman was breached in many places, and a large number of unfortunate non-combatants were killed and wounded.

Meanwhile the Arab irregulars, under Major Wortley, had been sharply engaged. That officer's orders were to co-operate with the flotilla by taking in rear the forts and fortified villages on the east bank of the river. As soon as the gunboats had silenced the lower forts, Major Wortley ordered the irregulars to advance on them and on the houses. He placed the Jaalin, who were practically the only trustworthy men in his force, in reserve, and formed the tribes according to their capabilities and prejudices. On the order to attack being given, the whole force, some 3,000 strong, advanced on the buildings, from which the Dervishes at once opened fire. Arrived within 500 yards they halted, and began to discharge their rifles in the air; they also indulged in frantic dances expressive of their fury and valour, but declined to advance any further.

Major Wortley then ordered the Jaalin to attack. These—formed in a long column, animated by the desire for vengeance, and being besides brave men—moved upon the village at a slow pace, and, surrounding one house after another, captured it and slew all its defenders; including the Dervish Emir and 350 of his followers. The Jaalin themselves suffered a loss of about sixty killed and wounded.

The village being captured, and the enemy on the east bank killed or dispersed, the gunboats proceeded to engage the batteries higher up the river. The howitzer battery was now landed, and at 1.30 began to bombard the Mahdi's Tomb. This part of the proceedings was plainly visible to us, waiting and watching on the ridge, and its interest even distracted attention from the Dervish army. The dome of the tomb rose tall and prominent above the mud houses of the city. A lyddite shell burst over it—a great flash, a white ball of smoke, and, after a pause, the dull thud of the distant explosion. Another followed. At the third shot, instead of the white smoke, there was a prodigious cloud of red dust, in which the whole tomb disappeared. When this cleared away we saw that, instead of being pointed, it was now flat-topped. Other shells continued to strike it with like effect, some breaking holes in the dome, others smashing off the cupolas, all enveloping it in dust.

All this time the Dervishes were coming nearer, and the steady and continuous advance of the great army compelled the Egyptian cavalry to mount their horses and trot off to some safer point of view. Colonel Broadwood conceived his direct line of retreat to camp threatened, and shortly after one o'clock he began a regular retirement. Eight squadrons of Egyptian cavalry and the Horse Artillery moved off first. Five companies of the Camel Corps, a Maxim gun section, and the ninth squadron of cavalry followed as a rear-guard under Major Tudway. The Dervish horsemen contented themselves with firing occasional shots, which were replied to by the Camel Corps with volleys whenever the ground was suited to dismounted action. From time to time one of the more daring Arabs would gallop after the retreating squadrons, but a shot from a carbine or a threatened advance always brought the adventurous horseman to a halt. The retirement was continued without serious interference, and the boggy ground of the Khor Shambat was recrossed in safety.

As soon as the Egyptian squadrons—a darker mass under the dark hills to the westward—were seen to be in retirement, the 21st Lancers were withdrawn slowly along the sandy ridge towards the rocks of Surgham—the position whence we had first seen the Dervish army. The regiment wheeled about and fell back by alternate wings, dropping two detached troops to the rear and flanks to make the enemy's patrols keep their distance. But when the Arab horsemen saw all the cavalry retiring they became very bold, and numerous small groups of fives and sixes began to draw nearer at a trot. Accordingly, whenever the ground was favourable, the squadrons halted in turn for a few minutes to fire on them. In this way perhaps half-a-dozen were killed or wounded. The others, however, paid little attention to the bullets, and continued to pry curiously, until at last it was thought necessary to send a troop to drive them away. The score of Lancers galloped back towards the inquisitive patrols in the most earnest fashion. The Dervishes, although more numerous, were scattered about in small parties, and, being unable to collect, they declined the combat. The great army, however, still advanced majestically, pressing the cavalry back before it; and it was evident that if the Khalifa's movement continued, in spite of it being nearly one o'clock, there would be a collision between the main forces before the night.

From the summit of the black hill of Surgham the scene was extraordinary. The great army of Dervishes was dwarfed by the size of the landscape to mere dark smears and smudges on the brown of the plain. Looking east, another army was now visible—the British and Egyptian army. All six brigades had passed the Kerreri Hills, and now stood drawn up in a crescent, with their backs to the Nile. The transport and the houses of the village of Egeiga filled the enclosed space. Neither force could see the other, though but five miles divided them. The array of the enemy was, without doubt, both longer and deeper. Yet there seemed a superior strength in the solid battalions, whose lines were so straight that they might have been drawn with a ruler.

The camp presented an animated appearance. The troops had piled arms after the march, and had already built a slender hedge of thorn-bushes around them. Now they were eating their dinners, and in high expectation of a fight. The whole army had been ordered to stand to arms at two o'clock in formation to resist the attack which it seemed the Dervishes were about to deliver. But at a quarter to two the Dervish army halted. Their drill was excellent, and they all stopped as by a single command. Then suddenly their riflemen discharged their rifles in the air with a great roar—a barbaric feu de joie. The smoke sprang up along the whole front of their array, running from one end to the other. After this they lay down on the ground, and it became certain that the matter would not be settled that day. We remained in our position among the sandhills of the ridge until the approach of darkness, and during the afternoon various petty encounters took place between our patrols and those of the enemy, resulting in a loss to them of about a dozen killed and wounded, and to us of one corporal wounded and one horse killed. Then, as the light failed, we returned to the river to water and encamp, passing into the zeriba through the ranks of the British division, where officers and men, looking out steadfastly over the fading plain, asked us whether the enemy were coming—and, if so, when. And it was with confidence and satisfaction that we replied, and they heard, 'Probably at daylight.'

When the gunboats had completed their bombardment, had sunk a Dervish steamer, had silenced all the hostile batteries, and had sorely battered the Mahdi's Tomb, they returned leisurely to the camp, and lay moored close to the bank to lend the assistance of their guns in case of attack. As the darkness became complete they threw their powerful searchlights over the front of the zeriba and on to the distant hills. The wheeling beams of dazzling light swept across the desolate, yet not deserted, plain. The Dervish army lay for the night along the eastern slope of the Shambat depression. All the 50,000 faithful warriors rested in their companies near the flags of their Emirs. The Khalifa slept in rear of the centre of his host, surrounded by his generals. Suddenly the whole scene was lit by a pale glare. Abdullah and the chiefs sprang up. Everything around them was bathed in an awful white illumination. Far away by the river there gleamed a brilliant circle of light—the cold, pitiless eye of a demon. The Khalifa put his hand on Osman Azrak's shoulder—Osman, who was to lead the frontal attack at dawn—and whispered, 'What is this strange thing?' 'Sire,' replied Osman, 'they are looking at us.' Thereat a great fear filled all their minds. The Khalifa had a small tent, which showed conspicuously in the searchlight. He had it hurriedly pulled down. Some of the Emirs covered their faces, lest the baleful rays should blind them. All feared that some terrible projectile would follow in the path of the light. And then suddenly it passed on—for the sapper who worked the lens could see nothing at that distance but the brown plain—and swept along the ranks of the sleeping army, rousing up the startled warriors, as a wind sweeps over a field of standing corn.

The Anglo-Egyptian army had not formed a quadrilateral camp, as on other nights, but had lain down to rest in the formation for attack they had assumed in the afternoon. Every fifty yards behind the thorn-bushes were double sentries. Every hundred yards a patrol with an officer was to be met. Fifty yards in rear of this line lay the battalions, the men in all their ranks, armed and accoutred, but sprawled into every conceivable attitude which utter weariness could suggest or dictate. The enemy, twice as strong as the Expeditionary Force, were within five miles. They had advanced that day with confidence and determination. But it seemed impossible to believe that they would attack by daylight across the open ground. Two explanations of their advance and halt presented themselves. Either they had offered battle in a position where they could not themselves be attacked until four o'clock in the afternoon, and hoped that the Sirdar's army, even though victorious, would have to fight a rear-guard action in the darkness to the river; or they intended to make a night attack. It was not likely that an experienced commander would accept battle at so late an hour in the day. If the Dervishes were anxious to attack, so much the worse for them. But the army would remain strictly on the defensive—at any rate, until there was plenty of daylight. The alternative remained—a night attack.

Here lay the great peril which threatened the expedition. What was to be done with the troops during the hours of darkness? In the daytime they recked little of their enemy. But at night, when 400 yards was the extreme range at which their fire could be opened, it was a matter of grave doubt whether the front could be kept and the attack repelled. The consequences of the line being penetrated in the darkness were appalling to think of. The sudden appearance of crowds of figures swarming to the attack through the gloom; the wild outburst of musketry and artillery all along the zeriba; the crowds still coming on in spite of the bullets; the fire getting uncontrolled, and then a great bunching and crumpling of some part of the front, and mad confusion, in which a multitude of fierce swordsmen would surge through the gap, cutting and slashing at every living thing; in which transport animals would stampede and rush wildly in all directions, upsetting every formation and destroying all attempts to restore order; in which regiments and brigades would shift for themselves and fire savagely on all sides, slaying alike friend and foe; and out of which only a few thousand, perhaps only a few hundred, demoralised men would escape in barges and steamers to tell the tale of ruin and defeat.

The picture—true or false—flamed before the eyes of all the leaders that night; but, whatever their thoughts may have been, their tactics were bold. Whatever advice was given, whatever opinions were expressed, the responsibility was Sir Herbert Kitchener's. Upon his shoulders lay the burden, and the decision that was taken must be attributed solely to him. He might have formed the army into a solid mass of men and animals, arranged the infantry four deep all round the perimeter, and dug as big a ditch or built as high a zeriba as time allowed. He might have filled the numerous houses with the infantry, making them join the buildings with hasty entrenchments, and so enclose a little space in which to squeeze cavalry, transport, and guns. Instead he formed his army in a long thin curve, resting on the river and enclosing a wide area of ground, about which baggage and animals were scattered in open order and luxurious accommodation. His line was but two deep; and only two companies per battalion and one Egyptian brigade (Collinson's) were in reserve. He thus obtained the greatest possible development of fire, and waited, prepared if necessary to stake everything on the arms of precision, but hoping with fervour that he would not be compelled to gamble by night.

The night was, however, undisturbed; and the moonlit camp, with its anxious generals, its weary soldiers, its fearful machinery of destruction, all strewn along the bank of the great river, remained plunged in silence, as if brooding over the chances of the morrow and the failures of the past. And hardly four miles away another army—twice as numerous, equally confident, equally brave—were waiting impatiently for the morning and the final settlement of the long quarrel.

CHAPTER XV:

THE BATTLE OF OMDURMAN

SEPTEMBER 2, 1898

The bugles all over the camp by the river began to sound at half-past four. The cavalry trumpets and the drums and fifes of the British division joined the chorus, and everyone awoke amid a confusion of merry or defiant notes. Then it grew gradually lighter, and the cavalry mounted their horses, the infantry stood to their arms, and the gunners went to their batteries; while the sun, rising over the Nile, revealed the wide plain, the dark rocky hills, and the waiting army. It was as if all the preliminaries were settled, the ground cleared, and nothing remained but the final act and 'the rigour of the game.'

Even before it became light several squadrons of British and Egyptian cavalry were pushed swiftly forward to gain contact with the enemy and learn his intentions. The first of these, under Captain Baring, occupied Surgham Hill, and waited in the gloom until the whereabouts of the Dervishes should be disclosed by the dawn. It was a perilous undertaking, for he might have found them unexpectedly near. As the sun rose, the 21st Lancers trotted out of the zeriba and threw out a spray of officers' patrols. As there had been no night attack, it was expected that the Dervish army would have retired to their original position or entered the town. It was hardly conceivable that they would advance across the open ground to attack the zeriba by daylight. Indeed, it appeared more probable that their hearts had failed them in the night, and that they had melted away into the desert. But these anticipations were immediately dispelled by the scene which was visible from the crest of the ridge.

It was a quarter to six. The light was dim, but growing stronger every minute. There in the plain lay the enemy, their numbers unaltered, their confidence and intentions apparently unshaken. Their front was now nearly five miles long, and composed of great masses of men joined together by thinner lines. Behind and near to the flanks were large reserves. From the ridge they looked dark blurs and streaks, relieved and diversified with an odd-looking shimmer of light from the spear-points. At about ten minutes to six it was evident that the masses were in motion and advancing swiftly. Their Emirs galloped about and before their ranks. Scouts and patrols scattered themselves all over the front. Then they began to cheer. They were still a mile away from the hill, and were concealed from the Sirdar's army by the folds of the ground. The noise of the shouting was heard, albeit faintly, by the troops down by the river. But to those watching on the hill a tremendous roar came up in waves of intense sound, like the tumult of the rising wind and sea before a storm.

The British and Egyptian forces were arranged in line, with their back to the river. The flanks were secured by the gunboats lying moored in the stream. Before them was the rolling sandy plain, looking from the slight elevation of the ridge smooth and flat as a table. To the right rose the rocky hills of the Kerreri position, near which the Egyptian cavalry were drawn up—a dark solid mass of men and horses. On the left the 21st Lancers, with a single squadron thrown out in advance, were halted watching their patrols, who climbed about Surgham Hill, stretched forward beyond it, or perched, as we did, on the ridge.

The ground sloped gently up from the river; so that it seemed as if the landward ends of the Surgham and Kerreri ridges curved in towards each other, enclosing what lay between. Beyond the long swell of sand which formed the western wall of this spacious amphitheatre the black shapes of the distant hills rose in misty confusion. The challengers were already in the arena; their antagonists swiftly approached.

Although the Dervishes were steadily advancing, a belief that their musketry was inferior encouraged a nearer view, and we trotted round the south-west slopes of Surgham Hill until we reached the sandhills on the enemy's side, among which the regiment had waited the day before. Thence the whole array was visible in minute detail. It seemed that every single man of all the thousands could be examined separately. The pace of their march was fast and steady, and it was evident that it would not be safe to wait long among the sandhills. Yet the wonder of the scene exercised a dangerous fascination, and for a while we tarried.

The emblems of the more famous Emirs were easily distinguishable. On the extreme left the chiefs and soldiers of the bright green flag gathered under Ali-Wad-Helu; between this and the centre the large dark green flag of Osman Sheikh-ed-Din rose above a dense mass of spearmen, preceded by long lines of warriors armed presumably with rifles; over the centre, commanded by Yakub, the sacred Black banner of the Khalifa floated high and remarkable; while on the right a great square of Dervishes was arrayed under an extraordinary number of white flags, amid which the red ensign of Sherif was almost hidden. All the pride and might of the Dervish Empire were massed on this last great day of its existence. Riflemen who had helped to destroy Hicks, spearmen who had charged at Abu Klea, Emirs who saw the sack of Gondar, Baggara fresh from raiding the Shillooks, warriors who had besieged Khartoum—all marched, inspired by the memories of former triumphs and embittered by the knowledge of late defeats, to chastise the impudent and accursed invaders.

The advance continued. The Dervish left began to stretch out across the plain towards Kerreri—as I thought, to turn our right flank. Their centre, under the Black Flag, moved directly towards Surgham. The right pursued a line of advance south of that hill. This mass of men were the most striking of all. They could not have mustered fewer than 6,000. Their array was perfect. They displayed a great number of flags—perhaps 500—which looked at the distance white, though they were really covered with texts from the Koran, and which by their admirable alignment made this division of the Khalifa's army look like the old representations of the Crusaders in the Bayeux tapestry.

The attack developed. The left, nearly 20,000 strong, toiled across the plain and approached the Egyptian squadrons. The leading masses of the centre deployed facing the zeriba and marched forthwith to the direct assault. As the whole Dervish army continued to advance, the division with the white flags, which had until now been echeloned in rear of their right, moved up into the general line and began to climb the southern slopes of Surgham Hill. Meanwhile yet another body of the enemy, comparatively insignificant in numbers, who had been drawn up behind the 'White Flags,' were moving slowly towards the Nile, echeloned still further behind their right, and not far from the suburbs of Omdurman. These men had evidently been posted to prevent the Dervish army being cut off from the city and to secure their line of retreat; and with them the 21st Lancers were destined to have a much closer acquaintance about two hours later.

The Dervish centre had come within range. But it was not the British and Egyptian army that began the battle. If there was one arm in which the Arabs were beyond all comparison inferior to their adversaries, it was in guns. Yet it was with this arm that they opened their attack. In the middle of the Dervish line now marching in frontal assault were two puffs of smoke. About fifty yards short of the thorn fence two red clouds of sand and dust sprang up, where the projectiles had struck. It looked like a challenge. It was immediately answered. Great clouds of smoke appeared all along the front of the British and Soudanese brigades. One after another four batteries opened on the enemy at a range of about 3,000 yards. The sound of the cannonade rolled up to us on the ridge, and was re-echoed by the hills. Above the heads of the moving masses shells began to burst, dotting the air with smoke-balls and the ground with bodies. But a nearer tragedy impended. The 'White Flags' were nearly over the crest. In another minute they would become visible to the batteries. Did they realise what would come to meet them? They were in a dense mass, 2,800 yards from the 32nd Field Battery and the gunboats. The ranges were known. It was a matter of machinery. The more distant slaughter passed unnoticed, as the mind was fascinated by the approaching horror. In a few seconds swift destruction would rush on these brave men. They topped the crest and drew out into full view of the whole army. Their white banners made them conspicuous above all. As they saw the camp of their enemies, they discharged their rifles with a great roar of musketry and quickened their pace. For a moment the white flags advanced in regular order, and the whole division crossed the crest and were exposed. Forthwith the gunboats, the 32nd British Field Battery, and other guns from the zeriba opened on them. About twenty shells struck them in the first minute. Some burst high in the air, others exactly in their faces. Others, again, plunged into the sand and, exploding, dashed clouds of red dust, splinters, and bullets amid their ranks. The white banners toppled over in all directions. Yet they rose again immediately, as other men pressed forward to die for the Mahdi's sacred cause and in the defence of the successor of the True Prophet. It was a terrible sight, for as yet they had not hurt us at all, and it seemed an unfair advantage to strike thus cruelly when they could not reply. Under the influence of the shells the mass of the 'White Flags' dissolved into thin lines of spearmen and skirmishers, and came on in altered formation and diminished numbers, but with unabated enthusiasm. And now, the whole attack being thoroughly exposed, it became the duty of the cavalry to clear the front as quickly as possible, and leave the further conduct of the debate to the infantry and the Maxim guns. All the patrols trotted or cantered back to their squadrons, and the regiment retired swiftly into the zeriba, while the shells from the gunboats screamed overhead and the whole length of the position began to burst into flame and smoke. Nor was it long before the tremendous banging of the artillery was swollen by the roar of musketry.

Taking advantage of the shelter of the river-bank, the cavalry dismounted; we watered our horses, waited, and wondered what was happening. And every moment the tumult grew louder and more intense, until even the flickering stutter of the Maxims could scarcely be heard above the continuous din. Eighty yards away, and perhaps twenty feet above us, the 32nd Field Battery was in action. The nimble figures of the gunners darted about as they busied themselves in their complicated process of destruction. The officers, some standing on biscuit-boxes, peered through their glasses and studied the effect. Of this I had one glimpse. Eight hundred yards away a ragged line of men were coming on desperately, struggling forward in the face of the pitiless fire—white banners tossing and collapsing; white figures subsiding in dozens to the ground; little white puffs from their rifles, larger white puffs spreading in a row all along their front from the bursting shrapnel.

The infantry fired steadily and stolidly, without hurry or excitement, for the enemy were far away and the officers careful. Besides, the soldiers were interested in the work and took great pains. But presently the mere physical act became tedious. The tiny figures seen over the slide of the backsight seemed a little larger, but also fewer at each successive volley. The rifles grew hot—so hot that they had to be changed for those of the reserve companies. The Maxim guns exhausted all the water in their jackets, and several had to be refreshed from the water bottles of the Cameron Highlanders before they could go on with their deadly work. The empty cartridge-cases, tinkling to the ground, formed a small but growing heap beside each man. And all the time out on the plain on the other side bullets were shearing through flesh, smashing and splintering bone; blood spouted from terrible wounds; valiant men were struggling on through a hell of whistling metal, exploding shells, and spurting dust—suffering, despairing, dying. Such was the first phase of the battle of Omdurman.

The Khalifa's plan of attack appears to have been complex and ingenious. It was, however, based on an extraordinary miscalculation of the power of modern weapons; with the exception of this cardinal error, it is not necessary to criticise it. He first ordered about 15,000 men, drawn chiefly from the army of Osman Sheikh-ed-Din and placed under the command of Osman Azrak, to deliver a frontal attack. He himself waited with an equal force near Surgham Hill to watch the result. If it succeeded, he would move forward with his bodyguard, the flower of the Arab army, and complete the victory. If it failed, there was yet another chance. The Dervishes who were first launched against the zeriba, although very brave men, were not by any means his best or most reliable troops. Their destruction might be a heavy loss, but it would not end the struggle. While the attack was proceeding, the valiant left, consisting of the rest of the army of Osman Sheikh-ed-Din, might move unnoticed to the northern flank and curve round on to the front of the zeriba held by the Egyptian brigade. Ali-Wad-Helu was meanwhile to march to the Kerreri Hills, and remain out of range and, if possible, out of sight among them. Should the frontal and flank attacks be unhappily repulsed, the 'enemies of God,' exulting in their easy victory over the faithful, would leave their strong place and march to the capture and sack of the city. Then, while they were yet dispersed on the plain, with no zeriba to protect them, the chosen warriors of the True Religion would abandon all concealment, and hasten in their thousands to the utter destruction of the accursed—the Khalifa with 15,000 falling upon them from behind Surgham; Ali-Wad-Helu and all that remained of Osman's army assailing them from Kerreri. Attacked at once from the north and south, and encompassed on every side, the infidels would abandon hope and order, and Kitchener might share the fate of Hicks and Gordon. Two circumstances, which will appear as the account proceeds, prevented the accomplishment of this plan. The second attack was not executed simultaneously by the two divisions of the Dervish army; and even had it been, the power of the musketry would have triumphed, and though the Expeditionary Force might have sustained heavier losses the main result could not have been affected. The last hopes of barbarism had passed with the shades of night.

Colonel Broadwood, with nine squadrons of cavalry, the Camel Corps, and the Horse Artillery, had been ordered to check the Dervish left, and prevent it enveloping the downstream flank of the zeriba, as this was held by the Egyptian brigade, which it was not thought desirable to expose to the full weight of an attack. With this object, as the Dervishes approached, he had occupied the Kerreri ridge with the Horse battery and the Camel Corps, holding his cavalry in reserve in rear of the centre.

The Kerreri ridge, to which reference has so frequently been made, consists of two main features, which rise to the height of about 300 feet above the plain, are each above a mile long, and run nearly east and west, with a dip or trough about 1,000 yards wide between them. The eastern ends of these main ridges are perhaps 1,000 yards from the river, and in this intervening space there are several rocky under-features and knolls. The Kerreri Hills, the spaces between them, and the smaller features are covered with rough boulders and angular stones of volcanic origin, which render the movements of horses and camels difficult and painful.

The cavalry horses and camels were in the dip between the two ridges; and the dismounted men of the Camel Corps were deployed along the crest of the most southerly of the ridges, with their right at the desert end. Next in order to the Camel Corps, the centre of the ridge was occupied by the dismounted cavalry. The Horse Artillery were on the left. The remainder of the cavalry waited in the hollow behind the guns.

The tempestuous advance of Osman soon brought him into contact with the mounted force. His real intentions are still a matter of conjecture. Whether he had been ordered to attack the Egyptian brigade, or to drive back the cavalry, or to disappear behind the Kerreri Hills in conformity with Ali-Wad-Helu, is impossible to pronounce. His action was, however, clear. He could not safely assail the Egyptians with a powerful cavalry force threatening his left rear. He therefore continued his move across the front of the zeriba. Keeping out of the range of infantry fire, bringing up his right, and marching along due north, he fell upon Broadwood. This officer, who had expected to have to deal with small bodies on the Dervish flank, found himself suddenly exposed to the attack of nearly 15,000 men, many of whom were riflemen. The Sirdar, seeing the situation from the zeriba, sent him an order to withdraw within the lines of infantry. Colonel Broadwood, however, preferred to retire through the Kerreri Hills to the northward, drawing Osman after him. He replied to that effect.

The first position had soon to be abandoned. The Dervishes, advancing in a north-easterly direction, attacked the Kerreri Hills obliquely. They immediately enveloped the right flank of the mounted troops holding them. It will be seen from the map that as soon as the Dervish riflemen gained a point west and in prolongation of the trough between the two ridges, they not only turned the right flank, but also threatened the retreat of the defenders of the southerly ridge; for they were able to sweep the trough from end to end with their fire. As soon as it became certain that the southerly ridge could not be held any longer, Colonel Broadwood retired the battery to the east end of the second or northern ridge. This was scarcely accomplished when the dip was enfiladed, and the cavalry and Camel Corps who followed lost about fifty men and many horses and camels killed and wounded. The Camel Corps were the most unfortunate. They were soon encumbered with wounded, and it was now painfully evident that in rocky ground the Dervishes could go faster on their feet than the soldiers on their camels. Pressing on impetuously at a pace of nearly seven miles an hour, and unchecked by a heavy artillery fire from the zeriba and a less effective fire from the Horse battery, which was only armed with 7-pounder Krupps of an obsolete pattern, the Arabs rapidly diminished the distance between themselves and their enemies. In these circumstances Colonel Broadwood decided to send the Camel Corps back to the zeriba under cover of a gunboat, which, watchfully observing the progress of the fight, was coming down stream to assist. The distance which divided the combatants was scarcely 400 yards and decreasing every minute. The cavalry were drawn up across the eastern or river end of the trough. The guns of the Horse battery fired steadily from their new position on the northern ridge. But the Camel Corps were still struggling in the broken ground, and it was clear that their position was one of great peril. The Dervishes already carpeted the rocks of the southern ridge with dull yellow swarms, and, heedless of the shells which still assailed them in reverse from the zeriba, continued to push their attack home. On the very instant that they saw the Camel Corps make for the river they realised that those they had deemed their prey were trying, like a hunted animal, to run to ground within the lines of infantry. With that instinctive knowledge of war which is the heritage of savage peoples, the whole attack swung to the right, changed direction from north to east, and rushed down the trough and along the southern ridge towards the Nile, with the plain intention of cutting off the Camel Corps and driving them into the river.

The moment was critical. It appeared to the cavalry commander that the Dervishes would actually succeed, and their success must involve the total destruction of the Camel Corps. That could not, of course, be tolerated. The whole nine squadrons of cavalry assumed a preparatory formation. The British officers believed that a terrible charge impended. They would meet in direct collision the swarms of men who were hurrying down the trough. The diversion might enable the Camel Corps to escape. But the ground was bad; the enemy's force was overwhelming; the Egyptian troopers were prepared to obey—but that was all. There was no exalted enthusiasm such as at these moments carries sterner breeds to victory. Few would return. Nevertheless, the operation appeared inevitable. The Camel Corps were already close to the river. But thousands of Dervishes were running swiftly towards them at right angles to their line of retreat, and it was certain that if the camelry attempted to cross this new front of the enemy they would be annihilated. Their only hope lay in maintaining themselves by their fire near the river-bank until help could reach them, and, in order to delay and weaken the Dervish attack the cavalry would have to make a desperate charge.

But at the critical moment the gunboat arrived on the scene and began suddenly to blaze and flame from Maxim guns, quick-firing guns, and rifles. The range was short; the effect tremendous. The terrible machine, floating gracefully on the waters—a beautiful white devil—wreathed itself in smoke. The river slopes of the Kerreri Hills, crowded with the advancing thousands, sprang up into clouds of dust and splinters of rock. The charging Dervishes sank down in tangled heaps. The masses in rear paused, irresolute. It was too hot even for them. The approach of another gunboat completed their discomfiture. The Camel Corps, hurrying along the shore, slipped past the fatal point of interception, and saw safety and the zeriba before them.

Exasperated by their disappointment, the soldiers of Osman Sheikh-ed-Din turned again upon the cavalry, and, forgetting in their anger the mobile nature of their foe, pursued the elusive squadrons three long miles to the north. The cavalry, intensely relieved by the escape of the Camel Corps, played with their powerful antagonist, as the banderillo teases the bull. Colonel Broadwood thus succeeded in luring this division of the Dervish army far away from the field of battle, where they were sorely needed. The rough ground, however, delayed the Horse battery. They lagged, as the Camel Corps had done, and caused constant anxiety. At length two of their guns stuck fast in a marshy spot, and as several men and horses were shot in the attempt to extricate them Broadwood wisely ordered them to be abandoned, and they were soon engulfed in the Dervish masses. Encouraged by this capture, the horsemen of Osman's command daringly attacked the retreating cavalry. But they were effectually checked by the charge of a squadron under Major Mahon.

Both gunboats, having watched the Camel Corps safely into the zeriba, now returned with the current and renewed their attack upon the Arabs. Opening a heavy and accurate fire upon the river flank, they drove them westward and away from the Nile. Through the gap thus opened Broadwood and his squadrons trotted to rejoin the main body, picking up on the way the two guns which had been abandoned.

While these things were passing on the northern flank, the frontal attack was in progress. The debris of the 'White Flags' joined the centre, and the whole 14,000 pressed forward against the zeriba, spreading out by degrees and abandoning their dense formations, and gradually slowing down. At about 800 yards from the British division the advance ceased, and they could make no headway. Opposite the Soudanese, who were armed only with the Martini-Henry rifle, the assailants came within 300 yards; and one brave old man, carrying a flag, fell at 150 paces from the shelter trench. But the result was conclusive all along the line. The attack was shattered. The leader, clad in his new jibba of many colours, rode on steadfastly towards the inexorable firing line, until, pierced by several bullets, he fell lifeless. Such was the end of that stubborn warrior of many fights—wicked Osman Azrak, faithful unto death. The surviving Dervishes lay down on the ground. Unable to advance, they were unwilling to retire; and their riflemen, taking advantage of the folds of the plain, opened and maintained an unequal combat. By eight o'clock it was evident that the whole attack had failed. The loss of the enemy was more than 2,000 killed, and perhaps as many wounded. To the infantry, who were busy with their rifles, it had scarcely seemed a fight. Yet all along the front bullets had whizzed over and into the ranks, and in every battalion there were casualties. Captain Caldecott, of the Warwicks, was killed; the Camerons had two officers,

Captain Clarke and Lieutenant Nicholson, severely wounded; the Grenadiers one, Captain Bagot. Colonel F. Rhodes, as he sat on his horse near the Maxim battery of the 1st British Brigade, was shot through the shoulder and carried from the field just as the attack reached its climax. There were, besides these officers, about 150 casualties among the soldiers.

The attack languished. The enemy's rifle fire continued, and as soon as the heavy firing ceased it began to be annoying. The ground, although it appeared flat and level to the eye, nevertheless contained depressions and swellings which afforded good cover to the sharpshooters, and the solid line behind the zeriba was an easy target. The artillery now began to clear out these depressions by their shells, and in this work they displayed a searching power very remarkable when their flat trajectory is remembered. As the shells burst accurately above the Dervish skirmishers and spearmen who were taking refuge in the folds of the plain, they rose by hundreds and by fifties to fly. Instantly the hungry and attentive Maxims and the watchful infantry opened on them, sweeping them all to the ground—some in death, others in terror. Again the shells followed them to their new concealment. Again they rose, fewer than before, and ran. Again the Maxims and the rifles spluttered. Again they fell. And so on until the front of the zeriba was clear of unwounded men for at least half a mile. A few escaped. Some, notwithstanding the vices of which they have been accused and the perils with which they were encompassed, gloriously carried off their injured comrades.

After the attack had been broken, and while the front of the zeriba was being cleared of the Dervish riflemen, the 21st Lancers were again called upon to act. The Sirdar and his generals were all agreed on one point. They must occupy Omdurman before the Dervish army could get back there. They could fight as many Dervishes as cared to come in the plain; among the houses it was different. As the Khalifa had anticipated, the infidels, exulting in their victory, were eager, though for a different reason, to seize the city. And this they were now in a position to do. The Arabs were out in the desert. A great part of their army was even as far away as Kerreri. The troops could move on interior lines. They were bound to reach Omdurman first. The order was therefore given to march on the city at once. But first the Surgham ridge must be reconnoitred, and the ground between the zeriba and Omdurman cleared of the Dervishes—

with infantry if necessary, but with cavalry if possible, because that would be quicker.

As the fusillade slackened, the Lancers stood to their horses. Then General Gatacre, with Captain Brooke and the rest of his Staff, came galloping along the rear of the line of infantry and guns, and shouted for Colonel Martin. There was a brief conversation—an outstretched arm pointing at the ridge—an order, and we were all scrambling into our saddles and straightening the ranks in high expectation. We started at a trot, two or three patrols galloping out in front, towards the high ground, while the regiment followed in mass—a great square block of ungainly brown figures and little horses, hung all over with water-bottles, saddle-bags, picketing-gear, tins of bully-beef, all jolting and jangling together; the polish of peace gone; soldiers without glitter; horsemen without grace; but still a regiment of light cavalry in active operation against the enemy.

The crest of the ridge was only half a mile away. It was found unoccupied. The rocky mass of Surgham obstructed the view and concealed the great reserve collected around the Black Flag. But southward, between us and Omdurman, the whole plain was exposed. It was infested with small parties of Dervishes, moving about, mounted and on foot, in tens and twenties. Three miles away a broad stream of fugitives, of wounded, and of deserters flowed from the Khalifa's army to the city. The mirages blurred and distorted the picture, so that some of the routed Arabs walked in air and some through water, and all were misty and unreal. But the sight was sufficient to excite the fiercest instincts of cavalry. Only the scattered parties in the plain appeared to prevent a glorious pursuit. The signalling officer was set to heliograph back to the Sirdar that the ridge was unoccupied and that several thousand Dervishes could be seen flying into Omdurman. Pending the answer, we waited; and looking back northwards, across the front of the zeriba, where the first attack had been stopped, perceived a greyish-white smudge, perhaps a mile long. The glass disclosed details—hundreds of tiny white figures heaped or scattered; dozens hopping, crawling, staggering away; a few horses standing stolidly among the corpses; a few unwounded men dragging off their comrades. The skirmishers among the rocks of Surgham soon began to fire at the regiment, and we sheltered among the mounds of sand, while a couple of troops replied with their carbines. Then the heliograph in the zeriba began to talk in flashes of light that opened and shut capriciously.

The actual order is important. 'Advance,' said the helio, 'and clear the left flank, and use every effort to prevent the enemy re-entering Omdurman.' That was all, but it was sufficient. In the distance the enemy could be seen re-entering Omdurman in hundreds. There was no room for doubt. They must be stopped, and incidentally these small parties in the plain might be brushed away. We remounted; the ground looked smooth and unbroken; yet it was desirable to reconnoitre. Two patrols were sent out. The small parties of Dervishes who were scattered all over the plain and the slopes of the hill prevented anything less than a squadron moving, except at their peril. The first patrol struck out towards Omdurman, and began to push in between the scattered Dervishes, who fired their rifles and showed great excitement. The other patrol, under Lieutenant Grenfell, were sent to see what the ground looked like from further along the ridge and on the lower slopes of Surgham. The riflemen among the rocks turned their fire from the regiment to these nearer objects. The five brown figures cantered over the rough ground, presenting difficult targets, but under continual fire, and disappeared round the spur. However, in two or three minutes they re-appeared, the riflemen on the hill making a regular rattle of musketry, amid which the Lancers galloped safely back, followed last of all by their officer. He said that the plain looked as safe from the other side of the hill as from where we were. At this moment the other patrol returned. They, too, had had good fortune in their adventurous ride. Their information was exact. They reported that in a shallow and apparently practicable khor about three-quarters of a mile to the south-west, and between the regiment and the fugitives, there was drawn up a formed body of Dervishes about 1,000 strong. Colonel Martin decided on this information to advance and attack this force, which alone interposed between him and the Arab line of retreat. Then we started.

But all this time the enemy had been busy. At the beginning of the battle the Khalifa had posted a small force of 700 men on his extreme right, to prevent his line of retreat to Omdurman being harassed. This detachment was composed entirely of the Hadendoa tribesmen of Osman Digna's flag, and was commanded by one of his subordinate Emirs, who selected a suitable position in the shallow khor. As soon as the 21st Lancers left the zeriba the Dervish scouts on the top of Surgham carried the news to the Khalifa. It was said that the English cavalry were coming to cut him off from Omdurman. Abdullah thereupon determined to strengthen his extreme right; and he immediately ordered four regiments, each 500 strong, drawn from the force around the Black Flag and under the Emir Ibrahim Khalil, to reinforce the Hadendoa in the khor. While we were waiting for orders on the ridge these men were hurrying southwards along the depression, and concealed by a spur of Surgham Hill. The Lancer patrol reconnoitred the khor, at the imminent risk of their lives, while it was only occupied by the original 700 Hadendoa. Galloping back, they reported that it was held by about 1,000 men. Before they reached the regiment this number was increased to 2,700. This, however, we had no means of knowing. The Khalifa, having despatched his reinforcement, rode on his donkey with a scanty escort nearly half a mile from the Black Flag towards the khor, in order to watch the event, and in consequence he was within 500 yards of the scene.

As the 21st Lancers left the ridge, the fire of the Arab riflemen on the hill ceased. We advanced at a walk in mass for about 300 yards. The scattered parties of Dervishes fell back and melted away, and only one straggling line of men in dark blue waited motionless a quarter of a mile to the left front. They were scarcely a hundred strong. The regiment formed into line of squadron columns, and continued at a walk until within 300 yards of this small body of Dervishes. The firing behind the ridges had stopped. There was complete silence, intensified by the recent tumult. Far beyond the thin blue row of Dervishes the fugitives were visible streaming into Omdurman. And should these few devoted men impede a regiment? Yet it were wiser to examine their position from the other flank before slipping a squadron at them. The heads of the squadrons wheeled slowly to the left, and the Lancers, breaking into a trot, began to cross the Dervish front in column of troops. Thereupon and with one accord the blue-clad men dropped on their knees, and there burst out a loud, crackling fire of musketry. It was hardly possible to miss such a target at such a range. Horses and men fell at once. The only course was plain and welcome to all. The Colonel, nearer than his regiment, already saw what lay behind the skirmishers. He ordered, 'Right wheel into line' to be sounded. The trumpet jerked out a shrill note, heard faintly above the trampling of the horses and the noise of the rifles. On the instant all the sixteen troops swung round and locked up into a long galloping line, and the 21st Lancers were committed to their first charge in war.

Two hundred and fifty yards away the dark-blue men were firing madly in a thin film of light-blue smoke. Their bullets struck the hard gravel into the air, and the troopers, to shield their faces from the stinging dust, bowed their helmets forward, like the Cuirassiers at Waterloo. The pace was fast and the distance short. Yet, before it was half covered, the whole aspect of the affair changed. A deep crease in the ground—a dry watercourse, a khor—appeared where all had seemed smooth, level plain; and from it there sprang, with the suddenness of a pantomime effect and a high-pitched yell, a dense white mass of men nearly as long as our front and about twelve deep. A score of horsemen and a dozen bright flags rose as if by magic from the earth. Eager warriors sprang forward to anticipate the shock. The rest stood firm to meet it. The Lancers acknowledged the apparition only by an increase of pace. Each man wanted sufficient momentum to drive through such a solid line. The flank troops, seeing that they overlapped, curved inwards like the horns of a moon. But the whole event was a matter of seconds. The riflemen, firing bravely to the last, were swept head over heels into the khor, and jumping down with them, at full gallop and in the closest order, the British squadrons struck the fierce brigade with one loud furious shout. The collision was prodigious. Nearly thirty Lancers, men and horses, and at least two hundred Arabs were overthrown. The shock was stunning to both sides, and for perhaps ten wonderful seconds no man heeded his enemy. Terrified horses wedged in the crowd, bruised and shaken men, sprawling in heaps, struggled, dazed and stupid, to their feet, panted, and looked about them. Several fallen Lancers had even time to re-mount. Meanwhile the impetus of the cavalry carried them on. As a rider tears through a bullfinch, the officers forced their way through the press; and as an iron rake might be drawn through a heap of shingle, so the regiment followed. They shattered the Dervish array, and, their pace reduced to a walk, scrambled out of the khor on the further side, leaving a score of troopers behind them, and dragging on with the charge more than a thousand Arabs. Then, and not till then, the killing began; and thereafter each man saw the world along his lance, under his guard, or through the back-sight of his pistol; and each had his own strange tale to tell.

Stubborn and unshaken infantry hardly ever meet stubborn and unshaken cavalry. Either the infantry run away and are cut down in flight, or they keep their heads and destroy nearly all the horsemen by their musketry. On this occasion two living walls had actually crashed together. The Dervishes fought manfully. They tried to hamstring the horses, They fired their rifles, pressing the muzzles into the very bodies of their opponents. They cut reins and stirrup-leathers. They flung their throwing-spears with great dexterity. They tried every device of cool, determined men practised in war and familiar with cavalry; and, besides, they swung sharp, heavy swords which bit deep. The hand-to-hand fighting on the further side of the khor lasted for perhaps one minute. Then the horses got into their stride again, the pace increased, and the Lancers drew out from among their antagonists. Within two minutes of the collision every living man was clear of the Dervish mass. All who had fallen were cut at with swords till they stopped quivering, but no artistic mutilations were attempted.

Two hundred yards away the regiment halted, rallied, faced about, and in less than five minutes were re-formed and ready for a second charge. The men were anxious to cut their way back through their enemies. We were alone together—the cavalry regiment and the Dervish brigade. The ridge hung like a curtain between us and the army. The general battle was forgotten, as it was unseen. This was a private quarrel. The other might have been a massacre; but here the fight was fair, for we too fought with sword and spear. Indeed the advantage of ground and numbers lay with them. All prepared to settle the debate at once and for ever. But some realisation of the cost of our wild ride began to come to those who were responsible. Riderless horses galloped across the plain. Men, clinging to their saddles, lurched helplessly about, covered with blood from perhaps a dozen wounds. Horses, streaming from tremendous gashes, limped and staggered with their riders. In 120 seconds five officers, 65 men, and 119 horses out of fewer than 400 had been killed or wounded.

The Dervish line, broken by the charge, began to re-form at once. They closed up, shook themselves together, and prepared with constancy and courage for another shock. But on military considerations it was desirable to turn them out of the khor first and thus deprive them of their vantage ground. The regiment again drawn up, three squadrons in line and the fourth in column, now wheeled to the right, and, galloping round the Dervish flank, dismounted and opened a heavy fire with their magazine carbines. Under the pressure of this fire the enemy changed front to meet the new attack, so that both sides were formed at right angles to their original lines. When the Dervish change of front was completed, they began to advance against the dismounted men. But the fire was accurate, and there can be little doubt that the moral effect of the charge had been very great, and that these brave enemies were no longer unshaken. Be this as it may, the fact remains that they retreated swiftly, though in good order, towards the ridge of Surgham Hill, where the Khalifa's Black Flag still waved, and the 21st Lancers remained in possession of the ground—and of their dead.

Such is the true and literal account of the charge; but the reader may care to consider a few incidents. Colonel Martin, busy with the direction of his regiment, drew neither sword nor revolver, and rode through the press unarmed and uninjured. Major Crole Wyndham had his horse shot under him by a Dervish who pressed the muzzle of his rifle into its hide before firing. From out of the middle of that savage crowd the officer fought his way on foot and escaped in safety. Lieutenant Molyneux fell in the khor into the midst of the enemy. In the confusion he disentangled himself from his horse, drew his revolver, and jumped out of the hollow before the Dervishes recoved from the impact of the charge. Then they attacked him. He fired at the nearest, and at the moment of firing was slashed across the right wrist by another. The pistol fell from his nerveless hand, and, being wounded, dismounted, and disarmed, he turned in the hopes of regaining, by following the line of the charge, his squadron, which was just getting clear. Hard upon his track came the enemy, eager to make an end. Beset on all sides, and thus hotly pursued, the wounded officer perceived a single Lancer riding across his path. He called on him for help. Whereupon the trooper, Private Byrne, although already severely wounded by a bullet which had penetrated his right arm, replied without a moment's hesitation and in a cheery voice, 'All right, sir!' and turning, rode at four Dervishes who were about to kill his officer. His wound, which had partly paralysed his arm, prevented him from grasping his sword, and at the first ineffectual blow it fell from his hand, and he received another wound from a spear in the chest. But his solitary charge had checked the pursuing Dervishes. Lieutenant Molyneux regained his squadron alive, and the trooper, seeing that his object was attained, galloped away, reeling in his saddle. Arrived at his troop, his desperate condition was noticed and he was told to fall out. But this he refused to do, urging that he was entitled to remain on duty and have 'another go at them.' At length he was compelled to leave the field, fainting from loss of blood.

Lieutenant Nesham had an even more extraordinary escape than Molyneux. He had scrambled out of the khor when, as his horse was nearly stopping, an Arab seized his bridle. He struck at the man with his sword, but did not prevent him cutting his off-rein. The officer's bridle-hand, unexpectedly released, flew out, and, as it did so, a swordsman at a single stroke nearly severed it from his body. Then they cut at him from all sides. One blow sheared through his helmet and grazed his head. Another inflicted a deep wound in his right leg. A third, intercepted by his shoulder-chains, paralysed his right arm. Two more, missing him narrowly, cut right through the cantel of the saddle and into the horse's back. The wounded subaltern—he was the youngest of all—reeled. A man on either side seized his legs to pull him to the ground; but the long spurs stuck into the horse's flanks, and the maddened animal, throwing up its head and springing forward, broke away from the crowd of foes, and carried the rider—bleeding, fainting, but still alive—to safety among the rallying squadrons. Lieutenant Nesham's experience was that of the men who were killed, only that he escaped to describe it.

The wounded were sent with a small escort towards the river and hospitals. An officer was despatched with the news to the Sirdar, and on the instant both cannonade and fusillade broke out again behind the ridge, and grew in a crashing crescendo until the whole landscape seemed to vibrate with the sound of explosions. The second phase of the battle had begun.

Even before the 21st Lancers had reconnoitred Surgham ridge, the Sirdar had set his brigades in motion towards Omdurman. He was determined, even at a very great risk, to occupy the city while it was empty and before the army in the plain could return to defend it. The advantage might be tremendous. Nevertheless the movement was premature. The Khalifa still remained undefeated west of Surgham Hill; Ali-Wad-Helu lurked behind Kerreri; Osman was rapidly re-forming. There were still at least 35,000 men on the field. Nor, as the event proved, was it possible to enter Omdurman until they had been beaten.

As soon as the infantry had replenished their ammunition, they wheeled to the left in echelon of brigades, and began to march towards Surgham ridge. The movements of a great force are slow. It was not desirable that the British division, which led the echelon, should remain in the low ground north of Surgham— where they were commanded, had no field of fire, and could see nothing—and accordingly both these brigades moved forward almost together to occupy the crest of the ridge. Thus two steps of the ladder were run into one, and Maxwell's brigade, which followed Wauchope's, was 600 yards further south than it would have been had the regular echelon been observed. In the zeriba MacDonald had been next to Maxwell. But a very significant change in the order was now made. General Hunter evidently conceived the rear of the echelon threatened from the direction of Kerreri. Had the earth swallowed all the thousands who had moved across the plain towards the hills? At any rate, he would have his best brigade and his most experienced general in the post of possible danger. He therefore ordered Lewis's brigade to follow Maxwell, and left MacDonald last of all, strengthening him with three batteries of artillery and eight Maxim guns. Collinson marched with the transport. MacDonald moved out westward into the desert to take his place in the echelon, and also to allow Lewis to pass him as ordered. Lewis hurried on after Maxwell, and, taking his distance from him, was thus also 600 yards further south than the regular echelon admitted. The step which had been absorbed when both British brigades moved off— advisedly—together, caused a double gap between MacDonald and the rest of the army. And this distance was further increased by the fact that while he was moving west, to assume his place in correct echelon, the other five brigades were drawing off to the southward. Hence MacDonald's isolation.

At 9.15 the whole army was marching south in echelon, with the rear brigade at rather more than double distance. Collinson had already started with the transport, but the field hospitals still remained in the deserted zeriba, busily packing up. The medical staff had about 150 wounded on their hands. The Sirdar's orders had been that these were to be placed on the hospital barges, and that the field hospitals were to follow the transport. But the moving of wounded men is a painful and delicate affair, and by a stupid and grievous mistake the three regular hospital barges, duly prepared for the reception of the wounded, had been towed across to the right bank. It was necessary to use three ammunition barges, which, although in no way arranged for the reception of wounded, were luckily at hand. Meanwhile time was passing, and the doctors, who worked with devoted energy, became suddenly aware that, with the exception of a few detachments from the British division and three Egyptian companies, there were no troops within half a mile, and none between them and the dark Kerreri Hills. The two gunboats which could have guarded them from the river were down stream, helping the cavalry; MacDonald with the rear brigade was out in the plain; Collinson was hurrying along the bank with his transport. They were alone and unprotected. The army and the river together formed a huge "V" pointing south. The northern extremity—the gorge of the redan, as it were—gaped open towards Kerreri; and from Kerreri there now began to come, like the first warning drops before a storm of rain, small straggling parties of Dervish cavalry. The interior of the "V" was soon actually invaded by these predatory patrols, and one troop of perhaps a score of Baggara horse watered their ponies within 300 yards of the unprotected hospitals. Behind, in the distance, the banners of an army began to re-appear. The situation was alarming. The wounded were bundled on to the barges, although, since there was no steamer to tow them, they were scarcely any safer when embarked. While some of the medical officers were thus busied, Colonel Sloggett galloped off, and, running the gauntlet of the Baggara horsemen, hurried to claim protection for the hospitals and their helpless occupants. In the midst of this excitement and confusion the wounded from the cavalry charge began to trickle in.

When the British division had moved out of the zeriba, a few skirmishers among the crags of Surgham Hill alone suggested the presence of an enemy. Each brigade, formed in four parallel columns of route, which closed in until they were scarcely forty paces apart, and both at deploying interval—the second brigade nearer the river, the first almost in line with it and on its right—hurried on, eager to see what lay beyond the ridge. All was quiet, except for a few 'sniping' shots from the top of Surgham. But gradually as Maxwell's brigade—the third in the echelon—approached the hill, these shots became more numerous, until the summit of the peak was spotted with smoke-puffs. The British division moved on steadily, and, leaving these bold skirmishers to the Soudanese, soon reached the crest of the ridge. At once and for the first time the whole panorama of Omdurman—the brown and battered dome of the Mahdi's Tomb, the multitude of mud houses, the glittering fork of water which marked the confluence of the rivers—burst on their vision. For a moment they stared entranced. Then their attention was distracted; for trotting, galloping, or halting and gazing stupidly about them, terrified and bewildered, a dozen riderless troop-horses appeared over the further crest—for the ridge was flat-topped—coming from the plain, as yet invisible, below. It was the first news of the Lancers' charge. Details soon followed in the shape of the wounded, who in twos and threes began to make their way between the battalions, all covered with blood and many displaying most terrible injuries—faces cut to rags, bowels protruding, fishhook spears still stuck in their bodies—realistic pictures from the darker side of war. Thus absorbed, the soldiers hardly noticed the growing musketry fire from the peak. But suddenly the bang of a field-gun set all eyes looking backward. A battery had unlimbered in the plain between the zeriba and the ridge, and was beginning to shell the summit of the hill. The report of the guns seemed to be the signal for the whole battle to reopen. From far away to the right rear there came the sound of loud and continuous infantry firing, and immediately Gatacre halted his division.

Almost before the British had topped the crest of the ridge, before the battery had opened from the plain, while Colonel Sloggett was still spurring across the dangerous ground between the river and the army, the Sirdar knew that his enemy was again upon him. Looking back from the slopes of Surgham, he saw that MacDonald, instead of continuing his march in echelon, had halted and deployed. The veteran brigadier had seen the Dervish formations on the ridge to the west of Surgham, realised that he was about to be attacked, and, resolving to anticipate the enemy, immediately brought his three batteries into action at 1,200 yards, Five minutes later the whole of the Khalifa's reserve, 15,000 strong, led by Yakub with the Black Flag, the bodyguard and 'all the glories' of the Dervish Empire, surged into view from behind the hill and advanced on the solitary brigade with the vigour of the first attack and thrice its chances of success. Thereupon Sir Herbert Kitchener ordered Maxwell to change front to the right and storm Surgham Hill. He sent Major Sandbach to tell Lewis to conform and come into line on Maxwell's right. He galloped himself to the British division—conveniently halted by General Gatacre on the northern crest of the ridge—and ordered Lyttelton with the 2nd Brigade to form facing west on Maxwell's left south of Surgham, and Wauchope with the 1st Brigade to hurry back to fill the wide gap between Lewis and MacDonald. Last of all he sent an officer to Collinson and the Camel Corps with orders that they should swing round to their right rear and close the open part of the "V". By these movements the army, instead of facing south in echelon, with its left on the river and its right in the desert, was made to face west in line, with its left in the desert and its right reaching back to the river. It had turned nearly a complete somersault.

In obedience to these orders Lyttelton's brigade brought up their left shoulders, deployed into line, and advanced west; Maxwell's Soudanese scrambled up the Surgham rocks, and, in spite of a sharp fire, cleared the peak with the bayonet and pressed on down the further side; Lewis began to come into action on Maxwell's right; MacDonald, against whom the Khalifa's attack was at first entirely directed, remained facing south-west, and was soon shrouded in the smoke of his own musketry and artillery fire. The three brigades which were now moving west and away from the Nile attacked the right flank of the Dervishes assailing MacDonald, and, compelling them to form front towards the river, undoubtedly took much of the weight of the attack off the isolated brigade. There remained the gap between Lewis and MacDonald. But Wauchope's brigade—still in four parallel columns of route—had shouldered completely round to the north, and was now doubling swiftly across the plain to fill the unguarded space. With the exception of Wauchope's brigade and of Collinson's Egyptians, the whole infantry and artillery force were at once furiously engaged.

The firing became again tremendous, and the sound was even louder than during the attack on the zeriba. As each fresh battalion was brought into line the tumult steadily increased. The three leading brigades continued to advance westward in one long line looped up over Surgham Hill, and with the right battalion held back in column. As the forces gradually drew nearer, the possibility of the Dervishes penetrating the gap between Lewis and MacDonald presented itself, and the flank battalion was wheeled into line so as to protect the right flank. The aspect of the Dervish attack was at this moment most formidable. Enormous masses of men were hurrying towards the smoke-clouds that almost hid MacDonald. Other masses turned to meet the attack which was developing on their right. Within the angle formed by the three brigades facing west and MacDonald facing nearly south a great army of not fewer than 15,000 men was enclosed, like a flock of sheep in a fold, by the thin brown lines of the British and Egyptian brigades. As the 7th Egyptians, the right battalion of Lewis's brigade and nearest the gap between that unit and MacDonald, deployed to protect the flank, they became unsteady, began to bunch and waver, and actually made several retrograde movements. There was a moment of danger; but General Hunter, who was on the spot, himself ordered the two reserve companies of the 15th Egyptians under Major Hickman to march up behind them with fixed bayonets. Their morale was thus restored and the peril averted. The advance of the three brigades continued.

Yakub found himself utterly unable to withstand the attack from the river. His own attack on MacDonald languished. The musketry was producing terrible losses in his crowded ranks. The valiant Wad Bishara and many other less famous Emirs fell dead. Gradually he began to give ground. It was evident that the civilised troops were the stronger. But even before the attack was repulsed, the Khalifa, who watched from a close position, must have known that the day was lost; for when he launched Yakub at MacDonald, it was clear that the only chance of success depended on Ali-Wad-Helu and Osman Sheikh-ed-Din attacking at the same time from Kerreri. And with bitter rage and mortification he perceived that, although the banners were now gathering under the Kerreri Hills, Ali and Osman were too late, and the attacks which should have been simultaneous would only be consecutive. The effect of Broadwood's cavalry action upon the extreme right was now becoming apparent.

Regrets and fury were alike futile. The three brigades advancing drove the Khalifa's Dervishes back into the desert. Along a mile of front an intense and destructive fire flared and crackled. The 32nd British Field Battery on the extreme left was drawn by its hardy mules at full gallop into action. The Maxim guns pulsated feverishly. Two were even dragged by the enterprise of a subaltern to the very summit of Surgham, and from this elevated position intervened with bloody effect. Thus the long line moved forward in irresistible strength. In the centre, under the red Egyptian flag, careless of the bullets which that conspicuous emblem drew, and which inflicted some loss among those around him, rode the Sirdar, stern and sullen, equally unmoved by fear or enthusiasm. A mile away to the rear the gunboats, irritated that the fight was passing beyond their reach, steamed restlessly up and down, like caged Polar bears seeking what they might devour. Before that terrible line the Khalifa's division began to break up. The whole ground was strewn with dead and wounded, among whose bodies the soldiers picked their steps with the customary Soudan precautions. Surviving thousands struggled away towards Omdurman and swelled the broad stream of fugitives upon whose flank the 21st Lancers already hung vengefully. Yakub and the defenders of the Black Flag disdained to fly, and perished where they stood, beneath the holy ensign, so that when their conquerors reached the spot the dark folds of the banner waved only over the dead.

While all this was taking place—for events were moving at speed—the 1st British Brigade were still doubling across the rear of Maxwell and Lewis to fill the gap between the latter and MacDonald. As they had wheeled round, the regiments gained on each other according to their proximity to the pivot flank. The brigade assumed a formation which may be described as an echelon of columns of route, with the Lincolns, who were actually the pivot regiment, leading. By the time that the right of Lewis's brigade was reached and the British had begun to deploy, it was evident that the Khalifa's attack was broken and that his force was in full retreat. In the near foreground the Arab dead lay thick. Crowds of fugitives were trooping off in the distance. The Black Flag alone waved defiantly over the corpses of its defenders. In the front of the brigade the fight was over. But those who looked away to the right saw a different spectacle. What appeared to be an entirely new army was coming down from the Kerreri Hills. While the soldiers looked and wondered, fresh orders arrived. A mounted officer galloped up. There was a report that terrible events were happening in the dust and smoke to the northward. The spearmen had closed with MacDonald's brigade; were crumpling his line from the flank; had already broken it. Such were the rumours. The orders were more precise. The nearest regiment—the Lincolnshire—was to hurry to MacDonald's threatened flank to meet the attack. The rest of the brigade was to change front half right, and remain in support. The Lincolnshires, breathless but elated, forthwith started off again at the double. They began to traverse the rear of MacDonald's brigade, dimly conscious of rapid movements by its battalions, and to the sound of tremendous independent firing, which did not, however, prevent them from hearing the venomous hiss of bullets.

Had the Khalifa's attack been simultaneous with that which was now developed, the position of MacDonald's brigade must have been almost hopeless. In the actual event it was one of extreme peril. The attack in his front was weakening every minute, but the far more formidable attack on his right rear grew stronger and nearer in inverse ratio. Both attacks must be met. The moment was critical; the danger near. All depended on MacDonald, and that officer, who by valour and conduct in war had won his way from the rank of a private soldier to the command of a brigade, and will doubtless obtain still higher employment, was equal to the emergency.

To meet the Khalifa's attack he had arranged his force facing south-west, with three battalions in line and the fourth held back in column of companies in rear of the right flank—an inverted L-shaped formation. As the attack from the south-west gradually weakened and the attack from the north-west continually increased, he broke off his battalions and batteries from the longer side of the L and transferred them to the shorter. He timed these movements so accurately that each face of his brigade was able to exactly sustain the attacks of the enemy. As soon as the Khalifa's force began to waver he ordered the XIth Soudanese and a battery on his left to move across the angle in which the brigade was formed, and deploy along the shorter face to meet the impending onslaught of Ali-Wad-Helu. Perceiving this, the IXth Soudanese, who were the regiment in column on the right of the original front, wheeled to the right from column into line without waiting for orders, so that two battalions faced towards the Khalifa and two towards the fresh attack. By this time it was clear that the Khalifa was practically repulsed, and MacDonald ordered the Xth Soudanese and another battery to change front and prolong the line of the IXth and XIth. He then moved the 2nd Egyptians diagonally to their right front, so as to close the gap at the angle between their line and that of the three other battalions. These difficult manoeuvres were carried out under a heavy fire, which in twenty minutes caused over 120 casualties in the four battalions—exclusive of the losses in the artillery batteries—and in the face of the determined attacks of an enemy who outnumbered the troops by seven to one and had only to close with them to be victorious. Amid the roar of the firing and the dust, smoke, and confusion of the change of front, the general found time to summon the officers of the IXth Soudanese around him, rebuked them for having wheeled into line in anticipation of his order, and requested them to drill more steadily in brigade.

The three Soudanese battalions were now confronted with the whole fury of the Dervish attack from Kerreri. The bravery of the blacks was no less conspicuous than the wildness of their musketry. They evinced an extraordinary excitement—firing their rifles without any attempt to sight or aim, and only anxious to pull the trigger, re-load, and pull it again. In vain the British officers strove to calm their impulsive soldiers. In vain they called upon them by name, or, taking their rifles from them, adjusted the sights themselves. The independent firing was utterly beyond control. Soon the ammunition began to be exhausted, and the soldiers turned round clamouring for more cartridges, which their officers doled out to them by twos and threes in the hopes of steadying them. It was useless. They fired them all off and clamoured for more. Meanwhile, although suffering fearfully from the close and accurate fire of the three artillery batteries and eight Maxim guns, and to a less extent from the random firing of the Soudanese, the Dervishes drew nearer in thousands, and it seemed certain that there would be an actual collision. The valiant blacks prepared themselves with delight to meet the shock, notwithstanding the overwhelming numbers of the enemy. Scarcely three rounds per man remained throughout the brigade. The batteries opened a rapid fire of case-shot. Still the Dervishes advanced, and the survivors of their first wave of assault were scarcely 100 yards away. Behind them both green flags pressed forward over enormous masses of armed humanity, rolling on as they now believed to victory.

At this moment the Lincoln Regiment began to come up. As soon as the leading company cleared the right of MacDonald's brigade, they formed line, and opened an independent fire obliquely across the front of the Soudanese. Groups of Dervishes in twos and threes were then within 100 yards. The great masses were within 300 yards. The independent firing lasted two minutes, during which the whole regiment deployed. Its effect was to clear away the leading groups of Arabs. The deployment having been accomplished with the loss of a dozen men, including Colonel Sloggett, who fell shot through the breast while attending to the wounded, section volleys were ordered. With excellent discipline the independent firing was instantly stopped, and the battalion began with machine-like regularity to carry out the principles of modern musketry, for which their training had efficiently prepared them and their rifles were admirably suited. They fired on an average sixty rounds per man, and finally repulsed the attack.

The Dervishes were weak in cavalry, and had scarcely 2,000 horsemen on the field. About 400 of these, mostly the personal retainers of the various Emirs, were formed into an irregular regiment and attached to the flag of Ali-Wad-Helu. Now when these horsemen perceived that there was no more hope of victory, they arranged themselves in a solid mass and charged the left of MacDonald's brigade. The distance was about 500 yards, and, wild as was the firing of the Soudanese, it was evident that they could not possibly succeed. Nevertheless, many carrying no weapon in their hands, and all urging their horses to their utmost speed, they rode unflinchingly to certain death. All were killed and fell as they entered the zone of fire—three, twenty, fifty, two hundred, sixty, thirty, five and one out beyond them all—a brown smear across the sandy plain. A few riderless horses alone broke through the ranks of the infantry.

After the failure of the attack from Kerreri the whole Anglo-Egyptian army advanced westward, in a line of bayonets and artillery nearly two miles long, and drove the Dervishes before them into the desert, so that they could by no means rally or reform. The Egyptian cavalry, who had returned along the river, formed line on the right of the infantry in readiness to pursue. At half-past eleven Sir H. Kitchener shut up his glasses, and, remarking that he thought the enemy had been given 'a good dusting,' gave the order for the brigades to resume their interrupted march on Omdurman—a movement which was possible, now that the forces in the plain were beaten. The brigadiers thereupon stopped the firing, massed their commands in convenient formations, and turned again towards the south and the city. The Lincolnshire Regiment remained detached as a rearguard.

Meanwhile the great Dervish army, who had advanced at sunrise in hope and courage, fled in utter rout, pursued by the Egyptian cavalry, harried by the 21st Lancers, and leaving more than 9,000 warriors dead and even greater numbers wounded behind them.

Thus ended the battle of Omdurman—the most signal triumph ever gained by the arms of science over barbarians. Within the space of five hours the strongest and best-armed savage army yet arrayed against a modern European Power had been destroyed and dispersed, with hardly any difficulty, comparatively small risk, and insignificant loss to the victors.

CHAPTER XVI:

THE FALL OF THE CITY

Now, when the Khalifa Abdullah saw that the last army that remained to him was broken, that all his attacks had failed, and that thousands of his bravest warriors were slain, he rode from the field of battle in haste, and, regaining the city, proceeded like a brave and stubborn soldier to make preparations for its defence, and, like a prudent man, to arrange for his own flight should further resistance be impossible. He ordered his great war-drum to be beaten and the ombya to be blown, and for the last time those dismal notes boomed through the streets of Omdurman. They were not heeded. The Arabs had had enough fighting. They recognised that all was lost. Besides, to return to the city was difficult and dangerous.

The charge of the 21st Lancers had been costly, but it was not ineffective. The consequent retirement of the Dervish brigade protecting the extreme right exposed their line of retreat. The cavalry were resolved to take full advantage of the position they had paid so much to gain, and while the second attack was at its height we were already trotting over the plain towards the long lines of fugitives who streamed across it. With the experience of the past hour in our minds, and with the great numbers of the enemy in our front, it seemed to many that a bloody day lay before us. But we had not gone far when individual Dervishes began to walk towards the advancing squadrons, throwing down their weapons, holding up their hands, and imploring mercy.

As soon as it was apparent that the surrender of individuals was accepted, the Dervishes began to come in and lay down their arms—at first by twos and threes, then by dozens, and finally by scores. Meanwhile those who were still intent on flight made a wide detour to avoid the cavalry, and streamed past our front at a mile's distance in uninterrupted succession. The disarming and escorting of the prisoners delayed our advance, and many thousands of Dervishes escaped from the field. But the position of the cavalry and the pressure they exerted shouldered the routed army out into the desert, so that retiring they missed the city of Omdurman altogether, and, disregarding the Khalifa's summons to defend it and the orders of their Emirs; continued their flight to the south. To harry and annoy the fugitives a few troops were dismounted with carbines, and a constant fire was made on such as did not attempt to come in and surrender. Yet the crowds continued to run the gauntlet, and at least 20,000 men made good their escape. Many of these were still vicious, and replied to our fire with bullets, fortunately at very long range. It would have been madness for 300 Lancers to gallop in among such masses, and we had to be content with the results of the carbine fire.

While all this had been going on, the advance of the army on Omdurman was continuing. Nor was it long before we saw the imposing array of infantry topping the sandhills near Surgham and flooding out into the plain which lay between them and the city. High over the centre brigade flew the Black Flag of the Khalifa, and underneath a smaller flash of red marked the position of the Headquarters Staff. The black masses of men continued to move slowly across the open ground while we fired at the flying Arabs, and at twelve o'clock we saw them halt near the river about three miles from the city. Orders now reached us to join them, and as the sun was hot, the day dragged, all were tired and hungry, and the horses needed water, we were not long in complying, and the remnants of the Dervish army made good their retreat unmolested.

We marched back to the Nile. The whole force had halted to drink, to eat, and to rest at Khor Shambat. The scene was striking. Imagine a six hundred yards stretch of the Suez Canal. Both banks are crowded with brown- or chocolate-clad figures. The northern side is completely covered with the swarming infantry of the British division. Thousands of animals—the horses of the cavalry, the artillery mules, the transport camels—fill the spaces and the foreground. Multitudes of khaki-clad men are sitting in rows on the slopes. Hundreds are standing by the brim or actually in the red muddy water. All are drinking deeply. Two or three carcasses, lying in the shallows, show that the soldiers are thirsty rather than particular. On all sides water-bottles are being filled from the welcome Nile, which has come into the desert to refresh the weary animals and men.

During the attack on MacDonald's brigade the Egyptian cavalry had watched from their position on the southern slopes of the Kerreri Hills, ready to intervene, if necessary, and support the infantry by a charge. As soon as the Dervish onsets had ended and the whole mass had begun to retreat, Broadwood's cavalry brigade formed in two lines, of four and of five squadrons respectively, and advanced in pursuit—first west for two miles, and then south-west for three miles more towards the Round-topped Hill. Like the 21st Lancers, they were delayed by many Dervishes who threw down their arms and surrendered, and whom it was necessary to escort to the river. But as they drew nearer the mass of the routed army, it became apparent that the spirit of the enemy was by no means broken. Stubborn men fired continually as they lay wounded, refusing to ask for quarter—doubting, perhaps, that it would be granted. Under every bush that gave protection from the lances of the horsemen little groups collected to make a desperate stand. Solitary spearmen awaited unflinching the charge of a whole squadron. Men who had feigned death sprang up to fire an unexpected shot. The cavalry began to suffer occasional casualties. In proportion as they advanced the resistance of the enemy increased. The direct pursuit had soon to be abandoned, but in the hope of intercepting some part of the retreating mob Major Le Gallais, who commanded the three leading squadrons, changed direction towards the river, and, galloping nearly parallel to Khor Shambat, charged and cut into the tail of the enemy's disordered array. The Arabs, however, stood their ground, and, firing their rifles wildly in all directions, killed and wounded a good many horses and men, so that the squadrons were content to bring up their right still more, and finally to ride out of the hornet swarm, into which they had plunged, towards Surgham Hill. The pursuit was then suspended, and the Egyptian cavalry joined the rest of the army by the Nile.

It was not until four o'clock that the cavalry received orders to ride round the outside of the city and harry such as should seek to escape. The Egyptian squadrons and the 21st Lancers started forthwith, and, keeping about a mile from the houses of the suburbs, proceeded to make the circle of the town. The infantry had already entered it, as was evident from a continual patter of shots and an occasional rattle of the Maxim guns. The leading Soudanese brigade—Maxwell's—had moved from Khor Shambat at 2.30, formed in line of company columns and in the following order:-

^ Direction of Advance ^

| XIVth | XIIth | Maxims | 8th | 32nd | XIIIth |
| Soudanese | Soudanese | | Egyptians | Field Battery | Soudanese |

The Sirdar, attended by his whole Staff, with the Black Flag of the Khalifa carried behind him and accompanied by the band of the XIth Soudanese, rode in front of the XIVth battalion. The regiments were soon enveloped by the numberless houses of the suburbs and divided by the twisting streets; but the whole brigade pressed forward on a broad front. Behind followed the rest of the army—battalion after battalion, brigade after brigade—until all, swallowed up by the maze of mud houses, were filling the open spaces and blocking and choking the streets and alleys with solid masses of armed men, who marched or pushed their way up to the great wall.

For two miles the progress through the suburbs continued, and the General, hurrying on with his Staff, soon found himself, with the band, the Maxims, and the artillery, at the foot of the great wall. Several hundred Dervishes had gathered for its defence; but the fact that no banquette had been made on which they could stand to fire prevented their resistance from being effective. A few ill-aimed shots were, however, fired, to which the Maxim guns replied with vigour. In a quarter of an hour the wall was cleared. The Sirdar then posted two guns of the 32nd Field Battery at its northern angle, and then, accompanied by the remaining four guns and the XIVth Soudanese, turned eastwards and rode along the foot of the wall towards the river, seeking some means of entry into the inner city. The breach made by the gunboats was found temporarily blocked by wooden doors, but the main gate was open, and through this the General passed into the heart of Omdurman. Within the wall the scenes were more terrible than in the suburbs. The effects of the bombardment were evident on every side. Women and children lay frightfully mangled in the roadway. At one place a whole family had been crushed by a projectile. Dead Dervishes, already in the fierce heat beginning to decompose, dotted the ground. The houses were crammed with wounded. Hundreds of decaying carcasses of animals filled the air with a sickening smell. Here, as without the wall, the anxious inhabitants renewed their protestations of loyalty and welcome; and interpreters, riding down the narrow alleys, proclaimed the merciful conditions of the conquerors and called on the people to lay down their arms. Great piles of surrendered weapons rose in the streets, guarded by Soudanese soldiers. Many Arabs sought clemency; but there were others who disdained it; and the whirring of the Maxims, the crashes of the volleys, and a continual dropping fire attested that there was fighting in all parts of the city into which the columns had penetrated. All Dervishes who did not immediately surrender were shot or bayoneted, and bullets whistled at random along or across the streets. But while women crowded round his horse, while sullen men fired carefully from houses, while beaten warriors cast their spears on the ground and others, still resisting, were despatched in corners, the Sirdar rode steadily onward through the confusion, the stench, and the danger, until he reached the Mahdi's Tomb.

At the mosque two fanatics charged the Soudanese escort, and each killed or badly wounded a soldier before he was shot. The day was now far spent, and it was dusk when the prison was reached. The General was the first to enter that foul and gloomy den. Charles Neufeld and some thirty heavily shackled prisoners were released. Neufeld, who was placed on a pony, seemed nearly mad with delight, and talked and gesticulated with queer animation. 'Thirteen years,' he said to his rescuer, 'have I waited for this day.' From the prison, as it was now dark, the Sirdar rode to the great square in front of the mosque, in which his headquarters were established, and where both British brigades were already bivouacking. The rest of the army settled down along the roadways through the suburbs, and only Maxwell's brigade remained in the city to complete the establishment of law and order—a business which was fortunately hidden by the shades of night.

While the Sirdar with the infantry of the army was taking possession of Omdurman, the British and Egyptian cavalry had moved round to the west of the city. There for nearly two hours we waited, listening to the dropping fusillade which could be heard within the great wall and wondering what was happening. Large numbers of Dervishes and Arabs, who, laying aside their jibbas, had ceased to be Dervishes, appeared among the houses at the edge of the suburbs. Several hundreds of these, with two or three Emirs, came out to make their submission; and we were presently so loaded with spears and swords that it was impossible to carry them, and many interesting trophies had to be destroyed. It was just getting dark when suddenly Colonel Slatin galloped up. The Khalifa had fled! The Egyptian cavalry were at once to pursue him. The 21st Lancers must await further orders. Slatin appeared very much in earnest. He talked with animated manner to Colonel Broadwood, questioned two of the surrendered Emirs closely, and hurried off into the dusk, while the Egyptian squadrons, mounting, also rode away at a trot.

It was not for some hours after he had left the field of battle that Abdullah realised that his army had not obeyed his summons, but were continuing their retreat, and that only a few hundred Dervishes remained for the defence of the city. He seems, if we judge from the accounts of his personal servant, an Abyssinian boy, to have faced the disasters that had overtaken him with singular composure. He rested until two o'clock, when he ate some food. Thereafter he repaired to the Tomb, and in that ruined shrine, amid the wreckage of the shell-fire, the defeated sovereign appealed to the spirit of Mohammed Ahmed to help him in his sore distress. It was the last prayer ever offered over the Mahdi's grave. The celestial counsels seem to have been in accord with the dictates of common-sense, and at four o'clock the Khalifa, hearing that the Sirdar was already entering the city, and that the English cavalry were on the parade ground to the west, mounted a small donkey, and, accompanied by his principal wife, a Greek nun as a hostage, and a few attendants, rode leisurely off towards the south. Eight miles from Omdurman a score of swift camels awaited him, and on these he soon reached the main body of his routed army. Here he found many disheartened friends; but the fact that, in this evil plight, he found any friends at all must be recorded in his favour and in that of his subjects. When he arrived he had no escort—was, indeed, unarmed. The fugitives had good reason to be savage. Their leaders had led them only to their ruin. To cut the throat of this one man who was the cause of all their sufferings was as easy as they would have thought it innocent. Yet none assailed him. The tyrant, the oppressor, the scourge of the Soudan, the hypocrite, the abominated Khalifa; the embodiment, as he has been depicted to European eyes, of all the vices; the object, as he was believed in England, of his people's bitter hatred, found safety and welcome among his flying soldiers. The surviving Emirs hurried to his side. Many had gone down on the fatal plain. Osman Azrak, the valiant Bishara, Yakub, and scores whose strange names have not obscured these pages, but who were, nevertheless, great men of war, lay staring up at the stars. Yet those who remained never wavered in their allegiance. Ali-Wad-Helu, whose leg had been shattered by a shell splinter, was senseless with pain; but the Sheikh-ed-Din, the astute Osman Digna, Ibrahim Khalil, who withstood the charge of the 21st Lancers, and others of less note rallied to the side of the appointed successor of Mohammed Ahmed, and did not, even in this extremity, abandon his cause. And so all hurried on through the gathering darkness, a confused and miserable multitude—dejected warriors still preserving their trashy rifles, and wounded men hobbling pitifully along; camels and donkeys laden with household goods; women crying, panting, dragging little children; all in thousands—nearly 30,000 altogether; with little food and less water to sustain them; the desert before them, the gunboats on the Nile, and behind the rumours of pursuit and a broad trail of dead and dying to mark the path of flight.

Meanwhile the Egyptian cavalry had already started on their fruitless errand. The squadrons were greatly reduced in numbers. The men carried food to suffice till morning, the horses barely enough to last till noon. To supplement this slender provision a steamer had been ordered up the river to meet them the next day with fresh supplies. The road by the Nile was choked with armed Dervishes, and to avoid these dangerous fugitives the column struck inland and marched southward towards some hills whose dark outline showed against the sky. The unknown ground was difficult and swampy. At times the horses floundered to their girths in wet sand; at others rocky khors obstructed the march; horses and camels blundered and fell. The darkness complicated the confusion. At about ten o'clock Colonel Broadwood decided to go no further till there was more light. He therefore drew off the column towards the desert, and halted on a comparatively dry spot. Some muddy pools, which were luckily discovered, enabled the bottles to be filled and the horses to be watered. Then, having posted many sentries, the exhausted pursuers slept, waking from time to time to listen to the intermittent firing which was still audible, both from the direction of Omdurman and from that in which the Dervish army was flying.

At 3 A.M. on the 3rd Colonel Broadwood's force moved on again. Men and horses seemed refreshed, and by the aid of a bright moon the ground was covered at a good pace. By seven o'clock the squadrons approached the point on the river which had been fixed for meeting the steamer. She had already arrived, and the sight of the funnel in the distance and the anticipation of a good meal cheered everyone, for they had scarcely had anything to eat since the night before the battle. But as the troopers drew nearer it became evident that 300 yards of shallow water and deep swamp intervened between them and the vessel. Closer approach was prevented. There was no means of landing the stores. In the hopes of finding a suitable spot further up the stream the march was resumed. The steamer kept pace along the river. The boggy ground delayed the columns, but by two o'clock seven more miles had been covered. Only the flag at the masthead was now visible; and an impassable morass separated the force from the river bank. It was impossible to obtain supplies. Without food it was out of the question to go on. Indeed, great privations must, as it was, accompany the return march. The necessity was emphasised by the reports of captured fugitives, who all told the same tale. The Khalifa had pushed on swiftly, and was trying to reorganise his army. Colonel Broadwood thereupon rested his horses till the heat of the day was over, and then began the homeward march. It was not until eleven o'clock on the 4th of September that the worn-out and famished cavalry reached their camp near Omdurman.

Such was the pursuit as conducted by the regular troops. Abdel-Azim, with 750 Arabs, persisted still further in the chase. Lightly equipped, and acquainted with the country, they reached Shegeig, nearly a hundred miles south of Khartoum, on the 7th. Here they obtained definite information. The Khalifa had two days' start, plenty of food and water, and many camels. He had organised a bodyguard of 500 Jehadia, and was, besides, surrounded by a large force of Arabs of various tribes. With this numerous and powerful following he was travelling day and night towards El Obeid, which town was held by an unbeaten Dervish garrison of nearly 3,000 men. On hearing these things the friendly Arabs determined—not unwisely—to abandon the pursuit, and came boastfully back to Omdurman.

In the battle and capture of Omdurman the losses of the Expeditionary Force included the following British officers killed: Capt. G. Caldecott, 1st Royal Warwickshire Regiment; Lieut. R.G. Grenfell, 12th Royal Lancers, attached 21st Lancers; Hon. H. Howard, correspondent of the TIMES. In total, the British Division and Egyptian Army suffered 482 men killed or wounded.

The Dervish losses were, from computations made on the field and corrected at a later date, ascertained to be 9,700 killed, and wounded variously estimated at from 10,000 to 16,000. There were, besides, 5,000 prisoners.

CHAPTER XVII:

'THE FASHODA INCIDENT'

The long succession of events, of which I have attempted to give some account, has not hitherto affected to any great extent other countries than those which are drained by the Nile. But this chapter demands a wider view, since it must describe an incident which might easily have convulsed Europe, and from which far-reaching consequences have arisen. It is unlikely that the world will ever learn the details of the subtle scheme of which the Marchand Mission was a famous part. We may say with certainty that the French Government did not intend a small expedition, at great peril to itself, to seize and hold an obscure swamp on the Upper Nile. But it is not possible to define the other arrangements. What part the Abyssinians were expected to play, what services had been rendered them and what inducements they were offered, what attitude was to be adopted to the Khalifa, what use was to be made of the local tribes: all this is veiled in the mystery of intrigue. It is well known that for several years France, at some cost to herself and at a greater cost to Italy, had courted the friendship of Abyssinia, and that the weapons by which the Italians were defeated at Adowa had been mainly supplied through French channels. A small quick-firing gun of continental manufacture and of recent make which was found in the possession of the Khalifa seems to point to the existence or contemplation of similar relations with the Dervishes. But how far these operations were designed to assist the Marchand Mission is known only to those who initiated them, and to a few others who have so far kept their own counsel.

The undisputed facts are few. Towards the end of 1896 a French expedition was despatched from the Atlantic into the heart of Africa under the command of Major Marchand. The re-occupation of Dongola was then practically complete, and the British Government were earnestly considering the desirability of a further advance. In the beginning of 1897 a British expedition, under Colonel

Macdonald, and comprising a dozen carefully selected officers, set out from England to Uganda, landed at Mombassa, and struck inland. The misfortunes which fell upon this enterprise are beyond the scope of this account, and I shall not dwell upon the local jealousies and disputes which marred it. It is sufficient to observe that Colonel Macdonald was provided with Soudanese troops who were practically in a state of mutiny and actually mutinied two days after he assumed command. The officers were compelled to fight for their lives. Several were killed. A year was consumed in suppressing the mutiny and the revolt which arose out of it. If the object of the expedition was to reach the Upper Nile, it was soon obviously unattainable, and the Government were glad to employ the officers in making geographical surveys.

At the beginning of 1898 it was clear to those who, with the fullest information, directed the foreign policy of Great Britain that no results affecting the situation in the Soudan could be expected from the Macdonald Expedition. The advance to Khartoum and the reconquest of the lost provinces had been irrevocably undertaken. An Anglo-Egyptian force was already concentrating at Berber. Lastly, the Marchand Mission was known to be moving towards the Upper Nile, and it was a probable contingency that it would arrive at its destination within a few months. It was therefore evident that the line of advance of the powerful army moving south from the Mediterranean and of the tiny expedition moving east from the Atlantic must intersect before the end of the year, and that intersection would involve a collision between the Powers of Great Britain and France.

I do not pretend to any special information not hitherto given to the public in this further matter, but the reader may consider for himself whether the conciliatory policy which Lord Salisbury pursued towards Russia in China at this time—a policy which excited hostile criticism in England—was designed to influence the impending conflict on the Upper Nile and make it certain, or at least likely, that when Great Britain and France should be placed in direct opposition, France should find herself alone.

With these introductory reflections we may return to the theatre of the war.

On the 7th of September, five days after the battle and capture of Omdurman, the Tewfikia, a small Dervish steamer—one of those formerly used by General Gordon—came drifting and paddling down the river. Her Arab crew soon perceived by the Egyptian flags which were hoisted on the principal buildings, and by the battered condition of the Mahdi's Tomb, that all was not well in the city; and then, drifting a little further, they found themselves surrounded by the white gunboats of the 'Turks,' and so incontinently surrendered. The story they told their captors was a strange one. They had left Omdurman a month earlier, in company with the steamer Safia, carrying a force of 500 men, with the Khalifa's orders to go up the White Nile and collect grain. For some time all had been well; but on approaching the old Government station of Fashoda they had been fired on by black troops commanded by white officers under a strange flag—and fired on with such effect that they had lost some forty men killed and wounded. Doubting who these formidable enemies might be, the foraging expedition had turned back, and the Emir in command, having disembarked and formed a camp at a place on the east bank called Reng, had sent the Tewfikia back to ask the Khalifa for instructions and reinforcements. The story was carried to the Sirdar and ran like wildfire through the camp. Many officers made their way to the river, where the steamer lay, to test for themselves the truth of the report. The woodwork of the hull was marked with many newly made holes, and cutting into these with their penknives the officers extracted bullets—not the roughly cast leaden balls, the bits of telegraph wire, or old iron which savages use, but the conical nickel-covered bullets of small-bore rifles such as are fired by civilised forces alone. Here was positive proof. A European Power was on the Upper Nile: which? Some said it was the Belgians from the Congo; some that an Italian expedition had arrived; others thought that the strangers were French; others, again, believed in the Foreign Office—it was a British expedition, after all. The Arab crew were cross-examined as to the flag they had seen. Their replies were inconclusive. It had bright colours, they declared; but what those colours were and what their arrangement might be they could not tell; they were poor men, and God was very great.

Curiosity found no comfort but in patience or speculation. The camp for the most part received the news with a shrug. After their easy victory the soldiers walked delicately. They knew that they belonged to the most powerful force that had ever penetrated the heart of Africa. If there was to be more war, the Government had but to give the word, and the Grand Army of the Nile would do by these newcomers as they had done by the Dervishes.

On the 8th the Sirdar started up the White Nile for Fashoda with five steamers, the XIth and XIIIth Battalions of Soudanese, two companies of the Cameron Highlanders, Peake's battery of artillery, and four Maxim guns. Three days later he arrived at Reng, and there found, as the crew of the Tewfikia had declared, some 500 Dervishes encamped on the bank, and the Safia steamer moored to it. These stupid fellows had the temerity to open fire on the vessels. Whereat the Sultan, steaming towards their dem, replied with a fierce shell fire which soon put them to flight. The Safia, being under steam, made some attempt to escape—whither, it is impossible to say—and Commander Keppel by a well-directed shell in her boilers blew her up, much to the disgust of the Sirdar, who wanted to add her to his flotilla.

After this incident the expedition continued its progress up the White Nile. The sudd which was met with two days' journey south of Khartoum did not in this part of the Nile offer any obstacle to navigation, as the strong current of the river clears the waterway; but on either side of the channel a belt of the tangled weed, varying from twelve to twelve hundred yards in breadth, very often prevented the steamers from approaching the bank to tie up. The banks themselves depressed the explorers by their melancholy inhospitality. At times the river flowed past miles of long grey grass and swamp-land, inhabited and habitable only by hippopotami. At times a vast expanse of dreary mud flats stretched as far as the eye could see. At others the forest, dense with an impenetrable undergrowth of thorn-bushes, approached the water, and the active forms of monkeys and even of leopards darted among the trees. But the country—whether forest, mud-flat, or prairie—was always damp and feverish: a wet land steaming under a burning sun and humming with mosquitoes and all kinds of insect life.

Onward and southward toiled the flotilla, splashing the brown water into foam and startling the strange creatures on the banks, until on the 18th of September they approached Fashoda. The gunboats waited, moored to the bank for some hours of the afternoon, to allow a message which had been sent by the Sirdar to the mysterious Europeans, to precede his arrival, and early in the morning of the 19th a small steel rowing-boat was observed coming down stream to meet the expedition. It contained a Senegalese sergeant and two men, with a letter from Major Marchand announcing the arrival of the French troops and their formal occupation of the Soudan. It, moreover, congratulated the Sirdar on his victory, and welcomed him to Fashoda in the name of France.

A few miles' further progress brought the gunboats to their destination, and they made fast to the bank near the old Government buildings of the town. Major Marchand's party consisted of eight French officers or non-commissioned officers, and 120 black soldiers drawn from the Niger district. They possessed three steel boats fitted for sail or oars, and a small steam launch, the Faidherbe, which latter had, however, been sent south for reinforcements. They had six months' supplies of provisions for the French officers, and about three months' rations for the men; but they had no artillery, and were in great want of small-arm ammunition. Their position was indeed precarious. The little force was stranded, without communications of any sort, and with no means of either withstanding an attack or of making a retreat. They had fired away most of their cartridges at the Dervish foraging party, and were daily expecting a renewed attack. Indeed, it was with consternation that they had heard of the approach of the flotilla. The natives had carried the news swiftly up the river that the Dervishes were coming back with five steamers, and for three nights the French had been sleeplessly awaiting the assault of a powerful enemy.

Their joy and relief at the arrival of a European force were undisguised. The Sirdar and his officers on their part were thrilled with admiration at the wonderful achievements of this small band of heroic men. Two years had passed since they left the Atlantic coast. For four months they had been absolutely lost from human ken. They had fought with savages; they had struggled with fever; they had climbed mountains and pierced the most gloomy forests. Five days and five nights they had stood up to their necks in swamp and water. A fifth of their number had perished; yet at last they had carried out their mission and, arriving at Fashoda on the 10th of July, had planted the tricolour upon the Upper Nile.

Moved by such reflections the British officers disembarked. Major Marchand, with a guard of honour, came to meet the General. They shook hands warmly. 'I congratulate you,' said the Sirdar, 'on all you have accomplished.' 'No,' replied the Frenchman, pointing to his troops; 'it is not I, but these soldiers who have done it.' And Kitchener, telling the story afterwards, remarked, 'Then I knew he was a gentleman.'

Into the diplomatic discussions that followed, it is not necessary to plunge. The Sirdar politely ignored the French flag, and, without interfering with the Marchand Expedition and the fort it occupied, hoisted the British and Egyptian colours with all due ceremony, amid musical honours and the salutes of the gunboats. A garrison was established at Fashoda, consisting of the XIth Soudanese, four guns of Peake's battery, and two Maxims, the whole under the command of Colonel Jackson, who was appointed military and civil commandant of the Fashoda district.

At three o'clock on the same afternoon the Sirdar and the gunboats resumed their journey to the south, and the next day reached the mouth of the Sobat, sixty-two miles from Fashoda. Here other flags were hoisted and another post formed with a garrison of half the XIIIth Soudanese battalion and the remaining two guns of Peake's battery. The expedition then turned northwards, leaving two gunboats—the Sultan and the Abu Klea—at the disposal of Colonel Jackson.

I do not attempt to describe the international negotiations and discussions that followed the receipt of the news in Europe, but it is pleasing to remember that a great crisis found England united. The determination of the Government was approved by the loyalty of the Opposition, supported by the calm resolve of the people, and armed with the efficiency of the fleet. At first indeed, while the Sirdar was still steaming southward, wonder and suspense filled all minds; but when suspense ended in the certainty that eight French adventurers were in occupation of Fashoda and claimed a territory twice as large as France, it gave place to a deep and bitter anger. There is no Power in Europe which the average Englishman regards with less animosity than France. Nevertheless, on this matter all were agreed. They should go. They should evacuate Fashoda, or else all the might, majesty, dominion, and power of everything that could by any stretch of the imagination be called 'British' should be employed to make them go.

Those who find it difficult to account for the hot, almost petulant, flush of resolve that stirred the nation must look back over the long history of the Soudan drama. It had always been a duty to reconquer the abandoned territory. When it was found that this might be safely done, the duty became a pleasure. The operations were watched with extravagant attention, and while they progressed the earnestness of the nation increased. As the tides of barbarism were gradually driven back, the old sea-marks came one after another into view. Names of towns that were half forgotten—or remembered only with sadness—re-appeared on the posters, in the gazettes, and in the newspapers. We were going back. 'Dongola,' 'Berber,' 'Metemma'—who had not heard of them before? Now they were associated with triumph. Considerable armies fought on the Indian Frontier. There was war in the South and the East and the West of Africa. But England looked steadfastly towards the Nile and the expedition that crawled forward slowly, steadily, unchecked, apparently irresistible.

When the final triumph, long expected, came in all its completeness it was hailed with a shout of exultation, and the people of Great Britain, moved far beyond their wont, sat themselves down to give thanks to their God, their Government, and their General. Suddenly, on the chorus of their rejoicing there broke a discordant note. They were confronted with the fact that a 'friendly Power' had, unprovoked, endeavoured to rob them of the fruits of their victories. They now realised that while they had been devoting themselves to great military operations, in broad daylight and the eye of the world, and prosecuting an enterprise on which they had set their hearts, other operations—covert and deceitful—had been in progress in the heart of the Dark Continent, designed solely for the mischievous and spiteful object of depriving them of the produce of their labours. And they firmly set their faces against such behaviour.

First of all, Great Britain was determined to have Fashoda or fight; and as soon as this was made clear, the French were willing to give way. Fashoda was a miserable swamp, of no particular value to them. Marchand, Lord Salisbury's 'explorer in difficulties upon the Upper Nile,' was admitted by the French Minister to be merely an 'emissary of civilisation.' It was not worth their while to embark on the hazards and convulsions of a mighty war for either swamp or emissary. Besides, the plot had failed. Guy Fawkes, true to his oath and his orders, had indeed reached the vault; but the other conspirators were less devoted. The Abyssinians had held aloof. The negro tribes gazed with wonder on the strangers, but had no intention of fighting for them. The pride and barbarism of the Khalifa rejected all overtures and disdained to discriminate between the various breeds of the accursed 'Turks.' Finally, the victory of Omdurman and its forerunner—the Desert Railway—had revolutionised the whole situation in the Nile valley. After some weeks of tension, the French Government consented to withdraw their expedition from the region of the Upper Nile.

Meanwhile events were passing at Fashoda. The town, the site of which had been carefully selected by the old Egyptian Government, is situated on the left bank of the river, on a gentle slope of ground which rises about four feet above the level of the Nile at full flood. During the rainy season, which lasts from the end of June until the end of October, the surrounding country is one vast swamp, and Fashoda itself becomes an island. It is not, however, without its importance; for it is the only spot on the west shore for very many miles where landing from the river is possible. All the roads—mere camel-tracks—from Lower Kordofan meet at the Government post, but are only passable in the dry season. The soil is fertile, and, since there is a superabundance of sun and water, almost any crop or plant can be grown. The French officers, with the adaptive thrift of their nation, had already, in spite of the ravages of the water-rats, created a good vegetable garden, from which they were able to supplement their monotonous fare. The natives, however—aboriginal negroes of the Dinka and Shillook tribes—are unwilling to work, except to provide themselves with the necessaries of life; and since these are easily obtained, there is very little cultivation, and the fertility of the soil may be said to increase the poverty of the country. At all seasons of the year the climate of Fashoda is pestilential, and the malarial fever attacks every European or Egyptian, breaking down the strongest constitutions, and in many cases causing death. [The place is most unhealthy, and in March 1899 (the driest season of the year) out of a garrison of 317 men only 37 were fit for duty.—Sir William Garstin's Report: EGYPT, No. 5, 1899.]

On this dismal island, far from civilisation, health, or comfort, the Marchand Mission and the Egyptian garrison lived in polite antagonism for nearly three months. The French fort stood at the northern end. The Egyptian camp lay outside the ruins of the town. Civilities were constantly exchanged between the forces, and the British officers repaid the welcome gifts of fresh vegetables by newspapers and other conveniences. The Senegalese riflemen were smart and well-conducted soldiers, and the blacks of the Soudanese battalion soon imitated their officers in reciprocating courtesies. A feeling of mutual respect sprang up between Colonel Jackson and Major Marchand. The dashing commandant of the XIth Soudanese, whose Egyptian medals bear no fewer than fourteen clasps, was filled with a generous admiration for the French explorer. Realising the difficulties, he appreciated the magnificence of the achievement; and as he spoke excellent French a good and almost cordial understanding was established, and no serious disagreement occurred. But, notwithstanding the polite relations, the greatest vigilance was exercised by both sides, and whatever civilities were exchanged were of a formal nature.

The Dinkas and Shillooks had on the first arrival of the French made submission, and had supplied them with provisions. They knew that white men were said to be coming, and they did not realise that there were different races among the whites. Marchand was regarded as the advance guard of the Sirdar's army. But when the negroes gradually perceived that these bands of white men were at enmity with each other—were, in fact, of rival tribes—they immediately transferred their allegiance to the stronger force, and, although their dread of the Egyptian flag was at first very marked, boycotted the French entirely.

In the middle of October despatches from France arrived for Marchand by steamer; and that officer, after reading them, determined to proceed to Cairo. Jackson, who was most anxious that no disagreement should arise, begged him to give positive orders to his subordinate to maintain the status quo, as had been agreed. Marchand gladly consented, and departed for Omdurman, where he visited the battlefield, and found in the heaps of slain a grim witness of the destruction from which he had been saved, and so on to Cairo, where he was moved to tears and speeches. But in his absence Captain Germain, who succeeded to the command, diverged from his orders, No sooner had Marchand left than Germain, anxious to win distinction, embarked upon a most aggressive policy. He occupied the Dinka country on the right bank of the river, pushed reconnoitring parties into the interior, prevented the Dinka Sheikhs from coming to make their submission at Fashoda, and sent his boats and the Faidherbe steam launch, which had returned from the south, beyond the northern limits which the Sirdar had prescribed and Marchand had agreed to recognise.

Colonel Jackson protested again and again. Germain sent haughty replies, and persisted in his provoking policy. At last the British officer was compelled to declare that if any more patrols were sent into the Dinka country, he would not allow them to return to the French post. Whereat Germain rejoined that he would meet force with force. All tempers were worn by fever, heat, discomfort, and monotony. The situation became very difficult, and the tact and patience of Colonel Jackson alone averted a conflict which would have resounded in all parts of the world. He confined his troops strictly to their lines, and moved as far from the French camp as was possible. But there was one dark day when the

French officers worked in their shirts with their faithful Senegalese to strengthen the entrenchments, and busily prepared for a desperate struggle. On the other side little activity was noticeable. The Egyptian garrison, although under arms, kept out of sight, but a wisp of steam above the funnels of the redoubtable gunboats showed that all was ready.

At length in a fortunate hour Marchand returned, reproved his subordinate, and expressed his regrets to Colonel Jackson. Then it became known that the French Government had ordered the evacuation of Fashoda. Some weeks were spent in making preparations for the journey, but at length the day of departure arrived. At 8.20 on the morning of the 11th of December the French lowered their flag with salute and flourish of bugle. The British officers, who remained in their own camp and did not obtrude themselves, were distant but interested spectators. On the flag ceasing to fly, a sous-officier rushed up to the flagstaff and hurled it to the ground, shaking his fists and tearing his hair in a bitterness and vexation from which it is impossible to withhold sympathy, in view of what these men had suffered uselessly and what they had done. The French then embarked, and at 9.30 steamed southward, the Faidherbe towing one oblong steel barge and one old steel boat, the other three boats sailing, all full of men. As the little flotilla passed the Egyptian camp a guard of honour of the XIth Soudanese saluted them and the band struck up their national anthem. The French acknowledged the compliment by dipping their flag, and in return the British and Egyptian flags were also lowered. The boats then continued their journey until they had rounded the bend of the river, when they came to land, and, honour being duly satisfied, Marchand and his officers returned to breakfast with Colonel Jackson. The meeting was very friendly. Jackson and Germain exchanged most elaborate compliments, and the commandant, in the name of the XIth Soudanese, presented the expedition with the banner of the Emir who had attacked them, which had been captured at Reng. Marchand shook hands all round, and the British officers bade their gallant opponents a final farewell.

Once again the eight Frenchmen, who had come so far and accomplished so much, set out upon their travels, to make a safe though tedious journey through Abyssinia to the coast, and thence home to the country they had served faithfully and well, and which was not unmindful of their services.

Let us settle the international aspect of the reconquest of the Soudan while we are in the way with it. The disputes between France and England about the valley of the Upper Nile were terminated, as far as material cause was concerned, by an Agreement, signed in London on the 21st of March, 1899, by Lord Salisbury and M. Cambon. The Declaration limiting the respective spheres of influence of the two Powers took the form of an addition to the IVth Article of the Niger Convention, concluded in the previous year. Its practical effect is to reserve the whole drainage system of the Nile to England and Egypt, and to engage that France shall have a free hand, so far as those Powers are concerned, in the rest of Northern Africa west of the Nile Valley not yet occupied by Europeans. This stupendous partition of half a continent by two European Powers could scarcely be expected to excite the enthusiasm of the rest. Germany was, however, soothed by the promise of the observance of the 'Open Door' policy upon the Upper Nile. Italy, protesting meekly, followed Germany. Russia had no interests in this quarter. France and England were agreed. The rest were not consulted: and the Declaration may thus be said to have been recognised by the world in general.

It is perhaps early to attempt to pronounce with which of the contracting Powers the advantage lies. France has acquired at a single stroke, without any serious military operations, the recognition of rights which may enable her ultimately to annex a vast African territory. At present what she has gained may be described as a recognised 'sphere of aspiration.' The future may convert this into a sphere of influence, and the distant future may witness the entire subjugation of the whole region. There are many difficulties to be overcome. The powerful influence of the Senussi has yet to be overthrown. The independent kingdom of Wadai must be conquered. Many smaller potentates will resist desperately. Altogether France has enough to occupy her in Central Africa for some time to come: and even when the long task is finished, the conquered regions are not likely to be of great value. They include the desert of the Great Sahara and wide expanses of equally profitless scrub or marsh. Only one important river, the Shari, flows through them, and never reaches the sea: and even Lake Chad, into which the Shari flows, appears to be leaking through some subterranean exit, and is rapidly changing from a lake into an immense swamp.

Great Britain and Egypt, upon the other hand, have secured a territory which, though smaller, is nevertheless of enormous extent, more fertile, comparatively easy of access, practically conquered, and containing the waterway of the Nile. France will be able to paint a great deal of the map of Africa blue, and the aspect of the continent upon paper may please the patriotic eye; but it is already possible to predict that before she can develop her property—can convert aspiration into influence, and influence into occupation—she will have to work harder, pay more, and wait longer for a return than will the more modest owners of the Nile Valley. And even when that return is obtained, it is unlikely that it will be of so much value.

It only remains to discuss the settlement made between the conquerors of the Soudan. Great Britain and Egypt had moved hand in hand up the great river, sharing, though unequally, the cost of the war in men and money. The prize belonged to both. The direct annexation of the Soudan by Great Britain would have been an injustice to Egypt. Moreover, the claim of the conquerors to Fashoda and other territories rested solely on the former rights of Egypt. On the other hand, if the Soudan became Egyptian again, it must wear the fetters of that imprisoned country. The Capitulations would apply to the Upper Nile regions, as to the Delta. Mixed Tribunals, Ottoman Suzerainty, and other vexatious burdens would be added to the difficulties of Soudan administration. To free the new country from the curse of internationalism was a paramount object. The Soudan Agreement by Great Britain and Egypt, published on the 7th of March, 1899, achieves this. Like most of the best work done in Egypt by the British Agency, the Agreement was slipped through without attracting much notice. Under its authority a State has been created in the Nile Valley which is neither British nor Ottoman, nor anything else so far known to the law of Europe. International jurists are confronted with an entirely new political status. A diplomatic 'Fourth Dimension' has been discovered. Great Britain and Egypt rule the country together. The allied conquerors have become the joint-possessors. 'What does this Soudan Agreement mean?' the Austrian Consul-General asked Lord Cromer; and the British Agent, whom twenty-two years' acquaintance with Egyptian affairs had accustomed to anomalies, replied, 'It means simply this'; and handed him the inexplicable document, under which the conquered country may some day march to Peace and Plenty.

CHAPTER XVIII:

ON THE BLUE NILE

The authority of the Khalifa and the strength of his army were for ever broken on the 2nd of September, and the battle of Omdurman is the natural climax of this tale of war. To those who fought, and still more to those who fell, in the subsequent actions the climax came somewhat later. After the victory the public interest was no longer centred in the Soudan. The last British battalion had been carried north of Assuan; the last Press correspondent had hurried back to Cairo or London. But the military operations were by no means over.

The enemy had been defeated. It remained to reconquer the territory. The Dervishes of the provincial garrisons still preserved their allegiance to the Khalifa. Several strong Arab forces kept the field. Distant Kordofan and even more distant Darfur were as yet quite unaffected by the great battle at the confluence of the Niles. There were rumours of Europeans in the Far South.

The unquestioned command of the waterways which the Sirdar enjoyed enabled the greater part of the Egyptian Soudan to be at once formally re-occupied. All towns or stations on the main rivers and their tributaries were at the mercy of the gunboats. It was only necessary to send troops to occupy them and to hoist the British and Egyptian flags. Two expeditions were forthwith sent up the White and Blue Niles to establish garrisons, and as far as possible to subdue the country. The first, under the personal command of the Sirdar, left Omdurman on the 8th of September, and steamed up the White Nile towards Fashoda. The events which followed that momentous journey have already been related. The second expedition consisted of the gunboats Sheikh and Hafir, together with two companies and the brass band of the Xth Soudanese and a Maxim battery, all under the command of General Hunter. Leaving Omdurman on the 19th of September, they started up the Blue Nile to Abu Haraz. The rest of the Xth Battalion followed as soon as other steamers were set free from the business of taking the British division to the Atbara and bringing supplies to Omdurman. The progress of the expedition up the river resembled a triumphal procession. The people of the riparian villages assembled on the banks, and, partly from satisfaction at being relieved from the oppression of the Khalifa and the scourge of war, partly from fear, and partly from wonder, gave vent to loud and long-continued cheers. As the gunboats advanced the inhabitants escorted them along the bank, the men dancing and waving their swords, and the women uttering shrill cries of welcome. The reception of the expedition when places of importance were passed, and the crowd amounted to several thousands, is described as very stirring, and, we are told, such was the enthusiasm of the natives that they even broke up their houses to supply the gunboats with wood for fuel. Whether this be true or not I cannot tell, but it is in any case certain that the vessels were duly supplied, and that the expedition in its progress was well received by the negroid tribes, who had long resented the tyranny of the Arabs.

On the 22nd of September a considerable part of the army of Osman Digna, which had not been present at the battle of Omdurman, was found encamped on the Ghezira, a few miles north of Rufaa. The Sheikhs and Emirs, on being summoned by General Hunter, surrendered, and a force of about 2,000 men laid down their arms. Musa Digna, a nephew of Osman and the commander of his forces, was put in irons and held prisoner. The rest, who were mostly from the Suakin district, were given a safe-conduct, and told to return to their homes—an order they lost no time in obeying.

The next day the general arrived at Wad Medina, where the Dervish garrison—1,000 strong—had already surrendered to the gunboat Sheikh. These men, who were regular Dervishes, were transported in sailing-boats to Omdurman; and augmented the number of prisoners of war already collected. On the 29th of September General Hunter reached Rosaires, 400 miles south of Khartoum, and the extreme limit of steam navigation on the Blue Nile. By the 3rd of October he had established garrisons of the Xth Soudanese in Rosaires, at Karkoj, at Sennar (the old seat of the Government of the province), and at Wad Medina. Having also arranged for gunboat patrolling, he returned to Omdurman.

But there was one Dervish force which had no intention of surrendering to the invaders, and whose dispersal was not accomplished until three fierce and critical actions had been fought. Ahmed Fedil, a zealous and devoted adherent of the Khalifa, had been sent, after the defeat on the Atbara, to collect all the Dervishes who could be spared from the Gedaref and Gallabat provinces, and bring them to join the growing army at Omdurman. The Emir had faithfully discharged his duty, and he was hurrying to his master's assistance with a strong and well disciplined force of no fewer than 8,000 men when, while yet sixty miles from the city, he received the news of 'the stricken field.' He immediately halted, and sought to hide the disaster from his soldiers by announcing that the Khalifa had been victorious and no longer needed their assistance. He even explained the appearance of gunboats upon the river by saying that these had run past the batteries at Omdurman and that the others were destroyed. The truth was not, however, long concealed; for a few days later two emissaries despatched by Slatin arrived at the Dervish camp and announced the destruction of the Omdurman army, the flight of the Khalifa, and the fall of the city. The messengers were authorised to offer Ahmed terms; but that implacable Dervish flew into a rage, and, having shot one, sent the other, covered with insults and stripes, to tell the 'Turks' that he would fight to the bitter end. He then struck his camp, and marched back along the east bank of the Blue Nile, with the intention of crossing the river near its confluence with the Rahad, and so joining the Khalifa in Kordofan. His Dervishes, however, did not view this project with satisfaction. Their families and women had been left with large stores of grain and ammunition in Gedaref, under a strong garrison of 3,000 men. They urged their commander to return and collect these possessions. Ahmed at first refused, but when on arriving at the place of passage he found himself confronted with a gunboat, he resolved to make a virtue of necessity and set out leisurely for Gedaref.

On the 5th of September Colonel Parsons, in command of the forces at Kassala, heard through the Italian Governor of Eritrea of the victory at Omdurman. The next day official news arrived from England, and in conformity with previous instructions he set out on the 7th for Gedaref. It was known that Ahmed Fedil had marched towards Omdurman. It was believed that Gedaref was only weakly held, and the opportunity of cutting the most powerful remaining Dervish army from its base was too precious to be neglected. But the venture was desperate. The whole available strength of the Kassala garrison was mustered. With these 1,350 motley soldiers, untried, little disciplined, worn with waiting and wasted by disease, without cavalry, artillery, or machine guns, and with only seven British officers, including the doctor, Gedaref was taken, and, having been taken, was held.

After two long marches Colonel Parsons and his force arrived at El Fasher, on the right bank of the Atbara. Their advance, which had hitherto led them through a waterless desert, was now checked by a raging torrent. The river was in full flood, and a channel of deep water, broader than the Thames below London Bridge and racing along at seven miles an hour, formed a serious obstacle. Since there were no boats the soldiers began forthwith to construct rafts from barrels that had been brought for the purpose. As soon as the first of these was completed, it was sent on a trial trip. The result was not encouraging. The raft supported ten men, occupied five hours in the passage, was carried ten miles down stream, and came back for its second journey on the afternoon of the next day. It was evident that this means of transport was out of the question. The only chance of success—indeed, of safety—lay in the force reaching and taking Gedaref before the return of Ahmed Fedil. All depended upon speed; yet here was a hopeless delay. After prolonged discussion it was resolved to act on the suggestion of an Egyptian officer and endeavour to build boats. The work proved easier than was anticipated. The elastic wood of the mimosa scrub supplied the frames; some tarpaulins—fortunately available—formed the outer covering. The Egyptian soldiers, who delighted in the work, succeeded in making daily from such materials one boat capable of carrying two tons; and in these ingenious contrivances the whole force crossed to the further bank. The camels, mules, and horses of the transport—their heads supported with inflated water-skins tied under their jowls—were made to swim across the river by the local Shukrieh Arabs. Such was the skill of these tribesmen that only one camel and one mule were drowned during the operation. The passage was completed on the 16th, and the next day the advance was resumed along the west bank of the Atbara. At midday on the 18th Mugatta was reached, and at dawn on the 20th the little force—having filled their water-skins, tightened their belts, and invoked the assistance of the various gods they worshipped—started off, and marched all day in single file through the thick bush which lies between the Atbara and Gedaref. The column retired to rest peacefully during the night of the 21st, although within twelve miles of Gedaref. But at midnight startling news arrived. A deserter from the Dervishes made his way into the camp and informed Colonel Parsons that the Emir Saadalla awaited him with 3,500 men two miles before the town. The situation was grave. A retreat through the broken country and thick bush in the face of a powerful and triumphant enemy seemed impossible. There was no alternative but to attack.

Very early on the morning of the 22nd—the same day on which General Hunter on the Blue Nile was compelling Musa Digna and his followers to surrender—Colonel Parsons and the Kassala column set forth to march into Gedaref and to fight whatever force it might contain. For the first two hours the road lay through doura plantations and high grass which rose above the heads even of men mounted on camels; but as the town was approached, the doura ceased, and the troops emerged from the jungle on to an undulating moorland with occasional patches of rushes and withered grass. At half-past seven, and about three miles from Gedaref, the enemy's scouts were encountered. A few shots were fired. The soldiers pressed their march, and at eight o'clock had reached a small knoll, from the top of which an extensive view was obtainable. The column halted, and Colonel Parsons and his officers ascended the eminence to reconnoitre.

A most menacing spectacle confronted them. Scarcely a mile away a strong force of Dervishes was rapidly advancing to meet the invaders. Four lines of white figures rising out of the grass showed by their length the number, and by their regularity the discipline, of the enemy. The officers computed the strength of their antagonists at not fewer than 4,000. Subsequent investigation has shown that the Emir Saadalla marched out of Gedaref with 1,700 riflemen, 1,600 spearmen, and 300 horse.

The swiftness of the Dervish advance and the short space that intervened between the forces made it evident that a collision would take place within half an hour. The valley was rocky, and overgrown with grass and reeds; but to the right of the track there rose a high saddleback hill, the surface of which looked more open, and which appeared to command the approaches from Gedaref. The troops knew nothing of the country; the Dervishes understood it thoroughly. The high ground gave at least advantage of view. Colonel Parsons resolved to occupy it. Time was however, very scanty.

The order was given, and the column began to double across the valley towards the saddleback. The Dervishes, perceiving the nature of the movement, hurried their advance in the hope of catching the troops on the move and perhaps of even seizing the hill itself. But they were too late. Colonel Parsons and his force reached the saddleback safely, and with a few minutes to spare climbed up and advanced along it in column in the direction of Gedaref—the Arab battalion leading, the 16th Egyptians next, and last of all the irregulars.

The Dervishes, seeing that the troops had already reached the hill and were moving along it towards the town, swung to their left and advanced to the attack. Thereupon at half-past eight the column wheeled into line to meet them, and standing in the long grass, which even on the summit of the hill was nearly breast-high, opened a heavy and destructive fire. The enemy, although suffering severe loss, continued to struggle bravely onward, replying vigorously to the musketry of the soldiers. At nine o'clock, while the frontal attack was still undecided, Colonel Parsons became aware that a strong force of Dervishes had moved round the left rear and were about to attack the hospital and transport. He at once sent to warn Captain Fleming, R.A.M.C., who combined the duties of medical officer and commander of the baggage column, of the impending assault, and directed him to close up the camels and meet it. The Arab Sheikhs, who in the absence of officers were acting as orderlies, had scarcely brought the news to Fleming, when the Dervish attack developed. The enemy, some 300 strong, rushed with great determination upon the baggage, and the escort of 120 Arab irregulars at once broke and fled. The situation became desperate; but Ruthven with thirty-four Supply Department camel-men hastened to meet the exultant enemy and protect the baggage column, and the transport was stubbornly defended. In spite of all their efforts the rear of the baggage column was broken and cut up. The survivors escaped along the saddleback. The British officers, with their small following, fell back towards their main body, hotly pressed by the enemy.

At this moment Captain Ruthven observed one of his native officers, lying wounded on the ground, about to fall into the hands of the Dervishes and perish miserably. He immediately went back and, being a man of great physical strength, carried the body off in his arms. The enemy were, however, so close that he was three times compelled to set his burden down and defend himself with his revolver. Meanwhile the retirement towards the main body continued and accelerated.

Colonel Parsons and his force were now between two fires. The frontal attack was within 200 yards. The rear attack, flushed with success, were hurrying impetuously forward. The defeat and consequent total destruction of the Kassala column appeared certain. But in the nick of time the Dervish frontal attack, which had been suffering heavily from the fire of the troops, wavered; and when the Arab battalion and the 16th Egyptians advanced upon them to complete their discomfiture, they broke and fled. Colonel Parsons at once endeavoured to meet the rear attack. The Arab battalion, whose valour was more admirable than their discipline, continued to pursue the beaten enemy down the hill; but the 16th Egyptians, on being called upon by their commanding officer, Captain McKerrell, faced steadily about and turned to encounter the fresh attack.

The heavy fire of the regular battalion checked the Dervish advance, and Captain Fleming, the rest of the dismounted camel-men, and Ruthven still carrying his native officer, found safety in their ranks. [For his gallantry on this occasion Captain Ruthven has since received the Victoria Cross.] A short fierce musketry combat followed at a range of less than a hundred yards, at the end of which the assailants of the baggage convoy were completely repulsed. The action was now practically over and success was won. The Arab battalion, and those of the irregulars that had rallied, advanced and drove the enemy before them towards Gedaref, until at ten o'clock, both their front and rear attacks having failed, the Dervishes abandoned all resistance and a general rout ensued. No cavalry or artillery being available, further pursuit was impossible.

The town of Gedaref surrendered at noon. The Dervish Emir, Nur Angara, who with 200 black riflemen and two brass guns had been left in command of the garrison, made haste to submit. The remainder of the Dervishes, continuing their flight under the Emir Saadalla, hurried to tell the tale of defeat to Ahmed Fedil.

The casualties suffered by the Kassala column in the action were severe in proportion to their numbers and the duration of the fight. The seven British officers escaped untouched; but of the 1,400 soldiers and irregulars engaged, 51 were killed and 80 wounded—a total of 131. The Dervishes left 500 dead on the field, including four Emirs of rank.

The victory had been won, the enemy were routed, and the town was taken: it had now to be defended. Colonel Parsons took possession of the principal buildings, and began immediately to put them in a state of defence. This was fortunately an easy matter. The position was good and adaptable. It consisted of three large enclosures, capable of holding the entire force, situated in echelon, so as to protect each other by their fire, and with strong brick walls six feet high. All were at once set to work to clear the approaches, to level the mud houses without, and to build ramparts or banquettes within the walls. The three enclosures thus became three forts, and in the principal work the two captured brass guns were mounted, in small bastions thrown out from the north and west corners. While the infantry were thus engaged, Ruthven and his camel-men made daily reconnaissances of the surrounding country, and eagerly looked for the first appearance of Ahmed Fedil.

By great good fortune a convoy of ammunition from Mugatta reached Gedaref on the afternoon of the 27th. At dawn the next day Ruthven reported that the advance guard of Ahmed Fedil was approaching the town. The attack began at half-past eight. The Dervishes, who fought with their customary gallantry, simultaneously assaulted the north, south, and west faces of the defences. Creeping forward through the high doura, they were able to get within 300 yards of the enclosures. But the intervening space had been carefully cleared of cover, and was swept by the musketry of the defenders. All attempts to cross this ground—even the most determined rushes—proved vain. While some made hopeless charges towards the walls, others crowded into a few straw shelters and mud huts which the troops had not found opportunity to remove, and thence maintained a ragged fire. After an hour's heavy fusillade the attack weakened, and presently ceased altogether. At ten o'clock, however, strong reinforcements having come up, the Dervishes made a second attempt. They were again repulsed, and at a quarter to eleven, after losing more than 500 men in killed and wounded, Ahmed Fedil admitted his defeat and retired to a clump of palm-trees two miles to the west of the town. The casualties among the defenders were five men killed, one British officer (Captain Dwyer) and thirteen men wounded.

The Dervishes remained for two days in the palm grove, and their leader repeatedly endeavoured to induce them to renew the attack. But although they closely surrounded the enclosures, and maintained a dropping fire, they refused to knock their heads against brick walls a third time; and on the 1st of October Ahmed Fedil was forced to retire to a more convenient camp eight miles to the southward. Here for the next three weeks he remained, savage and sulky; and the Kassala column were content to keep to their defences. A few convoys from Mugatta made their way into the forts under the cover of darkness, but for all practical purposes the blockade of the garrison was complete. Their losses in action had reduced their strength. They were not abundantly supplied with ammunition. The smell of the putrefying corpses which lay around the walls and in the doura crop, together with the unhealthy climate and the filth of the town, was a fertile source of disease. A painful and racking fever afflicted all ranks, and at one time as many as 270 of the 400 regular soldiers were prostrated. The recurring night alarms added to the fatigues of the troops and the anxieties of the seven officers. The situation was indeed so unsatisfactory that Colonel Parsons was compelled to ask for assistance.

Major-General Rundle, who in the Sirdar's absence held the chief command, immediately organised a relief expedition. The IXth, XIIth, and half of the XIIIth Soudanese, with three companies of the Camel Corps, under Colonel Collinson, were at once sent from Omdurman to the mouth of the Rahad river. The infantry were conveyed in steamers; the Camel Corps marched along the bank, completing the whole distance of 130 miles in fifty-six hours. The Blue Nile garrisons, with the exception of the post at Rosaires, were also concentrated. By the 8th of October the whole force was collected at Abu Haraz. Five hundred camels, which had marched from Omdurman, and every available local beast of burden joined the transport of the column. On the 9th the XIIth Soudanese started up the Rahad river for Ain el Owega. From this point the road leaves the river and strikes across the desert to Gedaref, a distance of 100 miles; and in the whole distance water is only found at the wells of El Kau. Owing to this scarcity of water it was necessary to carry a supply with the troops. The transport being insufficient to provide for the whole force, the march had to be made in two columns. The Camel Corps and the XIIth Soudanese, about 1,200 strong, set forth under Colonel Collinson from Ain el Owega on the 17th, and reached Gedaref safely on the 22nd. Warned of their arrival, Ahmed Fedil, having made a feeble night attack which was repulsed by the garrison with a loss to themselves of two Soudanese wounded, realised that he had now no chance of recapturing the town. Preparations were indeed made to attack him; but on the 23rd of October, when a reconnaissance was made in the direction of his camp, the Dervish force was seen moving off in a southerly direction, their retreat covered by a strong rearguard, which was intended to perform the double duty of protecting the retirement and preventing desertion.

The operations conducted by Colonel Parsons thus ended in complete success. Great difficulties were overcome, great perils were encountered, great results were obtained. But while we applaud the skill of the commander and the devotion of his subordinates, it is impossible not to criticise the rash and over-confident policy which sent such a weak and ill-equipped force on so hazardous an enterprise. The action of Gedaref, as has been shown, was, through no fault of the officers or men of the expedition, within an ace of being a disaster. But there were other critical occasions when only the extraordinary good fortune which attended the force saved it from destruction. First, the column was not discovered until it reached Mugatta; secondly, it was not attacked in the thick bush; thirdly, the Dervishes gave battle in the open instead of remaining within their walls, whence the troops could not have driven them without artillery; and, fourthly, the reserve ammunition arrived before the attack of Ahmed Fedil.

After his defeat before Gedaref, Ahmed Fedil reverted to his intention of joining the Khalifa in Kordofan, and he withdrew southwards towards the Dinder river with a following that still numbered more than 5,000. To pass the Nile in the face of the gunboats appeared impossible. He did not, however, believe that steamers could navigate the higher reaches of the rivers, and in the hopes of finding a safe crossing-place he directed his march so as to strike the Blue Nile south of Karkoj. Moving leisurely, and with frequent delays to pillage the inhabitants, he arrived on the Dinder, twenty-five miles to the east of Karkoj, on the 7th of November. Here he halted to reconnoitre. He had trusted in the Karkoj-Rosaires reach being too shallow for the gunboats; but he found two powerful vessels already patrolling it. Again frustrated, he turned southwards, meaning to cross above the Rosaires Cataract, which was without doubt impassable to steamers.

On the 22nd of October Colonel Lewis, with two companies of the Camel Corps and three squadrons of cavalry, started from Omdurman with the object of marching through the centre of the Ghezira and of re-establishing the Egyptian authority. His progress was in every way successful. The inhabitants were submissive, and resigned themselves with scarcely a regret to orderly government. Very little lawlessness had followed the defeat of the Khalifa, and whatever plundering there had been was chiefly the work of the disbanded irregulars who had fought at Omdurman under Major Wortley's command on the east bank of the Nile. In every village Sheikhs were appointed in the name of the Khedive, and the officers of the cavalry column concerned themselves with many difficult disputes about land, crops, and women—all of which they settled to their satisfaction. Marching through Awamra, Haloosen, and Mesalamia, Colonel Lewis reached Karkoj on the 7th of November, almost at the same time that Ahmed Fedil arrived on the Dinder.

For the next six weeks the movements of the two forces resembled a game of hide-and-seek. Ahmed Fedil, concealed in the dense forest and jungle of the east bank, raided the surrounding villages and worked his way gradually towards the Rosaires Cataract. Colonel Lewis, perplexed by false and vague information, remained halted at Karkoj, despatched vain reconnaissances in the hopes of obtaining reliable news, revolved deep schemes to cut off the raiding parties, or patrolled the river in the gunboats. And meanwhile sickness fell upon his force. The malarial fever, which is everywhere prevalent on the Blue Nile in the autumn, was now at its height. More than 30 per cent of every garrison and every post were affected. The company holding Rosaires were stricken to a man, and only the two British officers remained fit for duty. The cavalry force which had marched through the Ghezira suffered the most severely. One after another every British officer was stricken down and lay burning but helpless beneath the palm-leaf shelters or tottered on to the friendly steamers that bore the worst cases north. Of the 460 men who composed the force, ten had died and 420 were reported unfit for duty within a month of their arrival at Karkoj.

During the end of November the Sheikh Bakr, who had deserted the Dervishes after their retreat from Gedaref, arrived at Karkoj with 350 irregulars. He claimed to have defeated his former chief many times, and produced a sack of heads as evidence of his success. His loyalty being thus placed beyond doubt, he was sent to keep contact with the Dervishes and encouraged to the greatest efforts by the permission to appropriate whatever spoils of war he could capture.

Meanwhile Ahmed Fedil was working his way slowly southward along a deep khor which runs almost parallel to the Blue Nile and is perhaps twenty miles from it. As soon as the position of the Dervish Emir was definitely known, Colonel Lewis moved his force, which had been strengthened by detachments of the Xth Soudanese, from Karkoj to Rosaires. Here he remained for several days, with but little hope of obstructing the enemy's passage of the river. On the 20th of December, however, full—though, as was afterwards found, not very accurate—information was received. It was reported that on the 18th Ahmed Fedil had reached the village of Dakhila, about twenty miles south of the Rosaires post; that he himself had immediately crossed with his advanced guard, and was busily passing the women and children across the river on rafts.

On the 22nd, therefore, Colonel Lewis hurried the Sheikh Bakr up the west bank to cut off their flocks and harass the Dervishes who had already crossed the river. The irregulars accordingly departed; and the next day news was brought that the Dervish force was almost equally divided by the Blue Nile, half being on one bank and half on the other. At midday on the 24th the gunboats Melik and Dal arrived from Omdurman with a detachment of 200 more men of the Xth Soudanese under Major Fergusson, and thirty men of the IXth Soudanese under Captain Sir Henry Hill. With this addition the force at Colonel Lewis's disposal consisted of half the Xth Soudanese, a small detachment of the IXth Soudanese, two Maxim guns, and a doctor. Besides the regular troops, there were also the band of irregulars under the Sheikh Bakr, numbering 380 men, 100 men under the Sheikh of Rosaires, and a few other unclassified scallywags.

Colonel Lewis determined to attack what part of Ahmed Fedil's force still remained on the east bank of the river, and on Christmas Day, at five o'clock in the afternoon, he marched with every man he could muster in the direction of Dakhila.

Moving in single file along a track which led through a dense forest of thorny trees, the column reached Adu Zogholi, a village thought to be half, but really not one-third, of the way to Dakhila, at eleven o'clock on Christmas night. Here they bivouacked until 3 A.M. on the 26th, when the march was resumed in the same straggling order through the same tangled scrub. Daylight found them still several miles from the Dervish position, and it was not until eight o'clock that the enemy's outposts were discovered. After a few shots the Arab picket fell back, and the advance guard, hurrying after them, emerged from the forest upon the open ground of the river bank, broken only by palms and patches of high grass. Into this space the whole column gradually debouched. Before them the Blue Nile, shining in the early sunlight like a silver band, flowed swiftly; and beyond its nearest waters rose a long, bare, gravel island crowned with clumps of sandhills, to the shelter of which several hundred Dervishes, surprised by the sudden arrival of the troops, were scampering. Beyond the island, on the tall tree-clad cliff of the further bank, other minute figures moved and bustled. The discordant sound of horns and drums floating across the waters, and the unfurling of many bright flags, proclaimed the presence and the intention of the hostile force.

The Dervish position was well chosen and of great defensive strength. A little to the north of Dakhila the Blue Nile bifurcates—one rapid but shallow stream flowing fairly straight under the east bank; another very deep stream running in a wide curve under the west bank, cutting into it so that it is precipitous. These two branches of the river enclose an island a mile and a quarter long by 1,400 yards wide, and on this island, surrounded by a natural moat of swiftly flowing water, was the Dervish dem. The western side of the island rose into a line of low sandhills covered with scrub and grass, with a steep reverse slope towards the foreshore of the river-bank; and here, in this excellent cover, what eventually proved to be three-quarters of the force of Ahmed Fedil were drawn up. Backed against the deep arm of the river they had no choice, nor indeed any other wish, but to fight. Before them stretched a bare slope of heavy shingle, 1,000 yards wide, over which their enemies must advance to the attack, Behind them the high precipitous west bank of the river, which rose in some places to a height of fifty feet, was lined with the 300 riflemen who had already crossed; and from this secure position Ahmed Fedil and four of his Emirs were able to watch, assist, and direct the defence of the island. The force on the island was under the sole command of the Emir Saadalla, of Gedaref repute; but, besides his own followers, most of the men of the four other Emirs were concentrated there.

The prospect was uninviting. Colonel Lewis discovered that he had absurdly under-rated the strength and discipline of the Dervish force. It had been continually reported that the defeats at Gedaref had demoralised them, and that their numbers did not exceed 2,000 men. Moreover, he had marched to the attack in the belief that they were equally divided on both sides of the river. Retreat was, however, impossible. Strong as was the position of the enemy, formidable as was their strength, the direct assault was actually safer than a retirement through the nineteen miles of gloomy forest which lay between the adventurous column and Rosaires. The British officer immediately determined to engage. At nine o'clock the two Maxims, which represented the artillery of the little force, came into action in good positions, while the Xth Soudanese and most of the irregulars lined the east bank. Musketry and Maxim fire was now opened at long range. The Dervishes replied, and as the smoke of their rifles gradually revealed their position and their numbers, it soon became evident that no long-range fire could dislodge them; and Colonel Lewis resolved, in spite of the great disparity of force and disadvantage of ground, to attack them with the bayonet. Some time was spent in finding fords across the interposing arm of the river, and it was not until past ten o'clock that Bakr's men crossed on to the island, and, supported by a company of the Xth Soudanese, advanced towards the enemy's right and took up a position at about 800 yards from their line, to cover the rest of the passage.

Colonel Lewis now determined to turn the enemy's left from the north, attack them in flank, and roll them into the deep part of the river. With the Xth Soudanese, under Colonel Nason and Major Fergusson, he marched northwards along the river's edge, sheltering as far as possible under the curve of the bank from the fire, which now began to cause casualties. Having reached the position from which it was determined to deliver the attack, the battalion deployed into line, and, changing front half left, advanced obliquely by alternate companies across the bare shingle towards the sandhills. As they advanced, a galling fire was opened upon the left flank by two hundred Dervishes admirably placed on a knoll. Major Fergusson was detached with one company to dislodge them. The remaining four companies continued the attack.

The Dervish musketry now became intense. The whole front of the island position was lined with smoke, and behind it, from the high cliff of the west bank, a long half-circle of riflemen directed a second tier of converging bullets upon the 400 charging men. The shingle jumped and stirred in all directions as it was struck. A hideous whistling filled the air. The Soudanese began to drop on all sides, 'just like the Dervishes at Omdurman,' and the ground was soon dotted with the bodies of the killed and wounded. 'We did not,' said an officer, 'dare to look back.' But undaunted by fire and cross-fire, the heroic black soldiers—demons who would not be denied—pressed forward without the slightest check or hesitation, and, increasing their pace to a swift run in their eagerness to close with the enemy, reached the first sandhills and found cover beneath them. A quarter of the battalion had already fallen, and lay strewn on the shingle.

The rapidity of their advance had exhausted the Soudanese, and Lewis ordered Nason to halt under cover of the sandhills for a few minutes, so that the soldiers might get their breath before the final effort. Thereupon the Dervishes, seeing that the troops were no longer advancing, and believing that the attack was repulsed, resolved to clinch the matter. Ahmed Fedil from the west bank sounded the charge on drum and bugle, and with loud shouts of triumph and enthusiasm the whole force on the island rose from among the upper sandhills, and, waving their banners, advanced impetuously in counter-attack. But the Xth Soudanese, panting yet unconquerable, responded to the call of their two white officers, and, crowning the little dunes behind which they had sheltered, met the exultant enemy with a withering fire and a responding shout.

The range was short and the fire effective. The astonished Arabs wavered and broke; and then the soldiers, nobly led, swept forward in a long scattered line and drove the enemy from one sandy ridge to another—drove them across the rolling and uneven ground, every fold of which contained Dervishes—drove them steadily back over the sandhills, until all who were not killed or wounded were penned at the extreme southern end of the island, with the deep unfordable arm of the river behind them and the fierce black soldiers, roused to fury by their losses, in front.

The Sheikh Bakr, with his men and the rest of the irregulars, joined the victorious Soudanese, and from the cover of the sandhills, now in the hands of the troops, a terrible fire was opened upon the Dervishes crowded together on the bare and narrow promontory and on the foreshore. Some tried to swim across the rushing river to their friends on the west bank. Many were drowned—among them Saadalla, who sank horse and man beneath the flood. Others took refuge from the fire by standing up to their necks in the stream. The greater part, however, escaped to a smaller island a little further up the river. But the cover was bad, the deep water prevented further flight, and, after being exposed for an hour and a half to the musketry of two companies, the survivors—300 strong—surrendered.

By 11.30 the whole island was in the possession of the troops. It was, however, still swept and commanded by the fire from the west bank. The company which had been detached to subdue the Dervish riflemen were themselves pinned behind their scanty cover. Major Fergusson was severely wounded and a third of his men were hit. To withdraw this company and the wounded was a matter of great difficulty; and it was necessary to carry the Maxims across the river and bring them into action at 400 yards. Firing ceased at last at three o'clock, and the victors were left to measure their losses and their achievement.

There was neither time nor opportunity to count the enemy's dead, but it is certain that at least 500 Arabs were killed on the island. Two thousand one hundred and twenty-seven fighting men and several hundred women and children surrendered. Five hundred and seventy-six rifles, large quantities of ammunition, and a huge pile of spears and swords were captured. Ahmed Fedil, indeed, escaped with a numerous following across the Ghezira, but so disheartened were the Dervishes by this crushing defeat that the whole force surrendered to the gunboat Metemma at Reng, on the White Nile, on the 22nd of January, and their leader was content to fly with scarcely a dozen followers to join the Khalifa.

The casualties among the troops in the action amounted to 41 killed and 145 wounded, including Major Fergusson; and the Xth Soudanese, on whom the brunt of the fighting fell, suffered a loss of 25 non-commissioned officers and men killed, 1 British officer, 6 native officers, and 117 non-commissioned officers and men wounded, out of a total strength of 511. The rest of the loss was among the irregulars, 495 of whom took part in the engagement.

CHAPTER XIX:

THE END OF THE KHALIFA

By the operations described in the last chapter, the whole of the regions bordering on the Niles were cleared of hostile forces, dotted with military posts, and brought back to Egyptian authority. The Khalifa, however, still remained in Kordofan. After he had made good his escape from the battlefield of Omdurman, Abdullah had hurried in the direction of El Obeid, moving by the wells of Shat and Zeregia, which at that season of the year were full of water after the rains. At Abu Sherai, having shaken off the pursuit of the friendlies, he halted, encamped, and busily set to work to reorganise his shattered forces. How far he succeeded in this will presently be apparent. In the beginning of November the general drying-up of the country turned the wells at Abu Sherai into pools of mud, and the Khalifa moved westward to Aigaila. Here he was joined by the Emir El Khatem with the El Obeid garrison. This chief and his followers had never been engaged with the 'Turks,' and were consequently fresh and valiant. Their arrival greatly encouraged the force which the Khalifa had rallied. A large dem was formed at Aigaila, and here, since the water was plentiful during December, Abdullah abode quietly, sending his raiding parties far afield to collect grain and other supplies.

As soon as the Sirdar, who had returned from England, received the news of the success at Rosaires he determined to make an attempt to capture the Khalifa; and on the 29th of December sent for Colonel Kitchener, to whom as the senior available officer he had decided to entrust this honourable enterprise. The colonel was directed to take a small mixed force into Kordofan and to reconnoitre the enemy's position. If possible, he was to attack and capture Abdullah, whose followers were believed not to exceed 1,000 ill-armed men. The 'Kordofan Field Force,' as its officers called it, was formed as follows:

Commanding: COLONEL KITCHENER

Assistant Adjutant-General: LIEUT.-COLONEL MITFORD

Deputy-Assistant Adjutant-General: MAJOR WILLIAMS

Troops:

Two squadrons Egyptian Cavalry
2nd Egyptians
XIVth Soudanese
Two galloping Maxims
Two mule guns
One company Camel Corps.

Camel transport was drawn from the Atbara and from the Blue Nile. The troops were conveyed by steamer to Duem, and concentrated there during the first week in 1899. The camels were collected at Kawa, and, although several of the convoys had to march as much as 400 miles, the whole number had arrived by the 10th of January.

The prime difficulty of the operation was the want of water. The Khalifa's position was nearly 125 miles from the river. The intervening country is, in the wet season, dotted with shallow lakes, but by January these are reduced to mud puddles and only occasional pools remain. All the water needed by the men, horses, and mules of the column must therefore be carried. The camels must go thirsty until one of the rare pools—the likely places for which were known to the native guides—might be found. Now, the capacity of a camel for endurance without drinking is famous; but it has its limits. If he start having filled himself with water, he can march for five days without refreshment. If he then have another long drink, he can continue for five days more. But this strains his power to the extreme; he suffers acutely during the journey, and probably dies at its end. In war, however, the miseries of animals cannot be considered; their capacity for work alone concerns the commander. It was thought that, partly by the water carried in skins, partly by the drying-up pools, and partly by the camel's power of endurance, it might be just possible for a force of about

1,200 men to strike out 125 miles into the desert, to have three days to do their business in, and to come back to the Nile. This operation, which has been called the Shirkela Reconnaissance, occupied the Kordofan Field Force.

The report of the route from Kohi was considered encouraging. At Gedid the old wells promised sufficient water to refill the skins, and within seven miles of the wells were two large pools at which the camels could be watered. The column, therefore, prepared for the journey. Nothing was neglected which could increase the water carried or diminish the number of drinkers. Only twelve cavalry were taken. The horses of the Maxim guns and the mules of the battery were reduced to the lowest possible number. Every person, animal, or thing not vitally necessary was remorselessly excluded. In order to lighten the loads and make room for more water, even the ammunition was limited to 100 rounds per rifle. The daily consumption of water was restricted to one pint for men, six gallons for horses, and five for mules. To lessen the thirst caused by the heat Colonel Kitchener decided to march by night. An advanced depot was formed at Gedid and food for two days accumulated there. Besides this, each unit carried ten, and the column transport seven, days' rations. Thus the force were supplied with food up till the 9th of February, and their radius of action, except as restricted by water, was nineteen days. This was further extended five days by the arrangement of a convoy which was to set out on the 30th of January to meet them as they returned.

The column—numbering 1,604 officers and men and 1,624 camels and other beasts of burden—started from Kohi at 3 P.M. on the 23rd of January, having sent on a small advanced party to the wells of Gedid twelve hours before. The country through which their route lay was of barren and miserable aspect. They had embarked on a sandy ocean with waves of thorny scrub and withered grass. From the occasional rocky ridges, which allowed a more extended view, this sterile jungle could be seen stretching indefinitely on all sides. Ten miles from the river all vestiges of animal life disappeared. The land was a desert; not the open desert of the Northern Soudan, but one vast unprofitable thicket, whose interlacing thorn bushes, unable to yield the slightest nourishment to living creatures, could yet obstruct their path.

Through this the straggling column, headed in the daylight by the red Egyptian flag and at night by a lantern on a pole, wound its weary way, the advanced guard cutting a path with axes and marking the track with strips of calico, the rearguard driving on the laggard camels and picking up the numerous loads which were cast. Three long marches brought them on the 25th to Gedid. The first detachment had already arrived and had opened up the wells. None gave much water; all emitted a foul stench, and one was occupied by a poisonous serpent eight feet long—the sole inhabitant. The camels were sent to drink at the pool seven miles away, and it was hoped that some of the water-skins could be refilled; but, after all, the green slime was thought unfit for human consumption, and they had to come back empty.

The march was resumed on the 26th. The trees were now larger; the scrub became a forest; the sandy soil changed to a dark red colour; but otherwise the character of the country was unaltered. The column rested at Abu Rokba. A few starving inhabitants who occupied the huts pointed out the grave of the Khalifa's father and the little straw house in which Abdullah was wont to pray during his visits. Lately, they said, he had retired from Aigaila to Shirkela, but even from this latter place he had made frequent pilgrimages.

At the end of the next march, which was made by day, the guides, whose memories had been refreshed by flogging, discovered a large pool of good water, and all drank deeply in thankful joy. A small but strong zeriba was built near this precious pool, and the reserve food and a few sick men were left with a small garrison under an Egyptian officer. The column resumed their journey. On the 29th they reached Aigaila, and here, with feelings of astonishment scarcely less than Robinson Crusoe experienced at seeing the footprint in the sand, they came upon the Khalifa's abandoned camp. A wide space had been cleared of bush, and the trees, stripped of their smaller branches, presented an uncanny appearance. Beyond stood the encampment—a great multitude of yellow spear-grass dwellings, perfectly clean, neatly arranged in streets and squares, and stretching for miles. The aspect of this strange deserted town, rising, silent as a cemetery, out of the awful scrub, chilled everyone who saw it. Its size might indeed concern their leader. At the very lowest computation it had contained 20,000 people. How many of these were fighting men? Certainly not fewer than 8,000 or 9,000. Yet the expedition had been sent on the assumption that there were scarcely 1,000 warriors with the Khalifa!

Observing every precaution of war, the column crawled forward, and the cavalry and Camel Corps, who covered the advance, soon came in contact with the enemy's scouts. Shots were exchanged and the Arabs retreated. The column halted three miles to the east of this position, and, forming a strong zeriba, passed the night in expectation of an attack. Nothing, however, happened, and at dawn Mitford was sent out with some mounted 'friendlies' to reconnoitre. At ten o'clock he returned, and his report confirmed the conclusions which had been drawn from the size of the Aigaila camp. Creeping forward to a good point of view, the officer had seen the Dervish flags lining the crest of the hill. From their number, the breadth of front covered, and the numerous figures of men moving about them, he estimated not fewer than 2,000 Arab riflemen in the front line. How many more were in reserve it was impossible to say. The position was, moreover, of great strength, being surrounded by deep ravines and pools of water.

The news was startling. The small force were 125 miles from their base; behind them lay an almost waterless country, and in front was a powerful enemy. An informal council of war was held. The Sirdar had distinctly ordered that, whatever happened, there was to be no waiting; the troops were either to attack or retire. Colonel Kitchener decided to retire. The decision having been taken, the next step was to get beyond the enemy's reach as quickly as possible, and the force began their retreat on the same night. The homeward march was not less long and trying than the advance, and neither hopes of distinction nor glamour of excitement cheered the weary soldiers. As they toiled gloomily back towards the Nile, the horror of the accursed land grew upon all. Hideous spectacles of human misery were added to the desolation of the hot, thorny scrub and stinking pools of mud. The starving inhabitants had been lured from their holes and corners by the outward passage of the troops, and hoped to snatch some food from the field of battle. Disappointed, they now approached the camps at night in twos and threes, making piteous entreaties for any kind of nourishment. Their appeals were perforce unregarded; not an ounce of spare food remained.

Towards the end of the journey the camels, terribly strained by their privation of water, began to die, and it was evident that the force would have no time to spare. One young camel, though not apparently exhausted, refused to proceed, and even when a fire was lighted round him remained stubborn and motionless; so that, after being terribly scorched, he had to be shot. Others fell and died all along the route. Their deaths brought some relief to the starving inhabitants. For as each animal was left behind, the officers, looking back, might see first one, then another furtive figure emerge from the bush and pounce on the body like a vulture; and in many cases before life was extinct the famished natives were devouring the flesh.

On the 5th of February the column reached Kohi, and the Kordofan Field Force, having overcome many difficulties and suffered many hardships, was broken up, unsuccessful through no fault of its commander, its officers, or its men.

For nearly a year no further operations were undertaken against the Khalifa, and he remained all through the spring and summer of 1899 supreme in Kordofan, reorganising his adherents and plundering the country—a chronic danger to the new Government, a curse to the local inhabitants, and a most serious element of unrest. The barren and almost waterless regions into which he had withdrawn presented very difficult obstacles to any military expedition, and although powerful forces were still concentrated at Khartoum, the dry season and the uncertain whereabouts of the enemy prevented action. But towards the end of August trustworthy information was received by the Intelligence Department, through the agency of friendly tribesmen, that the Khalifa, with all his army, was encamped at Jebel Gedir—that same mountain in Southern Kordofan to which nearly twenty years before he and the Mahdi had retreated after the flight from Abba Island. Here among old memories which his presence revived he became at once a centre of fanaticism. Night after night he slept upon the Mahdi's stone; and day after day tales of his dreams were carried by secret emissaries not only throughout the Western Soudan, but into the Ghezira and even to Khartoum. And now, his position being definite and his action highly dangerous, it was decided to move against him.

On the 13th of October the first Soudanese battalion was despatched in steamers from Khartoum, and by the 19th a force of some 7,000 men, well equipped with camel transport, was concentrated at Kaka, a village on the White Nile not far north of Fashoda. The distance from here to Jebel Gedir was about eighty miles, and as for the first fifty no water existed; the whole supply had to be carried in tanks. Sir Reginald Wingate, who was in command of the infantry, reached Fungor, thirty miles from the enemy's position, with the two leading battalions (IXth and Xth Soudanese) on the 23rd of October, only to find news that the Khalifa had left his camp at Jebel Gedir on the 18th and had receded indefinitely into the desert. The cast having failed, and further progress involving a multiplication of difficulties, Lord Kitchener, who was at Kaka, stopped the operations, and the whole of the troops returned to Khartoum, which they reached in much vexation and disappointment on the 1st of November.

It was at first universally believed that the Khalifa's intention was to retire to an almost inaccessible distance—to El Obeid or Southern Darfur—and the officers of the Egyptian army passed an unhappy fortnight reading the Ladysmith telegrams and accusing their evil fortune which kept them so far from the scene of action. But soon strange rumours began to run about the bazaars of Omdurman of buried weapons and whispers of revolt. For a few days a vague feeling of unrest pervaded the native city, and then suddenly on the 12th of November came precise and surprising news. The Khalifa was not retreating to the south or to the west, but advancing northward with Omdurman, not El Obeid, as his object. Emboldened by the spectacle of two successive expeditions retreating abortive, and by, who shall say what wild exaggerated tales of disasters to the Turks far beyond the limits of the Soudan, Abdullah had resolved to stake all that yet remained to him in one last desperate attempt to recapture his former capital; and so, upon the 12th of November, his advanced guard, under the Emir Ahmed Fedil, struck the Nile opposite Abba Island, and audaciously fired volleys of musketry at the gunboat Sultan which was patrolling the river.

The name of Abba Island may perhaps carry the reader back to the very beginning of this story. Here, eighteen years before, the Mahdi had lived and prayed after his quarrel with the haughty Sheikh; here Abdullah had joined him; here the flag of the revolt had been set up, and the first defeat had been inflicted upon the Egyptian troops; and here, too, still dwelt—dwells, indeed, to this day—one of those same brothers who had pursued through all the vicissitudes and convulsions which had shaken the Soudan his humble industry of building wooden boats. It is surely a curious instance of the occasional symmetry of history that final destruction should have befallen the last remains of the Mahdist movement so close to the scene of its origin!

The news which had reached Khartoum set all wheels in motion. The IXth and XIIIth Soudanese Battalions were mobilised on the 13th of November and despatched at once to Abba Island under Colonel Lewis. Kitchener hurried south from Cairo, and arrived in Khartoum on the 18th. A field force of some 2,300 troops—one troop of cavalry, the 2nd Field Battery, the 1st Maxim Battery, the Camel Corps, IXth Soudanese, XIIIth Soudanese, and one company

2nd Egyptians—was immediately formed, and the command entrusted to Sir Reginald Wingate. There were besides some 900 Arab riflemen and a few irregular mounted scouts. On the 20th these troops were concentrated at Fashi Shoya, whence Colonel Lewis had obliged Ahmed Fedil to withdraw, and at 3.30 on the afternoon of the 21st the expedition started in a south-westerly direction upon the track of the enemy.

The troops bivouacked some ten miles south-west of Fashi Shoya, and then marched in bright moonlight to Nefisa, encountering only a Dervish patrol of about ten men. At Nefisa was found the evacuated camp of Ahmed Fedil, containing a quantity of grain which he had collected from the riverain district, and, what was of more value, a sick but intelligent Dervish who stated that the Emir had just moved to Abu Aadel, five miles further on. This information was soon confirmed by Mahmud Hussein, an Egyptian officer, who with an irregular patrol advanced boldly in reconnaissance. The infantry needed a short rest to eat a little food, and Sir Reginald Wingate ordered Colonel Mahon to press on immediately with the whole of the mounted troops and engage the enemy, so as to prevent him retreating before an action could be forced.

Accordingly cavalry, Camel Corps, Maxims, and irregulars—whose fleetness of foot enabled them, though not mounted, to keep pace with the rest—set off at their best pace: and after them at 9.15 hurried the infantry, refreshed by a drink at the water tanks and a hasty meal. As they advanced the scrub became denser, and all were in broken and obstructed ground when, at about ten o'clock, the sound of Maxim firing and the patter of musketry proclaimed that Mahon had come into contact. The firing soon became more rapid, and as the infantry approached it was evident that the mounted troops were briskly engaged. The position which they occupied was a low ridge which rose a little above the level of the plain and was comparatively bare of scrub; from this it was possible at a distance of 800 yards to overlook the Dervish encampment huddled around the water pools. It was immediately evident that the infantry and the battery were arriving none too soon. The Dervishes, who had hitherto contented themselves with maintaining a ragged and desultory fire from the scrub, now sallied forth into the open and delivered a most bold and determined charge upon the guns. The intervening space was little more than 200 yards, and for a moment the attack looked as if it might succeed. But upon the instant the IXth and XIIIth Soudanese, who had been doubled steadily for upwards of two miles, came into line, filling the gap between Mahon's guns and dismounted Camel Corps and the irregular riflemen; and so the converging fire of the whole force was brought to bear upon the enemy—now completely beaten and demoralised. Two Dervishes, brothers, bound together hand and foot, perished in valiant comradeship ninety-five paces from the line of guns. Many were slain, and the remainder fled. The whole Egyptian line now advanced upon the encampment hard upon the tracks of the retreating enemy, who were seen emerging from the scrub on to a grassy plain more than a mile away, across which and further for a distance of five miles they were pursued by the cavalry and the Camel Corps. Three hundred and twenty corpses were counted, and at least an equal number must have been wounded. Ahmed Fedil and one or two of his principal Emirs escaped to the southward and to the Khalifa. The Egyptian loss amounted to five men wounded. The troops bivouacked in square formation, at about four o'clock, near the scene of action.

A question of considerable difficulty and some anxiety now arose. It was learned from the prisoners that the Khalifa, with about 5,000 fighting men, was moving northwards towards the wells of Gedid, of which we have already heard in the Shirkela reconnaissance, and which were some twenty-five miles from the scene of the fight. The troops were already fatigued by their severe exertions. The water pool was so foul that even the thirsty camels refused to drink of it, and moreover scarcely any water remained in the tanks. It was therefore of vital importance to reach the wells of Gedid. But supposing exhausted troops famishing for water reached them only to be confronted by a powerful Dervish force already in possession! Sir Reginald Wingate decided, however, to face the risk, and at a few minutes before midnight the column set out again on its road. The ground was broken; the night was sultry: and as the hours passed by the sufferings of the infantry began to be most acute. Many piteous appeals were made for water. All had perforce to be refused by the commander, who dared not diminish by a mouthful his slender store until he knew the true situation at Gedid. In these circumstances the infantry, in spite of their admirable patience, became very restive. Many men fell exhausted to the ground; and it was with a feeling of immense relief that at nine o'clock on the morning of the 24th news was received from the cavalry that the wells had been occupied by them without opposition. All the water in the tanks was at once distributed, and thus refreshed the infantry struggled on and settled down at midday around a fine pool of comparatively pure water.

At Gedid, as at Nefisa, a single Dervish, and this time a sullen fellow, was captured, and from him it was learned that the Khalifa's army was encamped seven miles to the south-east. It was now clear that his position was strategically most unfavourable. His route to the north was barred; his retreat to the south lay through waterless and densely wooded districts; and as the seizure of the grain supplies which had resulted from Fedil's foraging excursions rendered his advance or retirement a matter of difficulty, it seemed probable he would stand. Wingate, therefore, decided to attack him at dawn. Leaving the transport under guard by the water with instructions to follow at four o'clock, the troops moved off at midnight, screened in front at a distance of half a mile by the cavalry and their flanks protected by the Camel Corps. The road was in places so thickly wooded that a path had to be cut by the infantry pioneers and the artillery. At three o'clock, when about three miles from the enemy's position, the force was deployed into fighting formation. The irregular riflemen covered the front; behind them the XIIIth and IXth Soudanese; and behind these, again, the Maxims and the artillery were disposed. Cautiously and silently the advance was resumed, and now in the distance the beating of war drums and the long booming note of the Khalifa's horn broke on the stillness, proclaiming that the enemy were not unprepared. At a few minutes before four o'clock another low ridge, also comparatively bare of scrub, was reached and occupied as a position. The cavalry were now withdrawn from the front, a few infantry picquets were thrown out, and the rest of the force lay down in the long grass of the little ridge and waited for daylight.

After about an hour the sky to the eastward began to grow paler with the promise of the morning and in the indistinct light the picquets could be seen creeping gradually in; while behind them along the line of the trees faint white figures, barely distinguishable, began to accumulate. Sir Reginald Wingate, fearing lest a sudden rush should be made upon him, now ordered the whole force to stand up and open fire; and forthwith, in sudden contrast to the silence and obscurity, a loud crackling fusillade began. It was immediately answered. The enemy's fire flickered along a wide half-circle and developed continually with greater vigour opposite the Egyptian left, which was consequently reinforced. As the light improved, large bodies of shouting Dervishes were seen advancing;

but the fire was too hot, and their Emirs were unable to lead them far beyond the edge of the wood. So soon as this was perceived Wingate ordered a general advance; and the whole force, moving at a rapid pace down the gentle slope, drove the enemy through the trees into the camp about a mile and a half away. Here, huddled together under their straw shelters, 6,000 women and children were collected, all of whom, with many unwounded combatants, made signals of surrender and appeals for mercy. The 'cease fire' was sounded at half-past six. Then, and not till then, was it discovered how severe the loss of the Dervishes had been. It seemed to the officers that, short as was the range, the effect of rifle fire under such unsatisfactory conditions of light could not have been very great. But the bodies thickly scattered in the scrub were convincing evidences. In one space not much more than a score of yards square lay all the most famous Emirs of the once far-reaching Dervish domination. The Khalifa Abdullah, pierced by several balls, was stretched dead on his sheepskin; on his right lay Ali-Wad-Helu, on his left Ahmed Fedil. Before them was a line of lifeless bodyguards; behind them a score of less important chiefs; and behind these, again, a litter of killed and wounded horses. Such was the grim spectacle which in the first light of the morning met the eyes of the British officers, to some of whom it meant the conclusion of a perilous task prolonged over many years. And while they looked in astonishment not unmingled with awe, there scrambled unhurt from under a heap of bodies the little Emir Yunes, of Dongola, who added the few links necessary to complete the chain.

At Omdurman Abdullah had remained mounted behind the hill of Surgham, but in this his last fight he had set himself in the forefront of the battle. Almost at the first discharge, his son Osman, the Sheikh-ed-Din, was wounded, and as he was carried away he urged the Khalifa to save himself by flight; but the latter, with a dramatic dignity sometimes denied to more civilised warriors, refused. Dismounting from his horse, and ordering his Emirs to imitate him, he seated himself on his sheepskin and there determined to await the worst of fortune. And so it came to pass that in this last scene in the struggle with Mahdism the stage was cleared of all its striking characters, and Osman Digna alone purchased by flight a brief ignoble liberty, soon to be followed by a long ignoble servitude.

Twenty-nine Emirs, 3,000 fighting men, 6,000 women and children surrendered themselves prisoners. The Egyptian losses were three killed and twenty-three wounded.

* * * * *

The long story now approaches its conclusion. The River War is over. In its varied course, which extended over fourteen years and involved the untimely destruction of perhaps 300,000 lives, many extremes and contrasts have been displayed. There have been battles which were massacres, and others that were mere parades. There have been occasions of shocking cowardice and surprising heroism, of plans conceived in haste and emergency, of schemes laid with slow deliberation, of wild extravagance and cruel waste, of economies scarcely less barbarous, of wisdom and incompetence. But the result is at length achieved, and the flags of England and Egypt wave unchallenged over the valley of the Nile.

At what cost were such advantages obtained? The reader must judge for himself of the loss in men; yet while he deplores the deaths of brave officers and soldiers, and no less the appalling destruction of the valiant Arabs, he should remember that such slaughter is inseparable from war, and that, if the war be justified, the loss of life cannot be accused. But I write of the cost in money, and the economy of the campaigns cannot be better displayed than by the table below:

Railway: EP 1,181,372
Telegraph: EP 21,825
Gunboats: EP 154,934
Military Expenditure: EP 996,223
    TOTAL EXPENDITURES: EP 2,354,354 (EP1 = British P1 0s.6d.)

For something less than two and a half millions sterling active military operations were carried on for nearly three years, involving the employment—far from its base—of an army of 25,000 disciplined troops, including an expensive British contingent of 8,000 men, and ending in the utter defeat of an enemy whose armed forces numbered at the beginning of the war upwards of 80,000 soldiers, and the reconquest and re-occupation of a territory measuring sixteen hundred miles from north to south and twelve hundred from east to west [Lieut.-Colonel Stewart's Report: Egypt, No.11, 1883], which at one time supported at least twenty millions of inhabitants. But this is not all. Of the total EP2,354,354 only EP996,223 can be accounted as military expenditure. For the remaining EP1,358,131 Egypt possesses 500 miles of railway, 900 miles of telegraph, and a flotilla of steamers. The railway will not, indeed, pay a great return upon the capital invested, but it will immediately pay something, and may ultimately pay much. The telegraph is as necessary as the railway to the development of the country; it costs far less, and, when the Egyptian system is connected with the South African, it will be a sure source of revenue. Lastly, there are the gunboats. The reader cannot have any doubts as to the value of these vessels during the war. Never was money better spent on military plant. Now that the river operations are over the gunboats discharge the duties of ordinary steamers; and although they are, of course, expensive machines for goods and passenger traffic, they are by no means inefficient. The movement of the troops, their extra pay, the supplies at the end of a long line of communications, the ammunition, the loss by wear and tear of uniforms and accoutrements, the correspondence, the rewards, all cost together less than a million sterling; and for that million Egypt has recovered the Soudan.

The whole EP2,354,354 had, however, to be paid during the campaigns. Towards this sum Great Britain advanced, as has been related, P800,000 as a loan; and this was subsequently converted into a gift. The cost to the British taxpayer of the recovery and part acquisition of the Soudan, of the military prestige, and of the indulgence of the sentiment known as 'the avenging of Gordon' has therefore been P800,000; and it may be stated in all seriousness that English history does not record any instance of so great a national satisfaction being more cheaply obtained. The rest of the money has been provided by Egypt; and this strange country, seeming to resemble the camel, on which so much of her wealth depends, has, in default of the usual sources of supply, drawn upon some fifth stomach for nourishment, and, to the perplexity even of those best acquainted with her amazing financial constitution, has stood the strain.

'The extraordinary expenditure in connection with the Soudan campaign,' wrote Mr. J.L. Gorst, the Financial Adviser to the Khedive in his Note of

December 20, 1898 [Note by the Financial Adviser on the Budget of 1899: EGYPT, No. 3, 1899], 'has been charged to the Special Reserve Fund. At the present moment this fund shows a deficit of EP336,000, and there are outstanding charges on account of the expedition amounting to EP330,000, making a total deficit of EP666,000.'

'On the other hand, the fund will be increased, when the accounts of the year are made up, by a sum of EP382,000, being the balance of the share of the Government in the surplus of 1898, after deduction of the excess administrative expenditure in that year, and by a sum of EP90,000, being part of the proceeds of the sale of the Khedivial postal steamers. The net deficit will, therefore, be EP194,000; and if the year 1899 is as prosperous as the present year, it may be hoped that the deficit will disappear when the accounts of 1899 are closed.'

A great, though perhaps academic, issue remains: Was the war justified by wisdom and by right?

If the reader will look at a map of the Nile system, he cannot fail to be struck by its resemblance to a palm-tree. At the top the green and fertile area of the Delta spreads like the graceful leaves and foliage. The stem is perhaps a little twisted, for the Nile makes a vast bend in flowing through the desert. South of Khartoum the likeness is again perfect, and the roots of the tree begin to stretch deeply into the Soudan. I can imagine no better illustration of the intimate and sympathetic connection between Egypt and the southern provinces. The water—the life of the Delta—is drawn from the Soudan, and passes along the channel of the Nile, as the sap passes up the stem of the tree, to produce a fine crop of fruit above. The benefit to Egypt is obvious; but Egypt does not benefit alone. The advantages of the connection are mutual; for if the Soudan is thus naturally and geographically an integral part of Egypt, Egypt is no less essential to the development of the Soudan. Of what use would the roots and the rich soil be, if the stem were severed, by which alone their vital essence may find expression in the upper air?

Here, then, is a plain and honest reason for the River War. To unite territories that could not indefinitely have continued divided; to combine peoples whose future welfare is inseparably intermingled; to collect energies which, concentrated, may promote a common interest; to join together what could not improve apart—these are the objects which, history will pronounce, have justified the enterprise.

The advantage to Great Britain is no less clear to those who believe that our connection with Egypt, as with India, is in itself a source of strength. The grasp of England upon Egypt has been strengthened twofold by the events of the war. The joint action and ownership of the two countries in the basin of the Upper Nile form an additional bond between them. The command of the vital river is an irresistible weapon. The influence of France over the native mind in Egypt has been completely destroyed by the result of the Fashoda negotiations; and although she still retains the legal power to meddle in and obstruct all financial arrangements, that power, unsupported by real influence, is like a body whence the soul has fled, which may, indeed, be an offensive encumbrance, but must ultimately decompose and crumble into dust.

But, apart from any connection with Egypt, Britain has gained a vast territory which, although it would be easy to exaggerate its value, is nevertheless coveted by every Great Power in Europe. The policy of acquiring large waterways, which has been pursued deliberately or unconsciously by British statesmen for three centuries, has been carried one step further; and in the valley of the Nile England may develop a trade which, passing up and down the river and its complement the railway, shall exchange the manufactures of the Temperate Zone for the products of the Tropic of Cancer, and may use the north wind to drive civilisation and prosperity to the south and the stream of the Nile to bear wealth and commerce to the sea.

APPENDIX

TEXT OF THE SOUDAN AGREEMENT OF THE 19TH OF JANUARY, 1899, AND OF THE DECLARATION OF THE 21ST OF MARCH, 1899

AGREEMENT BETWEEN HER BRITANNIC MAJESTY'S GOVERNMENT AND THE GOVERNMENT OF HIS HIGHNESS THE KHEDIVE OF EGYPT, RELATIVE TO THE FUTURE ADMINISTRATION OF THE SOUDAN

WHEREAS certain provinces in the Soudan which were in rebellion against the authority of His Highness the Khedive have now been reconquered by the joint military and financial efforts of Her Britannic Majesty's Government and the Government of His Highness the Khedive; AND whereas it has become necessary to decide upon a system for the administration of and for the making of laws for the said reconquered provinces, under which due allowance may be made for the backward and unsettled condition of large portions thereof, and for the varying requirements of different localities; AND whereas it is desired to give effect to the claims which have accrued to Her Britannic Majesty's Government, by right of conquest, to share in the present settlement and future working and development of the said system of administration and legislation; AND whereas it is conceived that for many purposes Wady Halfa and Suakin may be most effectively administered in conjunction with the reconquered provinces to which they are respectively adjacent: NOW, it is hereby agreed and declared by and between the Undersigned, duly authorised for that purpose, as follows:-

ART. I.

The word 'Soudan' in this Agreement means all the territories South of the 22nd parallel of latitude, which: 1. Have never been evacuated by Egyptian troops since the year 1882; or 2. Which having before the late rebellion in the Soudan been administered by the Government of His Highness the Khedive, were temporarily lost to Egypt, and have been reconquered by Her Majesty's Government and the Egyptian Government, acting in concert; or 3. Which may hereafter be reconquered by the two Governments acting in concert.

ART. II.

The British and Egyptian flags shall be used together, both on land and water, throughout the Soudan, except in the town of Suakin, in which locality the Egyptian flag alone shall be used.

ART. III.

The supreme military and civil command in the Soudan shall be vested in one officer, termed the 'Governor-General of the Soudan.' He shall be appointed by Khedivial Decree on the recommendation of Her Britannic Majesty's Government, and shall be removed only by Khedivial Decree, with the consent of Her Britannic Majesty's Government.

ART. IV.

Laws, as also Orders and Regulations with the full force of law, for the good government of the Soudan, and for regulating the holding, disposal, and devolution of property of every kind therein situate, may from time to time be made, altered, or abrogated by Proclamation of the Governor-General. Such Laws, Orders, and Regulations may apply to the whole or any named part of the Soudan, and may, either explicitly or by necessary implication, alter or abrogate any existing Law or Regulation. All such Proclamations shall be forthwith notified to Her Britannic Majesty's Agent and Consul-General in Cairo, and to the President of the Council of Ministers of His Highness the Khedive.

ART. V.

No Egyptian Law, Decree, Ministerial Arrete, or other enactment hereafter to be made or promulgated shall apply to the Soudan or any part thereof, save in so far as the same shall be applied by Proclamation of the Governor-General in manner hereinbefore provided.

ART. VI.

In the definition by Proclamation of the conditions under which Europeans, of whatever nationality, shall be at liberty to trade with or reside in the Soudan, or to hold property within its limits, no special privileges shall be accorded to the subjects of any one or more Power.

ART. VII.

Import duties on entering the Soudan shall not be payable on goods coming from Egyptian territory. Such duties may, however, be levied on goods coming from elsewhere than Egyptian territory; but in the case of goods entering the Soudan at Suakin, or any other port on the Red Sea Littoral, they shall not exceed the corresponding duties for the time being leviable on goods entering Egypt from abroad. Duties may be levied on goods leaving the Soudan, at such rates as may from time to time be prescribed by Proclamation.

ART. VIII.

The jurisdiction of the Mixed Tribunals shall not extend, nor be recognised for any purpose whatsoever, in any part of the Soudan, except in the town of Suakin.

ART .IX.

Until, and save so far as it shall be otherwise determined by Proclamation, the Soudan, with the exception of the town of Suakin, shall be and remain under martial law.

ART. X.

No Consuls, Vice-Consuls, or Consular Agents shall be accredited in respect of nor allowed to reside in the Soudan, without the previous consent of Her Britannic Majesty's Government.

ART. XI.

The importation of slaves into the Soudan, as also their exportation, is absolutely prohibited. Provision shall be made by Proclamation for the enforcement of this Regulation.

ART. XII.

It is agreed between the two Governments that special attention shall be paid to the enforcement of the Brussels Act of the 2nd of July, 1890, in respect to the import, sale, and manufacture of fire-arms and their munitions, and distilled or spirituous liquors.

Done in Cairo, the 19th of January, 1899.

Signed: BOURTROS GHALI-CROMER.

DECLARATION RELATIVE TO THE BRITISH AND FRENCH SPHERES OF INFLUENCE IN CENTRAL AFRICA

(Signed at London, March 21st, 1899)

THE Undersigned, duly authorised by their Governments, have signed the following declaration:-

The IVth Article of the Convention of the 14th of June, 1898, shall be completed by the following provisions, which shall be considered as forming an integral part of it:

1. Her Britannic Majesty's Government engages not to acquire either territory or political influence to the west of the line of frontier defined in the following paragraph, and the Government of the French Republic engages not to acquire either territory or political influence to the east of the same line.
2. The line of frontier shall start from the point where the boundary between the Congo Free State and French territory meets the water-parting between the watershed of the Nile and that of the Congo and its affluents. It shall follow in principle that water-parting up to its intersection with the 11th parallel of north latitude. From this point it shall be drawn as far as the 15th parallel in such manner as to separate, in principle, the Kingdom of Wadai from what constituted in 1882 the Province of Darfur; but it shall in no case be so drawn as to pass to the west beyond the 21st degree of longitude east of Greenwich (18 degrees 40' east of Paris), or to the east beyond the 23rd degree of longitude east of Greenwich (20 degrees 40' east of Paris).
3. It is understood, in principle, that to the north of the 15th parallel the French zone shall be limited to the north-east and east by a line which shall start from the point of intersection of the Tropic of Cancer with the 16th

degree of longitude east of Greenwich (18 degrees 40' east of Paris), shall run thence to the south-east until it meets the 24th degree of longitude east of Greenwich (21 degrees 40' east of Paris), and shall then follow the 24th degree until it meets, to the north of the 15th parallel of latitude, the frontier of Darfur as it shall eventually be fixed.

4. The two Governments engage to appoint Commissioners who shall be charged to delimit on the spot a frontier-line in accordance with the indications given in paragraph 2 of this Declaration. The result of their work shall be submitted for the approbation of their respective Governments. It is agreed that the provisions of Article IX of the Convention of the 14th of June, 1898, shall apply equally to the territories situated to the south of the 14 degrees 20' parallel of north latitude, and to the north of the 5th parallel of north latitude, between the 14 degrees 20' meridian of longitude east of Greenwich (12th degree east of Paris) and the course of the Upper Nile.

Done at London, the 21st of March, 1899.

(L.S.)   SALISBURY.
(L.S.)   PAUL CAMBON.

BIBLIOBAZAAR

The essential book market!

Did you know that you can get any of our titles in large print?

Did you know that we have an ever-growing collection of books in many languages?

Order online:
www.bibliobazaar.com

Find all of your favorite classic books!

Stay up to date with the latest government reports!

At BiblioBazaar, we aim to make knowledge more accessible by making thousands of titles available to you- *quickly and affordably*.

Contact us:
BiblioBazaar
PO Box 21206
Charleston, SC 29413

Lightning Source UK Ltd.
Milton Keynes UK
UKOW06n1850151115

262786UK00008B/30/P